Books are to be returned on or before
the last date below.

LIBREX —

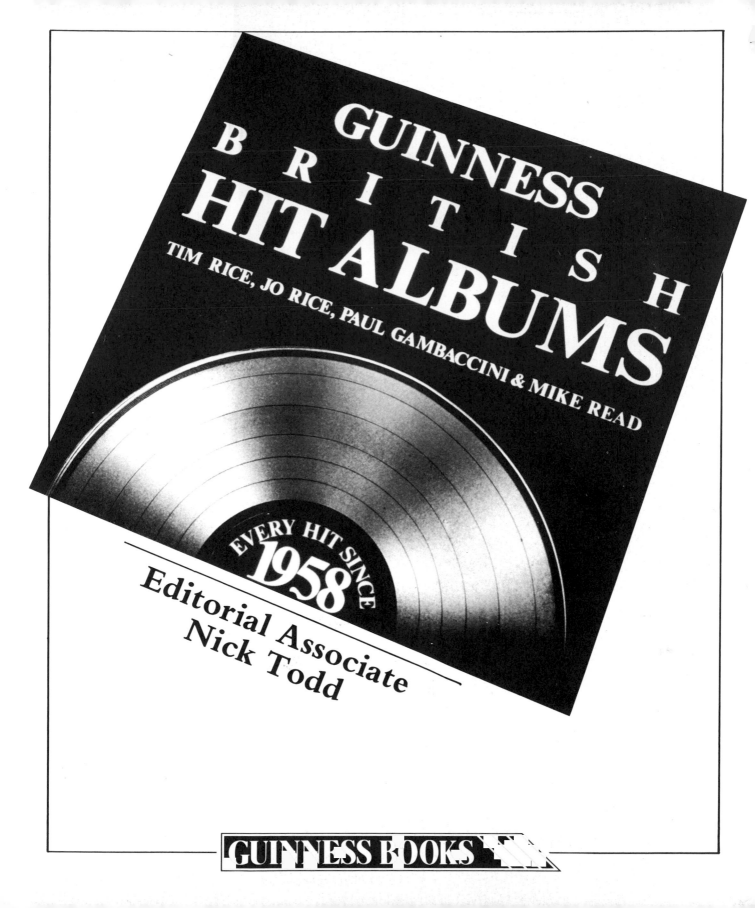

GUINNESS
BRITISH
HIT ALBUMS

TIM RICE, JO RICE, PAUL GAMBACCINI & MIKE READ

EVERY HIT SINCE 1958

Editorial Associate
Nick Todd

GUINNESS BOOKS

ACKNOWLEDGEMENTS

Our thanks to the many record company press officers for their patient help and for photographs. We also wish to thank *Melody Maker*, *Music Week*, Mismanagement, Derek Lewis and the BBC Record Library. Special thanks, too, to Eileen Heinink and Jan Rice for their continuing support.
Editorial Assistance: Honor Head; Alex E. Reid
Art Editor: David Roberts

Second Edition

First Edition 1983, reprinted once

Published in Great Britain by
Guinness Superlatives Ltd.,
33 London Road, Enfield, Middlesex
GRRR Books
196 Shaftesbury Avenue, London WC2

Guinness is a registered trademark of Guinness Superlatives Ltd.

British Library Cataloguing in Publication Data
The Guinness book of British hit albums.—2nd ed.
 1. Music, Popular (Songs, etc.)—Discography
 I. Rice, Jo
 016.7899'12   ML156.4.P6

ISBN 0-85112-480-1

Typeset by BPCC Graphics Ltd
and Hazell Watson & Viney Ltd

Printed and bound in England by Hazell Watson & Viney Ltd., Aylesbury, Bucks

THE AUTHORS

Rather than detail the early days of **PAUL GAM-BACCINI**, chronicled in the May 1986 Elm Tree book *Radio Boy*, or list his favourite LPs, which are in the September 1986 GRRR publication *Top 100 Albums*, let us celebrate our co-author's heroes, Carl Barks, Bob Dylan, Willie Mays, Arthur Rubinstein and Orson Welles, and wonder what they could possibly say to each other if locked in the same room except "What's for lunch?"

TIM RICE followed the album charts with particular enthusiasm towards the end of 1985, when he achieved what he thinks is a record in being represented on four of the top thirteen albums with the same track. This unparalleled (he hopes) event occurred on 14 December when 'I Know Him So Well' (which he wrote with Björn Ulvaeus and Benny Andersson) by Elaine Paige and Barbara Dickson was simultaneously at numbers 8, 10, 11 and 13 on 'The Greatest Hits Of 1985' (a former number one album), 'Love Hurts' by Elaine Paige, 'The Love Album' (another compilation) and Barbara Dickson's 'Gold' respectively. After this, all other biographical comment is superfluous.

JO RICE was born in a blizzard in Cricklewood, and at the age of nine failed his first audition for the school choir. At the age of eighteen he failed his first driving test and by the age of thirty-three and a third had failed to record his first album. However, his career has taken several turns for the better in recent months. He is now a star of the telephone (listen to the Golden Hitline on 246 8044) and his recent live appearances include guest spots as a trick question in a pop quiz and as an index entry in a cricket book.

MIKE READ is wisely hoarding LPs in readiness for the next vinyl shortage and has discovered that the the empty covers make jolly good hats. However, it is almost impossible to wear a compact disc cover on your head. To be honest, the above is all padding because he feels distraught that his voice isn't on the Golden Hitline, nor has he been remotely connected with a chart LP nor invited to lunch by any of Gambaccini's heroes.

GRRR GOLDEN HITLINE 0898 654321

Your 24 hour dial-a-disc service featuring nothing but hits from GUINNESS BRITISH HIT ALBUMS and GUINNESS BRITISH HIT SINGLES

Cover Design: David Roberts   *Artwork:* Rob Burns   *Photography:* Dave Page

INTRODUCTION

Listeners under thirty may have been perplexed when they heard Kevin Rowland sing on 'Don't Stand Me Down', "Bill, you know the newly wealthy peasants with their home bars and hi-fis?" (Copyright EMI Music Pub.) Not because *nouveau riche* Dexy's Midnight Runners fans were likely to be offended; they know the singer/songwriter sprinkles his lyrics with controversial opinions. But they may have wondered why he chose to use the word 'hi-fi' for a home music centre. Like 'gramophone' before it and 'stereo' after it, 'hi-fi' is a dated expression, referring to a type of record-player. It was part of everyday speech twenty-five years ago, but nowadays hardly anyone uses it in conversation. Most young people have probably never spoken the phrase.

A similar obsolescence seems to await the twelve-inch long-playing record, what is sometimes referred to in the music business as 'the black disc'. Since we published the first edition of *The Guinness Book of British Hit Albums* in 1983, dramatic developments have occurred that seem to foretell either the eventual disappearance or diminution in manufacture of the form.

The British Phonographic Industry reported in its *BPI Year Book 1985* that after 1981 retail sales of pre-recorded music increased annually in Britain at an average figure above the rate of inflation. The 1981 total of £427·6 million had surged to £549·3 million three years later. Yet in each one-year stage the revenue from LPs actually dropped by several million pounds.

The slack was more than taken up by the sale of other forms of album. 1983 was the first year in which Compact Disc sales were significant enough to be reported, totalling £2·6 million. The following twelve months CDs grossed £7·2 million. During 1985 music business publications on both sides of the Atlantic were full of reports of the astonishing growth of this new configuration. Supplies literally did not meet demand on hit titles, and at the end of 1985 there were still insufficient production facilities to cope with potential consumer interest. CD has been accepted earlier than expected on a larger scale than anticipated. Leading artists who value high quality sound reproduction, whether they work in rock or classical spheres, have stated it is on Compact Disc that they are best heard, and they have predicted it will take over completely from 'the black disc' as soon as is economically feasible.

Besides the consumer expense factor, there is another reason the twelve-inch LP has some life left in it. It is not yet fiscally wise or technically possible to manufacture all new popular releases on both twelve-inch and CD. Pop music generates a high proportion of unpredictable successes, and it is only after an artist has become established or an LP has enjoyed substantial sales that a record company will commit itself to a CD edition.

Alas for devotees of the black disc, there is another form encroaching upon its dominion. Pre-recorded cassette sales have boomed, moving from a quoted if unlikely figure of exactly £100·0 million in 1981 to £189·4 million in 1984. This was a dramatic surge, presaging the November 1985 front page *Music Week* story that cassette sales had finally overtaken LPs. During half a decade tape came from doing less than half the business of LP to surpassing it.

Reeling from the double blow it is sustaining from CD and cassette, the black disc seems truly doomed, likely to join the 78, the ten-inch LP and the 8-track cartridge as a format which will become the province of collectors and museums. It is with a massive sigh of relief that the authors of this book are able to report that its gradual passing will not affect us in the least! We will continue to record chart information on best-selling albums, regardless of the form of delivery.

Our first edition of *British Hit Albums* was published in 1983. For one glorious week it co-existed with our *British Hit Singles* in the *Sunday Times* Top 10 Best Seller list. Alas, that august newspaper decided to disqualify reference books from its chart, and out we went along with a couple of dictionaries, a thesaurus and a long-running number one road atlas. Armed with only these titles, a record collector would know what classic discs to buy, what routes to take to get to the shops, and what clever words to use in making one's requests. Without these books in the best sellers, readers would not even know how to find the *Sunday Times* offices.

We may have been out of sight, at least on the Best Seller page, but thank heaven we were not out of your mind. *Hit Albums* sold sufficiently well to justify its going into permanent rotation with *Hit Singles*, selling about 40% of our parent publication. This was near our most favourable expectations. We are delighted we will be able to issue *Hit Albums* every two years from now on to keep our research range up to date.

To first time readers we extend a hearty welcome and

the hope you will find the foibles of the British album chart during just over a quarter century as fascinating as we do. To old friends we offer another cup of your favourite hot beverage and the invitation to marvel with us at how all-time tables and artists' fortunes change in just a few years. We wish everyone who has charted in the thirty-six months since our last appearance the opportunity to make at least one hit CD before they go the way of the black disc.

The Charts

If ever a week went by without a chart being compiled, the previous week's chart was used again for the purposes of all the information and statistics used in this book. When albums began to be produced in both mono and stereo (1966) we list the stereo catalogue number only. The dates used in this book correspond to the Saturday of the week in which the chart was published.

A) MELODY MAKER
8 Nov 1958. First album chart published – Top Ten.
27 Jun–1 Aug 1959 inclusive: no charts published so 20 Jun chart repeated throughout.

B) RECORD RETAILER
26 Mar 1960. First Record Retailer chart published—Top Twenty. We now take our information from this chart though the MM chart continued.

14 Apr 1966: Chart increases to Top Thirty.

8 Dec 1966: Chart increases to Top Forty.

12 Feb 1969: Chart drops to Top Fifteen.

8 Mar 1969: This week's published chart is incorrect. The correct chart has been obtained by backtracking from the following week's listings.

11 Jun 1969: Chart increases to Top Twenty.

25 Jun 1969: Chart increases to Top Forty.

9 Aug 1969: 32 records in chart this week only.

11 Oct 1969: Chart drops to Top Twenty-five.

8 Nov 1969–24 Jan 1970: Chart varies between 20 and 24 records each week.

31 Jan 1970–9 Jan 1971: Chart varies between 47 and 77 records each week.

A Top 100 was compiled during this period but was only available to special subscribers.

9 Jan 1971: Record Retailer becomes RECORD AND TAPE RETAILER.

16 Jan 1971: Chart stabilises at Top Fifty.

6 Feb–27 Mar 1971: No charts published because of a postal strike. 30 Jan chart repeated throughout.

7 Aug 1971: Record and Tape Retailer combine their Full Price (the one we have been using) and the previously separate Budget charts. This means there is a sudden influx of budget label albums into the chart.

8 Jan 1972: The chart reverts to Full Price albums only so the budget albums exit as quickly as they appeared.

18 Mar 1972: Record and Tape Retailer becomes MUSIC WEEK.

13 Jan 1973: Top 24 only for this week.

5 Jan 1974: Top 42 only for this week.

5 Jul 1975: Chart increases to Top 60.

14 Jan 1978: Top 30 only for this week.

2 Dec 1978: Chart increases to Top 75.

13 Oct 1979: Two consecutive weeks' charts published simultaneously as a result of a speedy new chart compilation system which enabled Music Week, hitherto publishing the album chart more than a week after the survey period, to catch up a week. Both charts of this date are included in our calculations.

8 Aug 1981: Chart increases to Top 100.

BAT OUT OF HELL SOARS TO NEW HEIGHTS WITH A RECORD-MAKING 384 WEEKS ON CHART

Bat Out of Hell by Meat Loaf, released in 1978, peaked at number nine and spent only two weeks in the Top Ten in 1981, but in February 1986 it overtook the Sound of Music film soundtrack to become the most charted album since the album charts began in 1958

© Photograph of Meat Loaf courtesy Arista Records

HIT ALBUMS

ALPHABETICALLY BY ARTIST

The information given in this part of the book is as follows: date LP first hit the chart, title, label, catalogue number, highest position reached on chart, total number of weeks on the chart. Number one albums are highlighted with a green star and other Top Ten albums by a black dot. A black dagger indicates hits still on chart at 28 December 1985, as follows:

★ **Number one album**
● **Top Ten album**
† **Album still on chart at 28 December 1985**

For the purposes of this book, an album is considered a re-issue if it hits the chart for a second time with a new catalogue number.

Describing a recording act in one sentence is often fraught with danger, but we have attempted to do so above each act's list of hits. Although we are aware that many of the 'vocalists' thus described also play an instrument, we have only mentioned this fact where the artist's instrumental skills were an important factor in the album's success.

A

ABBA *Sweden, male/female vocal/instrumental group*
499 wks

8 Jun 74		WATERLOO	Epic EPC 80179	28	2 wks
31 Jan 76		ABBA	Epic EPC 80835	13	10 wks
10 Apr 76	★	GREATEST HITS	Epic EPC 69218	1	130 wks
27 Nov 76	★	ARRIVAL	Epic EPC 86108	1	92 wks
4 Feb 78	★	THE ALBUM	Epic EPC 86052	1	61 wks
19 May 79	★	VOULEZ-VOUS	Epic EPC 86086	1	43 wks
10 Nov 79	★	GREATEST HITS VOL.2	Epic EPC 10017	1	63 wks
22 Nov 80	★	SUPER TROUPER	Epic EPC 10022	1	43 wks
19 Dec 81	★	THE VISITORS	Epic EPC 10032	1	21 wks
20 Nov 82	★	THE SINGLES-THE FIRST TEN YEARS			
			Epic ABBA 10	1	22 wks
19 Nov 83		THANK YOU FOR THE MUSIC	Epic EPC 10043	17	12 wks

RUSS ABBOT *UK, male vocalist*
13 wks

5 Nov 83	RUSS ABBOT'S MADHOUSE	Ronco RTL 2096	41	7 wks
23 Nov 85	I LOVE A PARTY	K-Tel ONE 1313	12†	6 wks

ABC *UK, male vocal/instrumental group*
66 wks

3 Jul 82	★	THE LEXICON OF LOVE	Neutron NTRS 1	1	50 wks
26 Nov 83		BEAUTY STAB	Neutron NTRL 2	12	13 wks
26 Oct 85		HOW TO BE A ZILLIONAIRE	Neutron NTRH 3	28	3 wks

Father ABRAHAM and the SMURFS *Holland, male vocalist as himself and Smurfs*
11 wks

25 Nov 78	FATHER ABRAHAM IN SMURFLAND			
	Decca SMURF 1	19	11 wks

A.B.'s *US, male vocal/instrumental group*
2 wks

14 Apr 84	DEJA VU	Street Sounds XKHAN 503	80	2 wks

ACADEMY of ANCIENT MUSIC conducted by Christopher HOGWOOD *UK, male conductor/instrumentalist - harpisichord, UK chamber orchestra*
2 wks

16 Mar 85	THE FOUR SEASONS (VIVALDI)			
	L'Oiseau Lyre 4101261	85	2 wks

ACCEPT *Germany, male vocal/instrumental group*
3 wks

7 May 83	RESTLESS AND WILD			
	Heavy Metal Worldwide HMILP 6	98	2 wks
30 Mar 85	METAL HEART	Portrait PRT 26358	50	1 wk

AC/DC *Australia/UK, male vocal/instrumental group*
191 wks

5 Nov 77		LET THERE BE ROCK	Atlantic K 50366	17	5 wks
20 May 78		POWERAGE	Atlantic K 50483	26	9 wks
28 Oct 78		IF YOU WANT BLOOD YOU'VE GOT IT			
		Atlantic K 50532	13	58 wks
18 Aug 79	●	HIGHWAY TO HELL	Atlantic K 50628	8	32 wks
9 Aug 80	★	BACK IN BLACK	Atlantic K 50735	1	40 wks

5 Dec 81 ●	FOR THOSE ABOUT TO ROCK			3	29 wks
	Atlantic K 50851				
3 Sep 83 ●	FLICK OF THE SWITCH	*Atlantic 78-0100-1*		4	9 wks
13 Jul 85 ●	FLY ON THE WALL	*Atlantic 781263*		7	9 wks

Australia only for first four albums.

Bryan ADAMS *Canada, male vocalist/instrumentalist–guitar*
49 wks

2 Mar 85 ●	RECKLESS	*A & M AMA 5013*		7†	44 wks
24 Aug 85	YOU WANT IT, YOU GOT IT			78	5 wks
	A & M AMLH 64854				

Cliff ADAMS SINGERS *UK, male/female vocal group*
20 wks

16 Apr 60	SING SOMETHING SIMPLE	*Pye MPL 28013*		15	4 wks
24 Nov 62	SING SOMETHING SIMPLE			15	2 wks
	Pye Golden Guinea GGL 0150				
20 Nov 76	SING SOMETHING SIMPLE '76			23	8 wks
	Warwick WW 5016/17				
25 Dec 82	SING SOMETHING SIMPLE	*Ronco RTD 2087*		39	6 wks

All these identically titled albums are different.

King Sunny ADE and his AFRICAN BEATS
Nigeria, male vocalist and male vocal/instrumental group
1 wk

9 Jul 83	SYNCHRO SYSTEM	*Island ILPS 9737*		93	1 wk

ADICTS *UK, male vocal/instrumental group*
1 wk

4 Dec 82	SOUND OF MUSIC	*Razor RAZ 2*		99	1 wk

ADVERTS *UK, male/female vocal/instrumental group*
1 wk

11 Mar 78	CROSSING THE RED SEA WITH THE ADVERTS	*Bright BRL 201*		38	1 wk

AFTER THE FIRE *UK, male vocal/instrumental group*
4 wks

13 Oct 79	LASER LOVE	*CBS 83795*		57	1 wk
1 Nov 80	80 F	*Epic EPC 84545*		69	1 wk
3 Apr 82	BATTERIES NOT INCLUDED	*CBS 85566*		82	2 wks

A-HA *Norway, male vocal/instrumental group*
8 wks

9 Nov 85	HUNTING HIGH AND LOW			24†	8 wks
	Warner Bros WX 30				

ALARM *UK, male vocal/instrumental group*
15 wks

25 Feb 84 ●	DECLARATION	*IRS IRSA 7044*		6	11 wks
26 Oct 85	STRENGTH	*IRS MIRF 1004*		18	4 wks

ALEXANDER BROTHERS *UK, male vocal duo*
1 wk

10 Dec 66	THESE ARE MY MOUNTAINS	*Pye GGL 0375*		29	1 wk

ALIEN SEX FIEND *UK, male/female vocal/instrumental group*
1 wk

12 Oct 85	MAXIMUM SECURITY	*Anagram GRAM 24*		100	1 wk

Mose ALLISON *US, male vocalist/instrumentalist - piano*
1 wk

4 Jun 66	MOSE ALIVE	*Atlantic 587-007*		30	1 wk

ALLMAN BROTHERS BAND *US, male vocal/instrumental group*
4 wks

6 Oct 73	BROTHERS AND SISTERS	*Warner Bros. K 47507*		42	3 wks
6 Mar 76	THE ROAD GOES ON FOREVER			54	1 wk
	Capricorn 2637 101				

Marc ALMOND *UK, male vocalist*
5 wks

10 Nov 84	VERMIN IN ERMINE	*Some Bizzare BIZL 8*		36	2 wks
5 Oct 85	STORIES OF JOHNNY	*Virgin/*		22	3 wks
	Some Bizarre FAITH 1				

Vermin In Ermine credited to Marc Almond and the Willing Sinners- UK, male/female vocal/instrumental group.See also Marc and the Mambas.

Herb ALPERT and the TIJUANA BRASS *US, male band leader/instrumentalist - trumpet*
306 wks

29 Jan 66 ●	GOING PLACES	*Pye NPL 28065*		4	138 wks
23 Apr 66 ●	WHIPPED CREAM AND OTHER DELIGHTS			2	42 wks
	Pye NPL 28058				
28 May 66	WHAT NOW MY LOVE	*Pye NPL 28077*		18	17 wks
11 Feb 67	S.R.O.	*Pye NSPL 28088*		5	26 wks
15 Jul 67	SOUNDS LIKE	*A&M AMLS 900*		21	10 wks
3 Feb 68	NINTH	*A&M AMLS 905*		26	9 wks
29 Jun 68 ●	BEAT OF THE BRASS	*A&M AMLS 916*		4	21 wks
9 Aug 69	WARM	*A&M AMLS 937*		30	4 wks
14 Mar 70	THE BRASS ARE COMIN'	*A&M AMLS 962*		40	1 wk
30 May 70 ●	GREATEST HITS	*A&M AMLS 980*		8	27 wks
27 Jun 70	DOWN MEXICO WAY	*A&M AMLS 974*		64	1 wk
13 Nov 71	AMERICA	*A&M AMLB 1000*		45	1 wk
12 Nov 77	40 GREATEST	*K-Tel NE 1005*		45	2 wks
17 Nov 79	RISE	*A&M AMLH 64790*		37	7 wks

Rise credits only Herb Alpert. On 29 Jun 67 Going Places and What Now My Love changed labels and numbers to A&M AMLS 965 :and AMLS 977 respectively.

ALTERED IMAGES *UK, male/female vocal/instrumental group*
40 wks

19 Sep 81	HAPPY BIRTHDAY	*Epic EPC 84893*		26	21 wks
15 May 82	PINKY BLUE	*Epic EPC 85665*		12	10 wks
25 Jun 83	BITE	*Epic EPC 25413*		16	9 wks

AMEN CORNER *UK, male vocal/instrumental group*
8 wks

30 Mar 68	ROUND AMEN CORNER	*Deram SML 1021*		26	7 wks
1 Nov 69	EXPLOSIVE COMPANY	*Immediate IMSP 023*		19	1 wk

AMERICA *US, male vocal/instrumental group*
22 wks

22 Jan 72	AMERICA	*Warner Bros. K 46093*		14	13 wks
9 Dec 72	HOMECOMING	*Warner Bros. K 46180*		21	5 wks
10 Nov 73	HAT TRICK	*Warner Bros. K 56016*		41	3 wks
7 Feb 76	HISTORY - AMERICA'S GREATEST HITS			60	1 wk
	Warner Bros. K 56169				

ALTERED IMAGES (top left) The birthday celebration lasted 21 weeks for the Glaswegian band formed in March 1979.

BRYAN ADAMS (left) Canada's most successful world star of 1985. (Retna Pictures)

AC/DC (below) Hard rock bad boy image was paradoxically portrayed by schoolboy garbed Angus Young. After the death of Bon Scott in 1980 Brian Johnson joined as vocalist.

ADAM AND THE ANTS (bottom) Stuart Goddard, now out on his own, has charted three Antless albums. (Smash Hits)

Ian ANDERSON *UK, male vocalist/instrumentalist - flute*

1 wk

| 26 Nov 83 | **WALK INTO LIGHT** | Chrysalis CDL 1443 | ..... | **78** | 1 wk |

Jon ANDERSON *UK, male vocalist*

19 wks

24 Jul 76	● **OLIAS OF SUNHILLOW**	Atlantic K 50261	.....	**8**	10 wks
15 Nov 80	**SONG OF SEVEN**	Atlantic K 50756	....	**38**	3 wks
5 Jun 82	**ANIMATION**	Polydor POLD 5044	....	**43**	6 wks

See also Jon and Vangelis.

Laurie ANDERSON *US, female vocalist/multi-instrumentalist*

8 wks

| 1 May 82 | **BIG SCIENCE** | Warner Bros. K 57002 | | **29** | 6 wks |
| 10 Mar 84 | **MISTER HEARTBREAK** | Warner Bros 92-5077-1 | | **93** | 2 wks |

Lynn ANDERSON *US, female vocalist*

1 wk

| 17 Apr 71 | **ROSE GARDEN** | CBS 64333 | .... | **45** | 1 wk |

Moira ANDERSON *UK, female vocalist*

1 wk

| 20 Jun 70 | **THESE ARE MY SONGS** | Decca SKL 5016 | ..... | **50** | 1 wk |

See also Harry Secombe and Moira Anderson.

Julie ANDREWS *UK, female vocalist*

5 wks

| 16 Jul 83 | **LOVE ME TENDER** | Peach River JULIE 1 | ...... | **63** | 5 wks |

ANGELIC UPSTARTS *UK, male vocal/instrumental group*

20 wks

18 Aug 79	**TEENAGE WARNING**	Warner Bros. K 50634	...	**29**	7 wks
12 Apr 80	**WE'VE GOTTA GET OUT OF THIS PLACE**				
		Warner Bros. K 56806		**54**	3 wks
7 Jun 81	**2,000,000 VOICES**	Zonophone ZONO 104		**32**	3 wks
26 Sep 81	**ANGELIC UPSTARTS**	Zonophone ZEM 102	....	**27**	7 wks

ANIMAL NIGHTLIFE *UK, male vocal/instrumental group*

6 wks

| 24 Aug 85 | **SHANGRI-LA** | Island ILPS 9830 | .... | **36** | 6 wks |

ANIMALS *UK, male vocal/instrumental group*

86 wks

14 Nov 64	● **THE ANIMALS**	Columbia 33SX 1669	....	**6**	20 wks
22 May 65	● **ANIMAL TRACKS**	Columbia 33SX 1708	....	**6**	26 wks
16 Apr 66	● **MOST OF THE ANIMALS**	Columbia 33SX 6035		**4**	20 wks
28 May 66	● **ANIMALISMS**	Decca LK 4797	....	**4**	17 wks
25 Sep 71	**MOST OF THE ANIMALS**	MFP 5218	....	**18**	3 wks

Adam ANT *UK, male vocalist*

139 wks

15 Nov 80	★ **KINGS OF THE WILD FRONTIER**	CBS 84549		**1**	66 wks
17 Jan 81	**DIRK WEARS WHITE SOX**	Do It RIDE 3	....	**16**	29 wks
14 Nov 81	● **PRINCE CHARMING**	CBS 85268	....	**2**	21 wks
23 Oct 82	● **FRIEND OR FOE**	CBS 25040	....	**5**	12 wks
19 Nov 83	**STRIP**	CBS 25705	....	**20**	8 wks
14 Sep 85	**VIVE LE ROCK**	CBS 26583	....	**42**	3 wks

All the albums up to and including Prince Charming *credited to Adam and the Ants- UK, male vocal/instrumental group*

ANTI-NOWHERE LEAGUE *UK, male vocal/instrumental group*

12 wks

| 22 May 82 | **WE ARE...THE LEAGUE** | WXYZ LMNOP 1 | .. | **24** | 11 wks |
| 5 Nov 83 | **LIVE IN YUGOSLAVIA** | I.D. NOSE 3 | .... | **88** | 1 wk |

ANTI-PASTI *UK, male vocal/instrumental group*

7 wks

| 15 Aug 81 | **THE LAST CALL** | Rondelet ABOUT 5 | .... | **31** | 7 wks |

APRIL WINE *Canada, male vocal/instrumental group*

8 wks

15 Mar 80	**HARDER...FASTER**	Capitol EST 12013	....	**34**	5 wks
24 Jan 81	**THE NATURE OF THE BEAST**				
		Capitol EST 12125	....	**48**	3 wks

ARCADIA *UK, male vocal/instrumental group*

4 wks

| 7 Dec 85 | **SO RED THE ROSE** | Parlophone Odeon PCSD 101 | | **30†** | 4 wks |

ARGENT *UK, male vocal/instrumental group*

9 wks

| 29 Apr 72 | **ALL TOGETHER NOW** | Epic EPC 64962 | .... | **13** | 8 wks |
| 31 Mar 73 | **IN DEEP** | Epic EPC 65475 | .... | **49** | 1 wk |

Joan ARMATRADING *UK, female vocalist*

158 wks

4 Sep 76	**JOAN ARMATRADING**	A & M AMLH 64588		**12**	27 wks
1 Oct 77	● **SHOW SOME EMOTION**	A & M AMLH 68433		**6**	11 wks
14 Oct 78	**TO THE LIMIT**	A & M AMLH 64732		**13**	10 wks
24 May 80	● **ME MYSELF I**	A & M AMLH 64809		**5**	23 wks
12 Sep 81	● **WALK UNDER LADDERS**				
		A & M AMLH 64876	....	**6**	29 wks
12 Mar 83	● **THE KEY**	A & M AMLX 64912	....	**10**	14 wks
26 Nov 83	**TRACK RECORD**	A & M JA 2001	....	**18**	32 wks
16 Feb 85	**SECRET SECRETS**	A & M AMA 5040	......	**14**	12 wks

ARMOURY SHOW *UK, male vocal/instrumental group*

1 wk

| 21 Sep 85 | **WAITING FOR THE FLOODS** | | | | |
| | | Parlophone ARM 1 | .... | **57** | 1 wk |

Louis ARMSTRONG *US, male band leader vocalist/instrumentalist - trumpet*

14 wks

28 Oct 61	**JAZZ CLASSICS**	Ace Of Hearts AH 7		**20**	1 wk
22 Oct 60	**SATCHMO PLAYS KING OLIVER**				
		Audio Fidelity AFLP 1930	....	**20**	1 wk
27 Jun 64	**HELLO DOLLY**	London HAR 8190		**11**	6 wks
16 Nov 68	**WHAT A WONDERFUL WORLD**				
		Stateside SSL 10247	....	**37**	3 wks
20 Feb 82	**THE VERY BEST OF LOUIS ARMSTRONG**				
		Warwick WW 5112	....	**30**	3 wks

Steve ARRINGTON *US, male vocalist*

11 wks

| 13 Apr 85 | **DANCIN' IN THE KEY OF LIFE** | Atlantic 781245 | | **41** | 11 wks |

ART OF NOISE UK, male/female studio group under producer Trevor Horn
17 wks

3 Nov 84	(WHO'S AFRAID OF) THE ART OF NOISE ZTT ZTTIQ 2		27	17 wks

ASHFORD and SIMPSON US, male/female vocal duo
6 wks

16 Feb 85	SOLID Capitol SASH 1		42	6 wks

ASIA UK, male vocal/instrumental group
50 wks

10 Apr 82	ASIA Geffen GEF 85577		11	38 wks
20 Aug 83 ●	ALPHA Geffen GRF 25508		5	11 wks
14 Dec 85	ASTRA Geffen GEF 26413		68	1 wk

ASSOCIATES UK, male vocal/instrumental group
27 wks

22 May 82 ●	SULK Associates ASCL 1		10	20 wks
16 Feb 85	PERHAPS WEA WX 9		23	7 wks

ASWAD UK, male vocal/instrumental group
24 wks

24 Jul 82	NOT SATISFIED CBS 85666		50	6 wks
10 Dec 83	LIVE AND DIRECT Island IMA 6		57	16 wks
3 Nov 84	REBEL SOULS Island ILPS 9780		48	2 wks

ATHLETICO SPIZZ 80 UK, male vocal/instrumental group
5 wks

26 Jul 80	DO A RUNNER A & M AMLE 68514		27	5 wks

Chet ATKINS US, male instrumentalist - guitar
5 wks

18 Mar 61	THE OTHER CHET ATKINS RCA RD 27194		20	1 wk
17 Jun 61	CHET ATKINS' WORKSHOP RCA RD 27214		19	1 wk
30 Feb 63	CARIBBEAN GUITAR RCA RD 7519		17	3 wks

Rowan ATKINSON UK, male comedian
9 wks

7 Feb 81	LIVE IN BELFAST Arista SPART 1150		44	9 wks

ATLANTIC STARR US, male/female vocal/instrumental group
3 wks

15 Jun 85	AS THE BAND TURNS A & M AMA 5019		64	3 wks

ATOMIC ROOSTER UK, male vocal/instrumental group
13 wks

13 Jun 70	ATOMIC ROOSTER B & C CAS 1010		49	1 wk
16 Jan 71	DEATH WALKS BEHIND YOU Charisma CAS 1026		12	8 wks
21 Aug 71	IN HEARING OF ATOMIC ROOSTER Pegasus PEG 1		18	4 wks

ATTRACTIONS - See Elvis COSTELLO and the ATTRACTIONS

AU PAIRS UK, female/male vocal/instrumental group
10 wks

6 Jun 81	PLAYING WITH A DIFFERENT SEX Human HUMAN 1		33	7 wks
4 Sep 82	SENSE AND SENSUALITY Kamera KAM 010		79	3 wks

Brian AUGER TRINITY - See Julie DRISCOLL and the Brian AUGER TRINITY

Patti AUSTIN US, female vocalist
1 wk

26 Sep 81	EVERY HOME SHOULD HAVE ONE Quest K 56931		99	1 wk

AVERAGE WHITE BAND UK, male vocal/instrumental group
47 wks

1 Mar 75 ●	AVERAGE WHITE BAND Atlantic K 50058		6	14 wks
5 Jul 75	CUT THE CAKE Atlantic K 50146		28	4 wks
31 Jul 76	SOUL SEARCHING TIME Atlantic K 50272		60	1 wk
10 Mar 79	I FEEL NO FRET RCA XL 13063		15	15 wks
31 May 80	SHINE RCA XL 13123		14	13 wks

Pam AYERS UK, female vocalist
20 wks

27 Mar 76	SOME OF ME POEMS AND SONGS Galaxy GAL 6003		13	14 wks
18 Dec 76	SOME MORE OF ME POEMS AND SONGS Galaxy GAL 6010		23	6 wks

Roy AYERS US, male vocalist/instrumentalist - vibraphone
2 wks

26 Oct 85	YOU MIGHT BE SURPRISED CBS 26653		91	2 wks

Charles AZNAVOUR France, male vocalist
21 wks

29 Jun 74	AZNAVOUR SINGS AZNAVOUR VOL.3 Barclay 80472		23	7 wks
7 Sep 74 ●	A TAPESTRY OF DREAMS Barclay 90003		9	13 wks
2 Aug 80	HIS GREATEST LOVE SONGS K-Tel NE 1078		73	1 wk

AZTEC CAMERA UK, male vocal/instrumental group
24 wks

23 Apr 83	HIGH LAND HARD RAIN Rough Trade ROUGH 47		22	18 wks
29 Sep 84	KNIFE WEA WX 8		14	6 wks

B

BACCARA Spain, female vocal duo
6 wks

4 Mar 78	BACCARA RCA PL 28316		26	6 wks

Burt BACHARACH US, orchestra and chorus
43 wks

22 May 65 ●	HIT MAKER - BURT BACHARACH London HAR 8233		3	18 wks

28 Nov 70	REACH OUT A & M AMLS 908	52	3 wks
3 Apr 71 ●	PORTRAIT IN MUSIC A & M AMLS 2010	5	22 wks

BACHELORS Ireland, male vocal group 103 wks

27 Jun 64 ●	THE BACHELORS AND 16 GREAT SONGS Decca LK 4614	2	44 wks
9 Oct 65	MORE GREAT SONG HITS FROM THE BACHELORS Decca LK 4721	15	6 wks
9 Jul 66	HITS OF THE SIXTIES Decca TXL 102	12	9 wks
5 Nov 66	BACHELORS' GIRLS Decca LK 4827	24	8 wks
1 Jul 67	GOLDEN ALL TIME HITS Decca SKL 4849	19	7 wks
14 Jun 69 ●	WORLD OF THE BACHELORS Decca SPA 2	8	18 wks
23 Aug 69	WORLD OF THE BACHELORS VOL.2 Decca SPA 22	11	7 wks
22 Dec 79	25 GOLDEN GREATS Warwick WW 5068	38	4 wks

BACHMAN-TURNER OVERDRIVE Canada, male vocal/instrumental group 13 wks

14 Dec 74	NOT FRAGILE Mercury 9100 007	12	13 wks

B BOYS US, male vocal/instrumental group 1 wk

28 Jan 84	CUTTIN' HERBIE Streetwave X KHAN 501	90	1 wk

BAD COMPANY UK, male vocal/instrumental group 87 wks

15 Jun 74 ●	BAD COMPANY Island ILPS 9279	3	25 wks
12 Apr 75 ●	STRAIGHT SHOOTER Island ILPS 9304	3	27 wks
21 Feb 76 ●	RUN WITH THE PACK Island ILPS 9346	4	12 wks
19 Mar 77	BURNIN' SKY Island ILPS 9441	17	8 wks
17 Mar 79 ●	DESOLATION ANGELS Swansong SSK 59408	10	9 wks
28 Aug 82	ROUGH DIAMONDS Swansong SSK 59419	15	6 wks

BAD MANNERS UK, male vocal/instrumental group 44 wks

26 Apr 80	SKA 'N' B Magnet MAG 5033	34	13 wks
29 Nov 80	LOONEE TUNES Magnet MAG 5038	36	12 wks
24 Oct 81	GOSH IT'S BAD MANNERS Magnet MAGL 5043	18	12 wks
27 Nov 82	FORGING AHEAD Magnet MAGL 5050	78	1 wk
7 May 83	THE HEIGHT OF BAD MANNERS Telstar STAR 2229	23	6 wks

Joan BAEZ US, female vocalist 88 wks

18 Jul 64 ●	JOAN BAEZ IN CONCERT VOL.2 Fontana TFL 6033	8	19 wks
15 May 65 ●	JOAN BAEZ NO.5 Fontana TFL 6043	3	27 wks
19 Jun 65 ●	JOAN BAEZ Fontana TFL 6002	9	13 wks
27 Nov 65 ●	FAREWELL ANGELINA Fontana TFL 6058	5	23 wks
19 Jul 69	JOAN BAEZ ON VANGUARD Vanguard SVXL 100	15	5 wks
3 Apr 71	FIRST TEN YEARS Vanguard 6635 003	41	1 wk

Philip BAILEY US, male vocalist 17 wks

30 Mar 85	CHINESE WALL CBS 26161	29	17 wks

BAKER-GURVITZ ARMY UK, male vocal/instrumental group 5 wks

22 Feb 75	BAKER-GURVITZ ARMY Vertigo 9103 201	22	5 wks

See also Ginger Baker's Air Force.

Ginger BAKER'S AIR FORCE UK, male vocal/instrumental group 1 wk

13 Jun 70	GINGER BAKER'S AIR FORCE Polydor 2662-001	37	1 wk

See also Baker-Gurvitz Army.

Kenny BALL UK, male vocalist/instrumentalist - trumpet 26 wks

7 Sep 63 ●	KENNY BALL'S GOLDEN HITS Pye Golden Guinea GGL 0209	4	26 wks

See also Kenny Ball, Chris Barber and Acker Bilk.

Kenny BALL, Chris BARBER and Acker BILK UK, male jazz band leaders/vocalists/instrumentalists - trumpet, trombone and clarinet respectively 24 wks

25 Aug 62 ★	BEST OF BALL, BARBER AND BILK Pye Golden Guinea GGL 0131	1	24 wks

See also Kenny Ball; Chris Barber; Chris Barber and Acker Bilk; Mr Acker Bilk

BANANARAMA UK, female vocal group 27 wks

19 Mar 83 ●	DEEP SEA SKIVING London RAMA 1	7	16 wks
28 Apr 84	BANANARAMA London RAMA 2	16	11 wks

BAND Canada, male vocal/instrumental group 18 wks

31 Jan 70	THE BAND Capitol EST 132	25	11 wks
3 Oct 70	STAGE FRIGHT Capitol EA SW 425	15	6 wks
27 Nov 71	CAHOOTS Capitol EA-ST 651	41	1 wk

See film soundtracks for The Last Waltz

BANGLES US, female vocal/instrumental group 1 wk

16 Mar 85	ALL OVER THE PLACE CBS 26015	86	1 wk

Tony BANKS UK, male instrumentalist - keyboards 7 wks

20 Oct 79	A CURIOUS FEELING Charisma CAS 1148	21	5 wks
25 Jun 83	THE FUGITIVE Charisma TBLP 1	50	2 wks

BANSHEES - See SIOUXSIE and the BANSHEES

Chris BARBER UK, male vocalist/instrumentalist - trombone 3 wks

24 Sep 60	CHRIS BARBER BAND BOX NO.2 Columbia 33SCX 3277	17	1 wk
5 Nov 60	ELITE SYNCOPATIONS Columbia 33SX 1245	18	1 wk
12 Nov 60	BEST OF CHRIS BARBER Ace Of Clubs ACL 1037	17	1 wk

See also Kenny Ball, Chris Barber and Acker Bilk; Chris Barber and Acker Bilk.

Chris BARBER and Acker BILK UK, male band leaders/vocalists/instrumentalists - trombone and clarinet 61 wks

27 May 61 ●	BEST OF BARBER AND BILK VOL.1 Pye GGL 0075	4	43 wks

BAD COMPANY (left) Their members came from Free, Mott the Hoople and King Crimson.

AFTER THE FIRE (centre) They rode in on a laser and heated up to 80°F before their batteries gave out in the spring of 1982.

ATOMIC ROOSTER (right) Vincent Crane, Nick Graham and Carl Palmer. Three hit albums by the three-piece band on three different labels.

JOAN ARMATRADING (below) Joan Armatrading invites the audience to sing 'Willow' from her album 'Show Some Emotion'. (LFI)

11 Nov 61	●	**BEST OF BARBER AND BILK VOL.2**			
		Pye GGL 0096		**8**	18 wks

See also Kenny Ball, Chris Barber and Acker Bilk; Chris Barber; Mr Acker Bilk.

BARCLAY JAMES HARVEST *UK, male vocal/instrumental group*   *41 wks*

14 Dec 74	**BARCLAY JAMES HARVEST LIVE**			**40**	2 wks
	Polydor 2683 052				
18 Oct 75	**TIME HONOURED GHOST**	Polydor 2383 361		**32**	3 wks
23 Oct 76	**OCTOBERON**	Polydor 2442 144		**19**	4 wks
1 Oct 77	**GONE TO EARTH**	Polydor 2442 148		**30**	7 wks
21 Oct 78	**BARCLAY JAMES HARVEST XII**			**31**	2 wks
	Polydor POLD 5006				
23 May 81	**TURN OF THE TIDE**	Polydor POLD 5040		**55**	2 wks
24 Jul 82	**A CONCERT FOR THE PEOPLE (BERLIN)**			**15**	11 wks
	Polydor POLD 5052				
28 May 83	**RING OF CHANGES**	Polydor POLH 3		**36**	4 wks
14 Apr 84	**VICTIMS OF CIRCUMSTANCE**			**33**	6 wks
	Polydor POLD 5135				

Daniel BARENBOIM - *See John WILLIAMS and Daniel BARENBOIM*

Syd BARRETT *UK, male vocalist/instrumentalist - guitar*
1 wk

7 Feb 70	**MADCAP LAUGHS**	Harvest SHVL 765		**40**	1 wk

BARRON KNIGHTS *UK, male vocal/instrumental group*   *22 wks*

2 Dec 78	**NIGHT GALLERY**	Epic EPC 83221		**15**	13 wks
1 Dec 79	**TEACH THE WORLD TO LAUGH**			**51**	4 wks
	Epic EPC 83891				
13 Dec 80	**JUST A GIGGLE**	Epic EPC 84550		**62**	5 wks

John BARRY *UK, male arranger/conductor*   *9 wks*

29 Jan 72	**THE PERSUADERS**	CBS 64816		**18**	9 wks

Count BASIE *US, male orchestra leader/instrumentalist - piano*   *1 wk*

16 Apr 60	**CHAIRMAN OF THE BOARD**			**17**	1 wk
	Columbia 33SX 1209				

See also Frank Sinatra and Count Basie.

Toni BASIL *US, female vocalist*   *16 wks*

6 Feb 82	**WORD OF MOUTH**	Radialchoice BASIL 1		**15**	16 wks

Shirley BASSEY *UK, female vocalist*   *259 wks*

28 Jan 61	**FABULOUS SHIRLEY BASSEY**			**12**	2 wks
	Columbia 33SX 1178				
25 Feb 61	●	**SHIRLEY**	Columbia 33SX 1286	**9**	10 wks
17 Feb 62	**SHIRLEY BASSEY**	Columbia 33SX 1382		**14**	11 wks
15 Dec 62	**LET'S FACE THE MUSIC**	Columbia 33SX 1454		**12**	7 wks
4 Dec 65	**SHIRLEY BASSEY AT THE PIGALLE**			**16**	7 wks
	Columbia 33SX 1787				
27 Aug 66	**I'VE GOT A SONG FOR YOU**			**26**	1 wk
	United Artists ULP 1142				
17 Feb 68	**TWELVE OF THOSE SONGS**			**38**	3 wks
	Columbia SCX 6204				
7 Dec 68	**GOLDEN HITS OF SHIRLEY BASSEY**			**28**	40 wks
	Columbia SCX 6294				

11 Jul 70	**LIVE AT THE TALK OF THE TOWN**			**38**	6 wks
	United Artists UAS 29095				
29 Aug 70	●	**SOMETHING** United Artists UAS 29100		**5**	28 wks
15 May 71	●	**SOMETHING ELSE** United Artists UAG 29149		**7**	9 wks
2 Oct 71	**BIG SPENDER**	Sunset SLS 50262		**27**	8 wks
30 Oct 71	**IT'S MAGIC**	Starline SRS 5082		**32**	1 wk
6 Nov 71	**THE FABULOUS SHIRLEY BASSEY**	MFP 1398		**48**	1 wk
4 Dec 71	**WHAT NOW MY LOVE**	MFP 5230		**17**	5 wks
8 Jan 72	**THE SHIRLEY BASSEY COLLECTION**			**37**	1 wk
	United Artists UAD 60013/4				
19 Feb 72	**I CAPRICORN**	United Artists UAS 29246		**13**	11 wks
29 Nov 72	**AND I LOVE YOU SO**	United artists UAS 29385		**24**	9 wks
2 Jun 73	●	**NEVER NEVER NEVER**		**10**	10 wks
	United Artists UAG 29471				
15 Mar 75	●	**THE SHIRLEY BASSEY SINGLES ALBUM**		**2**	23 wks
	United Artists UAS 29728				
1 Nov 75	**GOOD, BAD BUT BEAUTIFUL**			**13**	7 wks
	United Artists UAS 29881				
15 May 76	**LOVE, LIFE AND FEELINGS**			**17**	5 wks
	United Artists UAS 29944				
4 Dec 76	**THOUGHTS OF LOVE**	United Artists UAS 30011		**15**	9 wks
25 Jun 77	**YOU TAKE MY HEART AWAY**			**34**	5 wks
	United Artists UAS 30037				
4 Nov 78	●	**25TH ANNIVERSARY ALBUM**		**3**	12 wks
	United Artists SBTV 601 4748				
12 May 79	**THE MAGIC IS YOU**	United Artists UATV 30230		**40**	5 wks
17 Jul 82	**LOVE SONGS**	Applause APKL 1163		**48**	5 wks
20 Oct 84	**I AM WHAT I AM**	Towerbell TOWLP 7		**25**	18 wks

Let's Face The Music has credit 'with The Nelson Riddle Orchestra'

BAUHAUS *UK, male vocal/instrumental group*   *24 wks*

15 Nov 80	**IN THE FLAT FIELD**	4AD CAD 13		**72**	1 wk
24 Oct 81	**MASK**	Beggars Banquet BEGA 29		**30**	5 wks
30 Oct 82	●	**THE SKY'S GONE OUT**		**4**	6 wks
	Beggars Banquet BEGA 42				
23 Jul 83	**BURNING FROM THE INSIDE**			**13**	10 wks
	Beggars Banquet BEGA 45				
30 Nov 85	**1979-1983**	Beggars Banquet BEGA 64		**36**	2 wks

BAY CITY ROLLERS *UK, male vocal/instrumental group*   *127 wks*

12 Oct 74	★	**ROLLIN'** Bell BELLS 244		**1**	62 wks
3 May 75	★	**ONCE UPON A STAR** Bell SYBEL 8001		**1**	37 wks
13 Dec 75	●	**WOULDN'T YOU LIKE IT** Bell SYBEL 8002		**3**	12 wks
25 Sep 76	●	**DEDICATION** Bell SYBEL 8005		**4**	12 wks
13 Aug 77	**IT'S A GAME**	Arista SPARTY 1009		**18**	4 wks

BBC SYMPHONY ORCHESTRA, SINGERS and CHORUS *UK, orchestra/choir and audience*   *6 wks*

4 Oct 69	**LAST NIGHT OF THE PROMS**			**36**	1 wk
	Philips SFM 23033				
11 Dec 82	**HIGHLIGHTS - LAST NIGHT OF THE PROMS**			**69**	5 wks
	'82 K-Tel NE 1198				

Last Night Of The Proms was conducted by Colin Davis and Highlights - Last Night Of The Proms '82 by James Loughran

BEACH BOYS *US, male vocal/instrumental group*   *524 wks*

25 Sep 65	**SURFIN' USA**	Capitol T 1890		**17**	7 wks
19 Feb 66	●	**BEACH BOYS PARTY** Capitol T 2398		**3**	14 wks
16 Apr 66	●	**BEACH BOYS TODAY** Capitol T 2269		**6**	25 wks
9 Jul 66	●	**PET SOUNDS** Capitol T 2458		**2**	39 wks
16 Jul 66	**SUMMER DAYS**	Capitol T 2354		**4**	22 wks
12 Nov 66	●	**BEST OF THE BEACH BOYS** Capitol T 20865		**2**	142 wks
11 Mar 67	**SURFER GIRL**	Capitol ST 1981		**13**	14 wks
21 Oct 67	●	**BEST OF THE BEACH BOYS VOL.2**		**3**	39 wks
	Capitol ST 20956				
18 Nov 67	●	**SMILEY SMILE** Capitol ST 9001		**9**	8 wks

16 Mar 68 ● **WILD HONEY** *Capitol ST 2859* .... **7** 15 wks
21 Sep 68 ● **FRIENDS** *Capitol ST 2895* **13** 8 wks
23 Nov 68 ● **BEST OF THE BEACH BOYS VOL. 3**
    Capitol ST 21142 .... **9** 12 wks
29 Mar 69 ● **20/20** *Capitol EST 133* .... **3** 10 wks
19 Sep 70 ● **GREATEST HITS** *Capitol ST 21628* **5** 30 wks
5 Dec 70 ● **SUNFLOWER** *Stateside SSL 8251* **29** 6 wks
27 Nov 71 **SURF'S UP** *Stateside SLS 10313* **15** 7 wks
24 Jun 72 **CARL AND THE PASSIONS/SO TOUGH**
    Reprise K 44184 .... **25** 1 wk
17 Feb 73 **HOLLAND** *Reprise K 54008* **20** 7 wks
10 Jul 76 ★ **20 GOLDEN GREATS** *Capitol EMTV 1* .... **1** 86 wks
24 Jul 76 **15 BIG ONES** *Reprise K 54079* **31** 3 wks
7 May 77 **THE BEACH BOYS LOVE YOU** *Brother/*
    Reprise K 54087 .... **28** ·1 wk
21 Apr 79 **LA (LIGHT ALBUM)** *Caribou CRB 86081* **32** 6 wks
12 Apr 80 **KEEPING THE SUMMER ALIVE**
    Caribou CRB 86109 .... **54** 3 wks
30 Jul 83 ★ **THE VERY BEST OF THE BEACH BOYS**
    Capitol BBTV 1867193 .... **1** 17 wks
22 Jun 85 **THE BEACH BOYS** *Caribou CRB 26378* .... **60** 2 wks

BEAKY - *See Dave DEE, DOZY, BEAKY, MICK and TICH*

The BEAT *UK, male vocal/instrumental group*   *69 wks*

31 May 80 ● **JUST CAN'T STOP IT** *Go-Feet BEAT 001* ...... **3** 32 wks
16 May 81 ● **WHA'PPEN** *Go-Feet BEAT 3* **3** 18 wks
9 Oct 82 **SPECIAL BEAT SERVICE** *Go Feet BEAT 5* .... **21** 6 wks
11 Jun 83 ● **WHAT IS BEAT? (THE BEST OF THE BEAT)**
    Go-Feet BEAT 6 .... **10** 13 wks

BEATLES *UK, male vocal/instrumental group*   *1021 wks*

6 Apr 63 ★ **PLEASE PLEASE ME** *Parlophone PMC 1202* .... **1** 70 wks
30 Nov 63 ★ **WITH THE BEATLES** *Parlophone PMC 1206* **1** 51 wks
18 Jul 64 ★ **A HARD DAY'S NIGHT** *Parlophone PMC 1230* .. **1** 38 wks
12 Dec 64 ★ **BEATLES FOR SALE** *Parlophone PMC 1240* **1** 46 wks
14 Aug 65 ★ **HELP** *Parlophone PMC 1255* **1** 37 wks
11 Dec 65 ★ **RUBBER SOUL** *Parlophone PMC 1267* **1** 42 wks
13 Aug 66 ★ **REVOLVER** *Parlophone PMC 7009* **1** 34 wks
10 Dec 66 ● **A COLLECTION OF BEATLES OLDIES**
    Parlophone PMC 7016 .... **7** 25 wks
3 Jun 67 ★ **SERGEANT PEPPER'S LONELY HEARTS CLUB
BAND** *Parlophone PMC 7027* .... **1** 148 wks
13 Jan 68 **MAGICAL MYSTERY TOUR (import)**
    Capitol SMAL 2835 .... **31** 2 wks
7 Dec 68 ★ **THE BEATLES** *Apple PCS 7167/8* **1** 22 wks
1 Feb 69 ● **YELLOW SUBMARINE** *Apple PCS 7070* **4** 10 wks
4 Oct 69 ★ **ABBEY ROAD** *Apple PCS 7088* **1** 76 wks
23 May 70 ★ **LET IT BE** *Apple PXS 1* **1** 59 wks
16 Jan 71 **A HARD DAY'S NIGHT (re-issue)**
    Parlophone PCS 3058 .... **39** 1 wk
24 Jul 71 **HELP (re-issue)** *Parlophone PCS 3071* **33** 2 wks
5 May 73 ● **THE BEATLES 1967-1970** *Apple PCSP 718* **2** 113 wks
5 May 73 ● **THE BEATLES 1962-1966** *Apple PCSP 717* ..... **3** 148 wks
25 Jun 76 **ROCK 'N' ROLL MUSIC** *Parlophone PCSP 719* .. **11** 15 wks
21 Aug 76 **THE BEATLES TAPES** *Polydor 2683 068* .... **45** 1 wk
21 May 77 ★ **THE BEATLES AT THE HOLLYWOOD BOWL**
    Parlophone EMTV 4 .... **1** 17 wks
17 Dec 77 ● **LOVE SONGS** *Parlophone PCSP 721* ..... **7** 17 wks
3 Nov 79 **RARITIES** *Parlophone PCM 1001* .... **71** 1 wk
15 Nov 80 **BEATLES BALLADS** *Parlophone PCS 7214* ..... **17** 16 wks
30 Oct 82 ● **20 GREATEST HITS** *Parlophone PCTC 260* ..... **10** 30 wks

Yellow Submarine *featured several tracks by the George Martin Orchestra.*

BE-BOP DELUXE *UK, male vocal/instrumental group*   *28 wks*

31 Jan 76 **SUNBURST FINISH** *Harvest SHSP 4053* .... **17** 12 wks
25 Sep 76 **MODERN MUSIC** *Harvest SHSP 4058* .... **12** 6 wks
6 Aug 77 ● **LIVE! IN THE AIR AGE** *Harvest SHVL 816* .... **10** 5 wks

25 Feb 78 **DRASTIC PLASTIC** *Harvest SHSP 4091* .... **22** 5 wks

Jeff BECK *UK, male vocalist/instrumentalist - guitar*   *11 wks*

13 Sep 69 **BECK-OLA** *Columbia SCX 6351* .... **39** 1 wk
24 Jul 76 **WIRED** *CBS 86012* .... **38** 5 wks
19 Jul 80 **THERE AND BACK** *Epic EPC 83288* .... **38** 4 wks
17 Aug 85 **FLASH** *Epic EPC 26112* .... **83** 1 wk

See also Jeff Beck, Tim Bogert and Carmine Appice.

Jeff BECK, Tim BOGERT and Carmine APPICE *UK/US, male vocal/instrumental group*   *3 wks*

28 Apr 73 **JEFF BECK, TIM BOGERT & CARMINE APPICE**
    Epic EPC 65455 .... **28** 3 wks

See also Jeff Beck.

BEE GEES *UK/Australia, male vocal/instrumental group*   *150 wks*

12 Aug 67 ● **BEE GEES FIRST** *Polydor 583-012* .... **8** 26 wks
24 Feb 68 ● **HORIZONTAL** *Polydor 582-020* .... **16** 15 wks
28 Sep 68 ● **IDEA** *Polydor 583-036* .... **4** 18 wks
5 Apr 69 ● **ODESSA** *Polydor 583-049/50* .... **10** 1 wk
8 Nov 69 ● **BEST OF THE BEE GEES** *Polydor 583-063* ..... **7** 22 wks
9 May 70 ● **CUCUMBER CASTLE** *Polydor 2383-010* ..... **57** 2 wks
17 Feb 79 ★ **SPIRITS HAVING FLOWN** *RSO RSBG 001* ..... **1** 33 wks
10 Nov 79 ● **BEE GEES GREATEST** *RSO RSDX 001* ..... **6** 25 wks
7 Nov 81 **LIVING EYES** *RSO RSBG 002* .... **73** 8 wks

All albums from Cucumber Castle onwards group were UK only

Sir Thomas BEECHAM *UK, conductor*   *2 wks*

26 Mar 60 **CARMEN** *HMV ALP 1762/4* .... **18** 2 wks

Full credit on sleeve reads 'Orchestre National de la Radio Diffusion Francaise, conducted by Sir Thomas Beecham'.

Captain BEEFHEART and his MAGIC BAND *US, male vocal/instrumental group*   *16 wks*

6 Dec 69 **TROUT MASK REPLICA** *Straight STS 1053* .... **21** 1 wk
23 Jan 71 **LICK MY DECALS OFF BABY**
    Straight STS 1063 .... **20** 10 wks
29 May 71 **MIRROR MAN** *Buddah 2365 002* .... **49** 1 wk
19 Feb 72 **THE SPOTLIGHT KID** *Reprise K 44162* .... **44** 2 wks
18 Sep 82 **ICE CREAM FOR CROW** *Virgin V 2337* .... **90** 2 wks

BELLAMY BROTHERS *US, male vocal duo*   *6 wks*

19 Jun 76 **BELLAMY BROTHERS** *Warner Bros. K 56242* .. **21** 6 wks

BELLE STARS *UK, female vocal/instrumental group*   *12 wks*

5 Feb 83 **THE BELLE STARS** *Stiff SEEZ 45* .... **15** 12 wks

Pierre BELMONDE *France, male instrumentalist - panpipes*   *10 wks*

7 Jun 80 **THEMES FOR DREAMS** *K-Tel ONE 1077* ..... **13** 10 wks

BARRON KNIGHTS (below) Laughalongabarronknights – Frank Carson, Mike Yarwood, Alfred Hitchcock, Mona Lisa and friends grace the cover.

BARBER AND BILK (top right) No ball!

THE BEACH BOYS (right) The classic Beach Boys line up: (L-R) Al Jardine, Mike Love, Dennis Wilson, Brian Wilson and Carl Wilson. (High Ridge Productions)

PAT BENATAR (bottom right) Holding her head in disbelief after finally scoring a significant UK success with 'Tropico'.

THE BAND The Band without a trace of stage fright. (LFI)

BELMONTS - *See DION and the BELMONTS*

Pat BENATAR *US, female vocalist* — *45 wks*

25 Jul 81	PRECIOUS TIME *Chrysalis CHR 1346*			30	7 wks
13 Nov 82	GET NERVOUS *Chrysalis CHR 1396*			73	6 wks
15 Oct 83	LIVE FROM EARTH *Chrysalis CHR 1451*			60	5 wks
17 Nov 84	TROPICO *Chrysalis CHR 1471*			31	25 wks
24 Aug 85	IN THE HEAT OF THE NIGHT				
	Chrysalis CHR 1236			98	1 wk
7 Dec 85	SEVEN THE HARD WAY *Chrysalis CHR 1507*			69	1 wk

Cliff BENNETT and the REBEL ROUSERS
UK, male vocal/instrumental group — *3 wks*

22 Oct 66	DRIVIN' ME WILD *MFP 1121*			25	3 wks

Tony BENNETT *US, male vocalist* — *63 wks*

29 May 65	I LEFT MY HEART IN SAN FRANCISCO				
	CBS BPG 62201			13	14 wks
19 Feb 66	● A STRING OF TONY'S HITS *CBS DP 66010*			9	13 wks
10 Jun 67	TONY'S GREATEST HITS *CBS SBPG 62821*			14	24 wks
23 Sep 67	TONY MAKES IT HAPPEN *CBS SBPG 63055*			31	3 wks
23 Mar 68	FOR ONCE IN MY LIFE *CBS SBPG 63166*			29	5 wks
26 Feb 77	THE VERY BEST OF TONY BENNETT - 20				
	GREATEST HITS *Warwick PA 5021*			23	4 wks

George BENSON *US, male vocalist/instrumentalist - guitar* — *196 wks*

19 Mar 77	IN FLIGHT *Warner Bros. K 56237*			19	23 wks
18 Feb 78	WEEKEND IN L.A. *Warner Bros. K 66074*			47	1 wk
24 Mar 79	LIVING INSIDE YOUR LOVE				
	Warner Bros. K 66085			24	14 wks
26 Jul 80	● GIVE ME THE NIGHT *Warner Bros. K 56823*			3	40 wks
14 Nov 81	GEORGE BENSON COLLECTION				
	Warner Bros. K 66107			19	35 wks
11 Jun 83	● IN YOUR EYES *Warner Brothers 92-3744-1*			3	53 wks
26 Jan 85	20/20 *Warner Bros 92-5178-1*			9	19 wks
19 Oct 85	★ THE LOVE SONGS *K-Tel NE 1308*			1†	11 wks

BERLIN PHILHARMONIC ORCHESTRA conducted by HERBERT VON KARAJAN
Germany, orchestra — *2 wks*

26 Sep 70	BEETHOVEN TRIPLE CONCERTO				
	HMV ASD 2582			51	2 wks

Soloists: David Oistrakh (violin), Mstislav Rostropovich (cello) and Sviatoslau Richter (piano)

LEONARD BERNSTEIN'S WEST SIDE STORY - *See Studio Cast Recordings*

Shelley BERMAN *US, male vocalist - comedian* — *4 wks*

19 Nov 60	INSIDE SHELLEY BERMAN *Capitol CLP 1300*			12	4 wks

Chuck BERRY *US, male vocalist/instrumentalist - guitar* — *53 wks*

25 May 63	CHUCK BERRY *Pye International NPL 28024*			12	16 wks
5 Oct 63	● CHUCK BERRY ON STAGE				
	Pye International NPL 28027			6	11 wks
7 Dec 63	● MORE CHUCK BERRY				
	Pye International NPL 28028			9	8 wks

30 May 64	● HIS LATEST AND GREATEST *Pye NPL 28037*		8	7 wks
3 Oct 64	YOU NEVER CAN TELL *Pye NPL 29039*		18	2 wks
12 Feb 77	● MOTORVATIN' *Chess 9288 690*		7	9 wks

Mike BERRY *UK, male vocalist* — *3 wks*

24 Jan 81	THE SUNSHINE OF YOUR SMILE			
	Polydor 2383 592		63	3 wks

BEVERLEY-PHILLIPS ORCHESTRA *UK, orchestra* — *9 wks*

9 Oct 76	GOLD ON SILVER *Warwick WW 5018*		22	9 wks

BIG AUDIO DYNAMITE *UK, male vocal/instrumental group* — *1 wk*

16 Nov 85	THIS IS BIG AUDIO DYNAMITE *CBS 26714*		100	1 wk

BIG BEN BANJO BAND *UK, male instrumental group* — *1 wk*

17 Dec 60	MORE MINSTREL MELODIES			
	Columbia 33SX 1254		20	1 wk

BIG COUNTRY *UK, male vocal instrumental group* — *99 wks*

6 Aug 83	● THE CROSSING *Mercury MERS 27*		3	78 wks
27 Oct 84	★ STEELTOWN *Mercury MERH 49*		1	21 wks

BIG ROLL BAND - *See Zoot MONEY and the BIG ROLL BAND*

BIG SOUND - *See Simon DUPREE and BIG SOUND*

Mr. Acker BILK *UK, male band leader, vocalist/instrumentalist - clarinet* — *76 wks*

19 Mar 60	● SEVEN AGES OF ACKER *Columbia 33SX 1205*		6	6 wks
9 Apr 60	ACKER BILK'S OMNIBUS *Pye NJL 22*		14	3 wks
4 Mar 61	ACKER *Columbia 33SX 1248*		17	1 wk
1 Apr 61	GOLDEN TREASURY OF BILK			
	Columbia 33SX 1304		11	6 wks
26 May 62	● STRANGER ON THE SHORE			
	Columbia 33SX 1407		6	28 wks
4 May 63	A TASTE OF HONEY *Columbia 33SX 1493*		17	4 wks
9 Oct 76	THE ONE FOR ME *Pye NSPX 41052*		38	6 wks
4 Jun 77	● SHEER MAGIC *Warwick WW 5028*		5	8 wks
11 Nov 78	EVERGREEN *Warwick PW 5045*		17	14 wks

See also Kenny Ball, Chris Barber and Acker Bilk; Chris Barber and Acker Bilk.

BIRTHDAY PARTY *Australia, male vocal/instrumental group* — *3 wks*

24 Jul 82	JUNKYARD *4AD CAD 207*		73	3 wks

Stephen BISHOP *US, male instrumentalist - piano* — *3 wks*

1 Apr 72	GREIG AND SCHUMANN PIANO CONCERTOS			
	Philips 6500 166		34	3 wks

Cilla BLACK *UK, female vocalist* *61 wks*

13 Feb 65 ●	CILLA *Parlophone PMC 1243*	**5**	11 wks
14 May 66 ●	CILLA SINGS A RAINBOW *Parlophone PMC 7004*	**4**	15 wks
13 Apr 68 ●	SHER-OO *Parlophone PCS 7041*	**7**	11 wks
30 Nov 68	BEST OF CILLA BLACK *Parlophone PCS 7065* ..	**21**	11 wks
25 Jul 70	SWEET INSPIRATION *Parlophone PCS 7103*	**42**	4 wks
29 Jan 83	THE VERY BEST OF CILLA BLACK *Parlophone EMTV 38*	**20**	9 wks

BLACK LACE *UK, male vocal/instrumental group* *18 wks*

8 Dec 84 ●	PARTY PARTY - 16 GREAT PARTY ICEBREAKERS *Telstar STAR 2250*	**4**	14 wks
7 Dec 85	PARTY PARTY 2 *Telstar STAR 2266*	**18†**	4 wks

BLACK SABBATH *UK/US, male vocal/instrumental group* *198 wks*

7 Mar 70 ●	BLACK SABBATH *Vertigo VO 6*	**8**	42 wks
26 Sep 70 ★	PARANOID *Vertigo 6360 011*	**1**	27 wks
21 Aug 71 ●	MASTER OF REALITY *Vertigo 6360 050*	**5**	13 wks
30 Sep 72 ●	BLACK SABBATH VOL.4 *Vertigo 6360 071*	**8**	10 wks
8 Dec 73 ●	SABBATH BLOODY SABBATH *WWA WWA 005*	**4**	11 wks
27 Sep 75 ●	SABOTAGE *NEMS 9119 001*	**7**	7 wks
7 Feb 76	WE SOLD OUR SOUL FOR ROCK 'N' ROLL *NEMS 6641 335*	**35**	5 wks
6 Nov 76	TECHNICAL ECSTASY *Vertigo 9102 750*	**13**	6 wks
14 Oct 78	NEVER SAY DIE *Vertigo 9102 751*	**12**	6 wks
26 Apr 80 ●	HEAVEN AND HELL *Vertigo 9102 752*	**9**	22 wks
5 Jul 80 ●	BLACK SABBATH LIVE AT LAST *NEMS BS 001*	**5**	15 wks
27 Sep 80	PARANOID (re-issue) *NEMS NEL 6003*	**54**	2 wks
14 Nov 81	MOB RULES *Mercury 6V02119*	**12**	14 wks
22 Jan 83	LIVE EVIL *Vertigo SAB 10*	**13**	11 wks
24 Sep 83 ●	BORN AGAIN *Vertigo VERL 8*	**4**	7 wks

BLACK UHURU *Jamaica, male/female vocal/instrumental group* *22 wks*

13 Jun 81	RED *Island ILPS 9625*	**28**	13 wks
22 Aug 81	BLACK UHURU *Virgin VX 1004*	**81**	2 wks
19 Jun 82	CHILL OUT *Island ILPS 9701*	**38**	6 wks
25 Aug 84	ANTHEM *Island ILPS 0773*	**90**	1 wk

Band Of The BLACK WATCH *UK, military band* *13 wks*

7 Feb 76	SCOTCH ON THE ROCKS *Spark SRLM 503* ...	**11**	13 wks

BLACK WIDOW *UK, male vocal/instrumental group* *2 wks*

4 Apr 70	SACRIFICE *CBS 63948*	**32**	2 wks

BLACKFOOT *US, male vocal/instrumental group* *22 wks*

18 Jul 81	MARAUDER *Atco K 50799*	**38**	12 wks
11 Sep 82	HIGHWAY SONG-BLACKFOOT LIVE *Atco K 50910*	**14**	6 wks
21 May 83	SIOGO *Atco 79-0080-1*	**28**	3 wks
29 Sep 84	VERTICAL SMILES *Atco 790218*	**82**	1 wk

Howard BLAKE conducting the SINFONIA OF LONDON *UK, conductor and orchestra* *5 wks*

22 Dec 84	THE SNOWMAN *CBS 71116*	**78†**	5 wks

Narration by Bernard Cribbins

BLANCMANGE *UK, male vocal/instrumental group* *57 wks*

9 Oct 82	HAPPY FAMILIES *London SH 8552*	**30**	38 wks
26 May 84 ●	MANGE TOUT *London SH 8554*	**8**	17 wks
26 Oct 85	BELIEVE YOU ME *London LONLP 10*	**54**	2 wks

BLIND FAITH *UK, male vocal/instrumental group* *10 wks*

13 Sep 69 ★	BLIND FAITH *Polydor 583-059*	**1**	10 wks

BLITZ *UK, male vocal/instrumental group* *3 wks*

6 Nov 82	VOICE OF A GENERATION *No Future PUNK 1*	**27**	3 wks

BLIZZARD OF OZ - *See Ozzy OSBOURNE*

BLOCKHEADS - *See Ian DURY and the BLOCKHEADS*

BLODWYN PIG *UK, male vocal/instrumental group* *11 wks*

16 Aug 69 ●	AHEAD RINGS OUT *Island ILPS 9101*	**9**	4 wks
23 Apr 70 ●	GETTING TO THIS *Island ILPS 9122*	**8**	7 wks

BLONDIE *US/UK, female/male vocal/instrumental group* *254 wks*

4 Mar 78 ●	PLASTIC LETTERS *Chrysalis CHR 1166*	**10**	54 wks
23 Sep 78 ★	PARALLEL LINES *Chrysalis CDL 1992*	**1**	105 wks
10 Mar 79	BLONDIE *Chrysalis CHR 1165*	**75**	1 wk
13 Oct 79 ★	EAT TO THE BEAT *Chrysalis CDL 1225*	**1**	38 wks
29 Nov 80 ●	AUTOAMERICAN *Chrysalis CDL 1290*	**3**	16 wks
31 Oct 81 ●	BEST OF BLONDIE *Chrysalis CDLTV 1*	**4**	28 wks
5 Jun 82 ●	THE HUNTER *Chrysalis CDL 1384*	**9**	12 wks

BLOOD SWEAT AND TEARS *US/Canada, male vocal/instrumental group* *21 wks*

13 Jul 68	CHILD IS FATHER TO THE MAN *CBS 63296*	**40**	1 wk
12 Apr 69	BLOOD SWEAT AND TEARS *CBS 63504*	**15**	8 wks
8 Aug 70	BLOOD SWEAT AND TEARS 3 *CBS 64024* ...	**14**	12 wks

BLUE NILE *UK, male vocal/instrumental group* *2 wks*

19 May 84	A WALK ACROSS THE ROOFTOPS *Linn/Virgin LKH 1*	**80**	2 wks

BLUE OYSTER CULT *US, male vocal/instrumental group* *40 wks*

3 Jul 76	AGENTS OF FORTUNE *CBS 81385*	**26**	10 wks
4 Feb 78	SPECTRES *CBS 86050*	**60**	1 wk
28 Oct 78	SOME ENCHANTED EVENING *CBS 86074* ...	**18**	4 wks
18 Aug 79	MIRRORS *CBS 86087*	**46**	5 wks
19 Jul 80	CULTOSAURUS ERECTUS *CBS 86120*	**12**	7 wks

25 Jul 81	**FIRE OF UNKNOWN ORIGIN** CBS 85137	**29** 7 wks
22 May 82	**EXTRATERRESTRIAL LIVE** CBS 22203	**39** 5 wks
19 Nov 83	**THE REVOLUTION BY NIGHT** CBS 25686 . . .	**95** 1 wk

BLUE RONDO A LA TURK *UK, male vocal/ instrumental group*   *2 wks*

6 Nov 82	**CHEWING THE FAT** Diable Noir/Virgin V 2240	**80** 2 wks

BLUES BAND *UK, male vocal/instrumental group*   *18 wks*

8 Mar 80	**OFFICIAL BOOTLEG ALBUM** Arista BBBP 101	**40** 9 wks
18 Oct 80	**READY** Arista BB 2	**36** 6 wks
17 Oct 81	**ITCHY FEET** Arista BB 3	**60** 3 wks

BLUEBELLES *UK, male vocal/instrumental group*   *10 wks*

11 Aug 84	**SISTERS** London LONLP 1	**22** 10 wks

Marc BOLAN - *See T.REX*

Graham BOND *UK, male vocalist/instrumentalist - keyboards*   *2 wks*

20 Jun 70	**SOLID BOND** Warner Bros. WS 3001	**40** 2 wks

Gary U.S. BONDS *US, male vocalist*   *8 wks*

22 Aug 81	**DEDICATION** EMI-America AML 3017	**43** 3 wks
10 Jul 82	**ON THE LINE** EMI America AML 3022	**55** 5 wks

BONEY M. *Various West Indian Islands, male/female vocal group*   *125 wks*

23 Apr 77	**TAKE THE HEAT OFF ME** Atlantic K 50314 . . .	**40** 15 wks
6 Aug 77	**LOVE FOR SALE** Atlantic K 50385	**60** 1 wk
29 Jul 78	★ **NIGHT FLIGHT TO VENUS** *Atlantic/ Hansa K 50498*	**1** 65 wks
29 Sep 79	★ **OCEANS OF FANTASY** Atmatic/Hansa K 50610	**1** 18 wks
12 Apr 80	★ **THE MAGIC OF BONEY M.** *Atlantic/ Hansa BMTV 1*	**1** 26 wks

BON JOVI *US, male vocal/instrumental group*   *9 wks*

28 Apr 84	**BON JOVI** Vertigo VERL 14	**71** 3 wks
11 May 85	**7800° FARENHEIT** Vertigo VERL 24	**28** 6 wks

Graham BONNET *UK, male vocalist*   *3 wks*

7 Nov 81	**LINE UP** Mercury 6302151	**62** 3 wks

BONZO DOG DOO-DAH BAND *UK, male vocal/instrumental group*   *4 wks*

18 Jan 69	**DOUGHNUT IN GRANNY'S GREENHOUSE** *Liberty LBS 83158*	**40** 1 wk
30 Aug 69	**TADPOLES** Liberty LBS 83257	**36** 1 wk
22 Jun 74	**THE HISTORY OF THE BONZOS** *United Artists UAD 60071*	**41** 2 wks

BOOKER T. and the MG'S *US, male instrumental group*   *5 wks*

25 Jul 64	**GREEN ONIONS** London HAK 8182	**11** 4 wks
11 Jul 70	**McLEMORE AVENUE** Stax SXATS 1031	**70** 1 wk

BOOMTOWN RATS *Ireland, male vocal/instrumental group*   *93 wks*

17 Sep 77	**BOOMTOWN RATS** Ensign ENVY 1	**18** 11 wks
8 Jul 78	● **TONIC FOR THE TROOPS** Ensign ENVY 3 . . .	**8** 44 wks
3 Nov 79	● **THE FINE ART OF SURFACING** Ensign ENROX 11	**7** 26 wks
24 Jan 81	● **MONDO BONGO** Mercury 6359 042	**6** 7 wks
3 Apr 82	**V DEEP** Mercury/Phonogram 6359 082	**64** 5 wks

Pat BOONE *US, male vocalist*   *12 wks*

22 Nov 58	● **STARDUST** London HAD 2127	**10** 1 wk
28 May 60	**HYMNS WE HAVE LOVED** London HAD 2228 . . .	**12** 2 wks
25 Jun 60	**HYMNS WE LOVE** London HAD 2092	**14** 1 wk
24 Apr 76	**PAT BOONE ORIGINALS** ABC ABSD 301 . . .	**16** 8 wks

BOSTON *US, male vocal/instrumental group*   *32 wks*

5 Feb 77	**BOSTON** Epic EPC 81611	**11** 20 wks
9 Sep 78	● **DON'T LOOK BACK** Epic EPC 86057	**9** 10 wks
4 Apr 81	**BOSTON** Epic EPC 32038	**58** 2 wks

BOW WOW WOW *UK, female/male vocal/instrumental group*   *13 wks*

24 Oct 81	**SEE JUNGLE! SEE JUNGLE! GO JOIN YOUR GANG YEAH CITY ALL OVER! GO APE CRAZY!** RCA RCALP 0027 3000 . . .	**26** 7 wks
7 Aug 82	**I WANT CANDY** EMI EMC 3416	**26** 6 wks

David BOWIE *UK, male vocalist*   *813 wks*

1 Jul 72	● **THE RISE AND FALL OF ZIGGY STARDUST AND THE SPIDERS FROM MARS** RCA Victor SF 8287	**5** 106 wks
23 Sep 72	● **HUNKY DORY** RCA Victor SF 8244	**3** 69 wks
29 Nov 72	**SPACE ODDITY** RCA Victor LSP 4813	**17** 37 wks
29 Nov 72	**THE MAN WHO SOLD THE WORLD** RCA Victor LSP 4816	**26** 22 wks
5 May 73	★ **ALADDIN SANE** RCA Victor RS 1001	**1** 47 wks
3 Nov 73	★ **PIN-UPS** RCA Victor RS 1003	**1** 21 wks
8 Jun 74	★ **DIAMOND DOGS** RCA Victor APLI 0576	**1** 17 wks
16 Nov 74	● **DAVID LIVE** RCA Victor APL 2 0771	**2** 12 wks
5 Apr 75	● **YOUNG AMERICANS** RCA Victor RS 1006 . . .	**2** 12 wks
7 Feb 76	● **STATION TO STATION** RCA Victor APLI 1327	**5** 16 wks
12 Jun 76	● **CHANGESONEBOWIE** RCA Victor RS 1055 . . .	**2** 28 wks
29 Jan 77	● **LOW** RCA Victor PL 12030	**2** 18 wks
29 Oct 77	● **HEROES** RCA Victor PL 12522	**3** 18 wks
14 Oct 78	● **STAGE** RCA Victor PL 02913	**5** 10 wks
9 Jun 79	● **LODGER** RCA Bow LP1	**4** 17 wks
27 Sep 80	★ **SCARY MONSTERS AND SUPER CREEPS** RCA Bow LP2	**1** 32 wks
10 Jan 81	● **VERY BEST OF DAVID BOWIE** K-Tel NE 1111	**3** 20 wks
17 Jan 81	**HUNKY DORY** (re-issue) RCA International INTS 5064	**32** 51 wks
31 Jan 81	**THE RISE AND FALL OF ZIGGY STARDUST AND THE SPIDERS FROM MARS** (re-issue) RCA International INTS 5063	**33** 62 wks
28 Nov 81	**CHANGESTWOBOWIE** RCA BOW LP 3	**24** 17 wks
6 Mar 82	**ALADDIN SANE** (re-issue) RCA International INTS 5067	**49** 24 wks
14 Jan 83	**RARE** RCA PL 45406	**34** 11 wks
23 Apr 83	★ **LETS DANCE** EMI America AML 3029	**1** 56 wks

BOOMTOWN RATS Bob Geldof is shown in performance at Loch Lomond. (LFI)

BIG COUNTRY Big Country climbed higher but fell faster with their second release. (LFI). DAVID BOWIE 198 weeks on the chart in 1983 – an all–time record. (Retna Pictures Int)

GEORGE BENSON (above right) The virtuoso guitarist has recorded albums with such jazz greats as Freddie Hubbard, Stanley Turrentine, Esther Phillips and Hank Crawford. (Debbie Leavitt)

Date		Title	Label/Number	Pos	Wks
30 Apr 83		PIN-UPS (re-issue) RCA International INTS 5236		57	15 wks
30 Apr 83		THE MAN WHO SOLD THE WORLD (re-issue) RCA International INTS 5237		64	8 wks
14 May 83		DIAMOND DOGS (re-issue) RCA International INTS 5068		60	14 wks
11 Jun 83		HEROES (re-issue) RCA International INTS 5066		75	8 wks
11 Jun 83		LOW (re-issue) RCA International INTS 5065		85	5 wks
20 Aug 83		GOLDEN YEARS RCA BOWLP 4		33	5 wks
5 Nov 83		ZIGGY STARDUST-THE MOTION PICTURE RCA PL 84862		17	6 wks
28 Apr 84		FAME AND FASHION (ALL TIME GREATEST HITS) RCA PL 84919		40	6 wks
19 May 84		LOVE YOU TILL TUESDAY Deram BOWIE 1		53	4 wks
6 Oct 84	★	TONIGHT EMI AMERICA DB 1		1	19 wks

BOXCAR WILLIE US, male vocalist — 12 wks

| 31 May 80 | ● | KING OF THE ROAD Warwick WW 5084 | | 5 | 12 wks |

Max BOYCE UK, male vocalist/comedian — 105 wks

5 Jul 75		LIVE AT TREORCHY One Up OU 2033		21	32 wks
1 Nov 75	★	WE ALL HAD DOCTORS' PAPERS EMI MB 101		1	17 wks
20 Nov 76	●	THE INCREDIBLE PLAN EMI MB 102		9	12 wks
7 Jan 78		THE ROAD AND THE MILES EMI MB 103		50	3 wks
11 Mar 78		LIVE AT TREORCHY (re-issue) One Up OU 54043		42	6 wks
27 May 78	●	I KNOW COS I WAS THERE EMI MAX 1001		6	14 wks
13 Oct 79		NOT THAT I'M BIASED EMI MAX 1002		27	13 wks
15 Nov 80		ME AND BILLY WILLIAMS EMI MAX 1003		37	8 wks

BOYS UK, male vocal/instrumental group — 1 wk

| 1 Oct 77 | | THE BOYS NEMS NEL 6001 | | 50 | 1 wk |

Billy BRAGG UK, male vocalist — 51 wks

| 21 Jan 84 | | LIFE'S A RIOT WITH SPY VS SPY Go! Discs UTILITY UTIL 1 | | 30 | 30 wks |
| 20 Oct 84 | | BREWING UP WITH BILLY BRAGG Go! Discs AGOLP 4 | | 16 | 21 wks |

Wilfred BRAMBELL and Harry H. CORBETT UK, male comic duo — 34 wks

23 Mar 63	●	STEPTOE AND SON Pye NPL 18081		4	28 wks
11 Mar 64		STEPTOE & SON Pye GGL 0217		14	5 wks
14 Mar 64		MORE JUNK Pye NPL18090		19	1 wk

BRAND X UK, male vocal/instrumental group — 6 wks

| 21 May 77 | | MOROCCAN ROLL Charisma CAS 1126 | | 37 | 5 wks |
| 11 Sep 82 | | IS THERE ANYTHING ABOUT? CBS 85967 | | 93 | 1 wk |

Laura BRANIGAN US, female vocalist — 18 wks

| 18 Aug 84 | | SELF CONTROL Atlantic 780147 | | 16 | 14 wks |
| 24 Aug 85 | | HOLD ME Atlantic 78-1265-1 | | 64 | 4 wks |

BRASS CONSTRUCTION US, male vocal/instrumental group — 12 wks

| 20 Mar 76 | ● | BRASS CONSTRUCTION United Artists UAS 29923 | | 9 | 11 wks |
| 30 Jun 84 | | RENEGADES Capitol EJ 24 0160 | | 94 | 1 wk |

BREAD US, male vocal/instrumental group — 176 wks

26 Sep 70		ON THE WATERS Elektra 2469-005		34	5 wks
18 Mar 72	●	BABY I'M A WANT-YOU Elektra K 42100		9	19 wks
28 Oct 72		BEST OF BREAD Elektra K 42115		7	100 wks
27 Jul 74		THE BEST OF BREAD VOL.2 Elektra K 42161		48	1 wk
29 Jan 77		LOST WITHOUT YOUR LOVE Elektra K 52044		17	6 wks
5 Nov 77	★	THE SOUND OF BREAD Elektra K 52062		1	45 wks

BREAK MACHINE US, male vocal/dance group — 16 wks

| 9 Jun 84 | | BREAK MACHINE Record Shack SOHO LP 3 | | 17 | 16 wks |

Adrian BRETT UK, male instrumentalist - flute — 11 wks

| 10 Nov 79 | | ECHOES OF GOLD Warwick WW 5062 | | 19 | 11 wks |

Paul BRETT UK, male instrumentalist - guitar — 7 wks

| 19 Jul 80 | | ROMANTIC GUITAR K-Tel ONE 1079 | | 24 | 7 wks |

BRIGHOUSE AND RASTRICK BRASS BAND UK, male brass band — 11 wks

| 28 Jan 78 | ● | FLORAL DANCE Logo 1001 | | 10 | 11 wks |

Johnny BRISTOL US, male vocalist — 7 wks

| 5 Oct 74 | | HANG ON IN THERE BABY MGM 2315 303 | | 12 | 7 wks |

June BRONHILL and Thomas ROUND Australia/UK, female/male vocal duo — 1 wk

| 18 Jun 60 | | LILAC TIME HMV CLP 1248 | | 17 | 1 wk |

BRONSKI BEAT UK, male vocal/instrumental group — 59 wks

| 20 Oct 84 | ● | THE AGE OF CONSENT Forbidden Fruit BITLP 1 | | 4 | 53 wks |
| 21 Sep 85 | | HUNDREDS AND THOUSANDS Forbidden Fruit BITLP 2 | | 24 | 6 wks |

Elkie BROOKS UK, female vocalist — 161 wks

18 Jun 77		TWO DAYS AWAY A & M AMLH 68409		16	20 wks
13 May 78		SHOOTING STAR A & M AMLH 64695		20	13 wks
13 Oct 79		LIVE AND LEARN A & M AMLH 68509		34	6 wks
14 Nov 81	●	PEARLS A & M ELK 1981		2	79 wks
13 Nov 82	●	PEARLS II A & M ELK 1982		5	25 wks
14 Jul 84		MINUTES A & M AML 68565		35	7 wks
8 Dec 84		SCREEN GEMS EMI SCREEN 1		35	11 wks

Nigel BROOKS SINGERS UK, male/female vocal choir — 17 wks

| 29 Nov 75 | ● | SONGS OF JOY K-Tel NE 706 | | 5 | 16 wks |
| 5 Jun 76 | | 20 ALL TIME EUROVISION FAVOURITES K-Tel NE 712 | | 44 | 1 wk |

BROTHERHOOD OF MAN *UK, male/female vocal group* 40 wks

24 Apr 76		LOVE AND KISSES FROM *Pye NSPL 18490* ...	20	8 wks
12 Aug 78		B FOR BROTHERHOOD *Pye NSPL 18567*	18	9 wks
7 Oct 78	●	BROTHERHOOD OF MAN *K-Tel BML 7980* ...	6	15 wks
29 Nov 80		SING 20 NUMBER ONE HITS *Warwick WW 5087*	14	8 wks

BROTHERS JOHNSON *US, male vocal/instrumental duo* 22 wks

19 Aug 78	BLAM!! *A & M AMLH 64714*	48	8 wks
23 Feb 80	LIGHT UP THE NIGHT *A & M AMLK 63716*	22	12 wks
18 Jul 81	WINNERS *A & M AMLK 63724*	42	2 wks

Edgar BROUGHTON BAND *UK, male vocal/instrumental group* 6 wks

20 Jun 70	SING BROTHER SING *Harvest SHVL 772*	18	4 wks
5 Jun 71	THE EDGAR BROUGHTON BAND *Harvest SHVL 791*	28	2 wks

Crazy World Of Arthur BROWN *UK, male vocal/instrumental group* 16 wks

6 Jul 68	● CRAZY WORLD OF ARTHUR BROWN *Track 612005*	2	16 wks

Dennis BROWN *Jamaica, male vocalist* 6 wks

26 Jun 82	LOVE HAS FOUND ITS WAY *A&M AMLH 64886*	72	6 wks

Joe BROWN *UK, male vocalist/instrumentalist - guitar* 47 wks

1 Sep 62	● A PICTURE OF YOU *Pye Golden Guinea GGL 0146*	3	39 wks
25 May 63	JOE BROWN - LIVE *Piccadilly NPL 38006*	14	8 wks

Jackson BROWNE *US, male vocalist* 24 wks

4 Dec 76	THE PRETENDER *Asylum K 53048*	26	5 wks
21 Jan 78	RUNNING ON EMPTY *Asylum K 53070*	28	7 wks
12 Jul 80	HOLD OUT *Asylum K 52226*	44	5 wks
13 Aug 83	LAWYERS IN LOVE *Asylum 96-0268-1*	37	7 wks

Dave BRUBECK QUARTET *US, male instrumental group* 17 wks

25 Jun 60	TIME OUT *Fontana TFL 5085*	11	1 wk
7 Apr 62	TIME FURTHER OUT *Fontana TFL 5161*	12	16 wks

Second album just credited to Dave Brubeck.

Jack BRUCE *UK, male vocalist/instrumentalist - bass* 9 wks

27 Sep 69	● SONGS FOR A TAILOR *Polydor 583-058*	6	9 wks

Peabo BRYSON and Roberta FLACK *US, male/female vocal duo* 10 wks

17 Sep 83	BORN TO LOVE *Capitol EST 7122841*	15	10 wks

See also Roberta Flack; Roberta Flack and Donny Hathaway.

BUCKS FIZZ *UK, male/female vocal group* 79 wks

8 Aug 81		BUCKS FIZZ *RCA RCALP 5050*	14	28 wks
18 May 82	●	ARE YOU READY? *RCA RCALP 8000*	10	23 wks
19 Mar 83		HAND CUT *RCA RCALP 6100*	17	13 wks
3 Dec 83		GREATEST HITS *RCA RCA PL 70022*	25	13 wks
24 Nov 84		I HEAR TALK *RCA PL 70397*	66	2 wks

BUDGIE *UK, male vocal/instrumental group* 10 wks

8 Jun 74	IN FOR THE KILL *MCA MCF 2546*	29	3 wks
27 Sep 75	BANDOLIER *MCA MCF 2723*	36	4 wks
31 Oct 81	NIGHT FLIGHT *RCA RCALP 6003*	68	2 wks
23 Oct 82	DELIVER US FROM EVIL *RCA RCALP 6054* ...	62	1 wk

BUGGLES *UK, male vocal/instrumental duo* 6 wks

16 Feb 80	THE AGE OF PLASTIC *Island ILPS 9585*	27	6 wks

BUNNYMEN - *See ECHO and the BUNNYMEN*

Eric BURDON and WAR *UK, male vocalist and US, male vocal/instrumental group* 2 wks

3 Oct 70	ERIC BURDON DECLARES WAR *Polydor 2310-041*	50	2 wks

Jean-Jacques BURNEL *UK, male vocalist/instrumentalist - bass guitar* 5 wks

21 Apr 79	EUROMAN COMETH *United Artists UAG 30214*	40	5 wks

See also Dave Greenfield and Jean-Jacques Burnel.

Kate BUSH *UK, female vocalist* 152 wks

11 Mar 78	●	THE KICK INSIDE *EMI EMC 3223*	3	70 wks
25 Nov 78	●	LIONHEART *EMI EMA 787*	6	36 wks
20 Sep 80	★	NEVER FOR EVER *EMI EMA 796*	1	23 wks
25 Sep 82	●	THE DREAMING *EMI EMC 3419*	3	9 wks
28 Sep 85	★	HOUNDS OF LOVE *EMI KAB 1*	1†	14 wks

BUZZCOCKS *UK, male vocal/instrumental group* 23 wks

25 Mar 78	ANOTHER MUSIC IN A DIFFERENT KITCHEN *United Artists UAG 30159*	15	11 wks
7 Oct 78	LOVE BITES *United Artists UAG 30184*	13	9 wks
6 Oct 79	A DIFFERENT KIND OF TENSION *United Artists UAG 30260*	26	3 wks

Max BYGRAVES *UK, male vocalist* 151 wks

23 Sep 72	●	SING ALONG WITH MAX *Pye NSPL 18361* ...	4	44 wks
2 Dec 72		SING ALONG WITH MAX VOL.2 *Pye NSPL 18383*	11	23 wks
5 May 73	●	SINGALONGAMAX VOL.3 *Pye NSPL 18401* ...	5	30 wks
29 Sep 73	●	SINGALONGAMAX VOL.4 *Pye NSPL 18410* ...	7	12 wks
15 Dec 73		SINGALONGPARTY SONG *Pye NSPL 18419* ...	15	6 wks

BROTHERS JOHNSON (above) When George was 12 and Louis 13, the Brothers Johnson opened shows for Bobby Womack, David Ruffin and the Supremes.

EDGAR BROUGHTON (above) 10 years on the Broughtons demonstrate they will not be dictated to by changing trends.
JOE BROWN (right) Joe Brown's best selling picture.

BREAD (above) Earned a crust for 176 weeks with 'The Best of Bread' retaining its freshness for 100 of them.

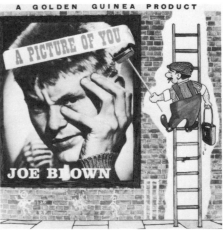

BONEY M (above) A hat trick of chart toppers. (LFI)

JOE BROWN (right) Joe Brown's best selling picture.

THE B52's (left) Is it a plane? Is it a haircut? No, it's a rock band from Georgia.

12 Oct 74	YOU MAKE ME FEEL LIKE SINGING A SONG				
	Pye NSPL 18436			39	3 wks
7 Dec 74	SINGALONGAXMAS *Pye NSPL 18439*			21	6 wks
13 Nov 76 ●	100 GOLDEN GREATS *Ronco RTDX 2019*			3	21 wks
28 Oct 78	LINGALONGAMAX *Ronco RPL 2033*			39	5 wks
16 Dec 78	THE SONG AND DANCE MEN			67	1 wk
	Pye NSPL 18574				

Charlie BYRD - *See Stan GETZ and Charlie BYRD*

Donald BYRD *US, male vocalist/instrumentalist – trumpet*
3 wks

10 Oct 81	LOVE BYRD *Elektra K 52301*		70	3 wks

BYRDS *US, male vocal/instrumental group*
42 wks

28 Aug 65 ●	MR. TAMBOURINE MAN *CBS BPG 62571*		7	12 wks
9 Apr 66	TURN, TURN, TURN *CBS BPG 62652*		11	5 wks
1 Oct 66	5TH DIMENSION *CBS BPG 62783*		27	2 wks
22 Apr 67	YOUNGER THAN YESTERDAY		37	4 wks
	CBS SBPG 62988			
4 May 68	THE NOTORIOUS BYRD BROTHERS		12	11 wks
	CBS 63169			
24 May 69	DR. BYRDS AND MR. HYDE *CBS 63545*		15	1 wk
14 Feb 70	BALLAD OF EASY RIDER *CBS 63795*		41	1 wk
28 Nov 70	UNTITLED *CBS 66253*		11	4 wks
14 Apr 73	BYRDS *Asylum SYLA 8754*		31	1 wk
19 May 73	HISTORY OF THE BYRDS *CBS 68242*		47	1 wk

David BYRNE - *See Brian ENO and David BYRNE*

B52s *US, male/female vocal/instrumental group*
28 wks

4 Aug 79	B-52S *Island ILPS 9580*		22	9 wks
13 Sep 80	WILD PLANET *Island ILPS 9622*		18	4 wks
11 Jul 81	THE PARTY MIX ALBUM *Island IPM 1001* ..		36	5 wks
27 Feb 82	MESOPOTAMIA *EMI ISSP 4006*		18	6 wks
21 May 83	WHAMMY! *Island ILPS 9759*		33	4 wks

C

CABARET VOLTAIRE *UK, male vocal/instrumental group*
11 wks

26 Jun 82	2 X 45 *Rough Trade ROUGH 42*		98	1 wk
13 Aug 83	THE CRACKDOWN *Some Bizzare CV 1*		31	5 wks
10 Nov 84	MICRO-PHONIES *Some Bizarre CV 2*		69	1 wk
3 Aug 85	DRINKING GASOLINE *Some Bizzare CVM 1* ..		71	2 wks
26 Oct 85	THE COVENANT, THE SWORD AND THE ARM			
	OF THE LORD *Virgin/Some Bizzare CV 3*		57	2 wks

J.J. CALE *US, male vocalist/instrumentalist – guitar*
22 wks

2 Oct 76	TROUBADOUR *Island ISA 5011*		53	1 wk
25 Aug 79	5 *Shelter ISA 5018*		40	6 wks
21 Feb 81	SHADES *Shelter ISA 5021*		44	7 wks
20 Mar 82	GRASSHOPPER *Shelter/Island IFA 5022*		36	5 wks
24 Sep 83	#8 *Mercury MERL 22*		47	3 wks

CAMEL *UK, male vocal/instrumental group*
47 wks

24 May 75	THE SNOW GOOSE *Decca SKL 5207*		22	13 wks
17 Apr 76	MOON MADNESS *Decca TXS 115*		15	6 wks
17 Sep 77	RAIN DANCES *Decca TXS 124*		20	8 wks
14 Oct 78	BREATHLESS *Decca TXS 132*		26	1 wk
27 Oct 79	I CAN SEE YOUR HOUSE FROM HERE			
	Decca TXS 137		45	3 wks
31 Jan 81	NUDE *Decca SKL 5323*		34	7 wks
15 May 82	THE SINGLE FACTOR *Decca FKL 5328*		57	5 wks
21 Apr 84	STATIONARY TRAVELLER *Decca SKL 5334* ..		57	4 wks

CAMEO *US, male vocal/instrumental group*
12 wks

10 Aug 85	SINGLE LIFE *Club JABH 11*		66	12 wks

Glen CAMPBELL *US, male vocalist*
179 wks

31 Jan 70	GLEN CAMPBELL LIVE *Capitol SB 21444*		16	14 wks
30 May 70	TRY A LITTLE KINDNESS *Capitol ESW 389* ..		37	10 wks
12 Dec 70	THE GLEN CAMPBELL ALBUM			
	Capitol ST 22493		16	5 wks
27 Nov 71 ●	GREATEST HITS *Capitol ST 21885*		8	113 wks
25 Oct 75	RHINESTONE COWBOY *Capitol E-SW 11430* ..		38	9 wks
20 Nov 76 ★	20 GOLDEN GREATS *Capitol EMTV 2*		1	27 wks
23 Apr 77	SOUTHERN NIGHTS *Capitol E-ST 11601*		51	1 wk

CANNED HEAT *US, vocal/instrumental group*
40 wks

29 Jun 68 ●	BOOGIE WITH CANNED HEAT			
	Liberty LBL 83103		5	21 wks
14 Feb 70 ●	CANNED HEAT COOKBOOK *Liberty LBS 83303*		8	12 wks
4 Jul 70	CANNED HEAT '70 CONCERT			
	Liberty LBS 83333		15	3 wks
10 Oct 70	FUTURE BLUES *Liberty LBS 83364*		27	4 wks

Freddy CANNON *US, male vocalist*
11 wks

27 Feb 60 ★	THE EXPLOSIVE FREDDY CANNON			
	Top Rank 25/108		1	11 wks

CAPTAIN and TENNILLE *US, male instrumentalist – keyboards and female vocalist*
6 wks

22 Mar 80	MAKE YOUR MOVE *Casablanca CAL 2060*		33	6 wks

CARAVAN *UK, male vocal/instrumental group*
2 wks

30 Aug 75	CUNNING STUNTS *Decca SKL 5210*		50	1 wk
15 May 76	BLIND DOG AT ST.DUNSTAN'S '			
	BTM BTM 1007		53	1 wk

CARMEL *UK, female/male vocal/instrumental group*
10 wks

1 Oct 83	CARMEL *Red Flame RFM 9*		94	2 wks
24 Mar 84	THE DRUM IS EVERYTHING *London SH 8555*		19	8 wks

Eric CARMEN *US, male vocalist*
1 wk

15 May 76	ERIC CARMEN *Arista ARTY 120*		58	1 wk

Kim CARNES *US, female vocalist*
16 wks

20 Jun 81	MISTAKEN IDENTITY *EMI-America AML 3018*		26	16 wks

CARPENTERS *US, male/female, vocal/instrumental duo*

470 wks

23 Jan	71		CLOSE TO YOU *A & M AMLS 998*		23	82 wks
30 Oct	71		THE CARPENTERS *A & M AMLS 63502*		12	36 wks
15 Apr	72		TICKET TO RIDE *A & M AMLS 64342*		20	3 wks
23 Sep	72		A SONG FOR YOU *A & M AMLS 63511*		13	37 wks
7 Jul	73	●	NOW AND THEN *A & M AMLH 63519*		2	65 wks
26 Jan	74	★	THE SINGLES 1969-1973 *A & M AMLH 63601*		1	116 wks
28 Jun	75	★	HORIZON *A & M AMLK 64530*		1	27 wks
23 Aug	75		TICKET TO RIDE (re-issue) *Hamlet AMLP 8001*		35	2 wks
3 Jul	76	●	A KIND OF HUSH *A & M AMLK 64581*		3	15 wks
8 Jan	77		LIVE AT THE PALLADIUM *A & M AMLS 68403*		28	3 wks
8 Oct	77		PASSAGE *A & M AMLK 64703*		12	12 wks
2 Dec	78	●	SINGLES 1974-78 *A & M AMLT 19748*		2	20 wks
27 Jun	81		MADE IN AMERICA *A & M AMLK 63723*		12	10 wks
15 Oct	83	●	VOICE OF THE HEART *A & M AMLX 64954*		6	19 wks
20 Oct	84	●	YESTERDAY ONCE MORE *EMI/ A & M SING 1*		10	23 wks

Vikki CARR *US, female vocalist*

12 wks

22 Jul	67	WAY OF TODAY *Liberty SLBY 1331*		31	2 wks
12 Aug	67	IT MUST BE HIM *Liberty LBS 83037*		12	10 wks

Jasper CARROTT *UK, male comedian*

63 wks

18 Oct	75	● RABBITS ON AND ON *DJM DJLPS 462*		10	7 wks
6 Nov	76	CARROTT IN NOTTS *DJM DJF 20482*		56	1 wk
25 Nov	78	THE BEST OF JASPER CARROTT *DJM DJF 20549*		38	13 wks
20 Oct	79	THE UNRECORDED JASPER CARROTT *DJM DJF 20560*		19	15 wks
19 Sep	81	BEAT THE CARROTT *DJM DJF 20575*		13	16 wks
25 Dec	82	CARROTT'S LIB *DJM DJF 20580*		80	3 wks
19 Nov	83	THE STUN (CARROTT TELLS ALL) *DJF 20582*		57	8 wks

CARS *US, male vocal/instrumental group*

50 wks

2 Dec	78	CARS *Elektra K 52088*		29	15 wks
7 Jul	79	CANDY-O *Elektra K 52148*		30	6 wks
6 Oct	84	HEARTBEAT CITY *Elektra 960296*		25	21 wks
9 Nov	85	THE CARS GREATEST HITS *Elektra EKT 25* ..		27†	8 wks

Johnny CASH *US, male vocalist*

285 wks

23 Jul	66	EVERYBODY LOVES A NUT *CBS BPG 62717*		28	1 wk
4 May	68	FROM SEA TO SHINING SEA *CBS 62972*		40	1 wk
6 Jul	68	OLD GOLDEN THROAT *CBS 63316*		37	2 wks
24 Aug	68	● FOLSOM PRISON *CBS 63308*		8	53 wks
23 Aug	69	● JOHNNY CASH AT SAN QUENTIN *CBS 63629*		2	114 wks
4 Oct	69	GREATEST HITS VOL.1 *CBS 63062*		23	25 wks
7 Mar	70	HELLO I'M JOHNNY CASH *CBS 63796*		6	16 wks
15 Aug	70	● WORLD OF JOHNNY CASH *CBS 66237*		5	31 wks
12 Dec	70	THE JOHNNY CASH SHOW *CBS 64089*		18	6 wks
18 Sep	71	MAN IN BLACK *CBS 64331*		18	7 wks
13 Nov	71	JOHNNY CASH *Hallmark SHM 739*		43	2 wks
20 May	72	● A THING CALLED LOVE *CBS 64898*		8	11 wks
14 Oct	72	STAR PORTRAIT *CBS 67201*		16	7 wks
10 Jul	76	ONE PIECE AT A TIME *CBS 81416*		49	3 wks
9 Oct	76	THE BEST OF JOHNNY CASH *CBS 10000*		48	2 wks
2 Sep	78	ITCHY FEET *CBS 10009*		36	4 wks

CASHMERE *US, male vocal/instrumental group*

5 wks

2 Mar	85	CASHMERE *Fourth and Broadway BRLP 503*		63	5 wks

David CASSIDY *US, male vocalist*

94 wks

20 May	72	● CHERISH *Bell BELLS 210*		2	43 wks
24 Feb	73	● ROCK ME BABY *Bell BELLS 218*		2	20 wks
24 Nov	73	★ DREAMS ARE NOTHIN' MORE THAN WISHES *Bell BELLS 231*		1	13 wks
3 Aug	74	● CASSIDY LIVE *Bell BELLS 243*		9	7 wks
9 Aug	75	THE HIGHER THEY CLIMB *RCA Victor RS 1012*		22	5 wks
8 Jun	85	ROMANCE *Arista 206 983*		20	6 wks

Nick CAVE featuring the BAD SEEDS
Australia, male vocalist with male vocal/instrumental group

4 wks

2 Jun	84	FROM HER TO ETERNITY *Mute STUMM 17*		40	3 wks
15 Jun	85	THE FIRST BORN IS DEAD *Mute STUMM 21*		53	1 wk

C.C.S. *UK, male vocal/instrumental group*

5 wks

8 Apr	72	C.C.S. *RAK SRAK 503*		23	5 wks

CENTRAL LINE *UK, male vocal/instrumental group*

5 wks

13 Feb	82	BREAKING POINT *Mercury/Phonogram MERA 001*		64	5 wks

CERRONE *France, male producer and multi-instrumentalist*

1 wk

30 Sep	78	SUPERNATURE *Atlantic K 50431*		60	1 wk

A CERTAIN RATIO *UK, male vocal/instrumental group*

3 wks

30 Jan	82	SEXTET *Factory FACT 55*		53	3 wks

Richard CHAMBERLAIN *US, male vocalist*

8 wks

16 Mar	63	● RICHARD CHAMBERLAIN SINGS *MGM C 923*		8	8 wks

CHAMELEONS *UK, male vocal/instrumental group*

2 wks

25 May	85	WHAT DOES ANYTHING MEAN? BASICALLY *Statik STAT LP 22*		60	2 wks

CHAMPAIGN *US, male/female vocal instrumental group*

4 wks

27 Jun	81	HOW 'BOUT US *CBS 84927*		38	4 wks

CHANGE *US, male/female vocal/instrumental group*

23 wks

19 May	84	CHANGE OF HEART *WEA WX 5*		34	17 wks
27 Apr	85	TURN ON THE RADIO *Cooltempo CHR 1504* ..		39	6 wks

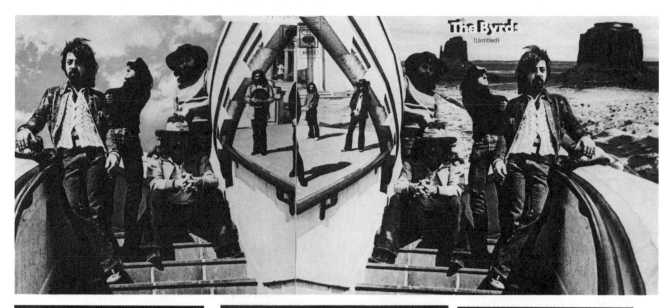

The Byrds
(Untitled)

KATE BUSH (right) She rolled back up that hill with 'Hounds of Love'. (Novercia–John Carder Bush)

BYRDS (above) The Byrds eleventh album and eighth British success was tentatively called 'The First Byrds Album' and then 'Phoenix' before being released as 'Untitled'.

THE CARPENTERS (below) Their 'Singles 1969–'73' album surged to number one four times knocking off Perry Como, Slade, Rick Wakeman and David Bowie.

JOHNNY CASH (below) Old Golden Throat seen eating his breakfast one piece at a time.

Michael CHAPMAN UK, male vocalist   1 wk

21 Mar 70	FULLY QUALIFIED SURVIVOR		
	Harvest SHVL 764	45	1 wk

CHAQUITO ORCHESTRA UK, orchestra arranged
and conducted by Johnny Gregory   2 wks

24 Feb 68	THIS CHAQUITO Fontana SFXL 50	36	1 wk
4 Mar 72	THRILLER THEMES Philips 6308 087	48	1 wk

First album credited to Chaquito and Quedo Brass.

CHARGE GBH UK, male vocal/instrumental group
6 wks

14 Aug 82	CITY BABY ATTACKED BY RATS		
	Clay CLAYLP 4	17	6 wks

CHARLENE US, female vocalist   4 wks

17 Jul 82	I'VE NEVER BEEN TO ME		
	Motown STML 12171	43	4 wks

Ray CHARLES US, male vocalist/instrumentalist – piano
39 wks

28 Jul 62	● MODERN SOUNDS IN COUNTRY & WESTERN MUSIC HMV CLP 1580	6	16 wks
23 Feb 63	MODERN SOUNDS IN COUNTRY AND WESTERN MUSIC VOL.2 HMV CLP 1613	15	5 wks
20 Jul 63	GREATEST HITS HMV CLP 1626	16	5 wks
5 Oct 68	GREATEST HITS VOL.2 Stateside SSL 10241	24	8 wks
19 Jul 80	HEART TO HEART – 20 HOT HITS London RAY TV 1	29	5 wks

Tina CHARLES UK, female vocalist   7 wks

3 Dec 77	HEART 'N' SOUL CBS 82180	35	7 wks

CHAS and DAVE UK, male vocal/instrumental duo
87 wks

5 Dec 81	CHAS AND DAVE'S CHRISTMAS JAMBOREE BAG Warwick WW 5166	25	15 wks
17 Apr 82	MUSTN'T GRUMBLE Rockney 909	35	11 wks
8 Jan 83	JOB LOT Rockney ROC 910	59	15 wks
15 Oct 83	● CHAS & DAVE'S KNEES UP- JAMBOREE BAG NO 2 Rockney ROC 911	7	17 wks
11 Aug 84	WELL PLEASED Rockney ROC 912	27	10 wks
17 Nov 84	CHAS & DAVE'S GREATEST HITS Rockney ROC 913	16	10 wks
15 Dec 84	CHAS & DAVE'S CHRISTMAS JAMBOREE BAG (re-issue) Rockney ROCM 001	87	1 wk
9 Nov 85	JAMBOREE BAG NUMBER 3 Rockney ROC 914	15†	8 wks

CHEAP TRICK US, male vocal/instrumental group
15 wks

24 Feb 79	CHEAP TRICK AT BUDOKAN Epic EPC 86083	29	9 wks
6 Oct 79	DREAM POLICE Epic EPC 83522	41	5 wks
5 Jun 82	ONE ON ONE Epic EPC 85740	95	1 wk

Chubby CHECKER US, male vocalist   7 wks

27 Jan 62	TWIST WITH CHUBBY CHECKER Columbia 33SX 1315	13	4 wks
3 Mar 62	FOR TWISTERS ONLY Columbia 33SX 1341	17	3 wks

CHER US, female vocalist   20 wks

2 Oct 65	● ALL I REALLY WANT TO DO Liberty LBY 3058	7	9 wks
7 May 66	SONNY SIDE OF CHER Liberty LBY 3072	11	11 wks

See also Sonny and Cher.

CHIC US, male/female vocal/instrumental group   44 wks

3 Feb 79	● C'EST CHIC Atlantic K 50565	2	24 wks
18 Aug 79	RISQUE Atlantic K 50634	29	12 wks
15 Dec 79	THE BEST OF CHIC Atlantic K 50686	30	8 wks

CHICAGO US, male vocal/instrumental group   92 wks

27 Sep 69	● CHICAGO TRANSIT AUTHORITY CBS 66221	9	14 wks
4 Apr 70	● CHICAGO CBS 66233	6	27 wks
3 Apr 71	CHICAGO 3 CBS 66260	31	1 wk
30 Sep 72	CHICAGO 5 CBS 69108	24	2 wks
23 Oct 76	CHICAGO X CBS 86010	21	11 wks
2 Oct 82	CHICAGO 16 Full Moon K 99235	44	9 wks
4 Dec 82	LOVE SONGS TV Records TVA 6	42	8 wks
1 Dec 84	CHICAGO 17 Full Moon 925060	24	20 wks

First album credited to Chicago Transit Authority.

CHICKEN SHACK UK, male/female vocal/instrumental
group   9 wks

22 Jul 68	40 BLUE FINGERS FRESHLY PACKED Blue Horizon 7-63203	12	8 wks
15 Feb 69	● OK KEN? Blue Horizon 7-63209	9	1 wk

CHINA CRISIS UK, male vocal/instrumental group
56 wks

20 Nov 82	DIFFICULT SHAPES AND PASSIVE RHYTHMS Virgin V 2243	21	18 wks
12 Nov 83	WORKING WITH FIRE AND STEEL - POSSIBLE POP SONGS VOL 2 Virgin V 2286	20	16 wks
11 May 85	● FLAUNT THE IMPERFECTION Virgin V 2342	9	22 wks

CHORDS UK, male vocal/instrumental group   3 wks

24 May 80	SO FAR AWAY Polydor POLS 1019	30	3 wks

Tony CHRISTIE UK, male vocalist   10 wks

24 Jul 71	I DID WHAT I DID FOR MARIA MCA MKPS 2016	37	1 wk
17 Feb 73	WITH LOVING FEELING MCA MUPS 468	19	2 wks
31 May 75	TONY CHRISTIE - LIVE MCA MCF 2703	33	3 wks
6 Nov 76	BEST OF TONY CHRISTIE MCA MCF 2769	28	4 wks

CHRON GEN UK, male vocal/instrumental group
3 wks

3 Apr 82	CHRONIC GENERATION Secret SEC 3	53	3 wks

DAVID CASSIDY David Cassidy cherished 1973.

CHICAGO Original music with unoriginal album titles.

GLEN CAMPBELL As a teenager, the seventh son of an Arkansas farmer joined his uncle Dick Bill's western band in New Mexico before putting his multi-instrumental talents to use as a top sixties session musician.

Sir Winston CHURCHILL UK, male statesman

8 wks

13 Feb 65	● THE VOICE OF CHURCHILL	Decca LXT 6200		6	8 wks

CLANCY BROTHERS and Tommy MAKEM
Ireland, male vocal/instrumental group and male vocalist

5 wks

16 Apr 66	ISN'T IT GRAND BOYS	CBS BPG 62674	......	22	5 wks

CLANNAD *Ireland, male/female vocal group*   60 wks

2 Apr 83	MAGICAL RING	RCA RCALP 6072	....	26	21 wks
12 May 84	LEGEND (MUSIC FROM ROBIN OF				
	SHERWOOD)	RCA PL 70188	.....	15	28 wks
2 Jun 84	MAGICAL RING (re-issue)	RCA PL 70003	.....	91	1 wk
26 Oct 85	MACALLA	RCA PL 70894	....	45†	10 wks

Eric CLAPTON UK, *male vocalist/instrumentalist - guitar*

159 wks

5 Sep 70	ERIC CLAPTON	Polydor 2383-021	......	17	8 wks
26 Aug 72	HISTORY OF ERIC CLAPTON				
		Polydor 2659 2478 027		20	6 wks
24 Aug 74	● 461 OCEAN BOULEVARD	RSO 2479 118	.....	3	19 wks
12 Apr 75	THERE'S ONE IN EVERY CROWD				
		RSO 2479 132	....	15	8 wks
13 Sep 75	E.C. WAS HERE	RSO 2394 160	......	14	6 wks
11 Sep 76	● NO REASON TO CRY	RSO 2479 179	.....	8	7 wks
26 Nov 77	SLOWHAND	RSO 2479 201	.....	23	13 wks
9 Dec 78	BACKLESS	RSO RSD 5001	.....	18	12 wks
10 May 80	● JUST ONE NIGHT	RSO RSDX 2	.....	3	12 wks
7 Mar 81	ANOTHER TICKET	RSO RSD 5008	.....	18	8 wks
24 Apr 82	TIME PIECES - THE BEST OF ERIC CLAPTON				
		RSO RSD 5010	....	20	13 wks
19 Feb 83	MONEY & CIGARETTES	Duck W 3773	.....	13	17 wks
9 Jun 84	BACKTRACKIN'	Starblend ERIC 1	.....	29	16 wks
23 Mar 85	● BEHIND THE SUN	Duck 92-5166-1	....	8	14 wks

Petula CLARK UK, *female vocalist*   43 wks

30 Jul 66	I COULDN'T LIVE WITHOUT YOUR LOVE				
		Pye NPL 18148	....	11	10 wks
4 Feb 67	HIT PARADE	Pye NPL 18159	.....	18	13 wks
18 Feb 67	COLOUR MY WORLD	Pye NSPL 18171	.....	16	9 wks
7 Oct 67	THESE ARE MY SONGS	Pye NSPL 18197	.....	38	3 wks
6 Apr 68	THE OTHER MAN'S GRASS IS ALWAYS				
	GREENER	Pye NSPL 18211	....	37	1 wk
5 Feb 77	20 ALL TIME GREATEST	K-Tel NE 945	......	18	7 wks

Dave CLARK FIVE UK, *male vocal/instrumental group*

26 wks

18 Apr 64	● A SESSION WITH THE DAVE CLARK FIVE				
		Columbia 33SX 1598	....	3	8 wks
14 Aug 65	● CATCH US IF YOU CAN	Columbia 33SX 1756	..	8	8 wks
4 Mar 78	● 25 THUMPING GREAT HITS	Polydor POLTV 7		7	10 wks

John Cooper CLARKE UK, *male vocalist*   9 wks

19 Apr 80	SNAP CRACKLE AND BOP	Epic EPC 84083	..	26	7 wks
5 Jun 82	ZIP STYLE METHOD	Epic EPC 85667	....	97	2 wks

Stanley CLARKE US, *male vocalist/instrumentalist - bass*

2 wks

12 Jul 80	ROCKS PEBBLES AND SAND	Epic EPC 84342		42	2 wks

Louis CLARK/ROYAL PHILHARMONIC ORCHESTRA *Australia, conductor/arranger and UK orchestra*

90 wks

19 Sep 81	● HOOKED ON CLASSICS	K-Tel ONE 1146	....	4	43 wks
31 Jul 82	CAN'T STOP THE CLASSICS - HOOKED ON				
	CLASSICS 2	K-Tel ONE 1173	.....	13	26 wks
9 Apr 83	JOURNEY THROUGH THE CLASSICS -				
	HOOKED ON CLASSICS 3	K-Tel ONE 1226		19	15 wks
10 Dec 83	THE BEST OF HOOKED ON CLASSICS				
		K-Tel ONE 1266	....	51†	6 wks

See also Royal Philharmonic Orchestra.

CLASH UK, *male vocal/instrumental group*   85 wks

30 Apr 77	CLASH	CBS 82000	....	12	16 wks
25 Nov 78	● GIVE 'EM ENOUGH ROPE	CBS 82431	......	2	14 wks
22 Dec 79	● LONDON CALLING	CBS CLASH 3	......	9	20 wks
20 Dec 80	SANDINISTA	CBS FSLN 1	......	19	9 wks
22 May 82	● COMBAT ROCK	CBS FMLN 2	......	2	23 wks
16 Nov 85	CUT THE CRAP	CBS 26601	....	16	3 wks

CLASSIX NOUVEAUX UK, *male vocal/instrumental group*

6 wks

30 May 81	NIGHT PEOPLE	Liberty LBG 30325	.....	66	2 wks
24 Apr 82	LA VERITE	Liberty LBG 30346	....	44	4 wks

Richard CLAYDERMAN *France, male instrumentalist - piano*

124 wks

13 Nov 82	● RICHARD CLAYDERMAN	Decca SKL 5329	....	2	64 wks
8 Oct 83	THE MUSIC OF RICHARD CLAYDERMAN				
		Decca SKL 5333	....	21	28 wks
24 Nov 84	THE MUSIC OF LOVE	Decca SKL 5340	....	28	21 wks
1 Dec 84	RICHARD CLAYDERMAN - CHRISTMAS				
		Decca SKL 5337	....	53	5 wks
23 Nov 85	THE CLASSIC TOUCH	Decca SKL 5343	....	18†	6 wks

The Classic Touch is credited to Richard Clayderman with the Royal Philharmonic Orchestra

John CLEESE UK, *male comedian*   7 wks

7 Feb 81	FAWLTY TOWERS VOL.2	BBC REB 405	.....	26	7 wks

Album also features Prunella Scales, Andrew Sachs and Connie Booth.

CLIMAX BLUES BAND UK, *male vocal/instrumental group*

1 wk

13 Nov 76	GOLD PLATED	BTM 1009	....	56	1 wk

Eddie COCHRAN US, *male vocalist/instrumentalist - guitar*

44 wks

30 Jul 60	SINGING TO MY BABY	London HAU 2093	....	19	1 wk
1 Oct 60	● EDDIE COCHRAN MEMORIAL ALBUM				
		London HAG 2267	....	9	12 wks
12 Jan 63	CHERISHED MEMORIES	Liberty LBY 1109	....	15	3 wks
20 Apr 63	EDDIE COCHRAN MEMORIAL ALBUM				
	(re-issue)	Liberty LBY 1127	....	11	18 wks

19 Oct 63	SINGING TO MY BABY (re-issue)		
	Liberty LBY 1158	20	1 wk
9 May 70	VERY BEST OF EDDIE COCHRAN		
	Liberty LBS 83337	34	3 wks
18 Aug 79	THE EDDIE COCHRAN SINGLES ALBUM		
	United Artists UAK 30244	39	6 wks

Joe COCKER UK, male vocalist   13 wks

26 Sep 70	MAD DOGS AND ENGLISHMEN		
	A & M AMLS 6002	16	8 wks
6 May 72	JOE COCKER/WITH A LITTLE HELP FROM MY		
	FRIENDS Double Back TOOFA 1/2	29	4 wks
30 Jun 84	A CIVILISED MAN Capitol EJ 24 0139 1	100	1 wk

COCKNEY REBEL - See Steve HARLEY and COCKNEY REBEL

COCKNEY REJECTS UK, male vocal/instrumental group   17 wks

15 Mar 80	GREATEST HITS VOL.1 Zonophone ZONO 101	22	11 wks
25 Oct 80	GREATEST HITS VOL.2 Zonophone ZONO 102	23	3 wks
18 Apr 81	GREATEST HITS VOL.3 (LIVE AND LOUD)		
	Zonophone ZEM 101	27	3 wks

COCTEAU TWINS UK, male/female vocal group   23 wks

29 Oct 83	HEAD OVER HEELS 4AD CAD 313	51	15 wks
24 Nov 84	TREASURE 4AD CAD 412	29	8 wks

Leonard COHEN Canada, male vocalist   129 wks

31 Aug 68	SONGS OF LEONARD COHEN CBS 63241	13	71 wks
3 May 69 ●	SONGS FROM A ROOM CBS 63587	2	26 wks
24 Apr 71 ●	SONGS OF LOVE AND HATE CBS 69004	4	18 wks
28 Sep 74	NEW SKIN FOR THE OLD CEREMONY		
	CBS 69087	24	3 wks
10 Dec 77	DEATH OF A LADIES' MAN CBS 86042	35	5 wks
16 Feb 85	VARIOUS POSITIONS CBS 26222	52	6 wks

Lloyd COLE and the COMMOTIONS UK, male vocalist and male vocal/instrumental group   35 wks

20 Oct 84	RATTLESNAKES Polydor LCLP 1	13	30 wks
30 Nov 85 ●	EASY PIECES Polydor LCLP 2	5†	5 wks

Nat King COLE US, male vocalist   93 wks

19 Aug 61	STRING ALONG WITH NAT KING COLE		
	Encore ENC 102	12	9 wks
27 Mar 65	UNFORGETTABLE NAT KING COLE		
	Capitol W 20664	19	8 wks
7 Dec 68 ●	BEST OF NAT KING COLE Capitol ST 21139	5	18 wks
5 Dec 70	BEST OF NAT KING COLE VOL.2		
	Capitol ST 21687	39	2 wks
8 Apr 78 ★	20 GOLDEN GREATS Capitol EMTV 9	1	30 wks
20 Nov 82 ●	GREATEST LOVE SONGS Capitol EMTV 35	7	26 wks

See also Nat King Cole and Dean Martin; Nat King Cole and the George Shearing Quintet.

Nat King COLE and Dean MARTIN US, male vocal duo   1 wk

27 Nov 71	WHITE CHRISTMAS MFP 5224	45	1 wk

See also Nat King Cole; Nat King Cole and the George Shearing Quintet.

Nat King COLE and the George SHEARING QUINTET US, male vocalist and UK/US instrumental group   7 wks

20 Oct 62 ●	NAT KING COLE SINGS AND THE GEORGE		
	SHEARING QUINTET PLAYS Capitol W 1675	8	7 wks

See also Nat King Cole; Nat King Cole and Dean Martin.

Dave and Ansil COLLINS Jamaica, male vocal duo   2 wks

7 Aug 71	DOUBLE BARREL Trojan TBL 162	41	2 wks

Judy COLLINS US, female vocalist   17 wks

10 Apr 71	WHALES AND NIGHTINGALES		
	Elektra EKS 75010	37	2 wks
31 May 75 ●	JUDITH Elektra K 52019	7	12 wks
14 Dec 85	AMAZING GRACE Telstar STAR 2265	34†	3 wks

Phil COLLINS UK, male vocalist/instrumentalist - drums   350 wks

21 Feb 81 ★	FACE VALUE Virgin V 2185	1†	193 wks
13 Nov 82 ●	HELLO I MUST BE GOING Virgin V 2252	2	113 wks
2 Mar 85 ★	NO JACKET REQUIRED Virgin V 2345	1†	44 wks

COLOSSEUM UK, male vocal/instrumental group   14 wks

17 May 69	COLOSSEUM Fontana S 5510	15	1 wk
22 Nov 69	VALENTYNE SUITE Vertigo VO 1	15	2 wks
5 Dec 70	DAUGHTER OF TIME Vertigo 6360 017	23	5 wks
26 Jun 71	COLOSSEUM LIVE Bronze ICD 1	17	6 wks

Alice COLTRANE - See Carlos SANTANA and Alice COLTRANE

COLOURBOX UK, male vocal/instrumental group   2 wks

24 Aug 85	COLOURBOX 4AD CAD 508	67	2 wks

COLOUR FIELD UK, male vocal/instrumental group   7 wks

4 May 85	VIRGINS & PHILISTINES Chrysalis CHR 1480	12	7 wks

COMETS - See Bill HALEY and his COMETS

COMMODORES US/UK, male vocal/instrumental group   121 wks

13 May 78	LIVE Motown TMSP 6007	60	1 wk
10 Jun 78 ●	NATURAL HIGH Motown STML 12087	8	23 wks
2 Dec 78	GREATEST HITS Motown STML 12100	19	16 wks
18 Aug 79	MIDNIGHT MAGIC Motown STMA 8032	15	25 wks
28 Jun 80	HEROES Motown STMA 8034	50	5 wks
18 Jul 81	IN THE POCKET Motown STML 12156	69	5 wks
14 Aug 82	LOVE SONGS K-Tel NE 1171	5	28 wks
23 Feb 85	NIGHTSHIFT Motown ZL 72343	13	10 wks
9 Nov 85	THE VERY BEST OF THE COMMODORES		
	Telstar STAR 2249	25†	8 wks

Group were US for first seven albums.

CLANNAD (above) Clannad are the only pop group to be nominated twice for a British Academy of Film and Television Arts award.

COCKNEY REJECTS (above right) The history books only record two Top 40 hit singles for Stink, Mick, Vince and Nig but they somehow spread over three greatest hits albums.

CHEAP TRICK Founded by writer/guitarist Rick Nelson in Illinois in 1972, they used Stones, Beatles and Who influences to great effect.

CLIMAX BLUES BAND Sixties blues band underrated. Next decade- success- elated. One chart album- so belated. For one week only- group 'gold plated'.

Perry COMO US, male vocalist   191 wks

8 Nov 58	● DEAR PERRY RCA RD 27078	6	5 wks
31 Jan 59	● COMO'S GOLDEN RECORDS RCA RD 27100	4	5 wks
10 Apr 71	IT'S IMPOSSIBLE RCA Victor SF 8175	13	13 wks
7 Jul 73	★ AND I LOVE YOU SO RCA Victor SF 8360	1	109 wks
24 Aug 74	PERRY RCA Victor APL1 0585	26	3 wks
19 Apr 75	MEMORIES ARE MADE OF HITS RCA Victor RS 1005	14	16 wks
25 Oct 75	★ 40 GREATEST HITS K-Tel NE 700	1	34 wks
3 Dec 83	FOR THE GOOD TIMES Telstar STAR 2235 ...	41	6 wks

COMPILATION ALBUMS - See VARIOUS ARTISTS

COMSAT ANGELS UK, male vocal/instrumental group   9 wks

5 Sep 81	SLEEP NO MORE Polydor POLS 1038	51	5 wks
18 Sep 82	FICTION Polydor POLS 1075	94	2 wks
8 Oct 83	LAND Jive HIP 8	91	2 wks

Ray CONNIFF US, male orchestra leader   96 wks

28 May 60	IT'S THE TALK OF THE TOWN Philips BBL 7354	15	1 wk
25 Jun 60	S'AWFUL NICE Philips BBL 7281	13	1 wk
26 Nov 60	● HI-FI COMPANION ALBUM Philips BET 101 ..	3	44 wks
20 May 61	MEMORIES ARE MADE OF THIS Philips BBL 7439	14	4 wks
29 Dec 62	WE WISH YOU A MERRY CHRISTMAS CBS BPG 62092	12	1 wk
29 Dec 62	'S WONDERFUL 'S MARVELLOUS CBS DPG 66001	18	3 wks
16 Apr 66	HI-FI COMPANION (re-issue) CBS DP 66011 ..	24	4 wks
9 Sep 67	SOMEWHERE MY LOVE CBS SBPG 62740 ..	34	3 wks
21 Jun 69	★ HIS ORCHESTRA, HIS CHORUS, HIS SINGERS, HIS SOUND CBS SPR 27	1	16 wks
23 May 70	BRIDGE OVER TROUBLED WATER CBS 64020	30	14 wks
12 Jun 71	LOVE STORY CBS 64294	34	1 wk
19 Feb 72	I'D LIKE TO TEACH THE WORLD TO SING CBS 64449	17	4 wks

Billy CONNOLLY UK, male vocalist   106 wks

20 Jul 74	● SOLO CONCERT Transatlantic TRA 279	8	33 wks
18 Jan 75	● COP YER WHACK OF THIS Polydor 2383 310 ..	10	29 wks
20 Sep 75	WORDS AND MUSIC Transatlantic TRA SAM 32	34	10 wks
6 Dec 75	● GET RIGHT INTAE HIM Polydor 2383 368	6	14 wks
11 Dec 76	ATLANTIC BRIDGE Polydor 2383 419	20	9 wks
28 Jan 78	RAW MEAT FOR THE BALCONY Polydor 2383 463	57	3 wks
5 Dec 81	PICK OF BILLY CONNOLLY Polydor POLTV 15	23	8 wks

Russ CONWAY UK, male instrumentalist - piano   69 wks

22 Nov 58	● PACK UP YOUR TROUBLES Columbia 33SX 1120	9	5 wks
2 May 59	● SONGS TO SING IN YOUR BATH Columbia 33SX 1149	8	10 wks
19 Sep 59	● FAMILY FAVOURITES Columbia 33SX 1169 ...	3	16 wks
19 Dec 59	● TIME TO CELEBRATE Columbia 33SX 1197 ...	3	7 wks
26 Mar 60	● MY CONCERTO FOR YOU Columbia 33SX 1214	5	17 wks
17 Dec 60	PARTY TIME Columbia 33SX 1279	7	11 wks
23 Apr 77	RUSS CONWAY PRESENTS 24 PIANO GREATS Ronco RTL 2022	25	3 wks

Ry COODER US, male vocalist/instrumentalist - guitar   27 wks

11 Aug 79	BOP TILL YOU DROP Warner Bros. K 56691	36	9 wks
18 Oct 80	BORDER LINE Warner Bros. K 56864	35	6 wks
24 Apr 82	THE SLIDE AREA Warner Bros K 56976	18	12 wks

Peter COOK and Dudley MOORE UK, male vocal duo   34 wks

21 May 66	ONCE MOORE WITH COOK Decca LK 4785	25	1 wk
18 Sep 76	DEREK AND CLIVE LIVE Island ILPS 9434 ...	12	25 wks
24 Dec 77	COME AGAIN Virgin V 2094	18	8 wks

See also Dudley Moore.

Rita COOLIDGE US, female vocalist   40 wks

6 Aug 77	● ANYTIME ANYWHERE A & M AMLH 64616	6	28 wks
8 Jul 78	● LOVE ME AGAIN A & M AMLH 64699	51	1 wk
14 Mar 81	● VERY BEST OF A & M AMLH 68520	6	11 wks

See also Kris Kristofferson and Rita Coolidge.

COOL NOTES UK, male/female vocal/instrumental group   2 wks

9 Nov 85	HAVE A GOOD FOREVER Abstract Dance ADLP 1	66	2 wks

Alice COOPER US, male vocalist   98 wks

5 Feb 72	KILLER Warner Bros. K 56005	27	18 wks
22 Jul 72	● SCHOOL'S OUT Warner Bros. K 56007	4	20 wks
9 Sep 72	LOVE IT TO DEATH Warner Bros. K 46177	28	7 wks
24 Mar 73	★ BILLION DOLLAR BABIES Warner Bros. K56013	1	23 wks
12 Jan 74	MUSCLE OF LOVE Warner Bros. K 56018 ...	34	4 wks
15 Mar 75	WELCOME TO MY NIGHTMARE Anchor ANCL 2011	19	8 wks
24 Jul 76	ALICE COOPER GOES TO HELL Warner Bros. K 56171	23	7 wks
28 May 77	LACE AND WHISKY Warner Bros. K 56365	33	3 wks
23 Dec 78	FROM THE INSIDE Warner Bros. K 56577	68	3 wks
17 May 80	FLUSH THE FASHION Warner Bros. K 56805 ...	56	3 wks
12 Sep 81	SPECIAL FORCES Warner Bros. K 56927	96	1 wk
12 Nov 83	DADA Warner Bros 92-3969-1	93	1 wk

Julian COPE UK, male vocalist   5 wks

3 Mar 84	WORLD SHUT YOUR MOUTH Mercury MERL 37	40	4 wks
24 Nov 84	FRIED Mercury MERL 48	87	1 wk

Harry H. CORBETT - See Wilfred BRAMBELL and Harry H. CORBETT

CORRIES UK, male vocal/instrumental duo   5 wks

9 May 70	SCOTTISH LOVE SONGS Fontana 6309-004	46	4 wks
16 Sep 72	SOUND OF PIBROCH Columbia SCX 6511	39	1 wk

Elvis COSTELLO and the ATTRACTIONS
UK, male vocalist and male vocal/instrumental group   145 wks

6 Aug 77	MY AIM IS TRUE Stiff SEEZ 3	14	12 wks
1 Apr 78	● THIS YEAR'S MODEL Radar RAD 3	4	14 wks
20 Jan 79	● ARMED FORCES Radar RAD 14	2	28 wks
23 Feb 80	● GET HAPPY F-Beat XXLP 1	2	14 wks
31 Jan 81	● TRUST F-Beat XXLP 11	9	7 wks

31 Oct 81	● ALMOST BLUE *F-Beat XXLP 13*	7	18 wks
10 Jul 82	● IMPERIAL BEDROOM *F-Beat XXLP 17*	6	12 wks
6 Aug 83	● PUNCH THE CLOCK *F-Beat XXLP 19*	3	13 wks
7 Jul 84	● GOODBYE CRUEL WORLD *F-Beat ZL 70317* ..	10	10 wks
20 Apr 85	● THE BEST OF ELVIS COSTELLO - THE MAN *Telstar STAR 2247*	8	17 wks

My Aim Is True, This Year's Model, Trust and The Best Of Elvis Costello - The Man are credited to Elvis Costello only.

Phil COULTER *Ireland, male orchestra leader/*
instrumentalist - piano   *15 wks*

13 Oct 84	SEA OF TRANQUILITY *K-Tel Ireland KLP 185*	46	14 wks
18 May 85	PHIL COULTER'S IRELAND *K-Tel ONE 1296*	86	1 wk

David COVERDALE *UK, male vocalist*   *1 wk*

27 Feb 82	NORTHWINDS *Purple TTS 3513*	78	1 wk

CRAMPS *US, male/female vocal/instrumental group*
                                                                        6 wks

25 Jun 83	OFF THE BONE *Illegal ILP 012*	44	4 wks
26 Nov 83	SMELL OF FEMALE *Big Beat NED 6*	74	2 wks

CRASS *UK, male vocal/instrumental group*   *2 wks*

28 Aug 82	CHRIST THE ALBUM *Crass BOLLOX 2U2*	26	2 wks

Randy CRAWFORD *US, female vocalist*   *114 wks*

28 Jun 80	● NOW WE MAY BEGIN *Warner Bros. K 56791* ..	10	16 wks
16 May 81	● SECRET COMBINATION *Warner Bros. K 56904*	2	60 wks
12 Jun 82	● WINDSONG *Warner Bros. K 57011*	7	17 wks
22 Oct 83	NIGHTLINE *Warner Bros 92-3976-1*	37	4 wks
13 Oct 84	● MISS RANDY CRAWFORD - THE GREATEST HITS *K-Tel NE 1281*	10	17 wks

---

Robert CRAY Band *US, male vocal/instrumental group*
                                                                        1 wk

12 Oct 85	FALSE ACCUSATIONS *Demon FIEND 43*	68	1 wk

CRAZY HORSE - *See Neil YOUNG*

CRAZY WORLD - *See Crazy World of Arthur BROWN*

CREAM *UK, male vocal/instrumental group*   *182 wks*

24 Dec 66	● FRESH CREAM *Reaction 593-001*	6	17 wks
18 Nov 67	● DISRAELI GEARS *Reaction 594-003*	5	42 wks
17 Aug 68	● WHEELS OF FIRE (double) *Polydor 583-031/2*	3	26 wks
17 Aug 68	● WHEELS OF FIRE (single) *Polydor 583-033*	7	13 wks
8 Feb 69	● FRESH CREAM (re-issue) *Reaction 594-001*	7	2 wks
15 Mar 69	★ GOODBYE *Polydor 583-053*	1	28 wks
8 Nov 69	● BEST OF CREAM *Polydor 583-060*	6	34 wks
4 Jul 70	● LIVE CREAM *Polydor 2383-016*	4	15 wks
24 Jun 72	LIVE CREAM VOL.2 *Polydor 2383 119*	15	5 wks

---

CREATURES *UK, male/female vocal/instrumental duo*
                                                                        9 wks

28 May 83	FEAST *Wonderland SHELP 1*	17	9 wks

---

CREEDENCE CLEARWATER REVIVAL
US, male vocal/instrumental group   *65 wks*

24 Jan 70	GREEN RIVER *Liberty LBS 83273*	20	6 wks
28 Mar 70	● WILLY AND THE POOR BOYS *Liberty LBS 83338*	10	24 wks
2 May 70	BAYOU COUNTRY *Liberty LBS 83261*	62	1 wk
12 Sep 70	★ COSMO'S FACTORY *Liberty LBS 83388*	1	15 wks
23 Jan 71	PENDULUM *Liberty LBG 83400*	23	12 wks
30 Jun 79	GREATEST HITS *Fantasy FT 558*	35	5 wks
19 Oct 85	THE CREEDENCE COLLECTION *Impression IMDP*	68	2 wks

CREME - *See GODLEY and CREME*

Kid CREOLE and the COCONUTS *US, male/*
female vocal instrumental group   *54 wks*

22 May 82	● TROPICAL GANGSTERS *Ze/Island ILPS 7016* ..	3	40 wks
26 Jun 82	FRESH FRUIT IN FOREIGN PLACES *Ze/ Island ILPS 7014*	99	1 wk
17 Sep 83	DOPPELGANGER *Island ILPS 9743*	21	6 wks
15 Sep 84	CRE-OLE *Island IMA 13*	21	7 wks

CRICKETS *US, male vocal/instrumental group*   *7 wks*

25 Mar 61	IN STYLE WITH THE CRICKETS *Coral LVA 9142*	13	7 wks

See also Buddy Holly and the Crickets; Bobby Vee and the Crickets.

Bing CROSBY *US, male vocalist*   *39 wks*

8 Oct 60	● JOIN BING AND SING ALONG *Warner Brothers WM 4021*	7	11 wks
21 Dec 74	WHITE CHRISTMAS *MCA MCF 2568*	45	3 wks
20 Sep 75	THAT'S WHAT LIFE IS ALL ABOUT *United Artists UAG 2973*	28	6 wks
5 Nov 77	THE BEST OF BING *MCA MCF 2540*	41	7 wks
5 Nov 77	● LIVE AT THE LONDON PALLADIUM *K-Tel NE 951*	9	2 wks
17 Dec 77	SEASONS *Polydor 2442 151*	25	7 wks
5 May 79	SONGS OF A LIFETIME *Philips 6641 923*	29	3 wks

---

Dave CROSBY *US, male vocalist*   *7 wks*

24 Apr 71	IF ONLY I COULD REMEMBER MY NAME *Atlantic 2401-005*	12	7 wks

See also Crosby, Stills and Nash; Crosby, Stills, Nash and Young; Graham Nash and David Crosby.

CROSBY, STILLS and NASH *US/UK/, male*
vocal/instrumental group   *14 wks*

23 Aug 69	CROSBY STILLS AND NASH *Atlantic 588-189* ..	25	5 wks
9 Jul 77	CSN *Atlantic K 50369*	23	9 wks

See also Dave Crosby; Crosby, Stills, Nash and Young; Graham Nash; Graham Nash and David Crosby; Stephen Stills; Stills-Young Band; Stephen Stills' Manassas.

CROSBY, STILLS, NASH and YOUNG *US/*
UK/Canada, male vocal/instrumental group   *79 wks*

30 May 70	● DEJA VU *Atlantic 2401-001*	5	61 wks
22 May 71	● FOUR-WAY STREET *Atlantic 2956 004*	5	12 wks
21 Sep 74	SO FAR *Atlantic K 50023*	25	6 wks

See also Dave Crosby; Crosby, Stills and Nash; Graham Nash; Graham Nash and David Crosby; Stephen Stills; Stills-Young Band; Stephen Stills' Manassas; Neil Young.

PHIL COLLINS (right) Being pulled out of the number one spot by Paul Young.

RY COODER (centre right) Former member of Captain Beefheart's Magic Band.

ELVIS COSTELLO (bottom right) His two number twos were kept from number one by compilation albums.

CREAM (below) Cream haunt the memory of the editor who ran this false headline.

Melody Maker

MARCH 7, 1970   1s weekly   USA 25 cents

Win a FREE week-end in New York

DON'T MISS NEXT WEEK'S Melody Maker

P.S. Tell your friends

SIMON AND GARFUNKEL BOUND FOR BRITAIN

SIMON and Garfunkel are bound for Britain! In a great business coup, agent Tito Burns has scooped the Americans on behalf of Gordon Mills' MAM organisation for the world-famous duo to make a brief European tour.

One British date has been set — a performance at London's Royal Albert Hall on Saturday, April 25. And only Simon and Garfunkel are appearing.

Commented Tito Burns on Tuesday: "At the moment I'm in negotiation with Simon and Garfunkel's management on the possibility of their doing TV during their stay in Britain."

CREAM RETURN FOR ONE CONCERT

Isle of Wight plan

CREAM to reform? There is a good chance the legendary group starring Eric Clapton, Jack Bruce and Ginger Baker may get together for one concert at this year's Isle Of Wight Festival, writes MM's Chris Welch.

If this happens, it would be the most startling development of 1970, following hard on the heels of the revival of Steve Winwood's Traffic.

It has always been believed that the group which formed in 1966 and broke up at the end of 1968 would never play together again. Each member has become involved in different projects, including the Blind Faith experiment, Airforce, Delaney and Bonnie and Jack Bruce and Friends.

In its heyday the band sold millions of albums in Britain and America, set a whole trend in "progressive rock" groups, and became the subject of a BBC-TV documentary.

But on the London group scene at the weekend it was widely believed the "impossible" could happen.

Effort

Promoters of the Isle of Wight Festival, Rikki Farr and Ronald Foulk said on Monday: "It would be beautiful for the Cream, if they reformed to play the Festival, but we have not even discussed the matter.

"There are many rumours as to who will appear at the Isle of Wight this year. We have been approached by many of the world's top artists to play the event and we shall make every effort to secure them. As for the Cream, no approaches have been made, but if they were we could not help but say yes.

TUBBY HAYES IN HOSPITAL

POLL-WINNING tenor man Tubby Hayes, who has been ill for the past two months and unable to work in recent weeks, went into hospital on Friday.

Tubby is in the Royal Free Hospital, Grays Inn Road, London, under observation for an unidentified infection.

He is not expected to be back at work for two or three months.

Doll Norman, Tubby's manager, told the MM on Monday that he was taking no bookings for the tenor star before June. A quarter recording scheduled for Fontana has had to be postponed. Although he will not be in condition to blow for some considerable time, Norman added, Tubby hopes to be able to resume his writing in a few weeks.

ERIC CLAPTON: could get together with Jack Bruce and Ginger Baker.

Christopher CROSS US, male vocalist — 93 wks

21 Feb 81	CHRISTOPHER CROSS Warner Bros. K 56789 ..	14	77 wks
19 Feb 83	● ANOTHER PAGE Warner Bros W 3757	4	16 wks

CROWN HEIGHTS AFFAIR US, male vocal/instrumental group — 3 wks

23 Sep 78	DREAM WORLD Philips 6372 754	40	3 wks

CRUSADERS US, male vocal/instrumental group — 30 wks

21 Jul 79	● STREET LIFE MCA MCF 3008	10	16 wks
19 Jul 80	RHAPSODY AND BLUE MCA MCG 4010	40	5 wks
12 Sep 81	STANDING TALL MCA MCF 3122	47	5 wks
7 Apr 84	GHETTO BLASTER MCA MCF 3176	46	4 wks

Bobby CRUSH UK, male instrumentalist – piano — 12 wks

29 Nov 72	BOBBY CRUSH Philips 6308 135	15	7 wks
18 Dec 82	THE BOBBY CRUSH INCREDIBLE DOUBLE DECKER PARTY Warwick WW 5126/7	53	5 wks

CULT UK, male vocal/instrumental group — 21 wks

18 Jun 83	SOUTHERN DEATH CULT Beggars Banquet BEGA 46	43	3 wks
8 Sep 84	DREAMTIME Beggars Banquet BEGA 57	21	8 wks
26 Oct 85	● LOVE Beggars Banquet BEGA 65	4†	10 wks

First album credited to Southern Death Cult.

CULTURE Jamaica, male vocal/instrumental group — 1 wk

1 Apr 78	TWO SEVENS CLASH Lightning LIP 1	60	1 wk

CULTURE CLUB UK, male vocal/instrumental group — 128 wks

16 Oct 82	● KISSING TO BE CLEVER Virgin V 2232	5	59 wks
22 Oct 83	★ COLOUR BY NUMBERS Virgin V 2285	1	56 wks
3 Nov 84	● WAKING UP WITH THE HOUSE ON FIRE Virgin V 2330	2	13 wks

CURE UK, male vocal/instrumental group — 76 wks

2 Jun 79	THREE IMAGINARY BOYS Fiction FIX 001 ...	44	3 wks
3 May 80	17 SECONDS Fiction FIX 004	20	10 wks
25 Apr 81	FAITH Fiction FIX 6	14	8 wks
15 May 82	● PORNOGRAPHY Fiction FIX D7	8	9 wks
3 Sep 83	BOYS DON'T CRY Fiction SPELP 26	93	1 wks
24 Dec 83	JAPANESE WHISPERS Fiction FIXM 8	26	14 wks
3 Mar 84	BOYS DON'T CRY Fiction SPELP 26	77	2 wks
12 May 84	● THE TOP Fiction FIXS 9	10	10 wks
3 Nov 84	CONCERT - THE CURE LIVE Fiction FIXH 10	26	4 wks
7 Sep 85	● THE HEAD ON THE DOOR Fiction FIXH 11 ..	7	13 wks

CURVED AIR UK, male/female vocal/instrumental group — 32 wks

5 Dec 70	● AIR CONDITIONING Warner Bros. WSX 3012 ..	8	21 wks
9 Oct 71	CURVED AIR Warner Bros. K 46092	11	6 wks
13 May 72	PHANTASMAGORIA Reprise K 46158	20	5 wks

Adge CUTLER and the WURZELS UK, male vocal/instrumental group — 4 wks

11 Mar 67	ADGE CUTLER AND THE WURZELS Columbia SX 6126	38	4 wks

See also the Wurzels.

D

DAKOTAS - See Billy J. KRAMER and the DAKOTAS

DALEK I UK, male vocal/instrumental group — 2 wks

9 Aug 80	COMPASS KUMPAS Backdoor OPEN 1	54	2 wks

DALIS' CAR UK, male vocal/instrumental duo — 1 wk

1 Dec 84	THE WAKING HOUR Paradox DOXLP 1	84	1 wk

Roger DALTREY UK, male vocalist — 24 wks

26 Jul 75	RIDE A ROCK HORSE Polydor 2660 111	14	10 wks
4 Jun 77	ONE OF THE BOYS Polydor 2442 146	45	1 wk
23 Aug 80	McVICAR (film soundtrack) Polydor POLD 5034	39	11 wks
2 Nov 85	UNDER A RAGING MOON 10 DIX 17	52	2 wks

Glen DALY UK, male vocalist — 2 wks

20 Nov 71	GLASGOW NIGHT OUT Golden Guinea GGL 0479	28	2 wks

DAMNED UK, male vocal/instrumental group — 47 wks

12 Mar 77	DAMNED DAMNED DAMNED Stiff SEEZ 1	36	10 wks
17 Nov 79	MACHINE GUN ETIQUETTE Chiswick CWK 3011	31	5 wks
29 Nov 80	THE BLACK ALBUM Chiswick CWK 3015	29	3 wks
28 Nov 81	BEST OF Chiswick DAM 1	43	12 wks
23 Oct 82	STRAWBERRIES Bronze BRON 542	15	4 wks
27 July 85	PHANTASMAGORIA MCA MCF 3275	11	13 wks

Vic DAMONE US, male vocalist — 4 wks

25 Apr 81	NOW! RCA INTS 5080	44	3 wks
2 Apr 83	VIC DAMONE SINGS THE GREAT SONGS CBS 32261	87	1 wk

Suzanne DANDO UK, female exercise instructor — 1 wk

17 Mar 84	SHAPE UP AND DANCE WITH SUZANNE DANDO Lifestyle LEG 21	87	1 wk

Charlie DANIELS BAND US, male vocal/instrumental group — 1 wk

10 Nov 79	MILLION MILE REFLECTIONS Epic EPC 83446	74	1 wk

Bobby DARIN US, male vocalist — 15 wks

19 Mar 60	● THIS IS DARIN London HA 2235	4	8 wks

9 Apr 60	**THAT'S ALL** *London HAE 2172*	**15**	1 wk
5 Oct 85	**THE LEGEND OF BOBBY DARIN - HIS GREATEST HITS** *Atlantic SMR 8504*	**39**	6 wks

DARTS UK, male/female vocal-instrumental group
57 wks

3 Dec 77	● **DARTS** *Magnet MAG 5020*	**9**	22 wks
3 Jun 78	**EVERYONE PLAYS DARTS** *Magnet MAG 5022*	**12**	18 wks
18 Nov 78	● **AMAZING DARTS** *K-Tel/Magnet DLP 7981*	**8**	13 wks
6 Oct 79	**DART ATTACK** *Magnet MAG 5030*	**38**	4 wks

DANSE SOCIETY UK, male vocal/instrumental group
4 wks

11 Feb 84	**HEAVEN IS WAITING** *Society 205 972*	**39**	4 wks

DAVE - *See CHAS and DAVE*

F.R. DAVID France, male vocalist
6 wks

7 May 83	**WORDS** *Carrere CAL 145*	**46**	6 wks

Miles DAVIS US, male instrumentalist - trumpet
2 wks

11 Jul 70	**BITCHES BREW** *CBS 66236*	**71**	1 wk
15 Jun 85	**YOU'RE UNDER ARREST** *CBS 26447*	**88**	1 wk

Windsor DAVIS - *See Don ESTELLE and Windsor DAVIS*

Spencer DAVIS GROUP UK, male vocal/instrumental group
47 wks

8 Jan 66	● **THEIR 1ST LP** *Fontana TL 5242*	**6**	9 wks
22 Jan 66	● **THE 2ND LP** *Fontana TL 5295*	**3**	18 wks
11 Sep 66	● **AUTUMN '66** *Fontana TL 5359*	**4**	20 wks

Sammy DAVIS JR. US, male vocalist
1 wk

13 Apr 63	**SAMMY DAVIS JR. AT THE COCONUT GROVE** *Reprise R 6063/2*	**19**	1 wk

DAWN US, male/female vocal group
2 wks

4 May 74	**GOLDEN RIBBONS** *Bell BELLS 236*	**46**	2 wks

Doris DAY US, female vocalist
11 wks

6 Jan 79	**20 GOLDEN GREATS** *Warwick PR 5053*	**12**	11 wks

Chris DE BURGH Ireland, male vocalist
90 wks

12 Sep 81	**BEST MOVES** *A & M AMLH 68532*	**65**	4 wks
9 Oct 82	**THE GETAWAY** *A & M AMLH 68549*	**30**	16 wks
19 May 84	**MAN ON THE LINE** *A & M AMLX 65002*	**11**	24 wks
29 Dec 84	● **THE VERY BEST OF CHRIS DE BURGH** *Telstar STAR 2248*	**6**	43 wks
24 Aug 85	**SPANISH TRAIN & OTHER STORIES** *A & M AMLH 68343*	**78**	3 wks

Waldo DE LOS RIOS Argentina, orchestra
26 wks

1 May 71	● **SYMPHONIES FOR THE SEVENTIES** *A & M AMLS 2014*	**6**	26 wks

Manitas DE PLATA Spanish, male instrumentalist - guitar
1 wk

29 Jul 67	**FLAMENCO GUITAR** *Philips SBL 7786*	**40**	1 wk

DEAD KENNEDYS US, male vocal/instrumental group
6 wks

13 Sep 80	**FRESH FRUIT FOR ROTTING VEGETABLES** *Cherry Red BRED 10*	**33**	6 wks

DEAD OR ALIVE UK, male vocal/instrumental group
18 wks

28 Apr 84	**SOPHISTICATED BOOM BOOM** *Epic EPC 25835*	**29**	3 wks
25 May 85	● **YOUTHQUAKE** *Epic EPC 26420*	**9**	15 wks

DeBARGE US, male/female vocal/instrumental group
2 wks

25 May 85	**RHYTHM OF THE NIGHT** *Gordy ZL 72340*	**94**	2 wks

DEAN - *See JAN and DEAN*

Kiki DEE UK, female vocalist
9 wks

26 Mar 77	**KIKI DEE** *Rocket ROLA 3*	**24**	5 wks
18 Jul 81	**PERFECT TIMING** *Ariola ARL 5050*	**47**	4 wks

Dave DEE, DOZY, BEAKY, MICK and TICH UK, male vocal/instrumental group
15 wks

2 Jul 66	**DAVE DEE, DOZY, BEAKY, MICK AND TICH** *Fontana STL 5350*	**11**	10 wks
7 Jan 67	**IF MUSIC BE THE FOOD OF LOVE...PREPARE FOR INDIGESTION** *Fontana STL 5388*	**27**	5 wks

DEEP PURPLE UK, male vocal/instrumental group
258 wks

24 Jan 70	**CONCERTO FOR GROUP AND ORCHESTRA** *Harvest SHVL 767*	**26**	4 wks
20 Jun 70	● **DEEP PURPLE IN ROCK** *Harvest SHVL 777*	**4**	68 wks
18 Sep 71	★ **FIREBALL** *Harvest SHVL 793*	**1**	25 wks
15 Apr 72	★ **MACHINE HEAD** *Purple TPSA 7504*	**1**	24 wks
6 Jan 73	**MADE IN JAPAN** *Purple TPSP 351*	**16**	14 wks
17 Feb 73	● **WHO DO WE THINK WE ARE** *Purple TPSA 7508*	**4**	11 wks
2 Mar 74	● **BURN** *Purple TPA 3505*	**3**	21 wks
23 Nov 74	● **STORM BRINGER** *Purple TPS 3508*	**6**	12 wks
5 Jul 75	**24 CARAT PURPLE** *Purple TPSM 2002*	**14**	17 wks
22 Nov 75	**COME TASTE THE BAND** *Purple TPS 7515*	**19**	4 wks
27 Nov 76	**DEEP PURPLE LIVE** *Purple TPSA 7517*	**12**	6 wks
21 Apr 79	**THE MARK II PURPLE SINGLES** *Purple TPS 3514*	**24**	6 wks
19 Jul 80	★ **DEEPEST PURPLE** *Harvest EMTV 25*	**1**	15 wks
13 Dec 80	**IN CONCERT** *Harvest SHDW 4121/4122*	**30**	8 wks
4 Sep 82	**DEEP PURPLE LIVE IN LONDON** *Harvest SHSP 4124*	**23**	5 wks
10 Nov 84	● **PERFECT STRANGERS** *Polydor POLH 16*	**5**	15 wks
29 Jun 85	**THE ANTHOLOGY** *Harvest PUR 1*	**50**	3 wks

DEF LEPPARD UK, male vocal/instrumental group

23 wks

22 Mar 80	ON THROUGH THE NIGHT	Vertigo 9102 040 ..	15	8 wks
25 Jul 81	HIGH AND DRY	Vertigo 6359 045	26	8 wks
12 Mar 83	PYROMANIA	Vertigo VERS 2	18	7 wks

Desmond DEKKER Jamaica, male vocalist

4 wks

5 Jul 69	THIS IS DESMOND DEKKER	Trojan TTL 4 ...	27	4 wks

DELANEY and BONNIE and FRIENDS US/UK, male/female vocal instrumental group

3 wks

6 Jun 70	ON TOUR	Atlantic 2400-013	39	3 wks

DEMON UK, male vocal/instrumental group

5 wks

14 Aug 82	THE UNEXPECTED GUEST	Carrere CAL 139	47	3 wks
2 Jul 83	THE PLAGUE	Clay CLAY LP 6	73	2 wks

Sandy DENNY UK, female vocalist

2 wks

2 Oct 71	THE NORTH STAR GRASSMAN AND THE RAVENS	Island ILPS 9165	31	2 wks

John DENVER US, male vocalist

201 wks

2 Jun 73	POEMS, PRAYERS AND PROMISES	RCA SF 8219	19	5 wks
23 Jun 73	RHYMES AND REASONS	RCA Victor SF 8348	21	5 wks
30 Mar 74 ●	THE BEST OF JOHN DENVER	RCA Victor APLI 0374	7	69 wks
7 Sep 74 ●	BACK HOME AGAIN	RCA Victor APLI 0548 ...	3	29 wks
22 Mar 75	AN EVENING WITH JOHN DENVER	RCA Victor LSA 3211/12	31	4 wks
11 Oct 75	WIND SONG RCA Victor APLI 1183		14	21 wks
15 May 76	LIVE IN LONDON RCA Victor RS 1050		2	29 wks
4 Sep 76	SPIRIT RCA Victor APLI 1694		9	11 wks
19 Mar 77 ●	BEST OF JOHN DENVER VOL.2	RCA Victor PL 42120	9	9 wks
11 Feb 78	I WANT TO LIVE RCA PL 12561		25	5 wks
21 Apr 79	JOHN DENVER RCA Victor PL 13075		68	1 wk
22 Oct 83	IT'S ABOUT TIME RCA RCALP 6087		90	2 wks
1 Dec 84	JOHN DENVER COLLECTION	Telstar STAR 2253	20	11 wks

See also Placido Domingo and John Denver.

Karl DENVER UK, male vocalist

27 wks

23 Dec 61 ●	WIMOWEH	Ace Of Clubs ACL 1098	7	27 wks

DEPECHE MODE UK, male vocal/instrumental group

78 wks

14 Nov 81 ●	SPEAK AND SPELL	Mute STUMM 5	10	33 wks
9 Oct 82 ●	A BROKEN FRAME	Mute STUMM 9	8	11 wks
3 Sep 83 ●	CONSTRUCTION TIME AGAIN	Mute STUMM 13	6	12 wks
6 Sep 84 ●	SOME GREAT REWARD	Mute STUMM 19 ...	5	12 wks
26 Oct 85 ●	THE SINGLES 81-85	Mute MUTEL 1	6†	10 wks

DEREK AND CLIVE - See Peter COOK and Dudley MOORE

DEREK and the DOMINOES UK/US, male vocal/instrumental group

1 wk

24 Mar 73	IN CONCERT	RSO 2659 020	36	1 wk

DESTROYERS - See George THOROGOOD and the DESTROYERS

DETROIT SPINNERS US, male vocal group

3 wks

14 May 77	DETROIT SPINNERS' SMASH HITS	Atlantic K 50363	37	3 wks

Sydney DEVINE UK, male vocalist

11 wks

10 Apr 76	DOUBLY DEVINE Philips 6625 019		14	10 wks
11 Dec 76	DEVINE TIME Philips 6308 283		49	1 wk

DEVO US, male vocal/instrumental group

22 wks

23 Jun 79	DUTY NOW FOR THE FUTURE Virgin V 2125		49	6 wks
16 Sep 78	Q: ARE WE NOT MEN? A: NO WE ARE DEVO!	Virgin V 2106	12	7 wks
24 May 80	FREEDOM OF CHOICE Virgin V 2162		47	5 wks
5 Sep 81	NEW TRADITIONALISTS Virgin V 2191		50	4 wks

Howard DEVOTO UK, male vocalist

2 wks

6 Aug 83	JERKY VERSIONS OF THE DREAM	Virgin V 2272	57	2 wks

DEXY'S MIDNIGHT RUNNERS UK, male/female vocal/instrumental group

64 wks

26 Jul 80 ●	SEARCHING FOR THE YOUNG SOUL REBELS	Parlophone PCS 7213	6	10 wks
7 Aug 82 ●	TOO-RYE-AY Mercury MERS 5		2	46 wks
26 Mar 83	GENO EMI EMS 1007		79	2 wks
21 Sep 85	DON'T STAND ME DOWN Mercury MERH 56		22	6 wks

Group were all male for first album.

Neil DIAMOND US, male vocalist

429 wks

3 Apr 71	TAP ROOT MANUSCRIPT Uni UNLS 117		19	12 wks
3 Apr 71	GOLD Uni UNLS 116		23	11 wks
11 Dec 71	STONES Uni UNLS 121		18	14 wks
5 Aug 72 ●	MOODS Uni UNLS 128		7	19 wks
12 Jan 74	HOT AUGUST NIGHT Uni ULD 1		32	2 wks
16 Feb 74	JONATHAN LIVINGSTON SEAGULL	CBS 69047	35	1 wk
9 Mar 74	RAINBOW MCA MCF 2529		39	5 wks
29 Jul 74	HIS 12 GREATEST HITS MCA MCF 2550 ...		13	78 wks
9 Nov 74	SERENADE CBS 69067		11	14 wks
10 Jul 76 ●	BEAUTIFUL NOISE CBS 86004		10	26 wks
12 Mar 77 ●	LOVE AT THE GREEK CBS 95001		3	32 wks
6 Aug 77	HOT AUGUST NIGHT (re-issue)	MCA MCSP 255	60	1 wk
17 Dec 77	I'M GLAD YOU'RE HERE WITH ME TONIGHT	CBS 86044	16	12 wks
25 Nov 78 ●	20 GOLDEN GREATS MCA EMTV 14		2	26 wks
6 Jan 79	YOU DON'T BRING ME FLOWERS CBS 86077		15	23 wks
19 Jan 80	SEPTEMBER MORN CBS 86096		14	11 wks
22 Nov 80	THE JAZZ SINGER Capitol EAST 12120		14	84 wks
28 Feb 81	LOVE SONGS MCA MCF 3092		43	6 wks
5 Dec 81	THE WAY TO THE SKY CBS 85343		39	13 wks
19 Jun 82	12 GREATEST HITS VOL 2 CBS 85844		32	8 wks
13 Nov 82	HEARTLIGHT CBS 25073		43	10 wks

DEXY'S MIDNIGHT RUNNERS (right) Their lead singer Kevin Rowland was a one-time candidate for the priesthood.

JOHN DENVER (above) Henry John Deutschendorf, Jr was born on New Year's Eve 1943 in Roswell, New Mexico. He changed his surname to that of his favourite city.

CHRIS DE BURGH (below) Nine albums, eleven million records sold worldwide and the first artist to enter the Swiss album charts at number one.

DAMNED

BARBARA DICKSON (below) One of Dunfermline's most celebrated exports has won awards as an actress (in Blood Brothers) as well as plenty of gold and platinum on record.

THE DAMNED Ahead of the Clash and the Sex Pistols – the first punk album to chart.

10 Dec 83	**THE VERY BEST OF NEIL DIAMOND** K-Tel NE 1265	33	11 wks
28 Jul 84 ●	**PRIMITIVE** CBS 86306	7	10 wks

DIAMOND HEAD UK, male vocal/instrumental group
9 wks

23 Oct 82	**BORROWED TIME** MCA DH 1001	24	5 wks
24 Sep 83	**CANTERBURY** MCA DH 1002	32	4 wks

DICKIES US, male vocal/instrumental group
19 wks

17 Feb 79	**THE INCREDIBLE SHRINKING DICKIES** A & M AMLE 64742	18	17 wks
24 Nov 79	**DAWN OF THE DICKIES** A & M AMLE 68510	60	2 wks

Barbara DICKSON UK, female vocalist
91 wks

18 Jun 77	**MORNING COMES QUICKLY** RSO 2394 188	58	1 wk
12 Apr 80 ●	**THE BARBARA DICKSON ALBUM** Epic EPC 84088	7	12 wks
16 May 81	**YOU KNOW IT'S ME** Epic EPC 84551	39	6 wks
6 Feb 82 ●	**ALL FOR A SONG** Epic 10030	3	38 wks
24 Sep 83	**TELL ME IT'S NOT TRUE** Legacy LLM 101	100	1 wk
23 Jun 84	**HEARTBEATS** Epic EPC 25706	21	8 wks
12 Jan 85 ●	**THE BARBARA DICKSON SONGBOOK** K-Tel NE 1287	5	19 wks
23 Nov 85	**GOLD** K-Tel ONE 1312	11†	6 wks

Tell Me It's Not True is a mini-album featuring songs from the musical Blood Brothers.

Bo DIDDLEY US, male vocalist/instrumentalist – guitar
16 wks

5 Oct 63	**BO DIDDLEY** Pye International NPL 28026	11	8 wks
9 Nov 63	**BO DIDDLEY IS A GUNSLINGER** Pye NJL 33	20	1 wk
30 Nov 63	**BO DIDDLEY RIDES AGAIN** Pye International NPL 28029	19	1 wk
15 Feb 64	**BO DIDDLEY'S BEACH PARTY** Pye NPL 28032	13	6 wks

DIFFORD and TILBROOK UK, male vocal/instrumental duo
3 wks

14 Jul 84	**DIFFORD AND TILBROOK** A & M AMLX 64985	47	3 wks

Richard DIMBLEBY UK, male broadcaster
5 wks

4 Jun 66	**VOICE OF RICHARD DIMBLEBY** MFP 1087	14	5 wks

DIO UK/US, male vocal/instrumental group
35 wks

11 Jun 83	**HOLY DIVER** Vertigo VERS 5	13	15 wks
21 Jul 84 ●	**THE LAST IN LINE** Vertigo VERL 16	4	14 wks
7 Sep 85 ●	**SACRED HEART** Vertigo VERH 30	4	6 wks

DION and the BELMONTS US, male vocal group
5 wks

12 Apr 80	**20 GOLDEN GREATS** K-Tel NE 1057	31	5 wks

DIRE STRAITS UK, male vocal/instrumental group
599 wks

22 Jul 78 ●	**DIRE STRAITS** Vertigo 9102 021	5	106 wks
23 Jun 79 ●	**COMMUNIQUE** Vertigo 9102 031	5	18 wks
25 Oct 80 ●	**MAKIN' MOVIES** Vertigo 6359 034	4†	209 wks
2 Oct 82 ★	**LOVE OVER GOLD** Vertigo 6359 109	1†	142 wks
24 Mar 84	**ALCHEMY – DIRE STRAITS LIVE** Vertigo VERY 11	3†	92 wks
25 May 85 ★	**BROTHERS IN ARMS** Vertigo VERH 25	1†	32 wks

DISCHARGE UK, male vocal/instrumental group
5 wks

15 May 82	**HEAR NOTHING, SEE NOTHING, SAY NOTHING** Clay CLAYLP 3	40	5 wks

Sacha DISTEL France, male vocalist
14 wks

2 May 70	**SACHA DISTEL** Warner Bros. WS 3003	21	14 wks

DR. FEELGOOD UK, male vocal/instrumental group
33 wks

18 Oct 75	**MALPRACTICE** United Artists UAS 29880	17	6 wks
2 Oct 76 ★	**STUPIDITY** United Artists UAS 29990	1	9 wks
4 Jun 77 ●	**SNEAKIN' SUSPICION** United Artists UAS 30075	10	6 wks
8 Oct 77	**BE SEEING YOU** United Artists UAS 30123	55	3 wks
7 Oct 78	**PRIVATE PRACTICE** United Artists UAG 30184	41	5 wks
2 Jun 79	**AS IT HAPPENS** United Artists UAK 30239	42	4 wks

DR. HOOK US, male vocal/instrumental group
130 wks

25 Jun 76 ●	**A LITTLE BIT MORE** Capitol E-ST 23795	5	42 wks
29 Oct 77	**MAKING LOVE AND MUSIC** Capitol EST 11632	39	4 wks
27 Oct 79	**PLEASURE AND PAIN** Capitol EAST 11859	47	6 wks
17 Nov 79	**SOMETIMES YOU WIN** Capitol EST 12018	14	44 wks
29 Nov 80	**RISING** Mercury 6302 076	44	5 wks
6 Dec 80 ●	**DR. HOOK'S GREATEST HITS** Capitol EST 26037	2	28 wks
14 Nov 81	**DR. HOOK LIVE IN THE UK** Capitol EST 26706	90	1 wk

Ken DODD UK, male vocalist
36 wks

25 Dec 65 ●	**TEARS OF HAPPINESS** Columbia 33SX 1793	6	12 wks
23 Jul 66	**HITS FOR NOW AND ALWAYS** Columbia SX 6060	14	11 wks
14 Jan 67	**FOR SOMEONE SPECIAL** Columbia SCX 6224	40	1 wk
29 Nov 80 ●	**20 GOLDEN GREATS OF KEN DODD** Warwick WW 5098	10	12 wks

Thomas DOLBY UK, male vocalist/instrumentalist – keyboards
24 wks

22 May 82	**THE GOLDEN AGE OF WIRELESS** Venice In Peril VIP 1001	65	10 wks
18 Feb 84	**THE FLAT EARTH** Parlophone ODEON PCS 2400341	14	14 wks

DOLLAR UK, male/female vocal duo
28 wks

15 Sep 79	**SHOOTING STARS** Carrere CAL 111	36	8 wks
24 Apr 82	**THE VERY BEST OF DOLLAR** Carrere CAL 3001	31	9 wks
30 Oct 82	**THE DOLLAR ALBUM** WEA DTV 1	18	11 wks

Placido DOMINGO Spain, male vocalist
8 wks

21 May 83	**MY LIFE FOR A SONG** CBS 73683	31	8 wks

See also Placido Domingo and John Denver.

DIRE STRAITS (above) The extraordinary staying power of their LPs and their great sales on compact disc give leader Mark Knopfler a lot to smile about. (LFI)

DOLLAR (top right) Dollarmites David Van Day and Thereze Bazar.

DONOVAN (centre right) Launched as Britain's Bob Dylan, Donovan discusses 'The Hollies Sing Dylan' album with Hollie Tony Hicks. (Richard Young)

DURAN DURAN (right) The famous five on their hols.

Placido DOMINGO and John DENVER *Spain/US, male vocal duo*   *21 wks*

| 28 Nov 81 | PERHAPS LOVE   CBS 73592 | 26 | 21 wks |

See also Placido Domingo; John Denver.

Fats DOMINO *US, male vocalist/instrumentalist – piano*   *1 wk*

| 16 May 70 | VERY BEST OF FATS DOMINO   Liberty LBS 83331 | 56 | 1 wk |

Lonnie DONEGAN *UK, male vocalist*   *29 wks*

1 Sep 62	● GOLDEN AGE OF DONEGAN Pye Golden Guinea GGL 0135	3	23 wks
9 Feb 63	GOLDEN AGE OF DONEGAN VOL.2 Pye Golden Guinea GGL 0170	15	3 wks
25 Feb 78	PUTTING ON THE STYLE Chrysalis CHR 1158	51	3 wks

DONOVAN *UK, male vocalist*   *73 wks*

5 Jun 65	● WHAT'S BIN DID AND WHAT'S BIN HID Pye NPL 18117	3	16 wks
6 Nov 65	FAIRY TALE Pye NPL 18128	20	7 wks
8 Jul 67	SUNSHINE SUPERMAN Pye NPL 18181	25	7 wks
14 Oct 67	● UNIVERSAL SOLDIER Marble Arch MAL 718	5	18 wks
11 May 68	A GIFT FROM A FLOWER TO A GARDEN Pye NSPL 20000	13	14 wks
12 Sep 70	OPEN ROAD Dawn DNLS 3009	30	4 wks
24 Mar 73	COSMIC WHEELS Epic EPC 65450	15	12 wks

DOOBIE BROTHERS *US, male vocal/instrumental group*   *30 wks*

30 Mar 74	WHAT WERE ONCE VICES ARE NOW HABITS Warner Bros. K 56206	19	10 wks
17 May 75	STAMPEDE Warner Bros. K 56094	14	11 wks
10 Apr 76	TAKIN' IT TO THE STREETS Warner Bros. K 56196	42	2 wks
17 Sep 77	LIVING ON THE FAULT LINE Warner Bros. K 56383	25	5 wks
11 Oct 80	ONE STEP CLOSER Warner Bros. K 56824	53	2 wks

DOOLEYS *UK, male/female vocal/instrumental group*   *27 wks*

30 Jun 79	● THE BEST OF THE DOOLEYS GTO GTTV 038	6	21 wks
3 Nov 79	THE CHOSEN FEW GTO GTLP 040	56	4 wks
25 Oct 80	FULL HOUSE GTO GTTV 050	54	2 wks

Val DOONICAN *Ireland, male vocalist*   *164 wks*

12 Dec 64	● LUCKY 13 SHADES OF VAL DOONICAN Decca LK 4648	2	27 wks
3 Dec 66	● GENTLE SHADES OF VAL DOONICAN Decca LK 4831	5	52 wks
2 Dec 67	★ VAL DOONICAN ROCKS BUT GENTLY Pye NSPL 18204	1	23 wks
30 Nov 68	● VAL Pye NSPL 18236	6	11 wks
14 Jun 69	● WORLD OF VAL DOONICAN Decca SPA 3	2	31 wks
13 Dec 69	SOUNDS GENTLE Pye NSPL 18321	22	9 wks
19 Dec 70	THE MAGIC OF VAL DOONICAN Philips 6642 003	34	3 wks
27 Nov 71	THIS IS VAL DOONICAN Philips 6382 017	40	1 wk
22 Feb 75	I LOVE COUNTRY MUSIC Philips 9299261	37	2 wks

| 21 May 77 | SOME OF MY BEST FRIENDS ARE SONGS   Philips 6641 607 | 29 | 5 wks |

DOORS *US, male vocal/instrumental group*   *28 wks*

28 Sep 68	WAITING FOR THE SUN Elektra EKS7 4024	16	10 wks
11 Apr 70	MORRISON HOTEL Elektra EKS 75007	12	8 wks
26 Sep 70	ABSOLUTELY LIVE Elektra 2665 002	69	1 wk
31 Jul 71	L.A. WOMAN Elektra K42090	28	3 wks
1 Apr 72	WEIRD SCENES INSIDE THE GOLD MINE Elektra K 62009	50	1 wk
29 Oct 83	ALIVE, SHE CRIED Elektra 96-0269-1	36	5 wks

Lee DORSEY *US, male vocalist*   *4 wks*

| 17 Dec 66 | NEW LEE DORSEY   Stateside SSL 10192 | 34 | 4 wks |

Craig DOUGLAS *UK, male vocalist*   *2 wks*

| 6 Aug 60 | CRAIG DOUGLAS   Top Rank BUY 049 | 17 | 2 wks |

DREAM ACADEMY *UK, male/female vocal/instrumental group*   *2 wks*

| 12 Oct 85 | THE DREAM ACADEMY   Blanco Y Negro BYN 6 | 58 | 2 wks |

DOZY - *See Dave DEE, DOZY, BEAKY, MICK and TICH*

DREAMERS - *See FREDDIE and the DREAMERS*

DRIFTERS *US, male vocal group*   *50 wks*

18 May 68	GOLDEN HITS Atlantic 588-103	27	7 wks
10 Jun 72	GOLDEN HITS Atlantic K 40018	26	8 wks
8 Nov 75	● 24 ORIGINAL HITS Atlantic K 60106	2	34 wks
13 Dec 75	LOVE GAMES Bell BELLS 246	51	1 wk

Julie DRISCOLL and The Brian AUGER TRINITY *UK, female vocalist/male instrumental group*   *13 wks*

| 8 Jun 68 | OPEN   Marmalade 608-002 | 12 | 13 wks |

D-TRAIN *US, male vocalist/multi-instrumentalist*   *4 wks*

| 8 May 82 | D-TRAIN   Epic EPC 85683 | 72 | 4 wks |

D-Train is a pseudonym for Hubert Eaves.

DUBLINERS *Ireland, male vocal/instrumental group*   *78 wks*

13 May 67	● A DROP OF THE HARD STUFF Major Minor MMLP 3	5	41 wks
9 Sep 67	BEST OF THE DUBLINERS Transatlantic TRA 158	25	11 wks
7 Oct 67	● MORE OF THE HARD STUFF Major Minor MMLP 5	8	23 wks
2 Mar 68	DRINKIN' AND COURTIN' Major Minor SMLP 14	31	3 wks

Stephen 'Tin Tin' DUFFY *UK, male vocalist*   *7 wks*

| 20 Apr 85 | THE UPS AND DOWNS   10 DIX 5 | 35 | 7 wks |

George DUKE US, male vocalist/instrumentalist – keyboards   4 wks

26 Jul 80	**BRAZILIAN LOVE AFFAIR** *Epic EPC 84311*	...	**33**	4 wks

Simon DUPREE and the BIG SOUND UK, male vocal/instrumental group   1 wk

13 Aug 67	**WITHOUT RESERVATIONS** *Parlophone PCS 7029*	**39**	1 wk

Duran DURAN UK, male vocal/instrumental group   305 wks

27 Jun 81	● **DURAN DURAN** *EMI EMC 3372*	**3**	118 wks
22 May 82	● **RIO** *EMI EMC 3411*	**2**	109 wks
3 Dec 83	★ **SEVEN AND THE RAGGED TIGER** *EMC 1654541*	**1**	47 wks
24 Nov 84	● **ARENA** *Parlophone DD 2*	**6**	31 wks

Deanna DURBIN US, female vocalist   4 wks

30 Jan 82	**THE BEST OF DEANNA DURBIN** *MCA Int MCL 1634*	**84**	4 wks

Ian DURY and The BLOCKHEADS UK, male vocal/instrumental group   118 wks

22 Oct 77	● **NEW BOOTS AND PANTIES!!** *Stiff SEEZ 4*	...	**5**	90 wks
2 Jun 79	● **DO IT YOURSELF** *Stiff SEEZ 14*	**2**	18 wks
6 Dec 80	**LAUGHTER** *Stiff SEEZ 30*	**48**	4 wks
10 Oct 81	**LORD UPMINSTER** *Polydor POLD 5042*	**53**	4 wks
4 Feb 84	**4,000 WEEKS HOLIDAY** *Polydor POLD 5112*	**54**	2 wks

4,000 Weeks Holiday credits the Music Students – UK, male vocal/instrumental group.

Bob DYLAN US, male vocalist   536 wks

23 May 64	★ **THE FREEWHEELIN' BOB DYLAN** *CBS BPG 62193*	**1**	49 wks
11 Jul 64	● **THE TIMES THEY ARE A-CHANGIN'** *CBS BPG 62251*	**4**	20 wks
21 Nov 64	● **ANOTHER SIDE OF BOB DYLAN** *CBS BPG 62429*	**8**	19 wks
8 May 65	**BOB DYLAN** *CBS BPG 62022*	**13**	6 wks
15 May 65	★ **BRINGING IT ALL BACK HOME** *CBS BPG 62515*	**1**	29 wks
9 Oct 65	● **HIGHWAY 61 REVISITED** *CBS BPG 62572*	**4**	15 wks
20 Aug 66	● **BLONDE ON BLONDE** *CBS DDP 66012*	**3**	15 wks
14 Jan 67	● **GREATEST HITS** *CBS SBPG 62847*	**6**	82 wks
2 Mar 68	★ **JOHN WESLEY HARDING** *CBS SBPG 63252*	**1**	29 wks
17 May 69	★ **NASHVILLE SKYLINE** *CBS 63601*	**1**	42 wks
11 Jul 70	★ **SELF PORTRAIT** *CBS 66250*	**1**	15 wks
28 Nov 70	★ **NEW MORNING** *CBS 69001*	**1**	18 wks
25 Dec 71	**MORE BOB DYLAN GREATEST HITS** *CBS 67238/9*	**12**	15 wks
29 Sep 73	**PAT GARRETT & BILLY THE KID (film soundtrack)** *CBS 69042*	**29**	11 wks
23 Feb 74	● **PLANET WAVES** *Island ILPS 9261*	**7**	8 wks
13 Jul 74	● **BEFORE THE FLOOD** *Asylum IDBD 1*	**8**	7 wks
15 Feb 75	● **BLOOD ON THE TRACKS** *CBS 69097*	**4**	16 wks
26 Jul 75	● **THE BASEMENT TAPES** *CBS 88147*	**8**	10 wks
31 Jan 76	● **DESIRE** *CBS 86003*	**3**	35 wks
9 Oct 76	● **HARD RAIN** *CBS 86016*	**3**	7 wks
1 Jul 78	● **STREET LEGAL** *CBS 86067*	**2**	20 wks
26 May 79	● **BOB DYLAN AT BUDOKAN** *CBS 96004*	**4**	19 wks
8 Sep 79	● **SLOW TRAIN COMING** *CBS 86095*	**2**	13 wks
28 Jun 80	● **SAVED** *CBS 86113*	**3**	8 wks
29 Aug 81	● **SHOT OF LOVE** *CBS 85178*	**6**	8 wks
12 Nov 83	● **INFIDELS** *CBS 25539*	**9**	12 wks
15 Dec 84	**REAL LIVE** *CBS 26334*	**54**	2 wks
22 Jun 85	**EMPIRE BURLESQUE** *CBS 86313*	**11**	6 wks

E

EAGLES US, male vocal/instrumental group   239 wks

27 Apr 74	**ON THE BORDER** *Asylum SYL 9016*	**28**	9 wks
12 Jul 75	● **ONE OF THESE NIGHTS** *Asylum SYLA 8759*	**8**	40 wks
12 Jul 75	**DESPERADO** *Asylum SYLL 9011*	**39**	9 wks
6 Mar 76	● **THEIR GREATEST HITS 1971-1975** *Asylum K 53017*	**2**	77 wks
25 Dec 76	● **HOTEL CALIFORNIA** *Asylum K 53051*	**2**	61 wks
13 Oct 79	● **THE LONG RUN** *Asylum K 52181*	**4**	16 wks
22 Nov 80	**LIVE** *Asylum K 62032*	**24**	4 wks
18 May 85	● **BEST OF THE EAGLES** *Asylum EKT 5*	**10**	23 wks

EARTH WIND AND FIRE US, male vocal/instrumental group   141 wks

21 Jan 78	**ALL 'N' ALL** *CBS 86051*	**13**	23 wks
16 Dec 78	● **THE BEST OF EARTH WIND AND FIRE VOL.1** *CBS 83284*	**6**	42 wks
23 Jun 79	● **I AM** *CBS 86084*	**5**	41 wks
1 Nov 80	● **FACES** *CBS 88498*	**10**	6 wks
14 Nov 81	**RAISE** *CBS 85272*	**14**	22 wks
19 Feb 83	**POWERLIGHT** *CBS 25120*	**22**	7 wks

EAST OF EDEN UK, male vocal/instrumental group   2 wks

14 Mar 70	**SNAFU** *Deram SML 1050*	**29**	2 wks

Sheena EASTON UK, female vocalist   20 wks

31 Jan 81	**TAKE MY TIME** *EMI EMC 3354*	**17**	9 wks
3 Oct 81	**YOU COULD HAVE BEEN WITH ME** *EMI EMC 3378*	**33**	6 wks
25 Sep 82	**MADNESS, MONEY AND MUSIC** *EMI EMC 3414*	**44**	4 wks
15 Oct 83	**BEST KEPT SECRET** *EMI EMC 1077951*	**99**	1 wk

Clint EASTWOOD and General SAINT Jamaica, male vocal duo   3 wks

6 Feb 82	**TWO BAD DJ** *Greensleeves GREL 24*	**99**	2 wks
28 May 83	**STOP THAT TRAIN** *Greensleeves GREL 53*	**98**	1 wk

ECHO and the BUNNYMEN UK, male vocal/instrumental group   71 wks

26 Jul 80	**CROCODILES** *Korova KODE 1*	**17**	6 wks
6 Jun 81	● **HEAVEN UP HERE** *Korova KODE 3*	**10**	16 wks
12 Feb 83	● **PORCUPINE** *Korova KODE 6*	**2**	17 wks
12 May 84	● **OCEAN RAIN** *Korova KODE 8*	**4**	26 wks
23 Nov 85	● **SONGS TO LEARN & SING** *Korova KODE 13*	**6†**	6 wks

EDDIE and the HOT RODS UK, male vocal/instrumental group   5 wks

18 Dec 76	**TEENAGE DEPRESSION** *Island ILPS 9457*	**43**	1 wk
3 Dec 77	**LIFE ON THE LINE** *Island ILPS 9509*	**27**	3 wks
24 Mar 79	**THRILLER** *Island ILPS 9563*	**50**	1 wk

Duane EDDY US, male instrumentalist - guitar 88 wks

6 Jun 59 ●	**HAVE TWANGY GUITAR WILL TRAVEL** London HAW 2160		**6**	3 wks
31 Oct 59 ●	**SPECIALLY FOR YOU** London HAW 2191		**6**	8 wks
19 Mar 60 ●	**THE TWANG'S THE THANG** London HAW 2236		**2**	25 wks
26 Nov 60	**SONGS OF OUR HERITAGE** London HAW 2285		**13**	5 wks
1 Apr 61 ●	**A MILLION DOLLARS' WORTH OF TWANG** London HAW 2325		**5**	19 wks
9 Jun 62	**A MILLION DOLLARS WORTH OF TWANG VOL.2** London HAW 2435		**18**	1 wk
21 Jul 62 ●	**TWISTIN' & TWANGIN'** RCA RD 27264		**8**	12 wks
8 Dec 62	**TWANGY GUITAR - SILKY STRINGS** RCA RD 7510		**13**	11 wks
16 Mar 63	**DANCE WITH THE GUITAR MAN** RCA RD 7545		**14**	4 wks

Dave EDMUNDS UK, male vocalist/instrumentalist - guitar 21 wks

23 Jun 79	**REPEAT WHEN NECESSARY** Swansong SSK 59409		**39**	12 wks
18 Apr 81	**TWANGIN'** Swansong SSK 59411		**37**	4 wks
3 Apr 82	**DE7** Arista SPART 1184		**60**	3 wks
30 Apr 83	**INFORMATION** Arista 205 348		**92**	2 wks

Dennis EDWARDS US, male vocalist 1 wk

14 Apr 84	**DON'T LOOK ANY FURTHER** Gordy ZL 72148	**91**	1 wk

EEK-A-MOUSE Jamaica, male vocalist 3 wks

14 Aug 82	**SKIDIP** Greensleeves GREL 41		**61**	3 wks

801 UK, male vocal/instrumental group 2 wks

20 Nov 76	**801 LIVE** Island ILPS 9444		**52**	2 wks

ELECTRIC LIGHT ORCHESTRA UK, male vocal/instrumental group 333 wks

12 Aug 72	**QUEEN OF THE HOURS** Harvest SHVL 797		**32**	4 wks
31 Mar 73	**ELO 2** Harvest SHVL 806		**35**	1 wk
11 Dec 76 ●	**A NEW WORLD RECORD** United Artists UAG 30017		**6**	100 wks
12 Nov 77 ●	**OUT OF THE BLUE** United Artists UAR 100		**4**	108 wks
6 Jan 79	**THREE LIGHT YEARS** Jet JET BX 1		**38**	9 wks
16 Jun 79 ★	**DISCOVERY** Jet JET LX 500		**1**	46 wks
1 Dec 79 ●	**ELO'S GREATEST HITS** Jet JET LX 525		**7**	18 wks
8 Aug 81 ★	**TIME** Jet LP 236		**1**	32 wks
2 Jul 83 ●	**SECRET MESSAGES** Jet JETLX 527		**4**	15 wks

A New World Record *changed to* JET LP 200 *and* Out Of The Blue *changed label number to* JET DP 400 *during their chart runs*

Duke ELLINGTON US, orchestra 2 wks

8 Apr 61	**NUT CRACKER SUITE** Philips BBL 7418		**11**	2 wks

ELECTRIC WIND ENSEMBLE UK, male instrumental group 9 wks

18 Feb 84	**HAUNTING MELODIES** Nouveau Music NML1007		**28**	9 wks

EMERSON, LAKE and PALMER UK, male instrumental group 135 wks

5 Dec 70 ●	**EMERSON, LAKE AND PALMER** Island ILPS 9132		**4**	28 wks
19 Jun 71 ★	**TARKUS** Island ILPS 9155		**1**	17 wks
4 Dec 71 ●	**PICTURES AT AN EXHIBITION** Island HELP 1		**3**	5 wks
8 Jul 72 ●	**TRILOGY** Island ILPS 9186		**2**	29 wks
22 Dec 73 ●	**BRAIN SALAD SURGERY** Manticore K 53501		**2**	17 wks
24 Aug 74 ●	**WELCOME BACK MY FRIENDS TO THE SHOW THAT NEVER ENDS - LADIES AND GENTLEMEN: EMERSON, LAKE AND PALMER** Manticore K 63500		**5**	5 wks
9 Apr 77 ●	**WORKS** Atlantic K 80009		**9**	25 wks
10 Dec 77	**WORKS VOL.2** Atlantic K 50422		**20**	5 wks
9 Dec 78	**LOVE BEACH** Atlantic K 50552		**48**	4 wks

See also Greg Lake.

ENGLAND FOOTBALL WORLD CUP SQUAD 1970 UK, male football team vocalists 8 wks

16 May 70 ●	**THE WORLD BEATERS SING THE WORLD BEATERS** Pye NSPL 18337		**4**	8 wks

ENGLAND FOOTBALL WORLD CUP SQUAD 1982 UK, male football team vocalists 10 wks

15 May 82	**THIS TIME** K-Tel NE 1169		**37**	10 wks

ENIGMA UK, male vocal/instrumental group 3 wks

5 Sep 81	**AIN'T NO STOPPIN'** Creole CRX 1		**80**	3 wks

Brian ENO UK, male instrumentalist-keyboards 3 wks

9 Mar 74	**HERE COME THE WARM JETS** Island ILPS 9268		**26**	2 wks
21 Oct 78	**MUSIC FOR FILMS** Polydor 2310 623		**55**	1 wk

See also Brian Eno and David Byrne.

Brian ENO and David BYRNE UK, male instrumentalist - keyboards and US, male vocalist 8 wks

21 Feb 81	**MY LIFE IN THE BUSH OF GHOSTS** Polydor EGLP 48		**29**	8 wks

See also Brian Eno.

EQUALS UK, male vocal/instrumental group 10 wks

18 Nov 67 ●	**UNEQUALLED EQUALS** President PTL 1006		**10**	9 wks
9 Mar 68	**EQUALS EXPLOSION** President PTLS 1015		**32**	1 wk

David ESSEX UK, male vocalist 133 wks

24 Nov 73 ●	**ROCK ON** CBS 65823		**7**	22 wks
19 Oct 74 ●	**DAVID ESSEX** CBS 69088		**2**	24 wks
27 Sep 75 ●	**ALL THE FUN OF THE FAIR** CBS 69160		**3**	20 wks
5 Jun 76	**ON TOUR** CBS 95000		**51**	1 wk
30 Oct 76	**OUT ON THE STREET** CBS 86017		**31**	9 wks
8 Oct 77	**GOLD AND IVORY** CBS 86038		**29**	4 wks
6 Jan 79	**DAVID ESSEX ALBUM** CBS 10011		**29**	7 wks
31 Mar 79	**IMPERIAL WIZARD** Mercury 9109 616		**12**	9 wks
12 Jun 80	**HOT LOVE** Mercury 6359 017		**75**	1 wk
19 Jun 82	**STAGE-STRUCK** Mercury MERS 4		**31**	15 wks
27 Nov 82	**THE VERY BEST OF DAVID ESSEX** TV Records TVA 4		**37**	11 wks

15 Oct 83	**MUTINY**	*Mercury MERH 30*	....	**39**	4 wks
17 Dec 83	**THE WHISPER**	*Mercury MERH 34*	....	**67**	6 wks

Mutiny is a studio recording of a musical that was not staged until 1985. Both this album and the eventual stage production starred David Essex and Frank Finlay.

Don ESTELLE and Windsor DAVIES *UK, male vocal duo* 8 wks

10 Jan 76	● **SING LOFTY**	*EMI EMC 3102*	....	**10**	8 wks

EUROPEANS *UK, male vocal/instrumental group* 1 wk

11 Feb 84	**LIVE**	*A & M SCOT 1*	....	**100**	1 wk

EURYTHMICS *UK, female/male vocal/instrumental group* 163 wks

12 Feb 83	● **SWEET DREAMS (ARE MADE OF THIS)** *RCA RCALP 6063*	....	**3**	59 wks
26 Nov 83	★ **TOUCH** *RCA PL 70109*	....	**1**	48 wks
9 Jun 84	**TOUCH DANCE** *RCA PG 70354*	......	**31**	5 wks
24 Nov 84	**1984 (FOR THE LOVE OF BIG BROTHER)** *Virgin V 1984*	....	**23**	17 wks
11 May 85	● **BE YOURSELF TONIGHT** *RCA PL 70711*	....	**3†**	34 wks

Phil EVERLY *US, male vocalist* 1 wk

7 May 83	**PHIL EVERLY**	*Capitol EST 27670*	....	**61**	1 wk

See also the Everly Brothers.

EVERLY BROTHERS *US, male vocal duo* 118 wks

2 Jul 60	● **IT'S EVERLY TIME** *Warner Bros. WM 4006*	....	**2**	23 wks
15 Oct 60	● **FABULOUS STYLE OF THE EVERLY BROTHERS** *London HAA 2266*	....	**4**	11 wks
4 Mar 61	● **A DATE WITH THE EVERLY BROTHERS** *Warner Bros. WM 4028*	....	**3**	14 wks
21 Jul 62	**INSTANT PARTY** *Warner Bros. WM 4061*	....	**20**	1 wk
12 Sep 70	● **ORIGINAL GREATEST HITS** *CBS 66255*	......	**7**	16 wks
8 Jun 74	**THE VERY BEST OF THE EVERLY BROTHERS** *Warner Bros. K 46008*	....	**43**	1 wk
29 Nov 75	● **WALK RIGHT BACK WITH THE EVERLYS** *Warner Bros. K56118*	....	**10**	10 wks
9 Apr 77	**LIVING LEGENDS** *Warwick WW 5027*	....	**12**	10 wks
18 Dec 82	**LOVE HURTS** *K-Tel NE 1197*	....	**31**	22 wks
7 Jan 84	**EVERLY BROTHERS REUNION CONCERT** *Impression IMDP 1*	....	**47**	6 wks
3 Nov 84	**THE EVERLY BROTHERS** *Mercury MERH 44*	......	**36**	4 wks

See also Phil Everly.

EVERYTHING BUT THE GIRL *UK, male/female vocal/instrumental group* 31 wks

16 Jun 84	**EDEN**	*Blanco Y Negro BYN 2*	....	**14**	22 wks
27 Apr 85	● **LOVE NOT MONEY**	*Blanco Y Negro BYN 3*	....	**10**	9 wks

EXPLOITED *UK, male vocal/instrumental group* 26 wks

16 May 81	**PUNK'S NOT DEAD**	*Secret SEC 1*	....	**20**	11 wks
14 Nov 81	**EXPLOITED LIVE**	*Superville EXPLP 2001*	......	**52**	3 wks
19 Jun 82	**TROOPS OF TOMORROW**	*Secret SEC 8*	....	**17**	12 wks

F

FACES *UK, male vocal/instrumental group* 56 wks

4 Apr 70	**FIRST STEP** *Warner Bros. WS 3000*	....	**45**	1 wk
8 May 71	**LONG PLAYER** *Warner Bros. W 3011*	....	**31**	7 wks
25 Dec 71	● **A NOD'S AS GOOD AS A WINK....TO A BLIND HORSE** *Warner Bros. K 56006*		**2**	22 wks
26 Jan 74	● **OVERTURE AND BEGINNERS** *Mercury 9100 001*		**3**	7 wks
21 Apr 73	★ **OOH-LA-LA** *Warner Bros. K 56011*		**1**	13 wks
21 May 77	**THE BEST OF THE FACES** *Riva RVLP 3*	.....	**24**	6 wks

Overture And Beginners credited to Rod Stewart and the Faces. See also Rod Stewart.

Donald FAGEN *US, male vocalist* 16 wks

30 Oct 82	**THE NIGHTFLY**	*Warner Bros. 923696*	....	**44**	16 wks

FAIRPORT CONVENTION *UK, male/female vocal/ instrumental group* 40 wks

2 Aug 69	**UNHALFBRICKING** *Island ILPS 9102*	......	**12**	8 wks
17 Jan 70	**LIEGE AND LIEF** *Island ILPS 9115*	......	**17**	15 wks
18 Jul 70	**FULL HOUSE** *Island ILPS 9130*	....	**13**	11 wks
3 Jul 71	● **ANGEL DELIGHT** *Island ILPS 9162*	......	**8**	5 wks
12 Jul 75	**RISING FOR THE MOON** *Island ILPS 9313*	....	**52**	1 wk

FAITH BROTHERS *UK, male vocal/instrumental group* 1 wk

9 Nov 85	**EVENTIDE**	*Siren SIRENLP 1*	....	**66**	1 wk

Adam FAITH *UK, male vocalist* 44 wks

19 Nov 60	● **ADAM** *Parlophone PMC 1128*	....	**6**	36 wks
11 Feb 61	**BEAT GIRL (film soundtrack)** *Columbia 33SX 1225*	....	**11**	3 wks
24 Mar 62	**ADAM FAITH** *Parlophone PMC 1162*	....	**20**	1 wk
25 Sep 65	**FAITH ALIVE** *Parlophone PMC 1249*	......	**19**	1 wk
19 Dec 81	**20 GOLDEN GREATS** *Warwick WW 5113*	......	**61**	3 wks

Marianne FAITHFULL *UK, female vocalist* 17 wks

5 Jun 65	**COME MY WAY** *Decca LK 4688*	......	**12**	7 wks
5 Jun 65	**MARIANNE FAITHFULL** *Decca LK 4689*	......	**15**	2 wks
24 Nov 79	**BROKEN ENGLISH** *Island M1*	......	**57**	3 wks
17 Oct 81	**DANGEROUS ACQUAINTANCES** *Island ILPS 9648*	....	**45**	4 wks
26 Mar 83	**A CHILD'S ADVENTURE** *Island ILPS 9734*	....	**99**	1 wk

FALL *UK, male vocal/instrumental group* 7 wks

20 Mar 82	**HEX ENDUCTION HOUR** *Kamera KAM 005*	..	**71**	3 wks
20 Oct 84	**THE WONDERFUL AND FRIGHTENING WORLD OF...** *Beggars Banquet BEGA 58*	......	**62**	2 wks
5 Oct 85	**THE NATION'S SAVING GRACE** *Beggars Banquet BEGA 67*	......	**54**	2 wks

Agnetha FALTSKOG *Sweden, female vocalist* 16 wks

11 Jun 83	**WRAP YOUR ARMS AROUND ME** *Epic EPC 25505*	....	**18**	13 wks

BOB DYLAN (left) 536 weeks in the chart – 112 of them in 1965.

JOSE FELICIANO (below) He has earned 32 gold and platinum albums worldwide, although recent UK album action has been a little modest.

IAN DURY The new boots are visible, the panties are not.

EURYTHMICS (above) Annie Lennox and Dave Stewart's greetings card – Christmas 1984.

FLEETWOOD MAC (left) 'Rumours' has been on the chart for over 300 weeks but never yielded a Top Twenty single in the UK. (LFI)

4 May 85	**EYES OF A WOMAN** *Epic EPC 26646*	....	**38**	3 wks

Georgie FAME   UK, male vocalist   *72 wks*

17 Oct 64	**FAME AT LAST** *Columbia 33SX 1638*	....	**15**	8 wks
14 May 66	● **SWEET THINGS** *Columbia SX 6043*	....	**6**	22 wks
15 Oct 66	● **SOUND VENTURE** *Columbia SX 6076*	....	**9**	9 wks
11 Mar 67	**HALL OF FAME** *Columbia SX 6120*	....	**12**	18 wks
1 Jul 67	**TWO FACES OF FAME** *CBS SBPG 63018*	.....	**22**	15 wks

FAMILY   UK, male vocal/instrumental group   *41 wks*

10 Aug 68	**MUSIC IN THE DOLLS HOUSE**			
	Reprise RLP 6312	....	**35**	3 wks
22 Mar 69	● **FAMILY ENTERTAINMENT** *Reprise RSLP 6340*		**6**	3 wks
7 Feb 70	● **A SONG FOR ME** *Reprise RSLP 9001*	....	**4**	13 wks
28 Nov 70	● **ANYWAY** *Reprise RSX 9005*	....	**7**	7 wks
20 Nov 71	**FEARLESS** *Reprise K 54003*	....	**14**	2 wks
30 Sep 72	**BANDSTAND** *Reprise K 54006*	....	**15**	10 wks
29 Sep 73	**IT'S ONLY A MOVIE** *Raft RA 58501*	......	**30**	3 wks

FAMILY STONE - *See SLY and the FAMILY STONE*

Chris FARLOWE   UK, male vocalist   *3 wks*

2 Apr 66	**14 THINGS TO THINK ABOUT**			
	Immediate IMLP 005	....	**19**	1 wk
10 Dec 66	**THE ART OF CHRIS FARLOWE**			
	Immediate IMLP 006	....	**37**	2 wks

FARMERS BOYS   UK, male vocal/instrumental group   *1 wk*

29 Oct 83	**GET OUT AND WALK** *EMI EMC 1077991*	....	**49**	1 wk

FASHION   UK, male vocal/instrumental group   *17 wks*

3 Jul 82	● **FABRIQUE** *Arista SPART 1185*	....	**10**	16 wks
16 Jun 84	**TWILIGHT OF IDOLS** *De Stijl EPC 25909*	.....	**69**	1 wk

FASTWAY   UK, male vocal/instrumental group   *2 wks*

30 Apr 83	**FASTWAY** *CBS 25359*	....	**43**	2 wks

FAT LARRY'S BAND   US, male vocal/instrumental group   *4 wks*

9 Oct 82	**BREAKIN' OUT** *Virgin V 2229*	....	**58**	4 wks

FATBACK BAND   US, male vocal/instrumental group   *6 wks*

6 Mar 76	**RAISING HELL** *Polydor 2391 203*	....	**19**	6 wks

Phil FEARON and GALAXY   UK, male/female vocal/instrumental group   *9 wks*

25 Aug 84	● **PHIL FEARON AND GALAXY** *Ensign ENCL 2*		**8**	8 wks
14 Feb 85	**THIS KIND OF LOVE** *Ensign ENCL 4*	....	**98**	1 wk

Jose FELICIANO   US, male vocalist/instrumentalist - guitar   *40 wks*

2 Nov 68	● **FELICIANO** *RCA Victor SF 7946*	....	**6**	36 wks
29 Nov 69	**JOSE FELICIANO** *RCA Victor SF 8044*	....	**29**	2 wks
14 Feb 70	**10 TO 23** *RCA SF 7946*	....	**38**	1 wk
22 Aug 70	**FIREWORKS** *RCA SF 8124*	....	**65**	1 wk

Wilton FELDER   US, male instrumentalist - tenor sax   *3 wks*

23 Feb 85	**SECRETS** *MCA MCF 3237*	....	**77**	3 wks

Also featuring Bobby Womack and introducing Alltrinna Grayson.

Julie FELIX   US, female vocalist   *4 wks*

11 Sep 66	**CHANGES** *Fontana TL 5368*	....	**27**	4 wks

Bryan FERRY   UK, male vocalist   *123 wks*

3 Nov 73	● **THESE FOOLISH THINGS** *Island ILPS 9249*	...	**5**	42 wks
20 Jul 74	● **ANOTHER TIME, ANOTHER PLACE**			
	Island ILPS 9284	....	**4**	25 wks
2 Oct 76	**LET'S STICK TOGETHER** *Island ILPSX 1*	.....	**19**	5 wks
5 Mar 77	● **IN YOUR MIND** *Polydor 2302 055*	....	**5**	17 wks
30 Sep 78	**THE BRIDE STRIPPED BARE**			
	Polydor POLD 5003	....	**13**	5 wks
15 Jun 85	★ **BOYS AND GIRLS** *EG EGLP 62*	....	**1†**	29 wks

Gracie FIELDS   UK, female vocalist   *3 wks*

20 Dec 75	**THE GOLDEN YEARS** *Warwick WW 5007*	....	**48**	3 wks

FINE YOUNG CANNIBALS   UK, male vocal/instrumental group   *2 wks*

21 Dec 85	**FINE YOUNG CANIBALS** *London LONLP 16*	..	**49†**	2 wks

The FIRM   UK, male vocal/instrumental group   *5 wks*

2 Mar 85	**THE FIRM** *Atlantic 78-1239-1*	....	**15**	5 wks

FISCHER-Z   UK, male vocal/instrumental group   *1 wk*

23 Jun 79	**WORD SALAD** *United Artists UAG 30232*	......	**66**	1 wk

Ella FITZGERALD   US, female vocalist   *13 wks*

11 Jun 60	**ELLA SINGS GERSHWIN** *Brunswick LA 8648*	...	**13**	3 wks
18 Jun 60	**ELLA AT THE OPERA HOUSE**			
	Columbia 3SX 10126	....	**16**	1 wk
23 Jul 60	**ELLA SINGS GERSHWIN VOL.5**			
	HMV CLP 1353	....	**18**	2 wks
10 May 80	**THE INCOMPARABLE ELLA** *Polydor POLTV 9*		**40**	7 wks

FIVE PENNY PIECE   UK, male/female vocal/instrumental group   *6 wks*

24 Mar 73	**MAKING TRACKS** *Columbia SCX 6536*	....	**37**	1 wk
3 Jul 76	● **KING COTTON** *EMI EMC 3129*	....	**9**	5 wks

FIVE STAR UK, male/female vocal/instrumental group
21 wks

3 Aug 85	**LUXURY OF LIFE** Tent PL 70735	**25**	21 wks

FIXX UK, male vocal/instrumental group
7 wks

22 May 82	**SHUTTERED ROOM** MCA FX 1001	**54**	6 wks
21 May 83	**REACH THE BEACH** MCA FX 1002	**91**	1 wk

Roberta FLACK US, female vocalist
18 wks

15 Jul 72	**FIRST TAKE** Atlantic K 40040	**47**	2 wks
13 Oct 73	**KILLING ME SOFTLY** Atlantic K 50021	**40**	2 wks
31 Mar 84	**GREATEST HITS** K-Tel NE 1269	**35**	14 wks

See also Roberta Flack and Donny Hathaway.

Roberta FLACK and Donny HATHAWAY
US, female/male vocal duo
7 wks

7 Jun 80	**ROBERTA FLACK AND DONNY HATHAWAY** Atlantic K 50696	**31**	7 wks

See also Roberta Flack.

FLASH and the PAN Australia, male vocal/instrumental group
2 wks

16 Jul 83	**PAN-ORAMA** Easy Beat EASLP 100	**69**	2 wks

FLEETWOOD MAC UK/US, male/female vocal/instrumental group
484 wks

2 Mar 68	● **FLEETWOOD MAC** Blue Horizon BPG 7-63200 ..	**4**	37 wks
7 Sep 68	● **MR. WONDERFUL** Blue Horizon 7-63205	**10**	11 wks
30 Aug 69	**PIOUS BIRD OF GOOD OMEN** Blue Horizon 7-63215	**18**	4 wks
4 Oct 69	● **THEN PLAY ON** Reprise RSLP 9000	**6**	11 wks
10 Oct 70	**KILN HOUSE** Reprise RSLP 9004	**39**	2 wks
19 Feb 72	**GREATEST HITS** CBS 69011	**36**	11 wks
6 Nov 76	**FLEETWOOD MAC** Reprise K 54043	**23**	19 wks
26 Feb 77	★ **RUMOURS** Warner Bros. K 56344	**1**	322 wks
27 Oct 79	★ **TUSK** Warner Bros. K 66088	**1**	23 wks
13 Dec 80	**FLEETWOOD MAC LIVE** Warner Bros. K 66097	**31**	9 wks
10 Jul 82	● **MIRAGE** Warner Bros K 56592	**5**	35 wks

Group were UK and male only for first 7 albums.

Berni FLINT UK, male vocalist
6 wks

2 Jul 77	**I DON'T WANT TO PUT A HOLD ON YOU** EMI EMC 3184	**37**	6 wks

FLOATERS US, male vocal/instrumental group
8 wks

20 Aug 77	**FLOATERS** ABC ABCL 5229	**17**	8 wks

FLOCK UK, male vocal/instrumental group
2 wks

2 May 70	**FLOCK** CBS 63733	**59**	2 wks

A FLOCK OF SEAGULLS UK, male vocal/instrumental group
59 wks

17 Apr 82	**A FLOCK OF SEAGULLS** Jive HOP 201	**32**	44 wks

7 May 83	**LISTEN** Jive HIP 4	**16**	10 wks
1 Sep 84	**THE STORY OF A YOUNG HEART** Jive HIP 14	**30**	5 wks

Eddie FLOYD US, male vocalist
5 wks

29 Apr 67	**KNOCK ON WOOD** Stax 589-006	**36**	5 wks

A FLUX OF PINK INDIANS UK, male vocal/instrumental group
2 wks

5 Feb 83	**STRIVE TO SURVIVE CAUSING LEAST SUFFERING POSSIBLE** Spiderleg SDL 8	**79**	2 wks

FLYING LIZARDS UK, male/female vocal/instrumental group
3 wks

16 Feb 80	**FLYING LIZARDS** Virgin V 2150	**60**	3 wks

FLYING PICKETS UK, male vocal group
22 wks

17 Dec 83	**LIVE AT THE ALBANY EMPIRE** AVM AVMLP 0001	**48**	11 wks
9 Jun 84	**LOST BOYS** 10 DIX 4	**11**	11 wks

FOCUS Holland, male instrumental group
65 wks

11 Nov 72	● **MOVING WAVES** Polydor 2931 002	**2**	34 wks
2 Dec 72	● **FOCUS 3** Polydor 2383 016	**6**	15 wks
20 Oct 73	**FOCUS AT THE RAINBOW** Polydor 2442 118 ..	**23**	5 wks
25 May 74	**HAMBURGER CONCERTO** Polydor 2442 124 ..	**20**	5 wks
9 Aug 75	**FOCUS** Polydor 2384 070	**23**	6 wks

Dan FOGELBERG US, male vocalist
3 wks

29 Mar 80	**PHOENIX** Epic EPC 83317	**42**	3 wks

John FOGERTY US, male vocalist/instrumentalist - guitar
11 wks

16 Feb 85	**CENTERFIELD** Warner Bros 92-5203-1	**48**	11 wks

Ellen FOLEY US, female vocalist
3 wks

17 Nov 79	**NIGHT OUT** Epic EPC 83718	**68**	1 wk
4 Apr 81	**SPIRIT OF ST.LOUIS** Epic EPC 84809	**57**	2 wks

Jane FONDA US, female exercise instructor
51 wks

29 Jan 83	● **JANE FONDA'S WORKOUT RECORD** CBS 88581	**7**	47 wks
22 Sep 84	**JANE FONDA'S WORKOUT RECORD:NEW AND IMPROVED** CBS 88640	**60**	4 wks

Wayne FONTANA and the MINDBENDERS
UK, male vocalist and male vocal/instrumental group
1 wk

20 Feb 65	**WAYNE FONTANA AND THE MINDBENDERS** Fontana TL 5230	**18**	1 wk

See also The Mindbenders.

ELLEN FOLEY Produced by
Bowie's ex-side kick Mick
Ronson and former Mott the Hoople
leader Ian Hunter.

FOREIGNER (left) At their most
successful in the UK with ballads –
their number one hit single 'I Want
To Know What Love Is' led to
excellent sales for 'Agent
Provocateur'. (LFI)

PETER FRAMPTON Peter
Frampton's double LP 'Frampton
Comes Alive' is his only Top Ten
entry. At least it was the biggest
selling live album in history.

Steve FORBERT US, male vocalist — 3 wks

9 Jun 79	**ALIVE ON ARRIVAL** Epic EPC 83308	**56**	1 wk
24 Nov 79	**JACK RABBIT SLIM** Epic EPC 83879	**54**	2 wks

Clinton FORD UK, male vocalist — 4 wks

26 May 62	**CLINTON FORD** Oriole PS 40021	**16**	4 wks

Lita FORD UK, female vocalist — 1 wk

26 May 84	**DANCIN' ON THE EDGE** Vertigo VERL 13	**96**	1 wk

FOREIGNER UK/US, male vocal/instrumental group — 110 wks

26 Aug 78	**DOUBLE VISION** Atlantic K 50476	**32**	5 wks
25 Jul 81 ●	**4** Atlantic K 50796	**5**	62 wks
18 Dec 82	**RECORDS** Atlantic A 0999	**58**	11 wks
22 Dec 84 ★	**AGENT PROVOCATEUR** Atlantic 78-1999-1	**1**	32 wks

FOSTER and ALLEN Ireland, male vocal duo — 30 wks

14 May 83	**MAGGIE** Ritz RITZLP 0012	**72**	6 wks
5 Nov 83	**I WILL LOVE YOU ALL OF MY LIFE** Ritz RITZLP 0015	**71**	6 wks
17 Nov 84	**THE VERY BEST OF FOSTER AND ALLEN** Ritz RITZ LP TV 1	**18**	18 wks

FOTHERINGAY UK, male/female vocal/instrumental group — 6 wks

11 Jul 70	**FOTHERINGAY** Island ILPS 9125	**18**	6 wks

FOUR PENNIES UK, male vocal/instrumental group — 5 wks

7 Nov 64	**TWO SIDES OF FOUR PENNIES** Philips BL 7642	**13**	5 wks

FOUR SEASONS US, male vocal group — 40 wks

6 Jul 63	**SHERRY** Stateside SL 10033	**20**	1 wk
10 Apr 71	**EDIZIONE D'ORO** Philips 6640-002	**11**	7 wks
20 Nov 71	**THE BIG ONES** Philips 6336-208	**37**	1 wk
6 Mar 76	**THE FOUR SEASONS STORY** Private Stock DAPS 1001	**20**	8 wks
6 Mar 76	**WHO LOVES YOU** Warner Bros. K 56179	**12**	17 wks
20 Nov 76 ●	**GREATEST HITS** K-Tel NE 942	**4**	6 wks

Greatest Hits album credited to Frankie Valli and the Four Seasons. It contains some solo Valli items.

4-SKINS UK, male vocal/instrumental group — 4 wks

17 Apr 82	**THE GOOD, THE BAD AND THE 4-SKINS** Secret SEC 4	**80**	4 wks

FOUR TOPS US, male vocal group — 233 wks

19 Nov 66 ●	**FOUR TOPS ON TOP** Tamla Motown TML 11037	**9**	23 wks
11 Feb 67 ●	**FOUR TOPS LIVE!** Tamla Motown STML 11041	**4**	72 wks
25 Nov 67 ●	**REACH OUT** Tamla Motown STML 11056	**4**	34 wks
20 Jan 68 ★	**GREATEST HITS** Tamla Motown STML 11061	**1**	67 wks
8 Feb 69	**YESTERDAY'S DREAMS** Tamla Motown STML 11087	**37**	1 wk
27 Jun 70	**STILL WATERS RUN DEEP** Tamla Motown STML 11149	**29**	8 wks
27 Nov 71	**FOUR TOPS' GREATEST HITS VOL.2** Tamla Motown STML 11195	**25**	10 wks
10 Nov 73	**THE FOUR TOPS STORY 1964-72** Tamla Motown TMSP 11241/2	**35**	5 wks
13 Feb 82	**THE BEST OF THE FOUR TOPS** K-Tel NE 1160	**13**	13 wks

See also Supremes and Four Tops.

FOX UK, male/female vocal instrumental group — 8 wks

17 May 75 ●	**FOX** GTO GTLP 001	**7**	8 wks

Bruce FOXTON UK, male vocalist — 4 wks

12 May 84	**TOUCH SENSITIVE** Arista 206 251	**68**	4 wks

John FOXX UK, male vocalist — 17 wks

2 Feb 80	**METAMATIX** Metalbeat V 2146	**18**	7 wks
3 Oct 81	**THE GARDEN** Virgin V 2194	**24**	6 wks
8 Oct 83	**THE GOLDEN SECTION** Virgin V 2233	**27**	3 wks
5 Oct 85	**IN MYSTERIOUS WAYS** Virgin V 2355	**85**	1 wk

FRAGGLES UK/US puppets — 4 wks

21 Apr 84	**FRAGGLE ROCK** RCA PL 70221	**38**	4 wks

Peter FRAMPTON UK, male vocalist — 49 wks

22 May 76 ●	**FRAMPTON COMES ALIVE** A & M AMLM 63703	**6**	39 wks
18 Jun 77	**I'M IN YOU** A & M AMLK 64039	**19**	10 wks

Connie FRANCIS US, female vocalist — 26 wks

26 Mar 60	**ROCK 'N' ROLL MILLION SELLERS** MGM C 804	**12**	1 wk
11 Feb 61	**CONNIE'S GREATEST HITS** MGM C 831	**16**	3 wks
18 Jun 77 ★	**20 ALL TIME GREATS** Polydor 2391 290	**1**	22 wks

FRANKIE GOES TO HOLLYWOOD UK, male vocal/instrumental group — 51 wks

10 Nov 84 ★	**WELCOME TO THE PLEASURE DOME** ZTT ZTTIQ 1	**1**	51 wks

Aretha FRANKLIN US, female vocalist — 31 wks

12 Aug 67	**I NEVER LOVED A MAN** Atlantic 587-006	**36**	2 wks
13 Apr 68	**LADY SOUL** Atlantic 588-099	**25**	18 wks
14 Sep 68 ●	**ARETHA NOW** Atlantic 588-114	**6**	11 wks

Rodney FRANKLIN US, male instrumentalist - piano — 2 wks

24 May 80	**YOU'LL NEVER KNOW** CBS 83812	**64**	2 wks

FREDDIE and the DREAMERS UK, male vocal/instrumental group — 26 wks

9 Nov 63	● FREDDIE AND THE DREAMERS *Columbia 33SX 1577*	**5**	26 wks

FREDERICK - *See NINA and FREDERICK*

FREE UK, male vocal/instrumental group — 62 wks

11 Jul 70	● FIRE AND WATER *Island ILPS 9120*	**2**	18 wks
23 Jan 71	HIGHWAY *Island ILPS 9138*	**41**	10 wks
26 Jun 71	● FREE LIVE! *Island ILPS 9160*	**4**	12 wks
17 Jun 72	● FREE AT LAST *Island ILPS 9192*	**9**	9 wks
3 Feb 73	● HEARTBREAKER *Island ILPS 9217*	**9**	7 wks
16 Mar 74	● THE FREE STORY *Island ISLD 4*	**2**	6 wks

FREEEZ UK, male instrumental group — 18 wks

7 Feb 81	SOUTHERN FREEEZ *Beggars Banquet BEGA 22*	**17**	15 wks
22 Oct 83	GONNA GET YOU *Beggars Banquet BEGA 48*	**46**	3 wks

Glenn FREY US, male vocalist — 9 wks

6 Jul 85	THE ALLNIGHTER *MCA MCF 3277*	**31**	9 wks

FRIDA Sweden, female vocalist — 8 wks

18 Sep 82	SOMETHING'S GOING ON *Epic EPC 85966*	**18**	7 wks
20 Oct 84	SHINE *Epic EPC 26178*	**67**	1 wk

Dean FRIEDMAN US, male vocalist — 14 wks

21 Oct 78	WELL, WELL, SAID THE ROCKING CHAIR *Lifesong LSLP 6019*	**21**	14 wks

Robert FRIPP UK, male vocalist/instrumentalist - guitar — 1 wk

12 May 79	EXPOSURE *Polydor EGLP 101*	**71**	1 wk

FUNBOY THREE UK, male vocal/instrumental group — 40 wks

20 Mar 82	● FUNBOY THREE *Chrysalis CHR 1383*	**7**	20 wks
19 Feb 83	WAITING *Chrysalis CHR 1417*	**14**	20 wks

FUNKADELIC US, male vocal/instrumental group — 5 wks

23 Dec 78	ONE NATION UNDER A GROOVE *Warner Bros. K 56539*	**56**	5 wks

FUREYS and DAVEY ARTHUR Ireland/UK, male vocal/instrumental group — 30 wks

8 May 82	WHEN YOU WERE SWEET SIXTEEN *Ritz RITZLP 0004*	**99**	1 wk
10 Nov 84	GOLDEN DAYS *K-Tel ONE 1283*	**17**	19 wks
26 Oct 85	AT THE END OF THE DAY *K-Tel ONE 1310*	**35†**	10 wks

Billy FURY UK, male vocalist — 51 wks

4 Jun 60	THE SOUND OF FURY *Decca LF 1329*	**18**	2 wks
23 Sep 61	● HALFWAY TO PARADISE *Ace Of Clubs ACL 1083*	**5**	9 wks
11 May 63	● BILLY *Decca LK 4533*	**6**	21 wks
26 Oct 63	WE WANT BILLY *Decca LK 4548*	**14**	2 wks
19 Feb 83	HIT PARADE *Decca TAB 37*	**44**	15 wks
26 Mar 83	THE ONE AND ONLY *Polydor POLD 5069*	**54**	2 wks

G

Kenny G US male instrumentalist - saxophone — 5 wks

17 Mar 84	G FORCE *Arusta 296 168*	**56**	5 wks

Peter GABRIEL UK, male vocalist — 73 wks

12 Mar 77	● PETER GABRIEL *Charisma CDS 4006*	**7**	19 wks
17 Jun 78	● PETER GABRIEL *Charisma CDS 4013*	**10**	8 wks
7 Jun 80	★ PETER GABRIEL *Charisma CDS 4019*	**1**	18 wks
18 Sep 82	● PETER GABRIEL *Charisma PG 4*	**6**	16 wks
18 Jun 83	● PETER GABRIEL PLAYS LIVE *Charisma PGDL 1*	**8**	9 wks
30 Apr 85	BIRDY - MUSIC FROM THE FILM *Charisma CAS 1167*	**51**	3 wks

First four albums are different.

GALLAGHER and LYLE UK, male vocal/instrumental duo — 44 wks

28 Feb 76	● BREAKAWAY *A & M AMLH 68348*	**6**	35 wks
29 Jan 77	LOVE ON THE AIRWAYS *A & M AMLH 64620*	**19**	9 wks

Rory GALLAGHER UK, male vocalist/instrumentalist - guitar — 43 wks

29 May 71	RORY GALLAGHER *Polydor 2383-044*	**32**	2 wks
4 Dec 71	DEUCE *Polydor 2383-076*	**39**	1 wk
20 May 72	● LIVE IN EUROPE *Polydor 2383 112*	**9**	15 wks
24 Feb 73	BLUE PRINT *Polydor 2383 189*	**12**	7 wks
17 Nov 73	TATTOO *Polydor 2383 230*	**32**	3 wks
27 Jul 74	IRISH TOUR '74 *Polydor 2659 031*	**36**	2 wks
30 Oct 76	CALLING CARD *Chrysalis CHR 1124*	**32**	1 wk
22 Sep 79	TOP PRIORITY *Chrysalis CHR 1235*	**56**	4 wks
8 Nov 80	STAGE STRUCK *Chrysalis CHR 1280*	**40**	3 wks
8 May 82	JINX *Chrysalis CHR 1359*	**68**	5 wks

James GALWAY Ireland, male instrumentalist - flute — 63 wks

27 May 78	THE MAGIC FLUTE OF JAMES GALWAY *RCA Red Seal LRLI 5131*	**43**	6 wks
1 Jul 78	THE MAN WITH THE GOLDEN FLUTE *RCA Red Seal LRLI 5127*	**52**	3 wks
9 Sep 78	● JAMES GALWAY PLAYS SONGS FOR ANNIE *RCA Red Seal RL 25163*	**7**	40 wks
15 Dec 79	SONGS OF THE SEASHORE *Solar RL 25253*	**39**	6 wks
18 Dec 82	THE JAMES GALWAY COLLECTION *Telstar STAR 2224*	**41**	8 wks

See also James Galway and Henry Mancini; Cleo Laine and James Galway.

GENERATION X (above) Idols of 1978.

BILLY FURY (left) Continued from *Guinness Book of British Hit Singles 5th edition* (page 17), Billy Fury and Joe Brown in the High Street (part two).

RORY GALLAGHER (above) The Irish bluesman came to England in 1969 fronting his band, Taste, and had two hit albums before going solo and notching up another 10.

THE J. GEILS BAND (left) Soon after lead singer Peter Wolf's split from Faye Dunaway he left the group. They never made the chart again.

GARY GLITTER (right) The double G. surprised by the camera while discussing his hit albums (4) with Dave Hill from Slade (14) and Suzi Quatro (2).

James GALWAY and Henry MANCINI with NATIONAL PHILHARMONIC ORCHESTRA *Ireland, male instrumentalist – flute. US conductor with UK orchestra* 6 wks

8 Dec 84	**IN THE PINK**	RCA Red Seal RL 85315	....	62	6 wks

See also James Galway; Cleo Laine and James Galway; Luciano Pavarotti with the Henry Mancini Orchestra.

GANG OF FOUR *UK, male vocal/instrumental group* 9 wks

13 Oct 79	**ENTERTAINMENT**	EMI EMC 3313	....	45	3 wks
21 Mar 81	**SOLID GOLD**	EMI EMC 3364	....	52	2 wks
29 May 82	**SONGS OF THE FREE**	EMI EMC 3412	....	61	4 wks

Art GARFUNKEL *US, male vocalist* 58 wks

13 Oct 73	**ANGEL CLARE**	CBS 69021	....	14	7 wks
1 Nov 75 ●	**BREAKAWAY**	CBS 86002	....	7	10 wks
18 Mar 78	**WATER MARK**	CBS 86054	....	25	5 wks
21 Apr 79 ●	**FATE FOR BREAKFAST**	CBS 86082	......	2	20 wks
19 Sep 81	**SCISSORS CUT**	CBS 85259	....	51	3 wks
17 Nov 84	**THE ART GARFUNKEL ALBUM**	CBS 10046	..	12	13 wks

See also Simon and Garfunkel.

Judy GARLAND *US, female vocalist* 3 wks

3 Mar 62	**JUDY AT CARNEGIE HALL**	Capitol W 1569		13	3 wks

Errol GARNER *US, male instrumentalist – piano* 1 wk

14 Jul 62	**CLOSE UP IN SWING**	Philips BBL 7579	....	20	1 wk

David GATES *US, male vocalist* 4 wks

31 May 75	**NEVER LET HER GO**	Elektra K 52012	......	32	1 wk
29 Jul 78	**GOODBYE GIRL**	Elektra K 52091	....	28	3 wks

Marvin GAYE *US, male vocalist* 76 wks

16 Mar 68	**GREATEST HITS**	Tamla Motown STML 11065	..	40	1 wk
10 Nov 73	**LET'S GET IT ON**	Tamla Motown STMA 8013	..	39	1 wk
15 May 76	**I WANT YOU**	Tamla Motown STML 12025	..	22	5 wks
30 Oct 76	**THE BEST OF MARVIN GAYE** Tamla Motown STML 12042		....	56	1 wk
28 Feb 81	**IN OUR LIFETIME**	Motown STML 12149	......	48	4 wks
20 Nov 82 ●	**MIDNIGHT LOVE**	CBS 85977	....	10	16 wks
12 Nov 83	**GREATEST HITS**	Telstar STAR 2234	....	13	44 wks
15 Jun 85	**DREAM OF A LIFETIME**	CBS 26239	....	46	4 wks

See also Marvin Gaye and Tammi Terrell; Diana Ross and Marvin Gaye.

Marvin GAYE and Tammi TERRELL *US male/female vocal duo* 4 wks

22 Aug 70	**GREATEST HITS**	Tamla Motown STML 11153	..	60	4 wks

See also Marvin Gaye; Diana Ross and Marvin Gaye.

Crystal GAYLE *US, female vocalist* 25 wks

21 Jan 78	**WE MUST BELIEVE IN MAGIC** United Artists UAG 30108		....	15	7 wks
23 Sep 78	**WHEN I DREAM**	United Artists UAG 30169	....	25	8 wks
22 Mar 80 ●	**THE CRYSTAL GAYLE SINGLES ALBUM** United Artists UAG 30287		....	7	10 wks

Gloria GAYNOR *US, female vocalist* 15 wks

8 Mar 75	**NEVER CAN SAY GOODBYE**	MGM 2315 321		32	8 wks
24 Mar 79	**LOVE TRACKS**	Polydor 2391 385	....	31	7 wks

J. GEILS BAND *US, male vocal/instrumental group* 15 wks

27 Feb 82	**FREEZE FRAME**	EMI America AML 3020	......	12	15 wks

GENERATION X *UK, male vocal/instrumental group* 9 wks

8 Apr 78	**GENERATION X**	Chrysalis CHR 1169	....	29	4 wks
17 Feb 79	**VALLEY OF THE DOLLS**	Chrysalis CHR 1193	..	51	5 wks

GENESIS *UK, male vocal/instrumental group* 278 wks

14 Oct 72	**FOXTROT**	Charisma CAS 1058	....	12	7 wks
11 Aug 73 ●	**GENESIS LIVE**	Charisma CLASS 1	....	9	10 wks
20 Oct 73 ●	**SELLING ENGLAND BY THE POUND** Charisma CAS 1074		....	3	21 wks
11 May 74	**NURSERY CRYME**	Charisma CAS 1052	....	39	1 wk
7 Dec 74 ●	**THE LAMB LIES DOWN ON BROADWAY** Charisma CGS 101		....	10	6 wks
28 Feb 76 ●	**A TRICK OF THE TRAIL**	Charisma CDS 4001	..	3	39 wks
15 Jan 77 ●	**WIND AND WUTHERING**	Charisma CDS 4005		7	22 wks
29 Oct 77 ●	**SECONDS OUT**	Charisma GE 2001	....	4	17 wks
15 Apr 78 ●	**AND THEN THERE WERE THREE** Charisma CDS 4010		....	3	32 wks
5 Apr 80 ★	**DUKE**	Charisma CBR 101	....	1	30 wks
26 Sep 81 ★	**ABACAB**	Charisma CBR 102	....	1	27 wks
12 Jun 82 ●	**3 SIDES LIVE**	Charisma GE 2002	....	2	19 wks
15 Oct 83 ★	**GENESIS**	Charisma GENLP 1	....	1	45 wks
31 Mar 84	**NURSERY CRYME** (re-issue)	Charisma/Virgin CHC 22		68	1 wk
21 Apr 84	**TRESPASS**	Charisma/Virgin CHC 12	.....	98	1 wk

Jackie GENOVA *UK, female exercise instructor* 2 wks

21 May 83	**WORK THAT BODY**	Island ILPS 9732	....	74	2 wks

Bobbie GENTRY *US, female vocalist* 1 wk

25 Oct 69	**TOUCH 'EM WITH LOVE**	Capitol EST 155	....	21	1 wk

See also Bobbie Gentry and Glen Campbell.

Bobbie GENTRY and Glen CAMPBELL *US, female/male vocal duo* 1 wk

28 Feb 70	**BOBBIE GENTRY AND GLEN CAMPBELL** Capitol ST 2928		....	50	1 wk

See also Bobbie Gentry, Glen Campbell.

Lowell GEORGE *US, male vocalist* 1 wk

21 Apr 79	**THANKS BUT I'LL EAT IT HERE** Warner Bros. K 56487		....	71	1 wk

Robin GEORGE *UK, male vocalist/instrumentalist - guitar*   *3 wks*

| 2 Mar 85 | **DANGEROUS MUSIC** *Bronze BRON 554* | ...... | **65** | 3 wks |

GERRY and the PACEMAKERS *UK, male vocal/instrumental group*   *29 wks*

| 26 Oct 63 | ● **HOW DO YOU LIKE IT?** *Columbia 33SX 1546* | .. | **2** | 28 wks |
| 6 Feb 65 | **FERRY CROSS THE MERSEY** *Columbia 33SX 1676* | .... | **19** | 1 wk |

Stan GETZ and Charlie BYRD *US, male instrumental duo - saxophone and guitar*   *7 wks*

| 23 Feb 63 | **JAZZ SAMBA** *Verve SULP 9013* | .... | **15** | 7 wks |

Andy GIBB *UK, male vocalist*   *9 wks*

| 19 Aug 78 | **SHADOW DANCING** *RSO RSS 0001* | .... | **15** | 9 wks |

Barry GIBB *UK, male vocalist*   *2 wks*

| 20 Oct 84 | **NOW VOYAGER** *Polydor POLH 14* | .... | **85** | 2 wks |

Steve GIBBONS BAND *UK, male vocal/instrumental group*   *3 wks*

| 22 Oct 77 | **CAUGHT IN THE ACT** *Polydor 2478 112* | ...... | **22** | 3 wks |

Don GIBSON *US, male vocalist*   *10 wks*

| 22 Mar 80 | **COUNTRY NUMBER ONE** *Warwick WW 5079* | **13** | 10 wks |

GIBSON BROTHERS *Martinique, male vocal/instrumental group*   *3 wks*

| 30 Aug 80 | **ON THE RIVIERA** *Island ILPS 9620* | .... | **50** | 3 wks |

GILLAN *UK, male vocal/instrumental group*   *53 wks*

17 Jul 76	**CHILD IN TIME** *Polydor 2490 136*	....	**55**	1 wk
20 Oct 79	**MR. UNIVERSE** *Acrobat ACRO 3*	....	**11**	6 wks
16 Aug 80	● **GLORY ROAD** *Virgin V 2171*	....	**3**	12 wks
25 Apr 81	● **FUTURE SHOCK** *Virgin VK 2196*	....	**2**	13 wks
7 Nov 81	**DOUBLE TROUBLE** *Virgin VGD 3506*	......	**12**	15 wks
2 Oct 82	**MAGIC** *Virgin V 2238*	....	**17**	6 wks

Child In Time *credited to Ian Gillan Band.*

David GILMOUR *UK, male instrumentalist - guitar*   *18 wks*

| 10 Jun 78 | **DAVID GILMOUR** *Harvest SHVL 817* | .... | **17** | 9 wks |
| 17 Mar 84 | **ABOUT FACE** *Harvest SHSP 2400791* | .... | **21** | 9 wks |

Gordon GILTRAP *UK, male instrumentalist - guitar*   *7 wks*

| 18 Feb 78 | **PERILOUS JOURNEY** *Electric TRIX 4* | .... | **29** | 7 wks |

GIRL *UK, male vocal/instrumental group*   *6 wks*

| 9 Feb 80 | **SHEER GREED** *Jet JETLP 224* | .... | **33** | 5 wks |
| 23 Jan 82 | **WASTED YOUTH** *Jet JETLP 238* | .... | **92** | 1 wk |

GIRLS AT OUR BEST *UK, male/female vocal/instrumental group*   *3 wks*

| 7 Nov 81 | **PLEASURE** *Happy Birthday RVLP 1* | .... | **60** | 3 wks |

GIRLSCHOOL *UK, female vocal/instrumental group*   *23 wks*

5 Jul 80	**DEMOLITION** *Bronze BRON 525*	.........,	**28**	10 wks
25 Apr 81	● **HIT 'N' RUN** *Bronze BRON 534*	....	**5**	6 wks
12 Jun 82	**SCREAMING BLUE MURDER** *Bronze BRON 541*		**27**	6 wks
12 Nov 83	**PLAY DIRTY** *Bronze BRON 548*	....	**66**	1 wk

---

Gary GLITTER *UK, male vocalist*   *92 wks*

21 Oct 72	● **GLITTER** *Bell BELLS 216*	....	**8**	40 wks
16 Jun 73	● **TOUCH ME** *Bell BELLS 222*	....	**2**	33 wks
29 Jun 74	● **REMEMBER ME THIS WAY** *Bell BELLS 237*	..	**5**	14 wks
27 Mar 76	**GARY GLITTER'S GREATEST HITS** *Bell BELLS 262*	....	**33**	5 wks

---

GLITTER BAND *UK, male vocal/instrumental group*   *17 wks*

14 Sep 74	**HEY** *Bell BELLS 241*	....	**13**	12 wks
3 May 75	**ROCK 'N' ROLL DUDES** *Bell BELLS 253*	......	**17**	4 wks
19 Jun 76	**GREATEST HITS** *Bell BELLS 264*	....	**52**	1 wk

---

GLOVE *UK, male vocal/instrumental group*   *3 wks*

| 17 Sep 83 | **BLUE SUNSHINE** *Wonderland SHELP 2* | .... | **35** | 3 wks |

GODLEY and CREME *UK, male vocal/instrumental duo*   *16 wks*

19 Nov 77	**CONSEQUENCES** *Mercury CONS 017*	....	**52**	1 wk
9 Sep 78	**L** *Mercury 9109 611*	....	**47**	2 wks
17 Oct 81	**ISMISM** *Polydor POLD 5043*	....	**29**	13 wks

Consequences *credited to Kevin Godley and Lol Creme.*

GO-GO s *US, female vocal/instrumental group*   *3 wks*

| 21 Aug 82 | **VACATION** *IRS/A&M SP 70031* | .... | **75** | 3 wks |

Andrew GOLD *US, male vocalist/instrumentalist - piano*   *7 wks*

| 15 Apr 78 | **ALL THIS AND HEAVEN TOO** *Asylum K 53072* | | **31** | 7 wks |

GOLDEN EARRING *Holland, male vocal/instrumental group*   *4 wks*

| 2 Feb 74 | **MOONTAN** *Track 2406 112* | .... | **24** | 4 wks |

GOODIES UK, male vocal group — 11 wks

8 Nov 75	THE NEW GOODIES LP	Bradley's BRADL 1010	25	11 wks

Benny GOODMAN US, male instrumentalist – clarinet — 1 wk

3 Apr 71	BENNY GOODMAN TODAY	Decca DDS 3 ...	49	1 wk

Ron GOODWIN UK, orchestra — 1 wk

2 May 70	LEGEND OF THE GLASS MOUNTAIN Studio two TWO 220		49	1 wk

GOOMBAY DANCE BAND Germany, male/female vocal group — 9 wks

10 Apr 82	SEVEN TEARS	Epic EPC 85702	16	9 wks

GOONS UK, male comic group — 31 wks

28 Nov 59 ●	BEST OF THE GOON SHOWS Parlophone PMC 1108		8	14 wks
17 Dec 60	BEST OF THE GOON SHOWS VOL.2 Parlophone PMC 1129		12	6 wks
4 Nov 72 ●	LAST GOON SHOW OF ALL BBC Radio Enterprises REB 142		8	11 wks

GO WEST UK, male vocal/instrumental group — 38 wks

13 Apr 85 ●	GO WEST	Chrysalis CHR 1495	9†	38 wks

Jaki GRAHAM UK, female vocalist — 5 wks

14 Sep 85	HEAVEN KNOWS	EMI JK 1	48	5 wks

GRANDMASTER FLASH and the FURIOUS FIVE US, male vocal group and male vocal — 20 wks

23 Oct 82	THE MESSAGE	Sugar Hill SHLP 1007	77	3 wks
23 Jun 84	GREATEST MESSAGES	Sugar Hill SHLP 5552	41	16 wks
23 Feb 85	THEY SAID IT COULDN'T BE DONE Elektra 9-60389-1		95	1 wk

GRANDMASTER MELLE MEL US, male vocalist — 5 wks

20 Oct 84	WORK PARTY	Sugar Hill SHLP 5553	45	5 wks

GORDON - See PETER and GORDON

GRAND PRIX UK, male vocal/instrumental group — 2 wks

18 Jun 83	SAMURAI	Chrysalis CHR 1430	65	2 wks

David GRANT UK, male vocalist — 7 wks

5 Nov 83	DAVID GRANT	Chrysalis CHR 1448	32	6 wks
18 May 85	HOPES & DREAMS	Chrysalis CHR 1483	96	1 wk

Eddy GRANT Guyana, male vocalist/multi-instrumentalist — 39 wks

30 May 81	CAN'T GET ENOUGH	Ice ICEL 21	39	6 wks
27 Nov 82 ●	KILLER ON THE RAMPAGE	Ice ICELP 3023 ..	7	23 wks
17 Nov 84	ALL THE HITS	K-Tel NE 1284	23	10 wks

GRATEFUL DEAD US, male vocal/instrumental group — 6 wks

19 Sep 70	WORKINGMAN'S DEAD	Warner Bros. WS 1869	69	2 wks
3 Aug 74	GRATEFUL DEAD FROM THE MARS HOTEL Atlantic K 59302		47	1 wk
1 Nov 75	BLUES FOR ALLAH	United Artists UAS 29895 ..	45	1 wk
4 Sep 76	STEAL YOUR FACE	United Artists UAS 60131/2	42	1 wk
20 Aug 77	TERRAPIN STATION	Arista SPARTY 1016	30	1 wk

David GRAY and Tommy TYCHO UK, male arrangers — 6 wks

16 Oct 76	ARMcHAIR MELODIES	K-Tel NE 927	21	6 wks

Al GREEN US, male vocalist — 16 wks

26 Apr 75	AL GREEN'S GREATEST HITS London SHU 8481		18	16 wks

Peter GREEN UK, male vocalist/instrumentalist - guitar — 17 wks

9 Jun 79	IN THE SKIES	Creole PULS 101	32	13 wks
24 May 80	LITTLE DREAMER	PUK PULS 102	34	4 wks

Dave GREENFIELD and Jean-Jacques BURNEL UK, male vocal/instrumental duo — 1 wk

3 Dec 83	FIRE AND WATER	Epic EPC 25707	94	1 wk

See also Jean-Jacques Burnel.

GREEN ON RED US, male vocal/instrumental group — 1 wk

26 Oct 85	NO FREE LUNCH	Mercury MERM 78	99	1 wk

GREENSLADE UK, male vocal/instrumental group — 3 wks

14 Sep 74	SPYGLASS GUEST	Warner Bros. K 56055	34	3 wks

Christina GREGG UK, female instructor - exercise record — 1 wk

27 May 78	MUSIC 'N' MOTION	Warwick WW 5041	51	1 wk

GROUNDHOGS UK, male vocal/instrumental group — 50 wks

6 Jun 70 ●	THANK CHRIST FOR THE BOMB Liberty LBS 83295		9	13 wks
3 Apr 71 ●	SPLIT	Liberty LBG 83401	5	27 wks
18 Mar 72 ●	WHO WILL SAVE THE WORLD United Artists UAG 29237		8	9 wks

HERBIE HANCOCK · SUNLIGHT

GRATEFUL DEAD (above) Legendary live band grateful for half-a-dozen weeks of record success. (LFI)

HERBIE HANCOCK (left) On this album Herbie's vocals were synthesised through a vocoder.

| 13 Jul 74 | SOLID *WWA WWA 004* .... | 31 | 1 wk |

GUILDFORD CATHEDRAL CHOIR *UK, choir*
4 wks

| 10 Dec 66 | CHRISTMAS CAROLS FROM GUILDFORD CATHEDRAL *MFP 1104* .... | 24 | 4 wks |

Record credits Barry Rose as conductor.

David GUNSON *US, male comedian*
2 wks

| 25 Dec 82 | WHAT GOES UP MIGHT COME DOWN *Big Ben BB0012* .... | 92 | 2 wks |

G.U.S. (FOOTWEAR) BAND and the MORRISTOWN ORPHEUS CHOIR *UK, male instrumental group and male/female vocal group*
1 wk

| 3 Oct 70 | LAND OF HOPE AND GLORY *Columbia SCX 6406* .... | 54 | 1 wk |

Arlo GUTHRIE *US, male vocalist*
1 wk

| 7 Mar 70 | ALICE'S RESTAURANT *Reprise RSLP 6267* .... | 44 | 1 wk |

GUYS 'N' DOLLS *UK, male/female vocal group*
1 wk

| 31 May 75 | GUYS 'N' DOLLS *Magnet MAG 5005* .... | 43 | 1 wk |

H

Steve HACKETT *UK, male vocalist/instrumentalist - guitar*
38 wks

1 Nov 75	VOYAGE OF THE ACOLYTE *Charisma CAS 1111*	26	4 wks
6 May 78	PLEASE DON'T TOUCH *Charisma CDS 4012* ..	38	5 wks
26 May 79	SPECTRAL MORNINGS *Charisma CDS 4017* ...	22	11 wks
21 Jun 80 ●	DEFECTOR *Charisma CDS 4018*	9	7 wks
29 Aug 81	CURED *Charisma CDS 4021*	15	5 wks
30 Apr 83	HIGHLY STRUNG *Charisma HACK 1*	16	3 wks
19 Nov 83	BAY OF KINGS *Lamborghini LMGLP 3000*	70	1 wk
22 Sep 84	TILL WE HAVE FACES *Lamborghini LMGLP 4000*	54	2 wks

Sammy HAGAR *US, male vocalist/instrumentalist - guitar*
17 wks

29 Sep 79	STREET MACHINE *Capitol EST 11983*	38	4 wks
22 Mar 80	LOUD AND CLEAR *Capitol EST 25330*	12	8 wks
7 Jun 80	DANGER ZONE *Capitol EST 12069*	25	3 wks
13 Feb 82	STANDING HAMPTON *Geffen GEF 85456*	84	2 wks

See also Hagar, Schon, Aaronson and Shrieve.

HAGAR, SCHON, AARONSON, SHRIEVE *US, male vocal/instrumental group*
1 wk

| 19 May 84 | THROUGH THE FIRE *Geffen GEF 25893* ...... | 92 | 1 wk |

See also Sammy Hagar.

Paul HAIG *UK, male vocalist*
2 wks

| 22 Oct 83 | RHYTHM OF LIFE *Crepuscule ILPS 9742* ...... | 82 | 2 wks |

HAIRCUT 100 *UK, male vocal/instrumental group*
34 wks

| 6 Mar 82 ● | PELICAN WEST *Arista HCC 100* .... | 2 | 34 wks |

Bill HALEY and his COMETS *US, male vocalist/guitarist, male vocal/instrumental backing group*
5 wks

| 18 May 68 | ROCK AROUND THE CLOCK *Ace Of Hearts AH 13* .... | 34 | 5 wks |

Daryl HALL and John OATES *US, male vocal duo*
128 wks

3 Jul 76	HALL AND OATES *RCA Victor APL1 1144*	56	1 wk
18 Sep 76	BIGGER THAN BOTH OF US *RCA Victor APL1 1467*	25	7 wks
15 Oct 77	BEAUTY ON A BACK STREET *RCA PL 12300*	40	2 wks
6 Feb 82 ●	PRIVATE EYES *RCA RCALP 6001*	8	21 wks
23 Oct 82	H2O *RCA RCALP 6056*	24	35 wks
29 Oct 83	ROCK 'N' SOUL (PART 1) *RCA PL 84858*	16	44 wks
27 Oct 84	BIG BAM BOOM *RCA 85309*	28	13 wks
28 Sep 85	LIVE AT THE APOLLO WITH DAVID RUFFIN & EDDIE KENDRICK *RCA PL 87035*	32	5 wks

HAMBURG STUDENTS' CHOIR *Germany, male vocal group*
6 wks

| 17 Dec 60 | HARK THE HERALD ANGELS SING *Pye GGL 0023* .... | 11 | 6 wks |

George HAMILTON IV *US, male vocalist*
11 wks

10 Apr 71	CANADIAN PACIFIC *RCA SF 8062*	45	1 wk
10 Feb 79	REFLECTIONS *Lotus WH 5008*	25	9 wks
13 Nov 82	SONGS FOR A WINTER'S NIGHT *Ronco RTL 2082*	94	1 wk

Herbie HANCOCK *US, male vocalist/instrumentalist - keyboards*
24 wks

9 Sep 78	SUNLIGHT *CBS 82240*	27	6 wks
24 Feb 79	FEETS DON'T FAIL ME NOW *CBS 83491*	28	8 wks
27 Aug 83	FUTURE SHOCK *CBS 25540*	27	10 wks

Tony HANCOCK *UK, male comedian*
42 wks

9 Apr 60 ●	THIS IS HANCOCK *Pye NPL 10845*	2	22 wks
12 Nov 60	PIECES OF HANCOCK *Pye NPL 18054*	17	2 wks
3 Mar 62	HANCOCK *Pye NPL 18068*	12	14 wks
14 Sep 63	THIS IS HANCOCK (re-issue) *Pye Golden Guinea GGL 0206*	16	4 wks

HANOI ROCKS *Finland/UK, male vocal/instrumental group*
4 wks

| 11 Jun 83 | BACK TO MYSTERY CITY *Lick LICLP 1* ..... | 87 | 1 wk |
| 20 Oct 84 | TWO STEPS FROM THE MOVE *CBS 26066* ... | 28 | 3 wks |

HALL AND OATES (left) The world's best selling duo of the 1980s first met in 1967 when they both led their own groups. Daryl headed the Temptones and John the Masters.

BILL HALEY (far left) Made his debut in the album chart thirteen years after 'Rock Around the Clock' was a number one single. (Harry Hammond)

JUSTIN HAYWARD (left) 296 weeks on chart as a Moody Blue, 18 as a duo with John Lodge and 10 as a soloist.

HAIRCUT 100 (left) The group who were nearly called Lemon Fire Brigade made their up-market debut in the Arnold Lumm library at the Ski Club in London's fashionable Eaton Square.

Bo HANNSON *Sweden, multi-instrumentalist* 2 wks

18 Nov 72	**LORD OF THE RINGS** *Charisma CAS 1059*	....	34	2 wks

John HANSON *UK, male vocalist* 12 wks

23 Apr 60	**THE STUDENT PRINCE** *Pye NPL 18046*	......	17	1 wk
2 Sep 61	● **THE STUDENT PRINCE/VAGABOND KING** *Pye GGL 0086*	....	9	7 wks
10 Dec 77	**JOHN HANSON SINGS 20 SHOWTIME GREATS** *K-Tel NE 1002*	....	16	4 wks

Paul HARDCASTLE *UK, male arranger/instrumentalist - synthesiser* 3 wks

30 Nov 85	**PAUL HARDCASTLE** *Chrysalis CHR 1517*	.....	53	3 wks

Mike HARDING *UK, male comedian* 24 wks

30 Aug 75	**MRS 'ARDIN'S KID** *Rubber RUB 011*	....	24	6 wks
10 Jul 76	**ONE MAN SHOW** *Philips 6625 022*	....	19	10 wks
11 Jun 77	**OLD FOUR EYES IS BACK** *Philips 6308 290*	...	31	6 wks
24 Jun 78	**CAPTAIN PARALYTIC AND THE BROWN ALE COWBOY** *Philips 6641 798*	....	60	2 wks

HARDY - *See LAUREL and HARDY*

Steve HARLEY and COCKNEY REBEL *UK, male vocalist and male vocal/instrumental group* 52 wks

22 Jun 74	● **THE PSYCHOMODO** *EMI EMC 3033*	....	8	20 wks
22 Mar 75	● **THE BEST YEARS OF OUR LIVES** *EMI EMC 3068*	....	4	19 wks
14 Feb 76	**TIMELESS FLIGHT** *EMI EMA 775*	....	18	6 wks
27 Nov 76	**LOVE'S A PRIMA DONNA** *EMI EMC 3156*	....	28	3 wks
30 Jul 77	**FACE TO FACE - A LIVE RECORDING** *EMI EMSP 320*	....	40	4 wks

First album credited to Cockney Rebel.

Roy HARPER *UK, male vocalist/instrumentalist - guitar* 5 wks

9 Mar 74	**VALENTINE** *Harvest SHSP 4027*	....	27	1 wk
21 Jun 75	**H.Q.** *Harvest SHSP 4046*	....	31	2 wks
12 Mar 77	**BULLINAMINGVASE** *Harvest SHSP 4060*	......	25	2 wks

See also Roy Harper and Jimmy Page

Roy HARPER and Jimmy PAGE *UK, male vocal/instrumental duo* 4 wks

16 Mar 85	**WHATEVER HAPPENED TO JUGULA?** *Second Sight/Beggars Banquet BEGA 60*	....	44	4 wks

See also Jimmy Page; Roy Harper

Anita HARRIS *UK, female vocalist* 5 wks

27 Jan 68	**JUST LOVING YOU** *CBS SBPG 63182*	....	29	5 wks

Emmylou HARRIS *US, female vocalist* 29 wks

14 Feb 76	**ELITE HOTEL** *Reprise K 54060*	....	17	11 wks
29 Jan 77	**LUXURY LINER** *Warner Bros. K 56344*	......	17	6 wks
4 Feb 78	**QUARTER MOON IN A TEN CENT TOWN** *Warner Bros. K 56443*	....	40	5 wks
29 Mar 80	**HER BEST SONGS** *K-Tel NE 1058*	....	36	3 wks

14 Feb 81	**EVANGELINE** *Warner Bros. K 56880*	....	53	4 wks

Keith HARRIS, ORVILLE and CUDDLES *UK, male ventriloquist vocalist with feathered dummies* 1 wk

4 Jun 83	**AT THE END OF THE RAINBOW** *BBC REH 465*	....	92	1 wk

George HARRISON *UK, male vocalist/instrumentalist - guitar* 53 wks

26 Dec 70	● **ALL THINGS MUST PASS** *Apple STCH 639*	...	4	24 wks
7 Jul 73	● **LIVING IN THE MATERIAL WORLD** *Apple PAS 10006*	....	2	12 wks
18 Oct 75	**EXTRA TEXTURE (read all about it)** *Apple PAS 10009*	....	16	4 wks
18 Dec 76	**THIRTY THREE AND A THIRD** *Dark Horse K 56319*	....	35	4 wks
17 Mar 79	**GEORGE HARRISON** *Dark Horse K 56562*	.....	39	5 wks
13 Jun 81	**SOMEWHERE IN ENGLAND** *Dark Horse K 56870*	....	13	4 wks

Debbie HARRY *US, female vocalist* 7 wks

8 Aug 81	● **KOO KOO** *Chrysalis CHR 1347*	....	6	7 wks

Keef HARTLEY BAND *UK, male vocal/instrumental group* 3 wks

5 Sep 70	**THE TIME IS NEAR** *Deram SML 1071*	....	41	3 wks

Sensational Alex HARVEY BAND *UK, male vocal/instrumental group* 42 wks

26 Oct 74	**THE IMPOSSIBLE DREAM** *Vertigo 6360 112*	...	16	4 wks
10 May 75	● **TOMORROW BELONGS TO ME** *Vertigo 9102 003*	....	9	10 wks
23 Aug 75	**NEXT** *Vertigo 6360 103*	....	37	5 wks
27 Sep 75	**SENSATIONAL ALEX HARVEY BAND LIVE** *Vertigo 6360 122*	....	14	7 wks
10 Apr 76	**PENTHOUSE TAPES** *Vertigo 9102 007*	....	14	7 wks
31 Jul 76	**SAHB STORIES** *Mountain TOPS 112*	......	11	9 wks

HATFIELD and The NORTH *UK, male/female vocal/instrumental group* 1 wk

29 Mar 75	**ROTTERS CLUB** *Virgin V 2030*	....	43	1 wk

Donny HATHAWAY - *See Roberta FLACK and Donny HATHAWAY*

HAWKWIND *UK, male vocal/instrumental group* 96 wks

6 Nov 71	**IN SEARCH OF SPACE** *United Artists UAS 29202*		18	19 wks
23 Dec 72	**DOREMI FASOL LATIDO** *United Artists UAS 29364*	....	14	5 wks
2 Jun 73	● **SPACE RITUAL ALIVE** *United Artists UAD 60037/8*	....	9	5 wks
21 Sep 74	**HALL OF THE MOUNTAIN GRILL** *United Artists UAG 29672*	....	16	5 wks
31 May 75	**WARRIOR ON THE EDGE OF TIME** *United Artists UAG 29766*	....	13	7 wks
24 Apr 76	**ROAD HAWKS** *United Artists UAK 29919*	.....	34	4 wks
18 Sep 76	**ASTONISHING SOUNDS, AMAZING MUSIC** *Charisma CDS 4004*	....	33	5 wks
9 Jul 77	**QUARK STRANGENESS AND CHARM** *Charisma CDS 4008*	....	30	6 wks

JIMI HENDRIX Jimi Hendrix wondering how many more parts of his anatomy he has to play his guitar with to please this crowd. (LFI)

DON HENLEY (top) His first album action following the demise of the Eagles was the duet 'Leather and Lace' on Stevie Nicks' album 'Bella Donna'. (Herb Ritts)

HERD (above) Nearly 300 years after John Milton wrote 'Paradise Lost', an LP of that title made the chart.

21 Oct 78	**25 YEARS ON**	*Charisma CD 4014*	....	**48**	3 wks
30 Jun 79	**PXR 5**	*Charisma CDS 4016*		**59**	5 wks
9 Aug 80	**LIVE 1979**	*Bronze Bron 527*		**15**	7 wks
8 Nov 80	**LEVITATION**	*Bronze Bron 530*		**21**	4 wks
24 Oct 81	**SONIC ATTACK**	*RCA RCALP 5004*		**19**	5 wks
22 May 82	**CHURCH OF HAWKWIND**	*RCA RCALP 9004*		**26**	6 wks
23 Oct 82	**CHOOSE YOUR MASQUES**	*RCA RCALP 6055*		**29**	5 wks
5 Nov 83	**ZONES**	*Flicknife SHARP 014*	....	**57**	2 wks
25 Feb 84	**HAWKWIND**	*Liberty SLS 1972921*		**75**	1 wk
16 Nov 85	**CHRONICLE OF THE BLACK SWORD**				
		Flicknife SHARP 033	....	**65**	2 wks

25 Years On credited to Hawklords, a pseudonym for Hawkwind.

Isaac HAYES *US, male vocalist/multi-instrumentalist*

14 wks

18 Dec 71	**SHAFT**	*Polydor 2659 007*	....	**17**	13 wks
12 Feb 72	**BLACK MOSES**	*Stax 2628 004*		**38**	1 wk

HAYSI FANTAYZEE *UK, male/female vocal duo*

5 wks

26 Feb 83	**BATTLE HYMNS FOR CHILDREN SINGING**				
		Regard RGLP 6000	....	**53**	5 wks

Justin HAYWARD *UK, male vocalist*

10 wks

5 Mar 77	**SONGWRITER**	*Deram SDL 15*		**28**	5 wks
19 Jul 80	**NIGHT FLIGHT**	*Decca TXS 138*		**41**	4 wks
19 Oct 85	**MOVING MOUNTAINS**	*Towerbell TOWLP 15*	..	**78**	1 wk

See also Justin Hayward and John Lodge.

Justin HAYWARD and John LODGE *UK, male vocal/instrumental duo*

18 wks

29 Mar 75	● **BLUE JAYS**	*Threshold THS 12*	....	**4**	18 wks

See also Justin Hayward.

HEART *Canada, female/male vocal/instrumental group*

15 wks

22 Jan 77	**DREAMBOAT ANNIE**	*Arista ARTY 139*	....	**36**	8 wks
23 Jul 77	**LITTLE QUEEN**	*Portrait PRT 82075*	....	**34**	4 wks
19 Jun 82	**PRIVATE AUDITION**	*Epic EPC 85792*	....	**77**	2 wks
26 Oct 85	**HEART**	*Capitol EJ 24-0372-1*	....	**79**	1 wk

HEARTBREAKERS *US, male vocal/instrumental group*

1 wk

5 Nov 77	**L.A.M.F.**	*Track 2409 218*	....	**55**	1 wk

Ted HEATH AND HIS MUSIC *UK, conductor and orchestra*

5 wks

21 Apr 62	**BIG BAND PERCUSSION**	*Decca PFM 24004*	...	**17**	5 wks

HEATWAVE *UK/US, male vocal/instrumental group*

26 wks

11 Jun 77	**TOO HOT TO HANDLE**	*GTO GTLP 013*	.....	**46**	2 wks
6 May 78	**CENTRAL HEATING**	*GTO GTLP 027*	....	**26**	15 wks
14 Feb 81	**CANDLES**	*GTO GTLP 047*	....	**29**	9 wks

HEAVEN 17 *UK, male vocal/instrumental group*

123 wks

26 Sep 81	**PENTHOUSE AND PAVEMENT**	*Virgin V 2208*		**14**	76 wks
7 May 83	● **THE LUXURY GAP**	*Virgin V 2253*	....	**4**	36 wks
6 Oct 84	**HOW MEN ARE**	*B.E.F V 2326*		**12**	11 wks

HEAVY PETTIN' *UK, male vocal/instrumental group*

4 wks

29 Oct 83	**LETTIN' LOOSE**	*Polydor HEPLP 1*	....	**55**	2 wks
13 Jul 85	**ROCK AIN'T DEAD**	*Polydor HEPLP 2*	....	**81**	2 wks

Jimi HENDRIX *US, male vocalist/instrumentalist - guitar*

187 wks

27 May 67	● **ARE YOU EXPERIENCED**	*Track 612-001*	......	**2**	33 wks
16 Dec 67	● **AXIS: BOLD AS LOVE**	*Track 613-003*	....	**5**	16 wks
27 Apr 68	● **SMASH HITS**	*Track 613-004*	....	**4**	25 wks
16 Nov 68	● **ELECTRIC LADYLAND**	*Track 613-008/9*	......	**6**	12 wks
4 Jul 70	● **BAND OF GYPSIES**	*Track 2406-001*	......	**6**	30 wks
3 Apr 71	● **CRY OF LOVE**	*Track 2408-101*	......	**2**	14 wks
28 Aug 71	● **EXPERIENCE**	*Ember NR 5057*	......	**9**	6 wks
20 Nov 71	**JIMI HENDRIX AT THE ISLE OF WIGHT**				
		Track 2302 016	......	**17**	2 wks
4 Dec 71	**RAINBOW BRIDGE**	*Reprise K 44159*	......	**16**	8 wks
5 Feb 72	● **HENDRIX IN THE WEST**	*Polydor 2302 018*	....	**7**	14 wks
11 Dec 72	**WAR HEROES**	*Polydor 2302 020*		**23**	3 wks
21 Jul 73	**SOUNDTRACK RECORDINGS FROM THE FILM**				
		'JIMI HENDRIX' *Warner Bros. K 64017*	......	**37**	1 wk
29 Mar 75	**JIMI HENDRIX**	*Polydor 2343 080*		**35**	4 wks
30 Aug 75	**CRASH LANDING**	*Polydor 2310 398*		**35**	3 wks
29 Nov 75	**MIDNIGHT LIGHTNING**	*Polydor 2310 415*		**46**	1 wk
14 Aug 82	**THE JIMI HENDRIX CONCERTS**	*CBS 88592*	..	**16**	11 wks
19 Feb 83	**THE SINGLES ALBUM**	*Polydor PODV 6*	......	**77**	4 wks

See also Jimi Hendrix and Curtis Knight. Act billed as Jimi Hendrix Experience, US/UK, male vocal/instrumental group, for first four hits.

Jimi HENDRIX and Curtis KNIGHT *US, male vocal/instrumental duo*

2 wks

18 May 68	**GET THAT FEELING**	*London HA 8349*	....	**39**	2 wks

See also Jimi Hendrix.

Don HENLEY *US, male vocalist*

11 wks

9 Mar 85	**BUILDING THE PERFECT BEAST**				
		Geffen GEF 25939	....	**14**	11 wks

Band and Chorus of HER MAJESTY'S GUARDS DIVISION *UK, military band*

4 wks

22 Nov 75	**30 SMASH HITS OF THE WAR YEARS**				
		Warwick WW 5006	....	**38**	4 wks

HERD *UK, male vocal/instrumental group*

1 wk

24 Feb 68	**PARADISE LOST**	*Fontana STL 5458*	....	**38**	1 wk

HERMAN'S HERMITS *UK, male vocal/instrumental group*

11 wks

18 Sep 65	**HERMAN'S HERMITS**	*Columbia 33SX 1727*		**16**	2 wks
25 Sep 71	**THE MOST OF HERMAN'S HERMITS**				
		MFP 5216	....	**14**	5 wks
8 Oct 77	**GREATEST HITS**	*K-Tel NE 1001*	....	**37**	4 wks

Nick HEYWARD UK, male vocalist   13 wks

29 Oct 83	●	NORTH OF A MIRACLE Arista NORTH 1	....	**10**	13 wks

HI TENSION UK, male vocal/instrumental group
                                                                        4 wks

6 Jan 79		HI TENSION Island ILPS 9564	....	**74**	4 wks

Benny HILL UK, male vocalist   8 wks

11 Dec 71	●	WORDS AND MUSIC Columbia SCX 6479	.....	**9**	8 wks

Vince HILL UK, male vocalist   10 wks

20 May 67		EDELWEISS Columbia SCX 6141	....	**23**	9 wks
29 Apr 78		THAT LOVING FEELING K-Tel NE 1017	.....	**51**	1 wk

Steve HILLAGE UK, male vocalist/instrumentalist – guitar
                                                                       41 wks

3 May 75		FISH RISING Virgin V 2031	....	**33**	3 wks
16 Oct 76	●	L Virgin V 2066	....	**10**	12 wks
22 Oct 77		MOTIVATION RADIO Virgin V 2777	.....	**28**	5 wks
29 Apr 78		GREEN VIRGIN V 2098	....	**30**	8 wks
17 Feb 79		LIVE HERALD Virgin VGD 3502	.....	**54**	5 wks
5 May 79		RAINBOW DOME MUSIC Virgin VR 1	.....	**52**	5 wks
27 Oct 79		OPEN Virgin V 2135	....	**71**	1 wk
5 Mar 83		FOR TO NEXT Virgin V 2244	.....	**48**	2 wks

Roger HODGSON UK, male vocalist   4 wks

20 Oct 84		IN THE EYE OF THE STORM A & M AMA 5004		**70**	4 wks

Gerrard HOFFNUNG UK, male comedian   19 wks

3 Sep 60	●	AT THE OXFORD UNION Decca LF 1330	.....	**4**	19 wks

Billie HOLIDAY US, female vocalist   7 wks

16 Nov 85		THE LEGEND OF BILLIE HOLIDAY MCA BHTV 1	.....	**60†**	7 wks

HOLLIES UK, male vocal/instrumental group   133 wks

15 Feb 64	●	STAY WITH THE HOLLIES Parlophone PMC 1220	....	**2**	25 wks
2 Oct 65	●	HOLLIES Parlophone PMC 1261	....	**8**	14 wks
16 Jul 66		WOULD YOU BELIEVE Parlophone PMC 7008		**16**	8 wks
17 Dec 66		FOR CERTAIN BECAUSE Parlophone PCS 17011		**23**	7 wks
17 Jun 67		EVOLUTION Parlophone PCS 7022		**13**	10 wks
17 Aug 68	★	GREATEST HITS Parlophone PCS 7057	....	**1**	27 wks
17 May 69	●	HOLLIES SING DYLAN Parlophone PCS 7078	.	**3**	7 wks
28 Nov 70		CONFESSIONS OF THE MIND Parlophone PCS 7117		**30**	5 wks
16 Mar 74		HOLLIES Polydor 2383 262		**38**	3 wks
19 Mar 77	●	HOLLIES LIVE HITS Polydor 2383 428	....	**4**	12 wks
22 Jul 78	●	20 GOLDEN GREATS EMI EMTV 11	....	**2**	15 wks

Buddy HOLLY and the CRICKETS US, male vocalist, male vocal/instrumental group
                                                                      308 wks

2 May 59	●	BUDDY HOLLY STORY Coral No. LVA 9105		**2**	156 wks

15 Oct 60	●	BUDDY HOLLY STORY VOL.2 Coral LVA 9127	....	**7**	14 wks
21 Oct 61	●	THAT'LL BE THE DAY Ace Of Hearts AH 3	..	**5**	14 wks
6 Apr 63	●	REMINISCING Coral LVA 9212	..	**2**	31 wks
13 Jun 64		BUDDY HOLLY SHOWCASE Coral LVA 9222		**3**	16 wks
26 Jun 65		HOLLY IN THE HILLS Coral LVA 9227	......	**13**	6 wks
15 Jul 67	●	BUDDY HOLLY'S GREATEST HITS Ace Of Hearts AH 148	....	**9**	40 wks
12 Apr 69		GIANT MCA MUPS 371		**13**	1 wk
21 Aug 71		BUDDY HOLLY'S GREATEST HITS (re-issue) Coral CP 8		**32**	6 wks
12 Jul 75		BUDDY HOLLY'S GREATEST HITS (2nd re-issue) MCA/Coral CDLM 8007	....	**42**	3 wks
11 Mar 78	★	20 GOLDEN GREATS MCA EMTV 8	....	**1**	20 wks
8 Sep 84		GREATEST HITS (3rd re-issue) MCA MCL 1618		**100**	1 wk

See also The Crickets; Bobby Vee and the Crickets. Most albums feature the Crickets on at least some tracks.

John HOLT Jamaica, male vocalist   2 wks

1 Feb 75		A THOUSAND VOLTS OF HOLT Trojan TRLS 75	....	**42**	2 wks

HOME UK, male vocal/instrumental group   1 wk

11 Nov 72		DREAMER CBS 67522	....	**41**	1 wk

HONEYDRIPPERS UK/US male vocal/instrumental group   10 wks

1 Dec 84		THE HONEYDRIPPERS VOLUME 1 Es Paranza 790220		**56**	10 wks

John Lee HOOKER US, male vocalist   2 wks

4 Feb 67		HOUSE OF THE BLUES Marble Arch MAL 663		**34**	2 wks

Mary HOPKIN UK, female vocalist   9 wks

1 Mar 69	●	POSTCARD Apple SAPCOR 5	....	**3**	9 wks

HORSLIPS Ireland, male vocal/instrumental group   3 wks

30 Apr 77		THE BOOK OF INVASIONS - A CELTIC SYMPHONY DJM DJF 20498		**39**	3 wks

HOT CHOCOLATE UK, male vocal/instrumental group   83 wks

15 Nov 75		HOT CHOCOLATE RAK SRAK 516		**34**	7 wks
7 Aug 76		MAN TO MAN RAK SRAK 522		**32**	7 wks
20 Nov 76	●	GREATEST HITS RAK SRAK 524		**6**	35 wks
8 Apr 78		EVERY 1'S A WINNER RAK SRAK 531	......	**30**	8 wks
15 Dec 79	●	20 HOTTEST HITS RAK EMTV 22		**3**	19 wks
25 Sep 82		MYSTERY RAK SRAK 549		**24**	7 wks

Whitney HOUSTON US, female vocalist   3 wks

14 Dec 85		WHITNEY HOUSTON Arista 206 978		**22†**	3 wks

Steve HOWE UK, male vocalist/instrumentalist – guitar   6 wks

15 Nov 75		BEGINNINGS Atlantic K 50151	....	**22**	4 wks

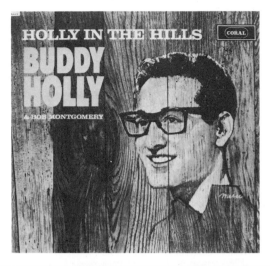

HOLLY IN THE HILLS
BUDDY HOLLY
& BOB MONTGOMERY

BUDDY HOLLY (far left) Buddy would've been 50 in 1986. How many great songs were lost to the world when he died at the age of 22?

INCREDIBLE STRING BAND (left) Charted seven albums in four years. (Jan Persson)

IT'S A BEAUTIFUL DAY Led by electric violinist David La Flamme, they also incorporated celeste, harpsichord, bells and gourds to obtain their post-psychedelic ethereal sound. (LFI)

24 Nov 79	**STEVE HOWE ALBUM** *Atlantic K 50621*		**68**	2 wks

Alan HULL *UK, male vocalist* — 3 wks

28 Jul 73	**PIPEDREAM** *Charisma CAS 1069*		**29**	3 wks

HUMAN LEAGUE *UK, male/female vocal/instrumental group* — 154 wks

31 May 80	**TRAVELOGUE** *Virgin V 2160*		**16**	42 wks
22 Aug 81	**REPRODUCTION** *Virgin V 2133*		**49**	23 wks
24 Oct 81	★ **DARE** *Virgin V 2192*		**1**	71 wks
19 May 84	● **HYSTERIA** *Virgin V 2315*		**3**	18 wks

HUMBLE PIE *UK, male vocal/instrumental group* — 10 wks

6 Sep 69	**AS SAFE AS YESTERDAY IS** *Immediate IMSP 025*		**32**	1 wk
22 Jan 72	**ROCKING AT THE FILLMORE** *A & M AMLH 63506*		**32**	2 wks
15 Apr 72	**SMOKIN'** *A & M AMLS 64342*		**28**	5 wks
7 Apr 73	**EAT IT** *A & M AMLS 6004*		**34**	2 wks

Engelbert HUMPERDINCK *UK, male vocalist* — 224 wks

20 May 67	● **RELEASE ME** *Decca SKL 4868*		**6**	58 wks
25 Nov 67	● **THE LAST WALTZ** *Decca SKL 4901*		**3**	33 wks
3 Aug 68	● **A MAN WITHOUT LOVE** *Decca SKL 4939*		**3**	45 wks
1 Mar 69	● **ENGELBERT** *Decca SKL 4985*		**3**	8 wks
6 Dec 69	● **ENGELBERT HUMPERDINCK** *Decca SKL 5030*		**5**	23 wks
11 Jul 70	**WE MADE IT HAPPEN** *Decca SKL 5054*		**17**	11 wks
18 Sep 71	**ANOTHER TIME, ANOTHER PLACE** *Decca SKL 5097*		**48**	1 wk
26 Feb 72	**LIVE AT THE RIVIERA LAS VEGAS** *Decca TXS 105*		**45**	1 wk
21 Dec 74	★ **ENGELBERT HUMPERDINCK - HIS GREATEST HITS** *Decca SKL 5198*		**1**	34 wks
4 May 85	**GETTING SENTIMENTAL** *Telstar STAR 2254*		**35**	10 wks

Ian HUNTER *UK, male vocalist* — 26 wks

12 Apr 75	**IAN HUNTER** *CBS 80710*		**21**	15 wks
29 May 76	**ALL AMERICAN ALIEN BOY** *CBS 81310*		**29**	4 wks
5 May 79	**YOU'RE NEVER ALONE WITH A SCHIZOPHRENIC** *Chrysalis CHR 1214*		**49**	3 wks
26 Apr 80	**WELCOME TO THE CLUB** *Chrysalis CJT 6* ...		**61**	2 wks
29 Aug 81	**SHORT BACK AND SIDES** *Chrysalis CHR 1326*		**79**	2 wks

HURRICANES - *See JOHNNY and the HURRICANES*

I

IQ *UK, male vocal/instrumental group* — 1 wk

22 Jun 85	**THE WAKE** *Sahara SAH 136*		**72**	1 wk

ICEHOUSE *Australia, male vocal/instrumental group* — 6 wks

5 Mar 83	**LOVE IN MOTION** *Chrysalis CHR 1390*		**64**	6 wks

ICICLE WORKS *UK, male vocal/instrumental group* — 9 wks

31 Mar 84	**THE ICICLE WORKS** *Beggars Banquet BEGA 50*		**24**	6 wks
28 Sep 85	**THE SMALL PRICE OF A BICYCLE** *Beggars Banquet BEGA 61*		**55**	3 wks

Billy IDOL *UK, male vocalist* — 37 wks

8 Jun 85	● **VITAL IDOL** *Chrysalis CUX 1502*		**7**	26 wks
28 Sep 85	**REBEL YELL** *Chrysalis CHR 1450*		**36**	11 wks

Frank IFIELD *UK, male vocalist* — 83 wks

16 Feb 63	● **I'LL REMEMBER YOU** *Columbia 33SX 1467*		**3**	36 wks
21 Sep 63	● **BORN FREE** *Columbia 33SX 1462*		**3**	32 wks
28 Mar 64	● **BLUE SKIES** *Columbia 33SX 1588*		**10**	12 wks
19 Dec 64	● **GREATEST HITS** *Columbia 33SX 1633*		**9**	3 wks

Julio IGLESIAS *Spain, male vocalist* — 82 wks

7 Nov 81	**DE NINA A MUJER** *CBS 85063*		**43**	5 wks
28 Nov 81	● **BEGIN THE BEGUINE** *CBS 85462*		**5**	28 wks
16 Oct 82	**AMOR** *CBS 25103*		**14**	14 wks
2 Jul 83	● **JULIO** *CBS 10038*		**5**	17 wks
1 Sep 84	**1100 BEL AIR PLACE** *CBS 86308*		**14**	14 wks
19 Oct 85	**LIBRA** *CBS 26623*		**61**	4 wks

I-LEVEL *UK, male vocal/instrumentalist group* — 4 wks

9 Jul 83	**I-LEVEL** *Virgin V 2270*		**50**	4 wks

IMAGINATION *UK, male vocal group* — 68 wks

24 Oct 81	**BODY TALK** *R & B RBLP 1001*		**22**	11 wks
11 Sep 82	● **IN THE HEAT OF THE NIGHT** *R&B RBLP 1002*		**7**	29 wks
14 May 83	● **NIGHT DUBBING** *R & B RBDUB 1*		**9**	20 wks
12 Nov 83	**SCANDALOUS** *R & B RBLP 1004*		**25**	8 wks

IMMACULATE FOOLS *UK, male vocal/instrumental group* — 2 wks

11 May 85	**HEARTS OF FORTUNE** *A & M AMA 5030* ...		**65**	2 wks

INCANTATION *UK, male instrumental group* — 37 wks

11 Dec 82	● **CACHARPAYA (PANPIPES OF THE ANDES)** *Beggars Banquet BEGA 39*		**9**	26 wks
17 Dec 83	**DANCE OF THE FLAMES** *Beggars Banquet BEGA 49*		**61**	10 wks
28 Dec 85	**BEST OF INCANTATION - MUSIC FROM THE ANDES** *West Five CODA 19*		**57†**	1 wk

INCOGNITO *France, male instrumental group* — 8 wks

18 Apr 81	**JAZZ FUNK** *Ensign ENVY 504*		**28**	8 wks

INCREDIBLE STRING BAND *UK, male/female vocal instrumental group* — 36 wks

21 Oct 67	**5,000 SPIRITS OR THE LAYERS OF THE ONION** *Elektra EUKS 257*		**26**	4 wks
6 Apr 68	● **HANGMAN'S BEAUTIFUL DAUGHTER** *Elektra EVKS7 258*		**5**	21 wks

Date	Title	Label/Cat	Pos	Wks

INCREDIBLE STRING BAND (continued)

20 Jul 68	INCREDIBLE STRING BAND *Elektra EKL 254*		34	3 wks
24 Jan 70	CHANGING HORSES *Elektra EKS 74057*		30	1 wk
9 May 70	I LOOKED UP *Elektra 2469-002*		30	4 wks
31 Oct 70	U *Elektra 2665-001*		34	2 wks
30 Oct 71	LIQUID ACROBAT AS REGARDS THE AIR *Island ILPS 9172*		46	1 wk

INFA RIOT UK, male vocal/instrumental group   4 wks

7 Aug 82	STILL OUT OF ORDER *Secret SEC 7*		42	4 wks

James INGRAM US, male vocalist   17 wks

31 Mar 84	IT'S YOUR NIGHT *Qwest 9239701*		25	17 wks

INTI ILLIMANI/GUAMARY Chile, male vocal/instrumental group - panpipes   7 wks

17 Dec 83	THE FLIGHT OF THE CONDOR - ORIGINAL TV SOUNDTRACK *BBC REB 440*		62	7 wks

INVISIBLE GIRLS - *See Pauline MURRAY and the INVISIBLE GIRLS*

IRON MAIDEN UK, male vocal instrumental group   97 wks

26 Apr 80	● IRON MAIDEN *EMI EMC 3330*		4	15 wks
28 Feb 81	KILLERS *EMI EMC 3357*		12	8 wks
10 Apr 82	★ THE NUMBER OF THE BEAST *EMI EMC 3400*		1	31 wks
28 May 83	● PIECE OF MIND *EMI EMA 800*		3	18 wks
15 Sep 84	● POWERSLAVE *EMI POWER 1*		2	13 wks
15 Jun 85	IRON MAIDEN (re-issue) *Fame FA 41-3121-1* ...		71	2 wks
26 Oct 85	● LIFE AFTER DEATH *EMI RIP 1*		2†	10 wks

Gregory ISAACS Jamaica, male vocalist   6 wks

12 Sep 81	MORE GREGORY *Charisma PREX 9*		93	1 wk
4 Sep 82	NIGHT NURSE *Island ILPS 9721*		32	5 wks

ISLEY BROTHERS US, male vocal/instrumental group   14 wks

14 Dec 68	THIS OLD HEART OF MINE *Tamla Motown STML 11034*		23	6 wks
14 Aug 76	HARVEST FOR THE WORLD *Epic EPC 81268*		50	5 wks
14 May 77	GO FOR YOUR GUNS *Epic EPC 86027*		46	2 wks
24 Jun 78	SHOWDOWN *Epic EPC 86039*		50	1 wk

IT'S A BEAUTIFUL DAY US, male/female vocal/instrumental group   3 wks

23 May 70	IT'S A BEAUTIFUL DAY *CBS 63722*		58	1 wk
18 Jul 70	MARRYING MAIDEN *CBS 66236*		45	2 wks

J

Freddie JACKSON US, male vocalist   6 wks

18 May 85	ROCK ME TONIGHT *Capitol EJ 2440316-1*		73	6 wks

Jermaine JACKSON US, male vocalist   12 wks

31 May 80	LET'S GET SERIOUS *Motown STML 12127*		22	6 wks
12 May 84	DYNAMITE *Arista 206 317*		57	6 wks

Joe JACKSON UK, male vocalist   85 wks

17 Mar 79	LOOK SHARP *A & M AMLH 64743*		40	11 wks
13 Oct 79	I'M THE MAN *A & M AMLH 64794*		12	16 wks
18 Oct 80	BEAT CRAZY *A & M AMLH 64837*		42	3 wks
4 Jul 81	JUMPIN' JIVE *A & M AMLH 68530*		14	14 wks
3 Jul 82	● NIGHT AND DAY *A&M AMLH 64906*		3	27 wks
7 Apr 84	BODY & SOUL *A & M AMLX 65000*		14	14 wks

Jumpin' Jive credited to Joe Jackson's Jumpin' Jive.

Michael JACKSON US, male vocalist   349 wks

3 Jun 72	GOT TO BE THERE *Tamla Motown STML 11205*		37	5 wks
13 Jan 73	BEN *Tamla Motown STML 11220*		17	7 wks
29 Sep 79	● OFF THE WALL *Epic EPC 83468*		5	158 wks
20 Jul 81	BEST OF *Motown STMR 9009*		11	18 wks
18 Jul 81	ONE DAY IN YOUR LIFE *Motown STML 12158*		29	8 wks
11 Dec 82	★ THRILLER *Epic EPC 85930*		1	134 wks
12 Feb 83	E.T. THE EXTRA TERRESTRIAL *MCA 7000*		82	2 wks
3 Dec 83	MICHAEL JACKSON 9 SINGLE PACK *Epic MJ1*		66	3 wks
9 Jun 84	● FAREWELL MY SUMMER LOVE *Motown ZL 72227*		9	14 wks

See also the Jacksons.

Millie JACKSON US, female vocalist   7 wks

18 Feb 84	E.S.P *Sire 250382*		59	5 wks
6 Apr 85	LIVE & UNCENSORED *Important TADLP 001* ...		81	2 wks

JACKSONS US, male vocal group   134 wks

21 Mar 70	DIANA ROSS PRESENTS THE JACKSON FIVE *Tamla Motown STML 11142*		16	4 wks
15 Aug 70	ABC *Tamla Motown STML 11153*		22	6 wks
7 Oct 72	GREATEST HITS *Tamla Motown STML 11212* ..		26	14 wks
18 Nov 72	LOOKIN' THROUGH THE WINDOWS *Tamla Motown STML 11214*		16	8 wks
16 Jul 77	THE JACKSONS *Epic EPC 86009*		54	1 wk
3 Dec 77	GOIN' PLACES *Epic EPC 86035*		45	1 wk
5 May 79	DESTINY *Epic EPC 83200*		33	7 wks
11 Oct 80	TRIUMPH *Epic EPC 86112*		13	16 wks
12 Dec 81	THE JACKSONS *Epic EPC 88562*		53	9 wks
9 Jul 83	★ 18 GREATEST HITS *Telstar STAR 2232*		1	55 wks
21 Jul 84	● VICTORY *Epic EPC 86303*		3	13 wks

First four albums credited to Jackson Five. 18 Greatest Hits, credited to Michael Jackson plus the Jackson Five, contains hits by both acts. All other albums credited to the Jacksons. See also Michael Jackson.

Mick JAGGER UK, male vocalist   11 wks

16 Mar 85	● SHE'S THE BOSS *CBS 86310*		6	11 wks

JAM UK, male vocal/instrumental group   148 wks

28 May 77	IN THE CITY *Polydor 2383 447*		20	18 wks
26 Nov 77	THIS IS THE MODERN WORLD *Polydor 2383 475*		22	5 wks
11 Nov 78	● ALL MOD CONS *Polydor POLD 5008*		6	17 wks
24 Nov 79	● SETTING SONS *Polydor POLD 5028*		4	19 wks
6 Dec 80	● SOUND AFFECTS *Polydor POLD 5035*		2	19 wks
20 Mar 82	★ THE GIFT *Polydor POLD 5055*		1	24 wks
18 Dec 82	● DIG THE NEW BREED *Polydor POLD 5075*		2	15 wks
27 Aug 83	IN THE CITY (re-issue) *Polydor SPELP 27*		100	1 wk
22 Oct 83	● SNAP *Polydor SNAP 1*		2	30 wks

Rick JAMES US, male vocalist — 2 wks

Date	Title	Label	Pos	Wks
24 Jul 82	THROWIN' DOWN Motown STML 12167		93	2 wks

JAN and DEAN US, male vocal duo — 2 wks

Date	Title	Label	Pos	Wks
12 Jul 80	THE JAN AND DEAN STORY K-Tel NE 1084		67	2 wks

JAPAN UK, male vocal/instrumental group — 136 wks

Date	Title	Label	Pos	Wks
9 Feb 80	QUIET LIFE Ariola Hansa AHAL 8011		53	8 wks
15 Nov 80	GENTLEMEN TAKE POLAROIDS Virgin V 2180		45	10 wks
26 Sep 81	ASSEMBLAGE Hansa HANLP 1		26	46 wks
28 Nov 81	TIN DRUM Virgin V 2209		12	50 wks
18 Jun 83	● OIL ON CANVAS Virgin VD 2513		5	14 wks
8 Dec 84	EXORCISING GHOSTS Virgin VGD 3510		45	8 wks

Jeff JARRATT and Don REEDMAN UK, male producers — 8 wks

Date	Title	Label	Pos	Wks
22 Nov 80	MASTERWORKS K-Tel ONE 1093		39	8 wks

Jean-Michel JARRE France, male instrumentalist/producer — 125 wks

Date	Title	Label	Pos	Wks
20 Aug 77	● OXYGENE Polydor 2310 555		2	23 wks
16 Dec 78	EQUINOXE Polydor POLD 5007		11	26 wks
6 Jun 81	● MAGNETIC FIELDS Polydor POLS 1033		6	17 wks
15 May 82	● THE CONCERTS IN CHINA Polydor PODV 3		6	17 wks
12 Nov 83	THE ESSENTIAL JEAN MICHEL JARRE Polystar PRO LP 3		14	28 wks
24 Nov 84	ZOOLOOK Dreyfus POLH 15		47	14 wks

Al JARREAU US, male vocalist — 27 wks

Date	Title	Label	Pos	Wks
5 Sep 81	BREAKING AWAY Warner Bros. K 56917		60	8 wks
30 Apr 83	JARREAU WEA International U 0070		39	18 wks
17 Nov 84	HIGH CRIME WEA 250807		81	1 wk

JEFFERSON AIRPLANE US, female/male vocal/instrumental group — 10 wks

Date	Title	Label	Pos	Wks
28 Jun 69	BLESS ITS POINTED LITTLE HEAD RCA SF 8019		38	1 wk
7 Mar 70	VOLUNTEERS RCA SF 8076		34	7 wks
2 Oct 71	BARK Grunt FTR 1001		42	1 wk
2 Sep 72	LONG JOHN SILVER Grunt FTR 1007		30	1 wk

JEFFERSON STARSHIP US, female/male vocal/instrumental group — 13 wks

Date	Title	Label	Pos	Wks
31 Jul 76	SPITFIRE Grunt RFL 1557		30	2 wks
9 Feb 80	FREEDOM AT POINT ZERO Grunt FL 13452		22	11 wks

JESUS and MARY CHAIN UK, male vocal/instrumental group — 3 wks

Date	Title	Label	Pos	Wks
30 Nov 85	PSYCHOCANDY Blanco Y Negro BYN 7		31	3 wks

JETHRO TULL UK, male vocal/instrumental group — 209 wks

Date	Title	Label	Pos	Wks
2 Nov 68	● THIS WAS Island ILPS 9085		10	22 wks
9 Aug 69	★ STAND UP Island ILPS 9103		1	29 wks
9 May 70	● BENEFIT Island ILPS 9123		3	13 wks
3 Apr 71	● AQUALUNG Island ILPS 9145		4	21 wks
18 Mar 72	● THICK AS A BRICK Chrysalis CHR 1003		5	14 wks
15 Jul 72	● LIVING IN THE PAST Chrysalis CJT 1		8	11 wks
28 Jul 73	A PASSION PLAY Chrysalis CHR 1040		13	8 wks
2 Nov 74	WAR CHILD Chrysalis CHR 1067		14	4 wks
27 Sep 75	MINSTREL IN THE GALLERY Chrysalis CHR 1082		20	6 wks
31 Jan 76	M.U. THE BEST OF JETHRO TULL Chrysalis CHR 1078		44	5 wks
15 May 76	TOO OLD TO ROCK 'N' ROLL TOO YOUNG TO DIE Chrysalis CHR 1111		25	10 wks
19 Feb 77	SONGS FROM THE WOOD Chrysalis CHR 1132		13	12 wks
29 Apr 78	HEAVY HORSES Chrysalis CHR 1175		20	10 wks
14 Oct 78	LIVE BURSTING OUT Chrysalis CJT 4		17	8 wks
6 Oct 79	STORM WATCH Chrysalis CDL 1238		27	4 wks
6 Sep 80	A Chrysalis CDL 1301		25	5 wks
17 Apr 82	BROADSWORD AND THE BEAST Chrysalis CDL 1380		27	19 wks
15 Sep 84	UNDER WRAPS Chrysalis CDL 1461		18	5 wks
2 Nov 85	ORIGINAL MASTERS Chrysalis JTTV 1		63	3 wks

JETS UK, male vocal/instrumental group — 6 wks

Date	Title	Label	Pos	Wks
10 Apr 82	100 PERCENT COTTON EMI EMC 3399		30	6 wks

Joan JETT and the BLACKHEARTS US, female/male vocal/instrumental group. — 7 wks

Date	Title	Label	Pos	Wks
8 May 82	I LOVE ROCK 'N' ROLL Epic EPC 85686		25	7 wks

JO BOXERS UK, male vocal/instrumental group — 5 wks

Date	Title	Label	Pos	Wks
24 Sep 83	LIKE GANGBUSTERS RCA BOXXLP 1		18	5 wks

Billy JOEL US, male vocalist — 238 wks

Date	Title	Label	Pos	Wks
25 Mar 78	THE STRANGER CBS 82311		25	40 wks
25 Nov 78	● 52ND STREET CBS 83181		10	43 wks
22 Mar 80	● GLASS HOUSES CBS 86108		9	24 wks
10 Oct 81	SONGS IN THE ATTIC CBS 85273		57	3 wks
2 Oct 82	NYLON CURTAIN CBS 85959		27	8 wks
10 Sep 83	● AN INNOCENT MAN CBS 25554		2	94 wks
4 Feb 84	COLD SPRING HARBOUR CBS 32400		95	1 wk
23 Jun 84	PIANO MAN CBS 32007		98	1 wk
20 Jul 85	● GREATEST HITS VOLUME 1 & VOLUME II CBS 88666		7†	24 wks

Elton JOHN UK, male vocalist/instrumentalist - piano — 570 wks

Date	Title	Label	Pos	Wks
23 May 70	ELTON JOHN DJM DJLPS 406		11	14 wks
16 Jan 71	● TUMBLEWEED CONNECTION DJM DJLPS 410		6	20 wks
1 May 71	THE ELTON JOHN LIVE ALBUM 17-11-70 DJM DJLPS 414		20	2 wks
20 May 72	MADMAN ACROSS THE WATER DJM DJLPH 420		41	2 wks
3 Jun 72	● HONKY CHATEAU DJM DJLPH 423		2	23 wks
10 Feb 73	★ DON'T SHOOT ME I'M ONLY THE PIANO PLAYER DJM DJLPH 427		1	42 wks
3 Nov 73	★ GOODBYE YELLOW BRICK ROAD DJM DJLPO 1001		1	84 wks
13 Jul 74	★ CARIBOU DJM DJLPH 439		1	18 wks
23 Nov 74	★ ELTON JOHN'S GREATEST HITS DJM DJLPH 442		1	84 wks
7 Jun 75	● CAPTAIN FANTASTIC AND THE BROWN DIRT COWBOY DJM DJLPX 1		2	24 wks
8 Nov 75	● ROCK OF WESTIES DJM DJLPH 464		5	12 wks
15 May 76	● HERE AND THERE DJM DJLPH 473		6	9 wks
6 Nov 76	● BLUE MOVES Rocket ROSP 1		3	15 wks

MICHAEL JACKSON (right)
Mr 1983.

THE JAM (above) Woking boys *circa* 1978. (LFI)

JANIS JOPLIN (top) Janis Joplin in London with pearls and other baubles. (LFI)

JUNIOR (left) Junior in the scrum with ex-Jam bassist Bruce Foxton and two unknowns.

15 Oct 77	●	**GREATEST HITS VOL. 2** *DJM DJH 20520*	**6**	24 wks
4 Nov 78	●	**A SINGLE MAN** *Rocket TRAIN 1*	**8**	26 wks
20 Oct 79		**VICTIM OF LOVE** *Rocket HISPD 125*	**41**	3 wks
8 Mar 80		**LADY SAMANTHA** *DJM 22085*	**56**	2 wks
31 May 80		**21 AT 33** *Rocket HISPD 126*	**12**	13 wks
25 Oct 80		**THE VERY BEST OF ELTON JOHN** *K-Tel NE 1094*	**24**	13 wks
30 May 81		**THE FOX** *Rocket TRAIN 16*	**12**	12 wks
17 Apr 82		**JUMP UP** *Rocket HISPD 127*	**13**	12 wks
6 Nov 82		**LOVE SONGS** *TV Records TVA 3*	**39**	13 wks
11 Jun 83	●	**TOO LOW FOR ZERO** *Rocket HIS PD 24*	**7**	73 wks
30 Jun 84	●	**BREAKING HEARTS** *Rocket HISPD 25*	**2**	23 wks
16 Nov 85	●	**ICE ON FIRE** *Rocket HISPD 26*	**3†**	7 wks

JOHNNY and The HURRICANES *US, male instrumental group*   *5 wks*

3 Dec 60	**STORMSVILLE** *London HAI 2269*	**18**	1 wk
1 Apr 61	**BIG SOUND OF JOHNNY AND THE HURRICANES** *London HAK 2322*	**14**	4 wks

Linton Kwesi JOHNSON *Jamaica, male poet*   *8 wks*

30 Jun 79	**FORCE OF VICTORY** *Island ILPS 9566*	**66**	1 wk
31 Oct 80	**BASS CULTURE** *Island ILPS 9605*	**46**	5 wks
10 Mar 84	**MAKING HISTORY** *Island ILPS 9770*	**73**	2 wks

Al JOLSON *US, male vocalist*   *11 wks*

14 Mar 81	**20 GOLDEN GREATS** *MCA MCTV 4*	**18**	7 wks
17 Dec 83	**THE AL JOLSON COLLECTION** *Ronco RON LP 5*	**67**	4 wks

JON and VANGELIS *UK, male vocalist and Greece, male instrumentalist - keyboards*   *53 wks*

26 Jan 80	●	**SHORT STORIES** *Polydor POLD 5030*	**4**	11 wks
11 Jul 81	●	**THE FRIENDS OF MR. CAIRO** *Polydor POLD 5039*	**6**	23 wks
2 Jul 83		**PRIVATE COLLECTION** *Polydor POLH 4*	**22**	10 wks
11 Aug 84		**THE BEST OF JON AND VANGELIS** *Polydor POLH 6*	**42**	9 wks

See also Jon Anderson; Vangelis.

Aled JONES with the BBC WELSH CHORUS *UK, male chorister with Welsh chorus*   *65 wks*

27 Apr 85	●	**VOICES FROM THE HOLY LAND** *BBC REC 564*	**6†**	32 wks
29 Jun 85	●	**ALL THROUGH THE NIGHT** *BBC REH 569* ..	**3†**	27 wks
23 Nov 85		**ALED JONES WITH THE BBC WELSH CHORUS** *10/BBC AJ 1*	**12†**	6 wks

All Through The Night credits the BBC Welsh Symphony Orchestra and was conducted by Robin Stapleton. Both other albums were conducted by John Hugh Thomas.

Grace JONES *US, female vocalist*   *49 wks*

30 Aug 80	**WARM LEATHERETTE** *Island ILPS 9592*	**45**	2 wks
23 May 81	**NIGHTCLUBBING** *Island ILPS 9624*	**35**	16 wks
20 Nov 82	**LIVING MY LIFE** *Island ILPS 9722*	**15**	22 wks,
9 Nov 85	**SLAVE TO THE RHYTHM** *ZTT/ Island GRACE 1*	**12**	6 wks
14 Dec 85	**ISLAND LIFE** *Island GJ 1*	**43†**	3 wks

Howard JONES *UK, male vocalist*   *114 wks*

17 Mar 84	★	**HUMAN'S LIB** *WEA WX 1*	**1**	56 wks
8 Dec 84		**THE 12" ALBUM** *WEA WX 14*	**15**	33 wks
23 Mar 85	●	**DREAM INTO ACTION** *WEA WX 15*	**2**	25 wks

Jack JONES *US, male vocalist*   *70 wks*

29 Apr 72	●	**A SONG FOR YOU** *RCA Victor SF 8228*	**9**	6 wks
3 Jun 72	●	**BREAD WINNERS** *RCA Victor SF 8280*	**7**	36 wks
7 Apr 73	●	**TOGETHER** *RCA Victor SF 8342*	**8**	10 wks
23 Feb 74		**HARBOUR** *RCA Victor APLI 0408*	**10**	5 wks
19 Feb 77		**THE FULL LIFE** *RCA Victor PL 12067*	**41**	5 wks
21 May 77		**ALL TO YOURSELF** *RCA TVL 2*	**13**	8 wks

Quincy JONES *US, male arranger/instrumentalist - keyboards*   *29 wks*

18 Apr 81	**THE DUDE** *A & M AMLK 63721*	**19**	25 wks
20 Mar 82	**THE BEST** *A&M AMLH 68542*	**41**	4 wks

Rickie Lee JONES *US, female vocalist*   *37 wks*

16 Jun 79	**RICKIE LEE JONES** *Warner Bros. K 56628*	**18**	19 wks
8 Aug 81	**PIRATES** *Warner Bros. K 56816*	**37**	11 wks
2 Jul 83	**GIRL AT HER VOLCANO** *Warner Bros 92-3805-1*	**51**	3 wks
13 Oct 84	**THE MAGAZINE** *Warner Bros 925117*	**40**	4 wks

Tammy JONES *UK, female vocalist*   *5 wks*

12 Jul 75	**LET ME TRY AGAIN** *Epic EPC 80853*	**38**	5 wks

Tom JONES *UK, male vocalist*   *392 wks*

5 Jun 65		**ALONG CAME JONES** *Decca LK 6693*	**11**	5 wks
8 Oct 66		**FROM THE HEART** *Decca LK 4814*	**23**	8 wks
8 Apr 67	●	**GREEN GREEN GRASS OF HOME** *Decca SKL 4855*	**3**	49 wks
24 Jun 67	●	**LIVE AT THE TALK OF THE TOWN** *Decca SKL 4874*	**6**	90 wks
30 Dec 67	●	**13 SMASH HITS** *Decca SKL 4909*	**5**	49 wks
27 Jul 68	★	**DELILAH** *Decca SKL 4946*	**1**	29 wks
21 Dec 68	●	**HELP YOURSELF** *Decca SKL 4982*	**4**	9 wks
28 Jun 69	●	**THIS IS TOM JONES** *Decca SKL 5007*	**2**	20 wks
15 Nov 69	●	**TOM JONES LIVE IN LAS VEGAS** *Decca SKL 5032*	**3**	45 wks
25 Apr 70	●	**TOM** *Decca SKL 5045*	**4**	18 wks
14 Nov 70	●	**I WHO HAVE NOTHING** *Decca SKL 5072*	**10**	10 wks
29 May 71	●	**SHE'S A LADY** *Decca SKL 5089*	**9**	7 wks
27 Nov 71		**LIVE AT CAESAR'S PALACE** *Decca 1/1-1/2*	**27**	5 wks
24 Jun 72		**CLOSE UP** *Decca SKL 5132*	**17**	4 wks
23 Jun 73		**THE BODY AND SOUL OF TOM JONES** *Decca SKL 5162*	**31**	1 wk
5 Jan 74		**GREATEST HITS** *Decca SKL 5162*	**15**	13 wks
22 Mar 75	★	**20 GREATEST HITS** *Decca TJD 1/11/2*	**1**	21 wks
7 Oct 78		**I'M COMING HOME** *Lotus WH 5001*	**12**	9 wks

Janis JOPLIN *US, female vocalist*   *7 wks*

17 Apr 71	**PEARL** *CBS 64188*	**50**	1 wk
22 Jul 72	**JANIS JOPLIN IN CONCERT** *CBS 67241*	**30**	6 wks

JOURNEY *US, male vocal/instrumental group*   *25 wks*

20 Mar 82		**ESCAPE** *CBS 85138*	**32**	16 wks
19 Feb 83	●	**FRONTIERS** *CBS 25361*	**6**	8 wks
6 Aug 83		**EVOLUTION** *CBS 32342*	**100**	1 wk

JOY DIVISION UK, *male vocal/instrumental group*

21 wks

26 Jul 80	●	CLOSER	*Factory FACT 25*	**6**	8 wks
30 Aug 80		UNKNOWN PLEASURES	*Factory FACT 10*	**71**	1 wk
17 Oct 81	●	STILL	*Factory FACT 40*	**5**	12 wks

JUDAS PRIEST UK, *male vocal/instrumental group*

64 wks

14 May 77		SIN AFTER SIN	*CBS 82008*	**23**	6 wks
25 Feb 78		STAINED GLASS	*CBS 82430*	**27**	5 wks
11 Nov 78		KILLING MACHINE	*CBS 83135*	**32**	9 wks
6 Oct 79	●	UNLEASHED IN THE EAST	*CBS 83852*	**10**	8 wks
19 Apr 80	●	BRITISH STEEL	*CBS 84160*	**4**	17 wks
7 Mar 81		POINT OF ENTRY	*CBS 84834*	**14**	5 wks
17 Jul 82		SCREAMING FOR VENGEANCE	*CBS 85941* ..	**11**	9 wks
28 Jan 84		DEFENDERS OF THE FAITH	*CBS 25713*	**19**	5 wks

JUDGE DREAD UK, *male vocalist*

14 wks

6 Dec 75	BEDTIME STORIES	*Cactus CTLP 113*	**26**	12 wks
7 Mar 81	40 BIG ONES	*Creole BIG 1*	**51**	2 wks

JUICY LUCY UK, *male vocal/instrumental group*

5 wks

18 Apr 70	JUICY LUCY	*Vertigo VO 2*	**41**	4 wks
21 Nov 70	LIE BACK AND ENJOY IT	*Vertigo 6360 014* ...	**53**	1 wk

JULUKA South Africa, *male/female vocal/instrumental group*

3 wks

23 Jul 83	SCATTERLINGS	*Safari SHAKA 1*	**50**	3 wks

JUNIOR UK, *male vocalist*

14 wks

5 Jun 82	JI	*Mercury/Phonogram MERS 3*	**28**	14 wks

K

Bert KAEMPFERT Germany, *orchestra*

104 wks

5 Mar 66	●	BYE BYE BLUES	*Polydor BM 84086*	**4**	22 wks
16 Apr 66		BEST OF BERT KAEMPFERT	*Polydor 84-012* ..	**27**	1 wk
28 May 66		SWINGING SAFARI	*Polydor LPHM 46-384*	**20**	15 wks
30 Jul 66		STRANGERS IN THE NIGHT *Polydor LPHM 84-053*		**13**	26 wks
4 Feb 67		RELAXING SOUND OF BERT KAEMPFERT *Polydor 583-501*		**33**	3* wks
18 Feb 67		BERT KAEMPFERT - BEST SELLER *Polydor 583-551*		**25**	18 wks
29 Apr 67		HOLD ME	*Polydor 184-072*	**36**	5 wks
26 Aug 67		KAEMPFERT SPECIAL	*Polydor 236-207*	**24**	5 wks
19 Jun 71		ORANGE COLOURED SKY	*Polydor 2310-091*	**49**	1 wk
5 Jul 80		SOUNDS SENSATIONAL	*Polydor POLTB 10* ...	**17**	8 wks

KAJAGOOGOO UK, *male vocal/instrumental group*

23 wks

30 Apr 83	●	WHITE FEATHERS	*EMI EMC 3433*	**5**	20 wks
26 May 84		ISLANDS	*EMI KAJA 1*	**35**	3 wks

KANE GANG UK, *male vocal/instrumental group*

8 wks

23 Feb 85	THE BAD AND LOWDOWN WORLD OF THE KANE GANG	*Kitchenware KWLP 2*	**21**	8 wks

Mick KARN UK, *male vocalist/instrumentalist - bass*

3 wks

20 Nov 82	TITLES	*Virgin V 2249*	**74**	3 wks

KATRINA and the WAVES UK/US, *male/female vocal/instrumental group*

6 wks

8 Jun 85	KATRINA AND THE WAVES	*Capitol KTW 1*	**28**	6 wks

K.C. and The SUNSHINE BAND US, *male vocal/instrumental group*

17 wks

30 Aug 75		K.C. AND THE SUNSHINE BAND	*Jayboy JSL 9*	**26**	7 wks
1 Mar 80	●	GREATEST HITS	*TK TKR 83385*	**10**	6 wks
27 Aug 83		ALL IN A NIGHT'S WORK	*Epic EPC 85847* ..	**46**	4 wks

Howard KEEL US, *male vocalist*

27 wks

14 Apr 84	●	AND I LOVE YOU SO	*Warwick WW 5137*	**6**	19 wks
9 Nov 85		REMINISCING - THE HOWARD KEEL COLLECTION	*Telstar STAR 2259*	**20†**	8 wks

Felicity KENDAL UK, *female exercise instructor*

47 wks

19 Jun 82	SHAPE UP AND DANCE (VOL 1) WITH FELICITY KENDAL	*Lifestyle LEG 1*	**29**	47 wks

KENNY UK, *male vocal/instrumental group*

1 wk

17 Jan 76	THE SOUND OF SUPER K	*RAK SRAK 518* ...	**56**	1 wk

Gerard KENNY US, *male vocalist*

4 wks

21 Jul 79	MADE IT THROUGH THE RAIN	*RCA Victor PL 25218*	**19**	4 wks

Nik KERSHAW UK, *male vocalist*

97 wks

10 Mar 84	●	HUMAN RACING	*MCA MCF 3197*	**5**	61 wks
1 Dec 84	●	THE RIDDLE	*MCA MCF 3245*	**8**	36 wks

Chaka KHAN US, *female vocalist*

22 wks

20 Oct 84	I FEEL FOR YOU	*Warner Bros 925 162*	**15**	22 wks

See also Rufus and Chaka Khan.

Aram KHATCHATURIAN/VIENNA PHILHARMONIC ORCHESTRA Russia, *male conductor* / Austria, *orchestra*

15 wks

22 Jan 72	SPARTACUS	*Decca SXL 6000*	**16**	15 wks

NIK KERSHAW (above) Lists his favourite artists in the human race as Steely Dan, Stevie Wonder, Thompson Twins, Howard Jones, Pinkies, Level 42 and Eurythmics.

KISS (above) Once they took their make-up off they hit the top ten.

KRAFTWERK (top left) They made the charts by both auto and train.

KIDS FROM FAME (below) Not quite so much fame second time round. (LFI)

B. B. KING (left) B. B. King feeling blue because he didn't chart in Britain until 1979.

KIDS FROM FAME US, male/female vocal/instrumental group
117 wks

24 Jul 82	★ KIDS FROM FAME BBC REP 447	**1**	45 wks
16 Oct 82	● KIDS FROM FAME AGAIN RCA RCALP 6057	**2**	21 wks
26 Feb 83	● THE KIDS FROM FAME LIVE BBC KIDLP 003	**8**	28 wks
14 May 83	THE KIDS FROM FAME SONGS BBC KIDLP 004	**14**	16 wks
20 Aug 83	SING FOR YOU BBC KIDLP 005	**28**	7 wks

KILLING JOKE UK, male vocal/instrumental group
28 wks

25 Oct 80	KILLING JOKE Polydor EGMD 545	**39**	4 wks
20 Jun 81	WHAT'S THIS FOR Malicious Damage EG MD 550	**42**	4 wks
8 May 82	REVELATIONS Malicious Damage EGMD 3	**12**	6 wks
27 Nov 82	'HA' - KILLING JOKE LIVE EG EGMDT 4 ...	**66**	2 wks
23 Jul 83	FIRE DANCES EG EGMD 5	**29**	3 wks
9 Mar 85	NIGHT TIME EG EGLP 61	**11**	9 wks

KIMERA with the LONDON SYMPHONY ORCHESTRA Korea, female vocalist with UK Orchestra
4 wks

26 Oct 85	HITS ON OPERA Stylus SMR 8505	**38**	4 wks

KING UK, male vocal/instrumental group
27 wks

9 Feb 85	● STEPS IN TIME CBS 26095	**6**	21 wks
23 Nov 85	BITTER SWEET CBS 86320	**16†**	6 wks

B.B. KING US, male vocalist/instrumentalist - guitar
5 wks

25 Aug 79	TAKE IT HOME MCA MCF 3010	**60**	5 wks

Ben E. KING UK, male vocalist
3 wks

1 Jul 67	SPANISH HARLEM Atlantic 590-001	**30**	3 wks

Carole KING US, female vocalist/instrumentalist - piano
102 wks

24 Jul 71	● TAPESTRY A & M AMLS 2025	**4**	90 wks
15 Jan 72	MUSIC A & M AMLH 67013	**18**	10 wks
2 Dec 72	RHYMES AND REASONS Ode 77016	**40**	2 wks

Evelyn KING US, female vocalist
9 wks

11 Sep 82	GET LOOSE RCA RCALP 3093	**35**	9 wks

Mark KING UK, male vocalist/instrumentalist - bass
2 wks

21 Jul 84	INFLUENCES Polydor MKLP 1	**77**	2 wks

Solomon KING US, male vocalist
1 wk

22 Jun 68	SHE WEARS MY RING Columbia SCX 6250	**40**	1 wk

KING CRIMSON UK, male vocal/instrumental group
53 wks

1 Nov 69	● IN THE COURT OF THE CRIMSON KING Island ILPS 9111	**5**	18 wks
30 May 70	● IN THE WAKE OF POSEIDON Island ILPS 9127	**4**	13 wks
16 Jan 71	LIZARD Island ILPS 9141	**30**	1 wk
8 Jan 72	ISLANDS Island ILPS 9175	**30**	1 wk
7 Apr 73	LARKS' TONGUES IN ASPIC Island ILPS 9230	**20**	4 wks
13 Apr 74	STARLESS AND BIBLE BLACK Island ILPS 9275	**28**	2 wks
26 Oct 74	RED Island ILPS 9308	**45**	1 wk
10 Oct 81	DISCIPLINE EG EGLP 49	**41**	4 wks
26 Jun 82	BEAT EG EGLP 51	**39**	5 wks
31 Mar 84	THREE OF A PERFECT PAIR E.G EGLP 55 ..	**30**	4 wks

KING KURT UK, male vocal/instrumental group
1 wk

10 Dec 83	OOH WALLAH WALLAH Stiff SEEZ 52	**99**	1 wk

The Choir Of KING'S COLLEGE, CAMBRIDGE UK, choir
3 wks

11 Dec 71	THE WORLD OF CHRISTMAS Argo SPAA 104	**38**	3 wks

KINGS OF SWING ORCHESTRA Australia, orchestra
11 wks

29 May 82	SWITCHED ON SWING K-Tel ONE 1166	**28**	11 wks

KINKS UK, male vocal/instrumental group
118 wks

17 Oct 64	● KINKS Pye NPL 18096	**3**	25 wks
13 Mar 65	● KINDA KINKS Pye NPL 18112	**3**	15 wks
4 Dec 65	● KINKS KONTROVERSY Pye NPL 18131	**9**	12 wks
11 Sep 66	● WELL RESPECTED KINKS Marble Arch MAL 612	**5**	31 wks
5 Nov 66	FACE TO FACE Pye NPL 18149	**12**	11 wks
14 Oct 67	SOMETHING ELSE Pye NSPL 18193	**35**	2 wks
2 Dec 67	● SUNNY AFTERNOON Marble Arch MAL 716 ..	**9**	11 wks
23 Oct 71	GOLDEN HOUR OF THE KINKS Golden Hour GH 501	**21**	4 wks
14 Oct 78	20 GOLDEN GREATS Ronco RPL 2031	**19**	6 wks
5 Nov 83	KINKS GREATEST HITS - DEAD END STREET PRT KINK 1	**96**	1 wk

Kathy KIRBY UK, female vocalist
8 wks

4 Jan 64	16 HITS FROM STARS AND GARTERS Decca LK 4575	**11**	8 wks

KISS US, male vocal/instrumental group
44 wks

29 May 76	DESTROYER Casablanca CBSP 4008	**22**	5 wks
25 Jun 76	ALIVE! Casablanca CBSP 401	**49**	2 wks
17 Dec 77	ALIVE Casablanca CALD 5004	**60**	1 wk
7 Jul 79	DYNASTY Casablanca CALH 2051	**50**	6 wks
28 Jun 80	UNMASKED Mercury 6302 032	**48**	3 wks
5 Dec 81	THE ELDER Casablanca 6302 163	**51**	3 wks
26 Jun 82	KILLERS Casablanca CANL 1	**42**	6 wks
6 Nov 82	CREATURES OF THE NIGHT Casablanca CANL 4	**22**	4 wks
8 Oct 83	● LICK IT UP Vertigo VERL 9	**7**	7 wks
6 Oct 84	ANIMALISE Vertigo VERL 18	**11**	4 wks
5 Oct 85	ASYLUM Vertigo VERH 32	**12**	3 wks

KISSING THE PINK UK, male/female vocal/instrumental group — 5 wks

4 Jun 83	**NAKED** *Magnet KTPL 1001*	**54**	5 wks

Eartha KITT US, female vocalist — 1 wk

11 Feb 61	**REVISITED** *London HA 2296*	**17**	1 wk

KLEEER US, male vocal/instrumental group — 1 wk

6 Jul 85	**SEEEKRET** *Atlantic 78-1254-1*	**96**	1 wk

KNACK US, male vocal/instrumental group — 2 wks

4 Aug 79	**GET THE KNACK** *Capitol EST 11948*	**65**	2 wks

Gladys KNIGHT and the PIPS US, female vocalist/male vocal backing group — 94 wks

31 May 75	**I FEEL A SONG** *Buddah BDLP 4030*	**20**	15 wks
28 Feb 76	● **THE BEST OF GLADYS KNIGHT & THE PIPS** *Buddah BDLH 5013*	**6**	43 wks
16 Jul 77	**STILL TOGETHER** *Buddah BDLH 5014*	**42**	3 wks
12 Nov 77	● **30 GREATEST** *K-Tel NE 1004*	**3**	22 wks
4 Oct 80	**A TOUCH OF LOVE** *K-Tel NE 1090*	**16**	6 wks
4 Feb 84	**THE COLLECTION - 20 GREATEST HITS** *Starblend NITE 1*	**43**	5 wks

KNIGHTSBRIDGE STRINGS UK, male orchestra — 1 wk

25 Jun 60	**STRING SWAY** *Top Rank BUY 017*	**20**	1 wk

David KNOPFLER UK, male vocalist/instrumentalist - guitar — 1 wk

19 Nov 83	**RELEASE** *Peach River DAVID 1*	**82**	1 wk

Mark KNOPFLER UK, male vocalist/instrumentalist - guitar — 14 wks

16 Apr 83	**LOCAL HERO** *Vertigo VERL 4*	**14**	11 wks
20 Oct 84	**CAL - MUSIC FROM THE FILM** *Vertigo VERH 17*	**65**	3 wks

John KONGOS South Africa, male vocalist/multi-instrumentalist — 2 wks

15 Jan 72	**KONGOS** *Fly HIFLY 7*	**29**	2 wks

KOOL AND THE GANG US, male vocal/instrumental group — 101 wks

21 Nov 81	● **SOMETHING SPECIAL** *De-Lite DSR 001*	**10**	20 wks
2 Oct 82	**AS ONE** *De-Lite/Phonogram DSR 3*	**49**	10 wks
7 May 83	● **TWICE AS KOOL** *De-Lite PROLP 2*	**4**	23 wks
14 Jan 84	**IN THE HEART** *De-Lite DSR 4*	**18**	23 wks
15 Dec 84	**EMERGENCY** *De-Lite DSR 6*	**47**	25 wks

KORGIS UK, male vocal/instrumental duo — 4 wks

26 Jul 80	**DUMB WAITERS** *Rialto TENOR 104*	**40**	4 wks

KRAFTWERK Germany, male vocal/instrumental group — 63 wks

17 May 75	● **AUTOBAHN** *Vertigo 6360 620*	**4**	18 wks
20 May 78	● **THE MAN-MACHINE** *Capitol EST 11728*	**9**	13 wks
23 May 81	**COMPUTER WORLD** *EMI EMC 3370*	**15**	22 wks
6 Feb 82	**TRANS-EUROPE EXPRESS** *Capitol EST 11603*	**56**	7 wks
22 Jun 85	**AUTOBAHN** (re-issue) *Parlophone AUTO 1*	**61**	3 wks

Billy J. KRAMER and The DAKOTAS UK, male vocalist/male instrumental backing group — 17 wks

16 Nov 63	**LISTEN TO BILLY J. KRAMER** *Parlophone PMC 1209*	**11**	17 wks

Kris KRISTOFFERSON and Rita COOLIDGE US, male/female vocal duo — 4 wks

6 May 78	**NATURAL ACT** *A & M AMLH 64690*	**35**	4 wks

See also Rita Coolidge.

KROKUS Switzerland/Malta, male vocal/instrumental group — 11 wks

21 Feb 81	**HARDWARE** *Ariola ARL 5064*	**44**	4 wks
20 Feb 82	**ONE VICE AT A TIME** *Arista SPART 1189* ...	**28**	5 wks
16 Apr 83	**HEADHUNTER** *Arista 205 255*	**74**	2 wks

Charlie KUNZ US, male instrumentalist - piano — 11 wks

14 Jun 69	● **THE WORLD OF CHARLIE KUNZ** *Decca SPA 15*	**9**	11 wks

L

Cleo LAINE UK, female vocalist — 1 wk

2 Dec 78	**CLEO** *Arcade ADEP 37*	**68**	1 wk

See also Cleo Laine and John Williams; Cleo Laine and James Galway.

Cleo LAINE and James GALWAY UK, female vocalist and Ireland, male instrumentalist - flute — 14 wks

31 May 80	**SOMETIMES WHEN WE TOUCH** *RCA PL 25296*	**15**	14 wks

See also Cleo Laine; Cleo Laine and John Williams; James Galway; James Galway and Henry Mancini.

Cleo LAINE and John WILLIAMS UK, female vocalist/male instrumentalist - guitar — 22 wks

7 Jan 78	**BEST OF FRIENDS** *RCA RS 1094*	**18**	22 wks

See also Cleo Laine; Cleo Laine and James Galway; John Williams; John Williams and the English Chamber Orchestar.

LED ZEPPELIN (above) Eight consecutive number ones. (Retna Pictures Ltd)

FRANKIE LAINE (above right) A stroll down memory lane in 1977.

JAMES LAST (right) More hit albums than anyone except Elvis.

Frankie LAINE US, male vocalist — 29 wks

Date	Title	Label	Pos	Wks
24 Jun 61	● HELL BENT FOR LEATHER *Philips BBL 7468*		7	23 wks
24 Sep 77	● THE VERY BEST OF FRANKIE LAINE *Warwick PR 5032*		7	6 wks

Greg LAKE UK, male vocalist — 3 wks

Date	Title	Label	Pos	Wks
17 Oct 81	GREG LAKE *Chrysalis CHR 1357*		62	3 wks

See also Emerson, Lake and Palmer.

Annabel LAMB UK, female vocalist — 1 wk

Date	Title	Label	Pos	Wks
28 Apr 84	THE FLAME *A & M AMLX 68564*		84	1 wk

LAMBRETTAS UK, male vocal/instrumental group — 8 wks

Date	Title	Label	Pos	Wks
5 Jul 80	BEAT BOYS IN THE JET AGE *Rocket TRAIN 10*		28	8 wks

LANDSCAPE UK, male vocal/instrumental group — 12 wks

Date	Title	Label	Pos	Wks
21 Mar 81	FROM THE TEAROOMS *RCA RCALP 5003*		16	12 wks

Ronnie LANE and the band SLIM CHANCE
UK, male vocal/instrumental group — 1 wk

Date	Title	Label	Pos	Wks
17 Aug 74	ANYMORE FOR ANYMORE *GM GML 1013*		48	1 wk

See also Pete Townshend and Ronnie Lane.

Mario LANZA US, male vocalist — 48 wks

Date	Title	Label	Pos	Wks
6 Dec 58	● THE STUDENT PRINCE/THE GREAT CARUSO *RCA RB 16113*		4	21 wks
23 Jul 60	● THE GREAT CARUSO *RCA RB 16112*		3	15 wks
9 Jan 71	HIS GREATEST HITS VOL.1 *RCA LSB 4000*		39	1 wk
5 Sep 81	THE LEGEND OF MARIO LANZA *K-Tel NE 1110*		29	11 wks

The Great Caruso side of the first album is a film soundtrack.

James LAST Germany, male orchestra leader — 334 wks

Date	Title	Label	Pos	Wks
15 Apr 67	● THIS IS JAMES LAST *Polydor 104-678*		6	48 wks
22 Jul 67	HAMMOND A-GO-GO *Polydor 249-043*		27	10 wks
26 Aug 67	NON-STOP DANCING *Polydor 236-203*		35	1 wk
26 Aug 67	LOVE THIS IS MY SONG *Polydor 583-553*		32	2 wks
22 Jun 68	JAMES LAST GOES POP *Polydor 249-160*		32	3 wks
8 Feb 69	DANCING '68 VOL. 1 *Polydor 249-216*		40	1 wk
31 May 69	TRUMPET A-GO-GO *Polydor 249-239*		13	1 wk
9 Aug 69	NON-STOP DANCING '69 *Polydor 249-294*		26	1 wk
24 Jan 70	NON-STOP DANCING '69/2 *Polydor 249-354*		27	3 wks
23 May 70	NON-STOP DANCING EVERGREENS *Polydor 249-370*		26	1 wk
11 Jul 70	CLASSICS UP TO DATE *Polydor 249-371*		44	1 wk
11 Jul 70	NON-STOP DANCING '70 *Polydor 2371-04*		67	1 wk
24 Oct 70	VERY BEST OF JAMES LAST *Polydor 2371-054*		45	4 wks
8 May 71	NON-STOP DANCING '71 *Polydor 2371-111*		21	4 wks
26 Jun 71	SUMMER HAPPENING *Polydor 2371-133*		38	1 wk
18 Sep 71	BEACH PARTY 2 *Polydor 2371-211*		47	1 wk
2 Oct 71	YESTERDAY'S MEMORIES *Contour 2870-117*		17	14 wks
16 Oct 71	NON-STOP DANCING 12 *Polydor 2371-141*		30	3 wks
5 Feb 72	NON-STOP DANCING 13 *Polydor 2371-189*		32	2 wks
4 Mar 72	POLKA PARTY *Polydor 2371-190*		22	3 wks
29 Apr 72	JAMES LAST IN CONCERT *Polydor 2371-191*		13	6 wks
24 Jun 72	VOODOO PARTY *Polydor 2371-235*		45	1 wk
16 Sep 72	CLASSICS UP TO DATE VOL.2 *Polydor 184-061*		49	1 wk
30 Sep 72	LOVE MUST BE THE REASON *Polydor 2371-281*		32	2 wks
27 Jan 73	THE MUSIC OF JAMES LAST *Polydor 2683 010*		19	12 wks
24 Feb 73	JAMES LAST IN RUSSIA *Polydor 2371 293*		12	9 wks
24 Feb 73	NON-STOP DANCING VOL. 14 *Polydor 2371-319*		27	3 wks
28 Jul 73	OLE *Polydor 2371 384*		24	5 wks
1 Sep 73	NON-STOP DANCING VOL. 15 *Polydor 2371-376*		34	2 wks
20 Apr 74	NON-STOP DANCING VOL. 16 *Polydor 2371-444*		43	2 wks
29 Jun 74	IN CONCERT VOL. 2 *Polydor 2371-320*		49	1 wk
23 Nov 74	GOLDEN MEMORIES *Polydor 2371-472*		39	2 wks
26 Jul 75	● TEN YEARS NON-STOP JUBILEE *Polydor 2660-111*		5	16 wks
2 Aug 75	VIOLINS IN LOVE *K-tel*		60	1 wk
22 Nov 75	● MAKE THE PARTY LAST *Polydor 2371-612*		3	19 wks
8 May 76	CLASSICS UP TO DATE VOL.3 *2371-538*		54	1 wk
6 May 78	EAST TO WEST *Polydor 2630-092*		49	4 wks
14 Apr 79	● LAST THE WHOLE NIGHT LONG *Polydor PTD 5008*		2	45 wks
23 Aug 80	THE BEST FROM 150 GOLD *Polydor 2681 211*		56	3 wks
1 Nov 80	CLASSICS FOR DREAMING *Polydor POLTV 11*		12	18 wks
14 Feb 81	ROSES FROM THE SOUTH *Polydor 2372 051*		41	5 wks
21 Nov 81	HANSIMANIA *Polydor POLTV 14*		18	13 wks
28 Nov 81	LAST FOREVER *Polydor 2630 135*		88	2 wks
5 Mar 83	BLUEBIRD *Polydor POLD 5072*		57	3 wks
30 Apr 83	THE BEST OF MY GOLD RECORDS *Polydor PODV 7*		42	5 wks
30 Apr 83	NON-STOP DANCING '83 - PARTY POWER *Polydor POLD 5094*		56	2 wks
3 Dec 83	THE GREATEST SONGS OF THE BEATLES *Polydor POLD 5119*		52	8 wks
13 Oct 84	PARADISE *Polydor POLD 5163*		74	2 wks
8 Dec 84	JAMES LAST IN SCOTLAND *Polydor POLD 5166*		68	9 wks
24 Mar 84	THE ROSE OF TRALEE AND OTHER IRISH FAVOURITES *Polydor POLD 5131*		21	11 wks
14 Sep 85	LEAVE THE BEST TO LAST *Polydor PROLP 7*		11†	16 wks

Cyndi LAUPER US, female vocalist — 31 wks

Date	Title	Label	Pos	Wks
18 Feb 84	SHE'S SO UNUSUAL *Portrait PRT 25792*		16	31 wks

LAUREL and HARDY US, male comic duo — 4 wks

Date	Title	Label	Pos	Wks
6 Dec 75	THE GOLDEN AGE OF HOLLYWOOD COMEDY *United Artists UAG 29676*		55	4 wks

Syd LAWRENCE UK, orchestra — 9 wks

Date	Title	Label	Pos	Wks
8 Aug 70	MORE MILLER AND OTHER BIG BAND MAGIC *Philips 6642 001*		14	4 wks
25 Dec 71	SYD LAWRENCE WITH THE GLENN MILLER SOUND *Fontana SFL 13178*		31	2 wks
25 Dec 71	MUSIC OF GLENN MILLER IN SUPER STEREO *Philips 6641-017*		43	2 wks
26 Feb 72	SOMETHING OLD, SOMETHING NEW *Philips 6308 090*		34	1 wk

Ronnie LAWS US, male vocalist/instrumentalist - saxophone — 1 wk

Date	Title	Label	Pos	Wks
17 Oct 81	SOLID GROUND *Liberty/EMI LBG 30336*		100	1 wk

LEAGUE UNLIMITED ORCHESTRA UK, male instrumental group — 52 wks

Date	Title	Label	Pos	Wks
17 Jul 82	● LOVE AND DANCING *Virgin OVED 6*		3	52 wks

This album is an instrumental version of previously recorded Human League songs re-mixed by UK producer Martin Rushent.

JOHN LENNON (above) At the statue of Liberty, 1974. (Bob Green)

JULIAN LENNON (right) Made the Top Twenty with his first attempt.

GORDON LIGHTFOOT Canada's Bob Dylan first tilted his lance at the chart in 1972. 'Dusk' fell in 1974.

LED ZEPPELIN UK, male vocal/instrumental group

411 wks

12 Apr 69 ●	LED ZEPPELIN Atlantic 588-171		6	79 wks
8 Nov 69 ★	LED ZEPPELIN 2 Atlantic 588-198		1	138 wks
7 Nov 70 ★	LED ZEPPELIN 3 Atlantic 2401-002		1	40 wks
27 Nov 71 ★	FOUR SYMBOLS Atlantic 2401-012		1	62 wks
14 Apr 73 ★	HOUSES OF THE HOLY Atlantic K 50014		1	13 wks
15 Mar 75 ★	PHYSICAL GRAFFITI Swan Song SSK 89400		1	27 wks
24 Apr 76 ★	PRESENCE Swan Song SSK 59402		1	14 wks
6 Nov 76 ★	THE SONG REMAINS THE SAME Swan Song SSK 89402		1	15 wks
8 Sep 79 ★	IN THROUGH THE OUT DOOR Swan Song SSK 59410		1	16 wks
4 Dec 82 ●	CODA Swansong A 0051		4	7 wks

Led Zeppelin 2 changed label/number to Atlantic K 40037, Four Symbols changed to Atlantic K 50008 during their runs. The fourth Led Zeppelin album appeared in the chart under various guises; The Fourth Led Zeppelin Album, Runes, The New Led Zeppelin Album, Led Zeppelin 4 and Four Symbols.

LEE - See PETERS and LEE

Brenda LEE US, female vocalist

57 wks

24 Nov 62	ALL THE WAY Brunswick LAT 8383		20	2 wks
16 Feb 63	BRENDA - THAT'S ALL Brunswick LAT 8516		13	9 wks
13 Apr 63 ●	ALL ALONE AM I Brunswick LAT 8530		8	20 wks
16 Jul 66	BYE BYE BLUES Brunswick LAT 8649		21	2 wks
1 Nov 80	LITTLE MISS DYNAMITE Warwick WW 5083		15	11 wks
7 Jan 84	25TH ANNIVERSARY MCA MALD 609		65	4 wks
30 Mar 85	THE VERY BEST OF BRENDA LEE MCA LETV 1		16	9 wks

Peggy LEE US, female vocalist

17 wks

4 Jun 60 ●	LATIN A LA LEE Capitol T 1290		8	15 wks
20 May 61	BEST OF PEGGY LEE VOL. 2 Brunswick LAT 8355		18	1 wk
21 Oct 61	BLACK COFFEE Ace of Hearts AH 5		20	1 wk

See also Peggy Lee and George Shearing.

Peggy LEE and George SHEARING US, female vocalist and UK and male instrumentalist - piano

6 wks

11 Jun 60	BEAUTY AND THE BEAT Capitol T 1219		16	6 wks

See also Peggy Lee, and Nat 'King' Cole and the George Shearing Quintet.

Raymond LEFEVRE France, orchestra

9 wks

7 Oct 67 ●	RAYMOND LEFEVRE Major Minor MMLP 4		10	7 wks
17 Feb 68	RAYMOND LEFEVRE VOL.2 Major Minor SMLP 13		37	2 wks

Tom LEHRER US, male comic vocalist

26 wks

8 Nov 58 ●	SONGS BY TOM LEHRER Decca LF 1311		7	19 wks
25 Jun 60 ●	AN EVENING WASTED WITH TOM LEHRER Decca LK 4332		7	7 wks

John LENNON UK, male vocalist

288 wks

16 Jan 71	JOHN LENNON AND THE PLASTIC ONO BAND Apple PCS 7124		11	11 wks
30 Oct 71 ★	IMAGINE Apple PAS 10004		1	101 wks
14 Oct 72	SOMETIME IN NEW YORK CITY Apple PCSP 716		11	6 wks
8 Dec 73	MIND GAMES Apple PCS 7165		13	12 wks
19 Oct 74 ●	WALLS AND BRIDGES Apple PCTC 253		6	10 wks
8 Mar 75 ●	ROCK 'N' ROLL Apple PCS 7169		6	28 wks
8 Nov 75 ●	SHAVED FISH Apple PCS 7173		8	29 wks
22 Nov 80 ★	DOUBLE FANTASY Geffen K 99131		1	36 wks
20 Nov 82 ★	THE JOHN LENNON COLLECTION Parlophone EMTV 37		1	42 wks
4 Feb 84 ●	MILK AND HONEY Polydor POLH 5		3	13 wks

Imagine changed its label credit to Parlophone PAS 10004 between its initial chart run and later runs. John Lennon and the Plastic Ono Band is credited to John Lennon and the Plastic Ono Band. Imagine is credited to John Lennon and the Plastic Ono Band with the Flux Fiddlers. Sometime In New York City is credited to John and Yoko Lennon with the Plastic Ono Band and Elephant's Memory. Double Fantasy and Milk And Honey are credited to John Lennon and Yoko Ono. Shaved Fish and The John Lennon Collection are compilations and so have various credits. See also Yoko Ono.

Julian LENNON UK, male vocalist

15 wks

3 Nov 84	VALOTTE Charisma JLLP 1		20	15 wks

Deke LEONARD UK, male vocalist/instrumentalist - guitar

1 wk

13 Apr 74	KAMIKAZE United Artists UAG 29544		50	1 wk

Paul LEONI UK, male instrumentalist - pan flute

18 wks

24 Sep 83	FLIGHTS OF FANCY Nouveau Music NML 1002		17	18 wks

LEVEL 42 UK, male vocal/instrumental group

76 wks

29 Aug 81	LEVEL 42 Polydor POLS 1036		20	18 wks
10 Apr 82	THE EARLY TAPES JULY-AUGUST 1980 Polydor POLS 1064		46	6 wks
18 Sep 82	THE PURSUIT OF ACCIDENTS Polydor POLD 5067		17	16 wks
3 Sep 83 ●	STANDING IN THE LIGHT Polydor POLD 5110		9	13 wks
13 Oct 84	TRUE COLOURS Polydor POLH 10		14	8 wks
6 Jul 85	A PHYSICAL PRESENCE Polydor POLH 23		28	5 wks
26 Oct 85 ●	WORLD MACHINE Polydor POLH 25		10†	10 wks

Huey LEWIS and the NEWS US, male vocal/instrumental group

8 wks

14 Sep 85	SPORTS Chrysalis CHR 1412		23	8 wks

Jerry Lee LEWIS US, male vocalist/instrumentalist - piano

6 wks

2 Jun 62	JERRY LEE LEWIS VOL.2 London HA 2440		14	6 wks

Linda LEWIS UK, female vocalist

4 wks

9 Aug 75	NOT A LITTLE GIRL ANYMORE Arista ARTY 109		40	4 wks

Ramsey LEWIS TRIO US, male vocal instrumental trio

4 wks

21 May 66	HANG ON RAMSEY Chess CRL 4520		20	4 wks

LIGHT OF THE WORLD UK, male vocal/instrumental group

1 wk

24 Jan 81	ROUND TRIP Ensign ENVY 14		73	1 wk

Gordon LIGHTFOOT *Canada, male vocalist*   *2 wks*

20 May 72	**DON QUIXOTE**	*Reprise K 44166*	**44**	1 wk
17 Aug 74	**SUNDOWN**	*Reprise K 54020*	**45**	1 wk

LIMAHL *UK, male vocalist*   *3 wks*

1 Dec 84	**DON'T SUPPOSE**	*EMI PLML 1*	**63**	3 wks

LINDISFARNE *UK, male vocal/instrumental group*   *119 wks*

30 Oct 71	★ **FOG ON THE TYNE**	*Charisma CAS 1050*	**1**	56 wks
15 Jan 72	● **NICELY OUT OF TUNE**	*Charisma CAS 1025* ...	**8**	30 wks
30 Sep 72	● **DINGLY DELL**	*Charisma CAS 1057* ...	**5**	10 wks
11 Aug 73	**LINDISFARNE LIVE**	*Charisma CLASS 2*	**25**	6 wks
18 Oct 75	**FINEST HOUR**	*Charisma CAS 1108*	**55**	1 wk
24 Jun 78	**BACK AND FOURTH**	*Mercury 9109 609*	**22**	11 wks
9 Dec 78	**MAGIC IN THE AIR**	*Mercury 6641 877*	**71**	1 wk
23 Oct 82	**SLEEPLESS NIGHT**	*LMP GET 1*	**59**	4 wks

LINX *UK, male vocal/instrumental group*   *23 wks*

28 Mar 81	● **INTUITION**	*Chrysalis CHR 1332*	**8**	19 wks
31 Oct 81	**GO AHEAD**	*Chrysalis CHR 1358*	**35**	4 wks

LIQUID GOLD *UK, male/female vocal instrumental group*   *3 wks*

16 Aug 80	**LIQUID GOLD**	*Polo POLP 101*	**34**	3 wks

LISA LISA and CULT JAM with FULL FORCE *US female vocalist with two US male vocal/instrumental groups*   *1 wk*

21 Sep 85	**LISA LISA AND CULT JAM WITH FULL FORCE** *CBS 26593*	**96**	1 wk

LITTLE FEAT *US, male vocal/instrumental group*   *19 wks*

6 Dec 75	**THE LAST RECORD ALBUM** *Warner Bros. K 56156*	**36**	3 wks
21 May 77	● **TIME LOVES A HERO** *Warner Bros. K 56349* ...	**8**	11 wks
11 Mar 78	**WAITING FOR COLUMBUS** *Warner Bros. K 66075*	**43**	1 wk
1 Dec 79	**DOWN ON THE FARM** *Warner Bros. K 56667* ..	**46**	3 wks
8 Aug 81	**HOY HOY** *Warner Bros. K 666100*	**76**	1 wk

Andrew LLOYD WEBBER *UK, male composer/producer*   *37 wks*

11 Feb 78	● **VARIATIONS**	*MCA MCF 2824*	**2**	19 wks
23 Mar 85	● **REQUIEM**	*HMV ALW 1*	**4**	18 wks

Variations features cellist Julian Lloyd Webber. Requiem credits Placido Domingo, Sarah Brightman, Paul Miles-Kingston, Winchester Cathedral Choir and the English Chamber Orchestra conducted by Lorin Maazel.

Julian LLOYD WEBBER and the LONDON SYMPHONY ORCHESTRA *UK, male instrumentalist - cello with UK orchestra*   *5 wks*

14 Sep 85	**PIECES**	*Polydor PROLP 6*	**59**	5 wks

See also the London Symphony Orchestra

Los LOBOS *US, male vocal/instrumental group*   *6 wks*

6 Apr 85	**HOW WILL THE WOLF SURVIVE?** *Slash SLMP 3*	**77**	6 wks

Josef LOCKE *Ireland, male vocalist*   *1 wk*

28 Jun 69	**THE WORLD OF JOSEF LOCKE TODAY** *Decca SPA 21*	**29**	1 wk

John LODGE *UK, male vocalist/instrumentalist - guitar*   *2 wks*

19 Feb 77	**NATURAL AVENUE**	*Decca TXS 120*	**38**	2 wks

See also Justin Hayward and John Lodge.

Nils LOFGREN *US, male vocalist/instrumentalsit - guitar*   *28 wks*

17 Apr 76	● **CRY TOUGH**	*A & M AMLH 64573*	**8**	11 wks
26 Mar 77	**I CAME TO DANCE**	*A & M AMLH 64628*	**30**	4 wks
5 Nov 77	**NIGHT AFTER NIGHT**	*A & M AMLH AMLM*	**38**	2 wks
26 Sep 81	**NIGHT FADES AWAY**	*Backstreet MCF 3121* ...	**50**	3 wks
1 May 82	**A RHYTHM ROMANCE**	*A&M AMLH 68543* ..	**100**	1 wk
6 Jul 85	**FLIP**	*Towerbell TOWLP 11*	**36**	7 wks

LONDON PHILHARMONIC CHOIR *UK, choir*   *17 wks*

3 Dec 60	● **THE MESSIAH**	*Pye Golden Guinea GGL 0062* ...	**10**	7 wks
13 Nov 76	● **SOUND OF GLORY**	*Arcade ADEP 25*	**10**	10 wks

The Messiah credits the London Orchestra conducted by Walter Susskind. Sound Of Glory credits the National Philharmonic Orchestra and conductor John Aldiss.

LONDON PHILHARMONIC ORCHESTRA *UK, orchestra*   *5 wks*

23 Apr 60	**RAVEL'S BOLERO**	*London HAV 2189*	**15**	4 wks
8 Apr 61	**VICTORY AT SEA**	*PYE GGL 0073*	**12**	1 wk

LONDON SYMPHONY ORCHESTRA *UK, orchestra*   *122 wks*

18 Mar 72	**TOP TV THEMES**	*Studio Two STWO 372*	**13**	7 wks
5 Jul 75	**MUSIC FROM 'EDWARD VII'**	*Polydor 2659 041*	**52**	1 wk
21 Jan 78	**STAR WARS (soundtrack)**	*20th Century BTD 541*	**21**	12 wks
8 Jul 78	● **CLASSIC ROCK**	*K-Tel ONE 1009*	**3**	39 wks
10 Feb 79	**CLASSIC ROCK - THE SECOND MOVEMENT** *K-Tel NE 1039*	**26**	8 wks
5 Jan 80	**RHAPSODY IN BLACK**	*K-Tel ONE 1063*	**34**	5 wks
1 Aug 81	● **CLASSIC ROCK-ROCK CLASSICS** *K-Tel ONE 1123*	**5**	23 wks
27 Nov 82	**THE BEST OF CLASSIC ROCK** *K-Tel ONE 1080*	**35**	11 wks
27 Aug 83	**ROCK SYMPHONIES**	*K-Tel ONE 1234*	**40**	9 wks

16 Nov 85	**THE POWER OF CLASSIC ROCK** Portrait PRT 10049	13†	7 wks

Last three albums credit the Royal Choral Society and Roger Smith Chorale

LONDON WELSH MALE VOICE CHOIR
UK, male choir — 10 wks

5 Sep 81	**SONGS OF THE VALLEYS** K-Tel NE 1117	61	10 wks

LONE JUSTICE US, male/female vocal/instrumental group — 2 wks

6 Jul 85	**LONE JUSTICE** Geffen GEF 26288	49	2 wks

LONE STAR UK, male vocal/instrumental group — 7 wks

2 Oct 76	**LONE STAR** Epic EPC 81545	47	1 wk
17 Sep 77	**FIRING ON ALL SIX** CBS 82213	36	6 wks

LONG RYDERS US, male vocal/instrumental group — 1 wk

16 Nov 85	**STATE OF OUR UNION** Island ILPS 9802	66	1 wk

LOOSE ENDS UK, male/female vocal/instrumental group — 22 wks

21 Apr 84	**A LITTLE SPICE** Virgin V 2381	46	9 wks
20 Apr 85	**SO WHERE ARE YOU?** Virgin V 2340	13	13 wks

Trini LOPEZ US, male vocalist — 42 wks

26 Oct 63	● **TRINI LOPEZ AT P.J.'S** Reprise R 6093	7	25 wks
25 Mar 67	● **TRINI LOPEZ IN LONDON** Reprise RSLP 6238	6	17 wks

Jeff LORBER US, male vocalist/instrumentalist - keyboards — 2 wks

18 May 85	**STEP BY STEP** Club JABH 9	97	2 wks

Sophia LOREN - See Peter SELLERS and Sophia LOREN

Joe LOSS UK, orchestra — 10 wks

30 Oct 71	**ALL-TIME PARTY HITS** MFP 5227	24	10 wks

See also the George Mitchell Minstrels.

LOTUS EATERS UK, male vocal/instrumental group — 1 wk

16 Jun 84	**NO SENSE OF SIN** Sylvan/Arista 206 263	96	1 wk

Jacques LOUSSIER French, male instrumentalist - piano — 3 wks

30 Mar 85	**THE BEST OF PLAY BACH** Start STL 1	58	3 wks

LOVE US, male vocal/instrumental group — 8 wks

24 Feb 68	**FOREVER CHANGES** Elektra EKS7 4013	24	6 wks
16 May 70	**OUT HERE** Harvest Show 3/4	29	2 wks

Geoff LOVE UK, orchestra — 28 wks

7 Aug 71	**BIG WAR MOVIE THEMES** MFP 5171	11	20 wks
21 Aug 71	**BIG WESTERN MOVIE THEMES** MFP 5204	38	3 wks
30 Oct 71	**BIG LOVE MOVIE THEMES** MFP 5171	28	5 wks

Lene LOVICH US, female vocalist — 17 wks

17 Mar 79	**STATELESS** Stiff SEEZ 7	35	11 wks
2 Feb 80	**FLEX** Stiff SEEZ 19	19	6 wks

LOVIN' SPOONFUL US/Canada, male vocal/instrumental group — 11 wks

7 May 66	● **DAYDREAM** Pye NPL 28078	8	11 wks

Nick LOWE UK, male vocalist — 17 wks

11 Mar 78	**THE JESUS OF COOL** Radar RAD 1	22	9 wks
23 Jun 79	**LABOUR OF LUST** Radar RAD 21	43	6 wks
20 Feb 82	**NICK THE KNIFE** F.Beat XXLP 14	99	2 wks

LULU UK, female vocalist — 6 wks

25 Sep 71	**THE MOST OF LULU** MFP 5215	15	6 wks

Bob LUMAN US, male vocalist — 1 wk

14 Jan 61	**LET'S THINK ABOUT LIVING** Warner Bros. WM 4025	18	1 wk

LURKERS UK, male vocal/instrumental group — 1 wk

1 Jul 78	**FULHAM FALLOUT** Beggars Banquet BEGA 2	57	1 wk

LYLE - See GALLAGHER and LYLE

Vera LYNN UK, female vocalist — 12 wks

21 Nov 81	**20 FAMILY FAVOURITES** EMI EMTV 28	25	12 wks

Philip LYNOTT Ireland, male vocalist — 6 wks

26 Apr 80	**SOLO IN SOHO** Vertigo 9102 038	28	6 wks

LYNYRD SKYNYRD US, male vocal/instrumental group — 19 wks

3 May 75	**NUTHIN' FANCY** MCA MCF 2700	43	1 wk
28 Feb 76	**GIMME BACK MY BULLETS** MCA MCF 2744	34	5 wks
6 Nov 76	**ONE MORE FOR THE ROAD** MCA MCPS 279	17	4 wks
12 Nov 77	**STREET SURVIVORS** MCA MCG 3525	13	4 wks
4 Nov 78	**SKYNYRD'S FIRST AND LAST** MCA MCG 3529	50	1 wk
9 Feb 80	**GOLD AND PLATINUM** MCA MCSP 308	49	4 wks

VERA LYNN Visiting the troops in 1944.

TRINI LOPEZ The Dallas-born singer's first hit in Britain came from a night club in Hollywood so it's little wonder he soon appeared in a movie (*The Dirty Dozen.*)

MADONNA (above) Her first album entered the chart in February 1984 but only made the Top Ten in August 1985. (Duncan Raban)

NILS LOFGREN (left) Before joining Bruce Springsteen's E. Street Band, Nils Lofgren's chart placings declined with every release. Since Bruce's tour things have improved.

M

Frankie McBRIDE *Ireland, male vocalist* *3 wks*

17 Feb 68	FRANKIE McBRIDE	*Emerald SLD 28*	**29**	3 wks

Paul McCARTNEY *UK, male vocalist* *454 wks*

2 May 70	● McCARTNEY *Apple PCS 7102*	**2**	32 wks
5 Jun 71	★ RAM *Apple PAS 10003*	**1**	24 wks
18 Dec 71	WINGS WILDLIFE *Apple PCS 7142*	**11**	9 wks
19 May 73	● RED ROSE SPEEDWAY *Apple PCTC 251*	**5**	16 wks
15 Dec 73	★ BAND ON THE RUN *Apple PAS 10007*	**1**	124 wks
21 Jun 75	★ VENUS AND MARS *Apple PCTC 254*	**1**	29 wks
17 Apr 76	● WINGS AT THE SPEED OF SOUND		
	Apple PAS 10010	**2**	35 wks
15 Jan 77	● WINGS OVER AMERICA *Parlophone PAS 720* ..	**8**	22 wks
15 Apr 78	● LONDON TOWN *Parlophone PAS 10012* ...	**4**	23 wks
16 Dec 78	WINGS GREATEST HITS *Parlophone PCTC 256*	**5**	32 wks
23 Jun 79	● BACK TO THE EGG *Parlophone PCTC 257*	**6**	15 wks
31 May 80	★ McCARTNEY II *Parlophone PCTC 258* ...	**1**	18 wks
7 Mar 81	McCARTNEY INTERVIEW *EMI CHAT 1*	**34**	4 wks
8 May 82	★ TUG OF WAR *Parlophone PCTC 259*	**1**	27 wks
12 Nov 83	● PIPES OF PEACE *Parlophone PCTC 1652301*	**4**	23 wks
3 Nov 84	★ GIVE MY REGARDS TO BROAD STREET -		
	ORIGINAL SOUNDTRACK		
	Parlophone PCTC 2	**1**	21 wks

Ram credited to Paul and Linda McCartney. Red Rose Speedway and Band On The Run credited to Paul McCartney and Wings. Wings Wildlife and the five albums from Venus and Mars to Wings Greatest Hits inclusive credited to Wings. All other albums credited to Paul McCartney.

Van McCOY and The SOUL CITY SYMPHONY *US, orchestra* *11 wks*

5 Jul 75	DISCO BABY *Avco 9109 004*	**32**	11 wks

George McCRAE *US, male vocalist* *29 wks*

3 Aug 74	ROCK YOUR BABY *Jayboy JSL 3*	**13**	28 wks
13 Sep 75	GEORGE McCRAE *Jayboy JSL 10*	**54**	1 wk

Kate and Anna McGARRIGLE *Canada, female vocal duo* *4 wks*

26 Feb 77	DANCER WITH BRUISED KNEES		
	Warner Bros. K 56356	**35**	4 wks

Mary MacGREGOR *US, female vocalist* *1 wk*

23 Apr 77	TORN BETWEEN TWO LOVERS		
	Ariola America AAS 1504	**59**	1 wk

McGUINNESS FLINT *UK, male vocal/instrumental group* *10 wks*

23 Jan 71	● McGUINNESS FLINT *Capitol EA-ST 22625*	**9**	10 wks

Kenneth McKELLAR *UK, male vocalist* *10 wks*

28 Jun 69	THE WORLD OF KENNETH McKELLAR		
	Decca SPA 11	**27**	7 wks

31 Jan 70	ECCO DI NAPOLI *Decca SKL 5018*	**45**	3 wks

Malcolm McLAREN *UK, male vocalist* *29 wks*

4 Jun 83	DUCK ROCK *Charisma MMLP 1*	**18**	17 wks
26 May 84	WOULD YA LIKE MORE SCRATCHIN'		
	Charisma CLAM 1	**44**	4 wks
29 Dec 84	FANS *Charisma MMDL 2*	**47**	8 wks

Would Ya Like More Scratchin' is credited to Malcolm McLaren and the World's Famous Supreme Team Show.

Don McLEAN *US, male vocalist* *89 wks*

11 Mar 72	● AMERICAN PIE *United Artists UAS 29285* ...	**3**	54 wks
17 Jun 72	TAPESTRY *United Artists UAS 29350*	**16**	12 wks
24 Nov 73	PLAYIN' FAVORITES *United Artists UAG 29528*	**42**	2 wks
14 Jun 80	CHAIN LIGHTNING *EMI International INS 3025*	**19**	9 wks
27 Sep 80	● THE VERY BEST OF DON McLEAN		
	United Artists UAG 30314	**4**	12 wks

Ralph McTELL *UK, male vocalist* *17 wks*

18 Nov 72	NOT TILL TOMORROW *Reprise K 44210*	**36**	1 wk
2 Mar 74	EASY *Reprise K 54013*	**31**	4 wks
15 Feb 75	STREETS *Warner Bros. K 56105*	**13**	12 wks

Christine McVIE *UK, female vocalist* *4 wks*

11 Feb 84	CHRISTINE McVIE *Warner Bros 92 5059*	**58**	4 wks

David McWILLIAMS *UK, male vocalist* *9 wks*

10 Jun 67	DAVID McWILLIAMS SINGS		
	Major Minor MMLP 2	**38**	2 wks
4 Nov 67	DAVID McWILLIAMS VOL.2		
	Major Minor MMLP 10	**23**	6 wks
9 Mar 68	DAVID McWILLIAMS VOL.3		
	Major Minor MMLP 11	**39**	1 wk

MADNESS *UK, male vocal/instrumental group* *291 wks*

3 Nov 79	● ONE STEP BEYOND *Stiff SEEZ 17*	**2**	78 wks
4 Oct 80	● ABSOLUTELY *Stiff SEEZ 29*	**2**	46 wks
10 Oct 81	● MADNESS 7 *Stiff SEEZ 39*	**5**	29 wks
1 May 82	★ COMPLETE MADNESS *Stiff HIT-TV 1*	**1**	88 wks
13 Nov 82	● THE RISE AND FALL *Stiff SEEZ 46*	**10**	22 wks
3 Mar 84	● KEEP MOVING *Stiff SEEZ 53*	**6**	19 wks
12 Oct 85	MAD NOT MAD *Zarjazz JZLP*	**16**	9 wks

MADONNA *US, female vocalist* *103 wks*

11 Feb 84	● MADONNA *Sire 923867*	**6†**	45 wks
24 Nov 84	★ LIKE A VIRGIN *Sire 925157*	**1†**	58 wks

From 22 Aug 85 Madonna was repackaged and was available as The First Album SIRE WX22.

MAGAZINE *UK, male vocal/instrumental group* *24 wks*

24 Jun 78	REAL LIFE *Virgin V 2100*	**29**	8 wks
14 Apr 79	SECONDHAND DAYLIGHT *Virgin V 2121*	**38**	8 wks
10 May 80	CORRECT USE OF SOAP *Virgin V 2156*	**28**	4 wks
13 Dec 80	PLAY *Virgin V 2184*	**69**	1 wk
27 Jun 81	MAGIC, MURDER AND THE WEATHER		
	Virgin V 2200	**39**	3 wks

MAGIC BAND - *See CAPTAIN BEEFHEART and his MAGIC BAND*

BOB MARLEY (right) Bob Marley about to achieve another of his goals – training with the Brazilians.

PAUL McCARTNEY (below) McCartney's 'Give My Regards to Broad Street' went staight in at number one the week Culture Club's 'Waking Up With The House on Fire' entered at number two.

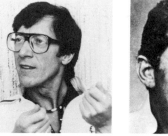

DEAN MARTIN (right) Ohio-born Dino Crocetti's first success was as one half of a comedy duo with Jerry Lewis.

HANK MARVIN (left) Honestly – I was playing it just a second ago.

MAGNA CARTA UK, male vocal/instrumental group
2 wks

8 Aug 70	SEASONS	Vertigo 6360 003	....	55	2 wks

MAGNUM UK, male vocal/instrumental group
24 wks

16 Sep 78	KINGDOM OF MADNESS	Jet JETLP 210	......	58	1 wk
19 Apr 80	MARAUDER	Jet JETLP 230	......	34	5 wks
6 Mar 82	CHASE THE DRAGON	Jet JETLP 235	....	17	7 wks
21 May 83	THE ELEVENTH HOUR	Jet JETLP 240	......	38	4 wks
25 May 85	ON A STORYTELLER'S NIGHT	FM WKFM LP 34	....	24	7 wks

MAHAVISHNU ORCHESTRA UK/US, male
instrumental group
5 wks

31 Mar 73	BIRDS OF FIRE	CBS 65321	....	20	5 wks

See also Carlos Santana and Mahavishnu John McLaughlin.

MAI TAI Holland, female vocal group
1 wk

6 Jul 85	HISTORY	Virgin V 2359	....	91	1 wk

Tommy MAKEM - *See* CLANCY BROTHERS *and* Tommy MAKEM

MAMA'S BOYS Ireland, male vocal/instrumental group
4 wks

6 Apr 85	POWER & PASSION	Jive HIP 24	....	55	4 wks

MAMAS and PAPAS US, male/female vocal group
61 wks

25 Jun 66 ●	THE MAMAS AND PAPAS	RCA Victor RD 7803		3	18 wks
28 Jan 67	CASS, JOHN, MICHELLE, DENNY	RCA Victor SF 7639		24	6 wks
24 Jun 67 ●	MAMAS AND PAPAS DELIVER	RCA Victor SF 7880	....	4	22 wks
26 Apr 69 ●	HITS OF GOLD	Stateside S 5007	....	7	2 wks
18 Jun 77 ●	THE BEST OF THE MAMAS AND PAPAS	Arcade ADEP 30	....	6	13 wks

MAN UK, male vocal/instrumental group
11 wks

20 Oct 73	BACK INTO THE FUTURE	United Artists UAD 60053/4	....	23	3 wks
25 May 74	RHINOS WINOS AND LUNATICS	United Artists UAG 29631	....	24	4 wks
11 Oct 75	MAXIMUM DARKNESS	United Artists UAG 29872	....	25	2 wks
17 Apr 76	WELSH CONNECTION	MCA MCF 2753	.....	40	2 wks

MANCHESTER BOYS CHOIR UK, male choir
2 wks

21 Dec 85	THE NEW SOUND OF CHRISTMAS	K-Tel ONE 1314	....	80†	2 wks

Henry MANCINI US, orchestra/chorus
8 wks

16 Oct 76	HENRY MANCINI	Arcade ADEP 24	....	26	8 wks

See also James Galway and Henry Mancini; Luciano Pavarotti with the Henry Mancini Orchestra.

MANFRED MANN UK, male vocal/instrumental group
72 wks

19 Sep 64 ●	FIVE FACES OF MANFRED MANN	HMV CLP 1731	....	3	24 wks
23 Oct 65 ●	MANN MADE	HMV CLP 1911	....	7	11 wks
17 Sep 66	MANN MADE HITS	HMV CLP 3559	....	11	18 wks
29 Oct 66	AS IS	Fontana TL 5377	....	22	4 wks
21 Jan 67	SOUL OF MANN	HMV CSD 3594	....	40	1 wk
15 Sep 79 ●	SEMI-DETACHED SUBURBAN	EMI EMTV 19	....	9	14 wks

MANHATTAN TRANSFER US, male/female vocal
group
85 wks

12 Mar 77	COMING OUT	Atlantic K 50291	....	12	20 wks
19 Mar 77	MANHATTAN TRANSFER	Atlantic K 50138	...	49	7 wks
25 Feb 78 ●	PASTICHE	Atlantic K 50444		10	34 wks
11 Nov 78 ●	LIVE	Atlantic K 50540		4	17 wks
17 Nov 79	EXTENSIONS	Atlantic K 50674		63	3 wks
18 Feb 84	BODIES AND SOULS	Atlantic 780104		53	4 wks

MANHATTANS US, male vocal group
3 wks

14 Aug 76	MANHATTANS	CBS 81513	....	37	3 wks

Barry MANILOW US, male vocalist
301 wks

23 Sep 78	EVEN NOW	Arista SPART 1047	....	12	28 wks
3 Mar 79 ●	MANILOW MAGIC	Arista ARTV 2	....	3	151 wks
20 Oct 79	ONE VOICE	Arista SPART 1106	....	18	7 wks
29 Nov 80 ●	BARRY	Arista DLART 2	....	5	34 wks
25 Apr 81	GIFT SET	Arista BOX 1	....	62	1 wk
3 Oct 81 ●	IF I SHOULD LOVE AGAIN	Arista BMAN 1	...	5	26 wks
1 May 82 ★	BARRY LIVE IN BRITAIN	Arista ARTV 4		1	23 wks
27 Nov 82 ●	I WANNA DO IT WITH YOU	Arista BMAN 2		7	9 wks
8 Oct 83 ●	A TOUCH MORE MAGIC	Arista BMAN 3		10	12 wks
1 Dec 84	2.00 AM PARADISE CAFE	Arista 206 496	......	28	6 wks
16 Nov 85	MANILOW	RCA PL 87044	....	40	4 wks

Roberto MANN UK, male orchestra leader
9 wks

9 Dec 67	GREAT WALTZES	Deram SML 1010	....	19	9 wks

Shelley MANNE US, male instrumentalist - drums
1 wk

18 Jun 60	MY FAIR LADY	Vogue LAC 12100	....	20	1 wk

Manfred MANN'S EARTH BAND UK, male
vocal/instrumental group
24 wks

18 Sep 76 ●	THE ROARING SILENCE	Bronze ILPS 9357	...	10	9 wks
17 Jun 78	WATCH	Bronze BRON 507	....	33	6 wks
24 Mar 79	ANGEL STATION	Bronze BRON 516	....	30	8 wks
26 Feb 83	SOMEWHERE IN AFRICA	Bronze BRON 543	..	87	1 wk

MANOWAR US, male vocal/instrumental group
3 wks

18 Feb 84	HAIL TO ENGLAND	Music For Nations MEN 19		83	2 wks
6 Oct 84	SIGN OF THE HAMMER	10 DIX 10	....	73	1 wk

MANTOVANI UK, orchestra
151 wks

21 Feb 59 ●	CONTINENTAL ENCORES	Decca LK 4298	....	4	12 wks
18 Feb 61	CONCERT SPECTACULAR	Decca LK 4377		16	2 wks
16 Apr 66 ●	MANTOVANI MAGIC	Decca LK 7949	....	3	15 wks

15 Oct 66	**MR MUSIC - MANTOVANI** *Decca LK 4809*	**24**	3 wks
14 Jan 67 ●	**MANTOVANI'S GOLDEN HITS** *Decca SKL 4818*	**10**	43 wks
30 Sep 67	**HOLLYWOOD** *Decca SKL 4887*	**37**	1 wk
14 Jun 69 ●	**THE WORLD OF MANTOVANI** *Decca SPA 1*	**6**	31 wks
4 Oct 69 ●	**THE WORLD OF MANTOVANI VOL 2** *Decca SPA 36*	**4**	19 wks
16 May 70	**MANTOVANI TODAY** *Decca SKL 5003*	**16**	8 wks
26 Feb 72	**TO LOVERS EVERYWHERE** *Decca SKL 5112* ..	**44**	1 wk
3 Nov 79 ●	**20 GOLDEN GREATS** *Warwick WW 5067*	**9**	13 wks
16 Mar 85	**MANTOVANI MAGIC** *Telstar STAR*	**52**	3 wks

Mantovani Magic on Telstar conducted by Roland Shaw.

MANUEL and his MUSIC OF THE MOUNTAINS *UK, orchestra, leader Geoff Love*

38 wks

10 Sep 60	**MUSIC OF THE MOUNTAINS** *Columbia 33SX 1212*	**17**	1 wk
7 Aug 71	**THIS IS MANUEL** *Studio Two STWO 5*	**18**	19 wks
31 Jan 76 ●	**CARNIVAL** *Studio Two TWO 337*	**3**	18 wks

See also Geoff Love.

Phil MANZANERA *UK, male vocalist/instrumentalist - guitar*

1 wk

24 May 75	**DIAMOND HEAD** *Island ILPS 9315*	**40**	1 wk

MARC and the MAMBAS *UK, male/female vocal/instrumental group*

9 wks

16 Oct 82	**UNTITLED** *Some Bizarre/Phonogram BZA 13*	**42**	4 wks
20 Aug 83	**TORMENT AND TOREROS** *Some Bizarre BIZL 4*	**28**	5 wks

See also Marc Almond.

MARILLION *UK, male vocal/instrumental group*

99 wks

26 Mar 83 ●	**SCRIPT FOR A JESTER'S TEARS** *EMI EMC 3429*	**7**	31 wks
24 Mar 84 ●	**FUGAZI** *EMI EMC 2400851*	**5**	20 wks
17 Nov 84 ●	**REAL TO REEL** *EMI JEST 1*	**8**	21 wks
29 Jun 85 ★	**MISPLACED CHILDHOOD** *EMI MRL 2*	**1†**	27 wks

Yannis MARKOPOULOS *Greece, orchestra*

8 wks

26 Aug 78	**WHO PAYS THE FERRYMAN** *BBC REB 315* ..	**22**	8 wks

Bob MARLEY and The WAILERS *Jamaica, male vocal/instrumental group*

239 wks

4 Oct 75	**NATTY DREAD** *Island ILPS 9281*	**43**	5 wks
20 Dec 75	**LIVE** *Island ILPS 9376*	**38**	11 wks
8 May 76	**RASTAMAN VIBRATION** *Island ILPS 9383*	**15**	13 wks
11 Jun 77 ●	**EXODUS** *Island ILPS 9498*	**8**	56 wks
1 Apr 78 ●	**KAYA** *Island ILPS 9517*	**4**	24 wks
16 Dec 78	**BABYLON BY BUS** *Island ISLD 11*	**40**	11 wks
13 Oct 79	**SURVIVAL** *Island ILPS 9542*	**20**	6 wks
28 Jun 80 ●	**UPRISING** *Island ILPS 9596*	**6**	17 wks
28 May 83 ●	**CONFRONTATION** *Island ILPS 9760*	**5**	19 wks
19 May 84 ★	**LEGEND** *Island BMW 1*	**1**	77 wks

Live Island ILPS 9376 returned to the chart in 1981 under the title Live At The Lyceum

Neville MARRINER and the ACADEMY OF ST MARTIN IN THE FIELDS *UK male conductor*
with UK chamber orchestra

6 wks

6 Apr 85	**AMADEUS - ORIGINAL SOUNDTRACK** *London LONDP 6*	**64**	6 wks

Bernie MARSDEN *UK, male vocalist/instrumentalist - guitar*

2 wks

5 Sep 81	**LOOK AT ME NOW** *Parlophone PCF 7217*	**71**	2 wks

Lena MARTELL *UK, female vocalist*

71 wks

25 May 74	**THAT WONDERFUL SOUND OF LENA MARTELL** *Pye SPL 18427*	**35**	2 wks
8 Jan 77	**THE BEST OF LENA MARTELL** *Pye NSPL 18506*	**13**	16 wks
27 May 78	**THE LENA MARTELL COLLECTION** *Ronco RTL 2028*	**12**	19 wks
20 Oct 79 ●	**LENA'S MUSIC ALBUM** *Pye N 123*	**5**	18 wks
19 Apr 80 ●	**BY REQUEST** *Ronco RTL 2046*	**9**	9 wks
29 Nov 80	**BEAUTIFUL SUNDAY** *Ronco RTL 2052*	**23**	7 wks

MARTHA and The MUFFINS *Canada, male/female vocal instrumental group*

6 wks

15 Mar 80	**METRO MUSIC** *DinDisc DID 1*	**34**	6 wks

Dean MARTIN *US, male vocalist*

24 wks

13 May 61	**THIS TIME I'M SWINGING** *Capitol T 1442*	**18**	1 wk
25 Feb 67	**AT EASE WITH DEAN** *Reprise RSLP 6322*	**35**	1 wk
4 Nov 67	**WELCOME TO MY WORLD** *Philips DBL 001*	**39**	1 wk
12 Oct 68	**GREATEST HITS VOL.1** *Reprise RSLP 6301*	**40**	1 wk
22 Feb 69 ●	**BEST OF DEAN MARTIN** *Capitol ST 21194*	**9**	1 wk
22 Feb 69 ●	**GENTLE ON MY MIND** *Reprise RSLP 6330*	**9**	8 wks
13 Nov 76 ●	**20 ORIGINAL DEAN MARTIN HITS** *Reprise K 54066*	**7**	11 wks

Juan MARTIN and the ROYAL PHILHARMONIC ORCHESTRA *Spain, male instrumentalist - guitar with UK orchestra*

9 wks

11 Feb 84	**SERENADE** *K-Tel NE 1267*	**21**	9 wks

John MARTYN *UK, male vocalist/instrumentalist - guitar*

19 wks

4 Feb 78	**ONE WORLD** *Island ILPS 9492*	**54**	1 wk
1 Nov 80	**GRACE AND DANGER** *Island ILPS 9560*	**54**	2 wks
26 Sep 81	**GLORIOUS FOOL** *Geffen K 99178*	**25**	7 wks
4 Sep 82	**WELL KEPT SECRET** *WEA K 99255*	**20**	7 wks
17 Nov 84	**SAPPHIRE** *Island ILPS 9779*	**57**	2 wks

Hank MARVIN *UK, male vocalist/instrumentalist - guitar*

5 wks

22 Nov 69	**HANK MARVIN** *Columbia SCX 6352*	**14**	2 wks
20 Mar 82	**WORDS AND MUSIC** *Polydor POLD 5054*	**66**	3 wks

See also Marvin, Welch and Farrar.

MEAT LOAF (left) Pictured with Meat is the writer/arranger of 'Bat Out of Hell' Jim Steinman.

JOHNNY MATHIS (below) The ex-Olympic high jumper defends himself with a bouquet while being threatened by a gaggle of microphones.

JOHN COUGAR MELLENCAMP John Cougar Mellencamp took just fifteen days to write, produce, arrange and record 'Uh-Huh'.

MARVIN, WELCH and FARRAR UK, male
vocal/instrumental group   **4 wks**

3 Apr 71	**MARVIN, WELCH AND FARRAR**		
	Regal Zonophone SRZA 8502	**30**	4 wks

See also Hank Marvin.

MARY JANE GIRLS US, *female vocal group*
    9 wks

28 May 83	**MARY JANE GIRLS** *Gordy STML 12189*	**51**	9 wks

MARY - *See PETER, PAUL and MARY*

MASSED WELSH CHOIRS UK, *male voice choir*
    7 wks

9 Aug 69 ●	**CYMANSA GANN** *BBC REC 53 M*	**5**	7 wks

MATCHBOX UK, *male vocal/instrumental group*
    14 wks

2 Feb 80	**MATCHBOX** *Magnet MAG 5031*	**44**	5 wks
11 Oct 80	**MIDNITE DYNAMOS** *Magnet MAG 5036*	**23**	9 wks

Mireille MATHIEU France, *female vocalist*   **1 wk**

2 Mar 68	**MIREILLE MATHIEU** *Columbia SCX 6210*	**39**	1 wk

Johnny MATHIS US, *male vocalist*   **193 wks**

8 Nov 58 ●	**WARM** *Fontana TBA TFL 5015*	**6**	2 wks
24 Jan 59 ●	**SWING SOFTLY** *Fontana TBA TFL 5039*	**10**	1 wk
13 Feb 60 ●	**RIDE ON A RAINBOW** *Fontana TFL 5061*	**10**	2 wks
10 Dec 60 ●	**RHYTHMS AND BALLADS OF BROADWAY**		
	Fontana SET 101	**6**	10 wks
17 Jun 61	**I'LL BUY YOU A STAR** *Fontana TFL 5143*	**18**	1 wk
16 May 70	**RAINDROPS KEEP FALLING ON MY HEAD**		
	CBS 63587	**23**	10 wks
3 Apr 71	**LOVE STORY** *CBS 64334*	**27**	5 wks
9 Sep 72	**FIRST TIME EVER I SAW YOUR FACE**		
	CBS 64930	**40**	3 wks
16 Dec 72	**MAKE IT EASY ON YOURSELF** *CBS 65161*	**49**	1 wk
8 Mar 75	**I'M COMING HOME** *CBS 65690*	**18**	11 wks
5 Apr 75	**THE HEART OF A WOMAN** *CBS 80533*	**39**	2 wks
26 Jul 75	**WHEN WILL I SEE YOU AGAIN** *CBS 80738*	**13**	10 wks
3 Jul 76	**I ONLY HAVE EYES FOR YOU** *CBS 81329*	**14**	12 wks
19 Feb 77	**GREATEST HITS VOL. IV** *CBS 86022*	**31**	5 wks
18 Jun 77 ★	**THE JOHNNY MATHIS COLLECTION**		
	CBS 10003	**1**	40 wks
17 Dec 77	**SWEET SURRENDER** *CBS 86036*	**55**	1 wk
29 Apr 78 ●	**YOU LIGHT UP MY LIFE** *CBS 86055*	**3**	19 wks
7 Apr 79	**THE BEST DAYS OF MY LIFE** *CBS 86080*	**38**	5 wks
3 Nov 79	**MATHIS MAGIC** *CBS 86103*	**59**	4 wks
8 Mar 80 ★	**TEARS AND LAUGHTER** *CBS 10019*	**1**	15 wks
12 Jul 80	**ALL FOR YOU** *CBS 86115*	**20**	8 wks
19 Sep 81 ●	**CELEBRATION** *CBS 10028*	**9**	16 wks
15 May 82	**FRIENDS IN LOVE** *CBS 85652*	**34**	7 wks
15 Sep 84	**A SPECIAL PART OF ME** *CBS 25475*	**45**	3 wks

See also Johnny Mathis and Deniece Williams.

Johnny MATHIS and Deniece WILLIAMS
US, *male/female vocal duo*   **11 wks**

26 Aug 78	**THAT'S WHAT FRIENDS ARE FOR** *CBS 86068*	**16**	11 wks

See also Johnny Mathis; Deniece Williams.

Johnny MATHIS and Natalie COLE US, *male/*
female vocal duo   **16 wks**

17 Sep 83 ●	**UNFORGETTABLE: A MUSICAL TRIBUTE TO NAT KING COLE** *CBS 10042*	**5**	16 wks

MATT BIANCO UK/Poland *male/female vocal/*
instrumental group   **49 wks**

8 Sep 84	**WHOSE SIDE ARE YOU ON** *WEA WX 7*	**35**	49 wks

MATTHEWS' SOUTHERN COMFORT UK,
male vocal/instrumental group   **4 wks**

25 Jul 70	**SECOND SPRING** *Uni UNLS 112*	**52**	4 wks

Brian MAY and FRIENDS UK, *male vocalist/*
instrumentalist - guitar, and UK/US male instrumental group
    4 wks

12 Nov 83	**STAR FLEET PROJECT** *EMI SFLT 1078061*	**35**	4 wks

John MAYALL UK, *male vocalist*   **97 wks**

4 Mar 67 ●	**A HARD ROAD** *Decca SKL 4853*	**10**	19 wks
23 Sep 67 ●	**CRUSADE** *Decca SKL 4890*	**8**	14 wks
25 Nov 67	**BLUES ALONE** *Ace Of Clubs SCL 1243*	**24**	5 wks
16 Mar 68	**DIARY OF A BAND VOL.1** *Decca SKL 4918*	**27**	9 wks
16 Mar 68	**DIARY OF A BAND VOL.2** *Decca SKL 4919*	**28**	5 wks
20 Jul 68 ●	**BARE WIRES** *Decca SKL 4945*	**3**	17 wks
18 Jan 69	**BLUES FROM LAUREL CANYON**		
	Decca SKL 4972	**33**	3 wks
23 Aug 69	**LOOKING BACK** *Decca SKL 5010*	**14**	7 wks
15 Nov 69	**TURNING POINT** *Polydor 583-571*	**11**	7 wks
11 Apr 70 ●	**EMPTY ROOMS** *Polydor 583-580*	**9**	8 wks
12 Dec 70	**U.S.A. UNION** *Polydor 2425-020*	**50**	1 wk
26 Jun 71	**BACK TO THE ROOTS** *Polydor 2657-005*	**31**	2 wks

First four Decca albums credited to John Mayall's Bluesbreakers.

John MAYALL and Eric CLAPTON UK, *male*
instrumental duo   **17 wks**

30 Jul 66 ●	**BLUES BREAKERS** *Decca LK 4804*	**6**	17 wks

See also John Mayall; Eric Clapton

Curtis MAYFIELD US, *male vocalist*   **2 wks**

31 Mar 73	**SUPER FLY** *Buddah 2318 065*	**26**	2 wks

MAZE featuring Frankie BEVERLY US, *male*
vocalist and male vocal/instrumental group   **18 wks**

7 May 83	**WE ARE ONE** *Capitol EST 12262*	**38**	6 wks
9 Mar 85	**CAN'T STOP THE LOVE** *Capitol MAZE 1*	**41**	12 wks

Vaughn MEADER US, *male comedian*   **8 wks**

29 Dec 62	**THE FIRST FAMILY** *London HAA 8048*	**12**	8 wks

MEAT LOAF US, *male vocalist*   **499 wks**

11 Mar 78 ●	**BAT OUT OF HELL** *Epic EPC 82419*	**9**	382 wks
12 Sep 81 ★	**DEAD RINGER** *Epic EPC 83645*	**1**	46 wks

7 May 83 ●	MIDNIGHT AT THE LOST AND FOUND		
	Epic EPC 25243	7	23 wks
10 Nov 84 ●	BAD ATTITUDE Arista 206 619	8	16 wks
26 Jan 85 ●	HITS OUT OF HELL Epic EPC 26156	2	32 wks

MELANIE   US, female vocalist   69 wks

19 Sep 70 ●	CANDLES IN THE RAIN Buddah 2318-009	5	27 wks
16 Jan 71	LEFTOVER WINE Buddah 2318-011	22	11 wks
29 May 71 ●	GOOD BOOK Buddah 2322 001	9	9 wks
8 Jan 72	GATHER ME Buddah 2322 002	14	14 wks
1 Apr 72	GARDEN IN THE CITY Buddah 2318 054	19	6 wks
7 Oct 72	THE FOUR SIDES OF MELANIE		
	Buddah 2659 013	23	2 wks

John Cougar MELLENCAMP   US, male vocalist   7 wks

6 Nov 82	AMERICAN FOOL Riva RVLP 16	37	6 wks
3 Mar 84	UH-HUH Riva RIVL 1	92	1 wk

American Fool *credited to John Cougar*

MEN AT WORK   Australia, male vocal/instrumental group   71 wks

15 Jan 83 ★	BUSINESS AS USUAL Epic EPC 85669	1	44 wks
30 Apr 83 ●	CARGO Epic EPC 25372	8	27 wks

MEN THEY COULDN'T HANG   UK, male vocal/instrumental group   2 wks

27 Jul 85	NIGHT OF A THOUSAND CANDLES		
	Imp FIEND 50	91	2 wks

MEN WITHOUT HATS   Canada, male vocal/instrumental group   1 wk

12 Nov 83	RHYTHM OF YOUTH Statik STATLP 10	96	1 wk

MEMBERS   UK, male vocal/instrumental group   5 wks

28 Apr 79	AT THE CHELSEA NIGHTCLUB Virgin V 2120	45	5 wks

Freddie MERCURY   UK, male vocalist   23 wks

11 May 85 ●	MR BAD GUY CBS 86312	6	23 wks

MERSEYBEATS   UK, male vocal/instrumental group   9 wks

20 Jun 64	THE MERSEYBEATS Fontana TL 5210	12	9 wks

METALLICA   US/Denmark, male vocal/instrumental group   2 wks

11 Aug 84	RIDE THE LIGHTNING		
	Music For Nations MFN 27	87	2 wks

METEORS   UK, male vocal/instrumental group   3 wks

26 Feb 83	WRECKIN' CREW I.D. NOSE 1	53	3 wks

MEZZOFORTE   Iceland, male instrumental group   10 wks

5 Mar 83	SURPRISE SURPRISE Steinar STELP 02	23	9 wks
2 Jul 83	CATCHING UP WITH MEZZOFORTE		
	Steinar STELP 03	95	1 wk

MG'S -   *See Booker T. and the MG's*

Keith MICHELL   Australia, male vocalist   12 wks

9 Feb 80	CAPTAIN BEAKY AND HIS BAND		
	Polydor 238 3462	28	12 wks

MIDNIGHT STAR   US, male/female vocal/instrumental group   2 wks

2 Feb 85	PLANETARY INVASION Solar MCF 3251	85	2 wks

MICK -   *See Dave DEE, DOZY, BEAKY, MICK and TICH*

MIGHTY WAH   UK, male vocal/instrumental group   6 wks

4 Aug 84	A WORD TO THE WISE GUY		
	Beggars Banquet BEGA 54	28	6 wks

Buddy MILES -   *See Carlos SANTANA and Buddy MILES*

John MILES   UK, male vocalist/multi-instrumentalist   25 wks

27 Mar 76 ●	REBEL Decca SKL 5231	9	10 wks
26 Feb 77	STRANGER IN THE CITY Decca TXS 118	37	3 wks
1 Apr 78	ZARAGON Decca TXS 126	43	5 wks
21 Apr 79	MORE MILES PER HOUR Decca TXS 135	46	5 wks
29 Aug 81	MILES HIGH EMI EMC 3374	96	2 wks

Frankie MILLER   UK, male vocalist   1 wk

14 Apr 79	FALLING IN LOVE Chrysalis CHR 1220	54	1 wk

Glenn MILLER   US, orchestra   68 wks

28 Jan 61 ●	GLENN MILLER PLAYS SELECTIONS FROM 'THE GLENN MILLER STORY' AND OTHER HITS RCA RD 27068 0023	10	18 wks
5 Jul 69 ●	THE BEST OF GLENN MILLER		
	RCA International 1002	5	14 wks
6 Sep 69	NEARNESS OF YOU		
	RCA International INTS 1019	30	2 wks
25 Apr 70	A MEMORIAL 1944-1969 RCA GM 1	18	17 wks
25 Dec 71	THE REAL GLENN MILLER AND HIS ORCHESTRA PLAY THE ORIGINAL MUSIC OF THE FILM 'THE GLENN MILLER STORY' AND OTHER HITS		
	RCA International INTS 1157	28	2 wks
14 Feb 76	A LEGENDARY PERFORMER		
	RCA Victor DPM 2065	41	5 wks
14 Feb 76	A LEGENDARY PERFORMER VOL 2		
	RCA Victor CPL 11349	53	2 wks
9 Apr 77 ●	THE UNFORGETTABLE GLENN MILLER		
	RCA Victor TVL 1	4	8 wks

The Real Glenn Miller And His Orchestra Play... *is a re-titled re-issue of the first album.*

Steve MILLER BAND US, male vocal/instrumental group
47 wks

12 Jun 76	FLY LIKE AN EAGLE	Mercury 9286 177		11	17 wks
4 Jun 77	BOOK OF DREAMS	Mercury 9286 456		12	12 wks
19 Jun 82	● ABRACADABRA	Mercury 6302 204		10	16 wks
7 May 83	STEVE MILLER BAND LIVE!	Mercury MERL 18		79	2 wks

MILLICAN and NESBIT UK, male vocal duo
24 wks

23 Mar 74	● MILLICAN AND NESBIT	Pye NSPL 18428		3	21 wks
4 Jan 75	EVERYBODY KNOWS MILLICAN & NESBIT				
		Pye NSPL 18446		23	3 wks

Spike MILLIGAN UK, male comedian
5 wks

25 Nov 61	MILLIGAN PRESERVED	Parlophone PMC 1152		11	4 wks
18 Dec 76	THE SNOW GOOSE	RCA RS 1088		49	1 wk

Second album also credited the London Symphony Orchestra. See also Harry Secombe, Peter Sellers and Spike Milligan.

Mrs. MILLS UK, female instrumentalist – piano
13 wks

10 Dec 66	COME TO MY PARTY	Parlophone PMC 7010		17	7 wks
28 Dec 68	MRS. MILLS' PARTY PIECES				
		Parlophone PCS 7066		32	3 wks
13 Dec 69	LET'S HAVE ANOTHER PARTY				
		Parlophone PCS 7035		23	2 wks
6 Nov 71	I'M MIGHTY GLAD	MFP 5225		49	1 wk

MINDBENDERS UK, male vocal/instrumental group
4 wks

25 Jun 66	THE MINDBENDERS	Fontana TL 5324		28	4 wks

See also Wayne Fontana and the Mindbenders.

Liza MINELLI US, female vocalist
16 wks

7 Apr 73	● LIZA WITH A 'Z'	CBS 65212		9	15 wks
16 Jun 73	THE SINGER	CBS 65555		45	1 wk

MINIPOPS UK, male/female vocal group
5 wks

19 Feb 83	WE'RE THE MINIPOPS	K-Tel ONE 1187		54	5 wks

Joni MITCHELL Canada, female vocalist
101 wks

6 Jun 70	● LADIES OF THE CANYON	Reprise RSLP 6376		8	25 wks
24 Jul 71	● BLUE	Reprise K 44128		3	18 wks
16 Mar 74	COURT AND SPARK	Asylum SYLA 8756		14	11 wks
1 Feb 75	MILES OF AISLES	Asylum SYSP 902		34	4 wks
27 Dec 75	THE HISSING OF SUMMER LAWNS				
		Asylum SYLA 8763		14	10 wks
11 Dec 76	HEJIRA	Asylum K 53063		11	5 wks
21 Jan 78	DON JUAN'S RECKLESS DAUGHTER				
		Asylum K 63003		20	7 wks
14 Jul 79	MINGUS	Asylum K 53091		24	7 wks
4 Oct 80	SHADOWS AND LIGHT	Elektra K 62030		63	3 wks
4 Dec 82	WILD THINGS RUN FAST	Geffen GEF 25102		32	8 wks
30 Nov 85	DOG EAT DOG	Geffen GEF 26455		57	3 wks

George MITCHELL MINSTRELS UK, male/female vocal group
240 wks

26 Nov 60	★ THE BLACK AND WHITE MINSTREL SHOW				
		HMV CLP 1399		1	90 wks
21 Oct 61	★ ANOTHER BLACK AND WHITE MINSTREL SHOW	HMV CLP 1460		1	64 wks
20 Oct 62	★ ON STAGE WITH THE GEORGE MITCHELL MINSTRELS	HMV CLP 1599		1	26 wks
2 Nov 63	● ON TOUR WITH THE GEORGE MITCHELL MINSTRELS	HMV CLP 1667		6	18 wks
12 Dec 64	● SPOTLIGHT ON THE GEORGE MITCHELL MINSTRELS	HMV CLP 1803		6	7 wks
4 Dec 65	● MAGIC OF THE MINSTRELS	HMV CLP 1917		9	7 wks
26 Nov 66	HERE COME THE MINSTRELS				
		HMV CLP 3579		11	11 wks
16 Dec 67	SHOWTIME	HMV CSD 3642		26	2 wks
14 Dec 68	SING THE IRVING BERLIN SONGBOOK				
		Columbia SCX 6267		33	1 wk
19 Dec 70	THE MAGIC OF CHRISTMAS				
		Columbia SCX 6431		32	4 wks
19 Nov 77	● 30 GOLDEN GREATS	EMI EMTV 7		10	10 wks

30 Golden Greats also credits the Joe Loss Orchestra.

MODERN EON UK, male vocal/instrumental group
1 wk

13 Jun 81	FICTION TALES	Dindisc DID 11		65	1 wk

MODERN LOVERS – See Jonathan RICHMAN and the MODERN LOVERS

MODERN ROMANCE UK, male vocal/instrumental group
13 wks

16 Apr 83	TRICK OF THE LIGHT	WEA X 0127		53	7 wks
3 Dec 83	PARTY TONIGHT	Ronco RON LP 3		45	6 wks

Zoot MONEY and the BIG ROLL BAND UK, male vocalist and male instrumental backing group
3 wks

15 Oct 66	ZOOT	Columbia SX 6075		23	3 wks

MONKEES US/UK, male vocal/instrumental group
92 wks

28 Jan 67	★ THE MONKEES	RCA Victor SF 7844		1	36 wks
15 Apr 67	★ MORE OF THE MONKEES	RCA Victor SF 7868		1	25 wks
8 Jul 67	● HEADQUARTERS	RCA Victor SF 7886		2	19 wks
13 Jan 68	● PISCES, AQUARIUS, CAPRICORN & JONES LTD.	RCA Victor SF 7912		5	11 wks
28 Nov 81	THE MONKEES	Arista DARTY 12		99	1 wk

MONOCHROME SET UK, male vocal/instrumental group
4 wks

3 May 80	STRANGE BOUTIQUE	Dindisc DID 4		62	4 wks

Tony MONOPOLY Australia, male vocalist
4 wks

12 Jun 76	TONY MONOPOLY	BUK BULP 2000		25	4 wks

Matt MONRO UK, male vocalist
15 wks

7 Aug 65	I HAVE DREAMED	Parlophone PMC 1250		20	1 wk
17 Sep 66	THIS IS THE LIFE	Capitol T 2540		25	2 wks

26 Aug 67	INVITATION TO THE MOVIES			
	Capitol ST 2730	30	1 wk
15 Mar 80 ●	HEARTBREAKERS EMI EMTV 23	5	11 wks

MONTROSE US, male vocal/instrumental group 1 wk

| 15 Jun 74 | MONTROSE Warner Bros. K 46276 .... | 43 | 1 wk |

MONTY PYTHON'S FLYING CIRCUS UK, male comedy group 31 wks

30 Oct 71	ANOTHER MONTY PYTHON RECORD			
	Charisma CAS 1049	26	3 wks
27 Jan 73	MONTY PYTHON'S PREVIOUS ALBUM			
	Charisma CAS 1063	39	3 wks
23 Feb 74	MATCHING TIE AND HANDKERCHIEF			
	Charisma CAS 1080	49	2 wks
27 Jul 74	LIVE AT DRURY LANE Charisma CLASS 4 ...	19	8 wks
9 Aug 75	MONTY PYTHON Charisma CAS 1003	45	4 wks
24 Nov 79	THE LIFE OF BRIAN Warner Bros. K 56751	63	3 wks
18 Oct 80	CONTRACTUAL OBLIGATION ALBUM			
	Charisma CAS 1152	13	8 wks

MOODY BLUES UK, male vocal/instrumental group 296 wks

27 Jan 68	DAYS OF FUTURE PASSED Deram SML 707 ..	27	16 wks
3 Aug 68 ●	IN SEARCH OF THE LOST CHORD			
	Deram SML 711	5	32 wks
3 May 69 ★	ON THE THRESHOLD OF A DREAM			
	Deram SML 1035	1	73 wks
6 Dec 69 ●	TO OUR CHILDREN'S CHILDREN'S CHILDREN			
	Threshold THS 1	2	44 wks
15 Aug 70 ★	A QUESTION OF BALANCE Threshold THS 3	1	19 wks
7 Aug 71 ★	EVERY GOOD BOY DESERVES FAVOUR			
	Threshold THS 5	1	21 wks
2 Dec 72 ●	SEVENTH SOJOURN Threshold THS 7	5	18 wks
16 Nov 74	THIS IS THE MOODY BLUES Threshold MB 1/2	14	18 wks
24 Jun 78 ●	OCTAVE Decca TXS 129	6	18 wks
10 Nov 79	OUT OF THIS WORLD K-Tel NE 1051	15	10 wks
23 May 81 ●	LONG DISTANCE VOYAGER			
	Threshold TXS 139	7	19 wks
10 Sep 83	THE PRESENT Threshold TXS 140	15	8 wks

Dudley MOORE UK, male instrumentalist - piano 19 wks

4 Dec 65	THE OTHER SIDE OF DUDLEY MOORE			
	Decca LK 4732	11	9 wks
11 Jun 66	GENUINE DUD Decca LK 4788	13	10 wks

Second album credited to the Dudley Moore Trio. See also Peter Cook and Dudley Moore.

Gary MOORE UK, male vocalist/instrumentalist - guitar 25 wks

3 Feb 79	BACK ON THE STREETS MCA MCF 2853 ...	70	1 wk
16 Oct 82	CORRIDORS OF POWER Virgin V 2245	30	6 wks
18 Feb 84	VICTIMS OF THE FUTURE 10 DIX 2	12	7 wks
13 Oct 84	WE WANT MOORE 10 GMDL 1	32	3 wks
14 Sep 85	RUN FOR COVER 10 DIX 16	12	8 wks

Patrick MORAZ Switzerland, male instrumentalist - keyboards 8 wks

| 10 Apr 76 | PATRICK MORAZ Charisma CDS 4002 .... | 28 | 7 wks |
| 23 Jul 77 | OUT IN THE SUN Charisma CDS 4007 .... | 44 | 1 wk |

Ennio MORRICONE Italy, orchestra 11 wks

| 2 May 81 | THIS IS ENNIO MORRICONE EMI THIS 33 .. | 23 | 5 wks |
| 9 May 81 | CHI MAI BBC REH 414 .... | 29 | 6 wks |

Van MORRISON UK, male vocalist 60 wks

18 Apr 70	MOONDANCE Warner Bros. WS 1835	32	2 wks
11 Aug 73	HARD NOSE THE HIGHWAY			
	Warner Bros. K 46242	22	3 wks
16 Nov 74	VEEDON FLEECE Warner Bros. K 56068	41	1 wk
7 May 77	A PERIOD OF TRANSITION			
	Warner Bros. K 56322	23	5 wks
21 Oct 78	WAVELENGTH Warner Bros. K 56526	27	6 wks
8 Sep 79	INTO THE MUSIC Vertigo 9120 852	21	9 wks
20 Sep 80	THE COMMON ONE Mercury 6302 021	53	3 wks
27 Feb 82	BEAUTIFUL VISION Mercury/Phonogram 6302 122	31	14 wks
26 Mar 83	INARTICULATE SPEECH OF THE HEART			
	Mercury MERL 16	14	8 wks
3 Mar 84	LIVE AT THE GRAND OPERA HOUSE			
	Mercury MERL 36	47	4 wks
9 Feb 85	A SENSE OF WONDER Mercury MERH 54	25	5 wks

MORRISSEY MULLEN UK, male vocal/instrumental duo 11 wks

18 Jul 81	BADNESS Beggars Banquet BEGA 27	43	5 wks
3 Apr 82	LIFE ON THE WIRE Beggars Banquet BEGA 33 ..	47	5 wks
23 Apr 83	IT'S ABOUT TIME Beggars Banquet BEGA 44 ..	95	1 wk

MOTHERS OF INVENTION US, male vocal/instrumental group 12 wks

29 Jun 68	WE'RE ONLY IN IT FOR THE MONEY			
	Verve SVLP 9199	32	5 wks
28 Mar 70	BURNT WEENY SANDWICH Reprise RSLP 6370	17	3 wks
3 Oct 70	WEASELS RIPPED MY FLESH			
	Reprise RSLP 2028	28	4 wks

MOTLEY CRUE US, male vocal/instrumental group 3 wks

| 13 Jul 85 | THEATRE OF PAIN Elektra EKT 8 .... | 36 | 3 wks |

MOTORHEAD UK, male vocal/instrumental group 76 wks

24 Sep 77	MOTORHEAD Chiswick WIK 2	43	5 wks
24 Mar 79	OVERKILL Bronze BRON 515	24	11 wks
8 Dec 79	ON PARADE United Artists LBR 1004	65	2 wks
8 Nov 80 ●	ACE OF SPADES Bronze BRON 531	4	16 wks
27 Jun 81 ★	NO SLEEP TILL HAMMERSMITH			
	Bronze BRON 535	1	21 wks
17 Apr 82 ●	IRONFIST Bronze BRNA 539	6	9 wks
26 Feb 83	WHAT'S WORDS WORTH Big Beat NED 2 ...	71	2 wks
4 Jun 83	ANOTHER PERFECT DAY Bronze BRON 546	20	4 wks
15 Sep 84	NO REMORSE			
	Bronze PROTV MOTOR 1	14	6 wks

MOTORS UK, male vocal/instrumental group 6 wks

| 15 Oct 77 | THE MOTORS Virgin V 2089 .... | 46 | 5 wks |
| 3 Jun 78 | APPROVED BY THE MOTORS Virgin V 2101 .... | 60 | 1 wk |

MOTT THE HOOPLE UK, male vocal/instrumental
group 32 wks

2 May 70	**MOTT THE HOOPLE** *Island ILPS 9108*	**66**	1 wk
17 Oct 70	**MAD SHADOWS** *Island ILPS 9119*	**48**	2 wks
17 Apr 71	**WILD LIFE** *Island ILPS 9144*	**44**	2 wks
23 Sep 72	**ALL THE YOUNG DUDES** *CBS 65184*	**21**	4 wks
11 Aug 73 ●	**MOTT** *CBS 69038*	**7**	15 wks
13 Apr 74	**THE HOOPLE** *CBS 69062*	**11**	5 wks
23 Nov 74	**LIVE** *CBS 69093*	**32**	2 wks
4 Oct 75	**DRIVE ON** *CBS 69154*	**45**	1 wk

MOUNTAIN US/Canada, male vocal/instrumental group
4 wks

5 Jun 71	**NANTUCKET SLEIGHRIDE** *Island ILPS 9148* ..	**43**	1 wk
8 Jul 72	**THE ROAD GOES EVER ON** *Island ILPS 9199*	**21**	3 wks

Nana MOUSKOURI Greece, female vocalist 190 wks

7 Jun 69 ●	**OVER AND OVER** *Fontana S 5511*	**10**	105 wks
4 Apr 70 ●	**THE EXQUISITE NANA MOUSKOURI**		
	Fontana STL 5536	**10**	25 wks
10 Oct 70	**RECITAL '70** *Fontana 6312 003*	**68**	1 wk
3 Apr 71	**TURN ON THE SUN** *Fontana 6312 008*	**16**	15 wks
29 Jul 72	**BRITISH CONCERT** *Fontana 6651 003*	**29**	11 wks
28 Apr 73	**SONGS FROM HER TV SERIES**		
	Fontana 6312 036	**29**	11 wks
28 Sep 74	**SPOTLIGHT ON NANA MOUSKOURI**		
	Fontana 6641 197	**38**	6 wks
10 Jul 76 ●	**PASSPORT** *Philips 9101 061*	**3**	16 wks

MOVE UK, male vocal/instrumental group 9 wks

13 Apr 68	**MOVE** *Regal Zonophone SLPZ 1002*	**15**	9 wks

Alison MOYET UK, female vocalist 57 wks

17 Nov 84 ★	**ALF** *CBS 26229*	**1†**	57 wks

MTUME US, male/female vocal/instrumental group
1 wk

6 Oct 84	**YOU, ME & HE** *Epic EPC 26077*	**85**	1 wk

MUD UK, male vocal/instrumental group 58 wks

28 Sep 74 ●	**MUD ROCK** *RAK SRAK 508*	**8**	35 wks
26 Jul 75 ●	**MUD ROCK VOL 2** *RAK SRAK 513*	**6**	12 wks
1 Nov 75	**MUD'S GREATEST HITS** *RAK SRAK 6755*	**25**	6 wks
27 Dec 75	**USE YOUR IMAGINATION**		
	Private Stock PVLP 1003	**33**	5 wks

MUFFINS - *See MARTHA and the MUFFINS*

Gerry MULLIGAN and Ben WEBSTER US,
male instrumental duo – baritone and tenor sax 1 wk

24 Sep 60	**GERRY MULLIGAN MEETS BEN WEBSTER**		
	HMV CLP 1373	**15**	1 wk

MUNGO JERRY UK, male vocal/instrumental group
14 wks

8 Aug 70	**MUNGO JERRY** *Dawn DNLS 3008*	**13**	6 wks

10 Apr 71	**ELECTRONICALLY TESTED** *Dawn DNLS 3020*	**14**	8 wks

MUPPETS US, puppets 45 wks

11 Jun 77 ★	**THE MUPPET SHOW** *Pye NSPH 19*	**1**	35 wks
25 Feb 78	**THE MUPPET SHOW VOL.2** *Pye NSPH 21* ...	**16**	10 wks

Anne MURRAY Canada, female vocalist 10 wks

3 Oct 81	**VERY BEST OF ANNE MURRAY**		
	Capitol EMTV 31	**14**	10 wks

Pauline MURRAY and the INVISIBLE
GIRLS UK, female vocalist with male vocal/instrumental group
4 wks

11 Oct 80	**PAULINE MURRAY AND THE INVISIBLE**		
	GIRLS *Elusive 2394 227*	**25**	4 wks

MUSIC OF THE MOUNTAINS - *See MANUEL and his MUSIC OF THE MOUNTAINS*

MUSICAL YOUTH UK, male vocal/instrumental group
22 wks

4 Dec 82	**THE YOUTH OF TODAY** *MCA YOULP 1*	**24**	22 wks

N

Graham NASH UK, male vocalist 8 wks

26 Jun 71	**SONGS FOR BEGINNERS** *Atlantic 2401-011*	**13**	8 wks

See also Crosby, Stills and Nash; Crosby, Stills, Nash and Young; Graham Nash and David Crosby.

Graham NASH and David CROSBY UK/US,
male vocal duo 5 wks

13 May 72	**GRAHAM NASH AND DAVID CROSBY**		
	Atlantic K 50011	**13**	5 wks

See also Dave Crosby; Crosby, Stills and Nash; Crosby, Stills, Nash and Young; Graham Nash.

Johnny NASH US, male vocalist 17 wks

5 Aug 72	**I CAN SEE CLEARLY NOW** *CBS 64860*	**39**	6 wks
10 Dec 77	**JOHNNY NASH COLLECTION** *Epic EPC 10008*	**18**	11 wks

NASH THE SLASH Canada, male vocalist/
multi-instrumentalist 1 wk

21 Feb 81	**CHILDREN OF THE NIGHT** *DinDisc DID 9* ...	**61**	1 wk

NATASHA UK, female vocalist 3 wks

9 Oct 82	**CAPTURED** *Towerbell TOWLP 2*	**53**	3 wks

THE NOLANS (left) Watching the camera but not their weight.

STEVIE NICKS (below centre) The Fleetwood Mac vocalist just missed the Top Ten with her first solo attempt in 1981.

MUSICAL YOUTH (left) The youth of 1982.

YOKO ONO (below) 'Season of Glass' was her first album to break.

ESTHER AND ABI OFARIM (below) The most successful Israeli act in UK chart history.

NATIONAL BRASS BAND UK, orchestra

10 wks

10 May 80	**GOLDEN MEMORIES**	*K-Tel ONE 1075*	......	**15**	10 wks

NAZARETH UK, male vocal/instrumental group

51 wks

26 May 73	**RAZAMANAZ**	*Mooncrest CREST 1*	....	**11**	25 wks
24 Nov 73 ●	**LOUD 'N' PROUD**	*Mooncrest CREST 4*	....	**10**	7 wks
18 May 74	**RAMPANT**	*Mooncrest CREST 15*	....	**13**	3 wks
13 Dec 75	**GREATEST HITS**	*Mountain TOPS 108*	....	**54**	1 wk
3 Feb 79	**NO MEAN CITY**	*Mountain TOPS 123*	....	**34**	9 wks
28 Feb 81	**THE FOOL CIRCLE**	*NEMS NEL 6019*	......	**60**	3 wks
3 Oct 81	**NAZARETH LIVE**	*NEMS NELD 102*	....	**78**	3 wks

Bill NELSON UK, male vocalist/multi-instrumentalist

20 wks

24 Feb 79	**SOUND ON SOUND**	*Harvest SHSP 4095*	.....	**33**	5 wks
23 May 81 ●	**QUIT DREAMING AND GET ON THE BEAM**				
		Mercury 6359 055		**7**	6 wks
3 Jul 82	**THE LOVE THAT WHIRLS (DIARY OF A THINKING HEART)**	*Mercury/*			
		Phonogram WHIRL 3		**28**	4 wks
14 May 83	**CHIMERA**	*Mercury MERB 19*	....	**30**	5 wks

First album credited to Bill Nelson's Red Noise – UK male vocal/instrumental group.

Phyllis NELSON US, female vocalist

10 wks

20 Apr 85	**MOVE CLOSER**	*Carrere CAL 203*	....	**29**	10 wks

NENA Germany, female/male vocal/instrumental group

5 wks

24 Mar 84	**NENA**	*Epic EPC 25925*	....	**31**	5 wks

NEW MODEL ARMY UK, male vocal/instrumental group

8 wks

12 May 84	**VENGENCE**	*Abstract ABT 008*	....	**73**	5 wks
25 May 85	**NO REST FOR THE WICKED**	*EMI NMAL 1*	..	**22**	3 wks

NEW MUSIK UK, male vocal/instrumental group

11 wks

17 May 80	**FROM A TO B**	*GTO GTLP 041*	....	**35**	9 wks
14 Mar 81	**ANYWHERE**	*GTO GTLP 044*	....	**68**	2 wks

NEW ORDER UK, male/female vocal/instrumental group

49 wks

28 Nov 81	**MOVEMENT**	*Factory FACT 50*	....	**30**	10 wks
14 May 83 ●	**POWER, CORRUPTION AND LIES**				
		Factory FACT 75		**4**	29 wks
25 May 85 ●	**LOW-LIFE**	*Factory FACT 100*	....	**7**	10 wks

NEW SEEKERS UK, male/female vocal instrumental group

49 wks

5 Feb 72	**NEW COLOURS**	*Polydor 2383 066*	....	**40**	4 wks
1 Apr 72 ●	**WE'D LIKE TO TEACH THE WORLD TO SING**				
		Polydor 2883 103	....	**2**	25 wks

---

12 Aug 72	**NEVER ENDING SONG OF LOVE**				
		Polydor 2383 126	....	**35**	4 wks
14 Oct 72	**CIRCLES**	*Polydor 2442 102*	....	**23**	5 wks
21 Apr 73	**NOW**	*Polydor 2383 195*	....	**47**	2 wks
30 Mar 74	**TOGETHER**	*Polydor 2383 264*	....	**12**	9 wks

NEW WORLD THEATRE ORCHESTRA
UK, orchestra

1 wk

24 Dec 60	**LET'S DANCE TO THE HITS OF THE 30'S AND 40'S**	*Pye Golden Guinea GGL 0026*		**20**	1 wk

NEWCLEUS US, male vocal/instrumental group

2 wks

25 Aug 84	**JAM ON REVENGE**	*Sunnyview SVLP 6600*	.....	**84**	2 wks

Bob NEWHART US, male comedian

37 wks

1 Oct 60 ●	**BUTTON-DOWN MIND OF BOB NEWHART**				
		Warner Bros. WM 4010	....	**2**	37 wks

Anthony NEWLEY UK, male vocalist

14 wks

14 May 60	**LOVE IS A NOW AND THEN THING**				
		Decca LK 4343	....	**19**	2 wks
8 Jul 61 ●	**TONY**	*Decca LK 4406*	....	**5**	12 wks

See also Anthony Newley, Peter Sellers and Joan Collins.

Anthony NEWLEY, Peter SELLERS, Joan COLLINS UK, male/female vocalists

10 wks

28 Sep 63 ●	**FOOL BRITANNIA**	*Ember CEL 902*	....	**10**	10 wks

See also Anthony Newley; Peter Sellers and Harry Secombe, and Spike Milligan; Peter Sellers and Sophia Loren.

Olivia NEWTON-JOHN UK, female vocalist

90 wks

2 Mar 74	**MUSIC MAKES MY DAY**	*Pye NSPL 28186*	....	**37**	3 wks
29 Jun 74	**LONG LIVE LOVE**	*EMI EMC 3028*	....	**40**	2 wks
26 Apr 75	**HAVE YOU NEVER BEEN MELLOW**				
		EMI EMC 3069	....	**37**	2 wks
29 May 76	**COME ON OVER**	*EMI EMC 3124*	....	**49**	4 wks
27 Aug 77	**MAKING A GOOD THING BETTER**				
		EMI EMC 3192	....	**60**	1 wk
21 Jan 78	**GREATEST HITS**	*EMI EMA 785*	....	**19**	9 wks
9 Dec 79	**TOTALLY HOT**	*EMI EMA 789*	....	**30**	9 wks
31 Oct 81	**PHYSICAL**	*EMI EMC 3386*	....	**11**	22 wks
23 Oct 82 ●	**GREATEST HITS**	*EMI EMTV 36*	....	**8**	38 wks

NICE UK, male instrumental group

38 wks

13 Sep 69 ●	**NICE**	*Immediate IMSP 026*	....	**3**	6 wks
27 Jun 70 ●	**FIVE BRIDGES**	*Charisma CAS 1014*	....	**2**	21 wks
17 Apr 71 ●	**ELEGY**	*Charisma CAS 1030*	....	**5**	11 wks

Stevie NICKS US, female vocalist

37 wks

8 Aug 81	**BELLA DONNA**	*WEA K 99169*	....	**11**	15 wks
2 Jul 83	**THE WILD HEART**	*WEA 25-0071-1*	....	**28**	19 wks
14 Dec 85	**ROCK A LITTLE**	*Modern PCS 7300*	....	**83†**	3 wks

Hector NICOL UK, male vocalist

1 wk

28 Apr 84	**BRAVO JULIET**	*Igus/Klub KLP 42*	....	**92**	1 wk

NICOLE *Germany, female vocalist* — *2 wks*

2 Oct 82	**A LITTLE PEACE**	*CBS 85011*	....	85	2 wks

NILSSON *US, male vocalist* — *43 wks*

29 Jan 72	**THE POINT**	*RCA Victor SF 8166*	....	46	1 wk
5 Feb 72 ●	**NILSSON SCHMILSSON**	*RCA Victor SF 8242*	..	4	22 wks
19 Aug 72	**SON OF SCHMILSSON**	*RCA Victor SF 8297*	..	41	1 wk
28 Jul 73	**A LITTLE TOUCH OF SCHMILSSON IN THE NIGHT**	*RCA Victor SF 8371*	..	20	19 wks

NINA and FREDERICK *Denmark, male/female vocal duo* — *6 wks*

13 Feb 60 ●	**NINA AND FREDERICK**	*Pye NPT 19023*	......	9	2 wks
29 Apr 61	**NINA AND FREDERICK**	*Columbia COL 1314*	..	11	4 wks

These two albums, although identically named, are different.

9 BELOW ZERO *UK, male vocal/instrumental group* — *12 wks*

14 Mar 81	**DON'T POINT YOUR FINGER**	*A & M AMLH 68521*	....	56	6 wks
20 Mar 82	**THIRD DEGREE**	*A&M AMLH 68537*	....	38	6 wks

999 *UK, male vocal/instrumental group* — *1 wk*

25 Mar 78	**999**	*United Artists UAG 30199*	....	53	1 wk

NOLANS *Ireland, female vocal group* — *84 wks*

20 Jul 78 ●	**20 GIANT HITS**	*Target TGS 502*	....	3	12 wks
19 Jan 80	**NOLANS**	*Epic EPC 83892*		15	13 wks
25 Oct 80	**MAKING WAVES**	*Epic EPC 10023*		11	33 wks
27 Mar 82 ●	**PORTRAIT**	*Epic EPC 10033*		7	10 wks
20 Nov 82	**ALTOGETHER**	*Epic EPC 10037*		52	8 wks
17 Nov 84	**GIRLS JUST WANNA HAVE FUN**	*Towerbell TOWLP 10*	....	39	8 wks

First album credited to Nolan Sisters.

NORTH - *See HATFIELD and the NORTH*

NOT THE 9 O'CLOCK NEWS CAST *UK, male/female TV cast* — *51 wks*

8 Nov 80 ●	**NOT THE 9 O'CLOCK NEWS**	*BBC REB 400*	...	5	23 wks
17 Oct 81 ●	**HEDGEHOG SANDWICH**	*BBC REB 421*	......	5	24 wks
23 Oct 82	**THE MEMORY KINDA LINGERS**	*BBC REF 453*		63	4 wks

NUCLEUS *UK, male instrumental group* — *1 wk*

11 Jul 70	**ELASTIC ROCK**	*Vertigo 6360 006*	....	46	1 wk

Ted NUGENT *US, male vocalist/instrumentalist - guitar* — *14 wks*

4 Sep 76	**TED NUGENT**	*Epic EPC 81268*		56	1 wk
30 Oct 76	**FREE FOR ALL**	*Epic EPC 81397*		33	2 wks
2 Jul 77	**CAT SCRATCH FEVER**	*Epic EPC 82010*		28	5 wks
11 Mar 78	**DOUBLE LIVE GONZO**	*Epic EPC 88282*	......	47	2 wks
14 Jun 80	**SCREAM DREAM**	*Epic EPC 86111*		37	3 wks
25 Apr 81	**IN 10 CITIES**	*Epic EPC 84917*	....	75	1 wk

Gary NUMAN *UK, male vocalist* — *127 wks*

9 Jun 79 ★	**REPLICAS**	*Beggars Banquet BEGA 7*		1	31 wks
25 Aug 79	**TUBEWAY ARMY**	*Beggars Banquet BEGA 4*	....	14	10 wks
22 Sep 79 ★	**THE PLEASURE PRINCIPLE**	*Beggars Banquet BEGA 10*		1	21 wks
13 Sep 80 ★	**TELEKON**	*Beggars Banquet BEGA 19*		1	11 wks
2 May 81 ●	**LIVING ORNAMENTS 1979-1980**	*Beggars Banquet BOX 1*		2	4 wks
2 May 81	**LIVING ORNAMENTS 1979**	*Beggars Banquet BEGA 24*		47	3 wks
2 May 81	**LIVING ORNAMENTS 1980**	*Beggars Banquet BEGA 25*		39	3 wks
12 Sep 81 ●	**DANCE**	*Beggars Banquet BEGA 28*		3	8 wks
18 Sep 82 ●	**I, ASSASSIN**	*Beggars Banquet BEGA 40*		8	6 wks
27 Nov 82	**NEW MAN NUMAN - THE BEST OF GARY NUMAN**	*TV Records TVA 7*	....	45	7 wks
24 Sep 83	**WARRIORS**	*Beggars Banquet BEGA 47*		12	6 wks
6 Oct 84	**THE PLAN**	*Beggars Banquet BEGA 55*		29	4 wks
24 Nov 84	**BERSERKER**	*Numa NUMA 1001*		45	3 wks
13 Apr 85	**WHITE NOISE-LIVE**	*Numa NUMAD 1002*	.....	29	5 wks
28 Sep 85	**THE FURY**	*Numa NUMA 1003*		24	5 wks

First two albums credited to Tubeway Army. The Plan is credited to Tubeway Army and Gary Numan. All other albums are credited to Gary Numan. Living Ornaments 1979-1980 is a boxed set of Living Ornaments 1979 and Living Ornaments 1980.

O

Philip OAKEY and Georgio MORODER *UK/Italy male vocal/instrumental duo* — *5 wks*

10 Aug 85	**PHILIP OAKEY AND GEORGIO MORODER**	*Virgin V 2351*	....	52	5 wks

OASIS *UK, male/female vocal group* — *14 wks*

28 Apr 84	**OASIS**	*WEA WX 3*	....	23	14 wks

OATES - *See Daryl HALL and John OATES*

Billy OCEAN *UK, male vocalist* — *39 wks*

24 Nov 84 ●	**SUDDENLY**	*Jive JIP 12*	....	9	39 wks

Des O'CONNOR *UK, male vocalist* — *41 wks*

7 Dec 68 ●	**I PRETEND**	*Columbia SCX 6295*	....	8	10 wks
5 Dec 70	**WITH LOVE**	*Columbia SCX 6417*		40	4 wks
2 Dec 72	**SING A FAVOURITE SONG**	*Pye NSPL 18390*	..	25	6 wks
2 Feb 80	**JUST FOR YOU**	*Warwick WW 5071*	....	17	7 wks
13 Oct 84	**DES O'CONNOR NOW**	*Telstar STAR 2245*		24	14 wks

Hazel O'CONNOR *UK, female vocalist* — *44 wks*

9 Aug 80 ●	**BREAKING GLASS (film soundtrack)**	*A & M AMLH 64820*		5	37 wks
12 Sep 81	**COVER PLUS**	*Albion ALB 108*	....	32	7 wks

ODYSSEY *US, male/female vocal group* — *24 wks*

16 Aug 80	**HANG TOGETHER**	*RCA PL 13526*		38	3 wks
4 Jul 81	**I'VE GOT THE MELODY**	*RCA RCALP 5028*	..	29	7 wks
3 Jul 82	**HAPPY TOGETHER**	*RCA RCALP 6036*		21	9 wks
20 Nov 82	**THE MAGIC TOUCH OF ODYSSEY**	*Telstar STAR 2223*	....	69	5 wks

ROBERT PLANT Trying to figure out how long a Big Log is.

MIKE OLDFIELD Even more hits than images in this picture.

GRAHAM PARKER Rumour has it Ron and Russell Mael resisted the temptation to issue an album entitled 'Squeezing Out Graham Parker'.

ELAINE PAIGE Four hit albums – the last three platinum.

Esther and Abi OFARIM *Israel, female/male vocal duo*

24 wks

24 Feb 68	●	**2 IN 3**	*Philips SBL 7825*	**6**	20 wks
12 Jul 69		**OFARIM CONCERT - LIVE '69**	*Philips XL 4* ...	**29**	4 wks

Mary O'HARA *UK, female vocalist/instrumentalist - harp*

12 wks

8 Apr 78	**MARY O'HARA AT THE ROYAL FESTIVAL HALL** *Chrysalis CHR 1159*	**37**	3 wks
1 Dec 79	**TRANQUILLITY** *Warwick WW 5072*	**12**	9 wks

Mike OLDFIELD *UK, male multi-instrumentalist/vocalist*

449 wks

14 Jul 73	★ **TUBULAR BELLS** *Virgin V 2001*	**1**	264 wks
14 Sep 74	★ **HERGEST RIDGE** *Virgin V 2013*	**1**	17 wks
8 Feb 75	**THE ORCHESTRAL TUBULAR BELLS (WITH THE ROYAL PHILHARMONIC ORCHESTRA)** *Virgin V 2026*	**17**	7 wks
15 Nov 75	● **OMMADAWN** *Virgin V 2043*	**4**	23 wks
20 Nov 76	**BOXED** *Virgin V BOX 1*	**22**	13 wks
9 Dec 78	**INCANTATIONS** *Virgin VDT 101*	**14**	17 wks
11 Aug 79	**EXPOSED** *Virgin VD 2511*	**16**	9 wks
8 Dec 79	**PLATINUM** *Virgin V 2141*	**24**	9 wks
8 Nov 80	**QE 2** *Virgin V 2181*	**27**	8 wks
27 Mar 82	● **FIVE MILES OUT** *Virgin V 2222*	**7**	27 wks
4 Jun 83	● **CRISES** *Virgin V 2262*	**6**	29 wks
7 Jul 84	**DISCOVERY** *Virgin V 2308*	**15**	▪16 wks
15 Dec 84	**THE KILLING FIELDS-ORIGINAL SOUNDTRACK** *Virgin V 2328*	**97**	1 wk
2 Nov 85	**THE COMPLETE MIKE OLDFIELD** *Virgin MOC 1*	**36†**	9 wks

ONE HUNDRED & ONE STRINGS *Germany, orchestra*

35 wks

26 Sep 59	● **GYPSY CAMPFIRES** *Pye GGL 0009*	**9**	7 wks
26 Mar 60	**SOUL OF SPAIN** *Pye GGL 0017*	**17**	1 wk
16 Apr 60	● **GRAND CANYON SUITE** *Pye GGL 0048*	**10**	1 wk
27 Aug 60	★ **DOWN DRURY LANE TO MEMORY LANE** *Pye GGL 0061*	**1**	21 wks
15 Oct 83	**MORNING, NOON & NIGHT** *Ronco RTL 2094*	**32**	5 wks

The orchestra was American based for last album.

Alexander O'NEAL *US, male vocalist*

5 wks

1 Jun 85	**ALEXANDER O'NEAL** *Tabu TBU 26485*	**53**	5 wks

ONLY ONES *UK, male vocal/instrumental group*

8 wks

3 Jun 78	**THE ONLY ONES** *CBS 82830*	**56**	1 wk
31 Mar 79	**EVEN SERPENTS SHINE** *CBS 83451*	**42**	2 wks
3 May 80	**BABY'S GOT A GUN** *CBS 84089*	**37**	5 wks

Yoko ONO *Japan, female vocalist*

2 wks

20 Jun 81	**SEASON OF GLASS** *Geffen K 99164*	**47**	2 wks

See also John Lennon.

ORANGE JUICE *UK, male vocal/instrumental group*

18 wks

6 Mar 82	**YOU CAN'T HIDE YOUR LOVE FOREVER** *Polydor POLS 1057*	**21**	6 wks
20 Nov 82	**RIP IT UP** *Holden Caulfield Universal/ Polydor POLS 1076*	**39**	8 wks
10 Mar 84	**TEXAS FEVER** *Polydor OJMLP 1*	**34**	4 wks

Roy ORBISON *US, male vocalist*

142 wks

8 Jun 63	**LONELY AND BLUE** *London HAU 2342*	**15**	8 wks
29 Jun 63	**CRYING** *London HAU 2437*	**17**	3 wks
30 Nov 63	● **IN DREAMS** *London HAU 8108*	**6**	57 wks
25 Jul 64	**EXCITING SOUNDS OF ROY ORBISON** *Ember NR 5013*	**17**	2 wks
5 Dec 64	● **OH PRETTY WOMAN** *London HAU 8207*	**4**	16 wks
25 Sep 65	● **THERE IS ONLY ONE ROY ORBISON** *London HAU 8252*	**10**	12 wks
26 Feb 66	**THE ORBISON WAY** *London HAU 8279*	**11**	10 wks
24 Sep 66	**THE CLASSIC ROY ORBISON** *London HAU 8297*	**12**	8 wks
22 Jul 67	**ORBISONGS** *Monument SMO 5004*	**40**	1 wk
30 Sep 67	**ROY ORBISON'S GREATEST HITS** *Monument SMO 5007*	**40**	1 wk
27 Jan 73	**ALL-TIME GREATEST HITS** *Monument MNT 67290*	**39**	3 wks
29 Nov 75	★ **THE BEST OF ROY ORBISON** *Arcade ADEP 19*	**1**	20 wks
18 Jul 81	**GOLDEN DAYS** *CBS 10026*	**63**	1 wk

ORCHESTRAL MANOEUVRES IN THE DARK *UK, male vocal/instrumental duo*

145 wks

1 Mar 80	**ORCHESTRAL MANOEUVRES IN THE DARK** *DinDisc DID 2*	**27**	29 wks
1 Nov 80	● **ORGANISATION** *DinDisc DID 6*	**6**	25 wks
14 Nov 81	● **ARCHITECTURE AND MORALITY** *DinDisc DID 12*	**3**	39 wks
12 Mar 83	● **DAZZLE SHIPS** *Telegraph V 2261*	**5**	13 wks
12 May 84	● **JUNK CULTURE** *Virgin V 2310*	**9**	27 wks
29 Jun 85	**CRUSH** *Virgin V 2349*	**13**	12 wks

L'ORCHESTRE ELECTRONIQUE *UK, male synthesized orchestra*

1 wk

29 Oct 83	**SOUND WAVES** *Nouveau Musique NML 1005* ...	**75**	1 wk

Cyril ORNADEL/LONDON SYMPHONY ORCHESTRA *UK, conductor and orchestra*

21 wks

16 Dec 72	● **THE STRAUSS FAMILY** *Polydor 2659 014*	**2**	21 wks

See also London Symphony Orchestra.

Jeffrey OSBORNE *US, male vocalist*

10 wks

5 May 84	**STAY WITH ME TONIGHT** *A & M AMLX 64940*	**56**	7 wks
13 Oct 84	**DON'T STOP** *A & M AMA 5017*	**59**	3 wks

Ozzy OSBOURNE *UK, male vocalist*

33 wks

20 Sep 80	● **OZZY OSBOURNE'S BLIZZARD OF OZ** *Jet JETLP 234*	**7**	8 wks
7 Nov 81	**DIARY OF A MADMAN** *Jet JETLP 237*	**14**	12 wks
27 Nov 82	**TALK OF THE DEVIL** *Jet JETDP 401*	**21**	6 wks
10 Dec 83	**BARK AT THE MOON** *Epic EPC 25739*	**24**	7 wks

Ozzy Osbourne's Blizzard Of Oz are a UK/US male vocal/instrumental group.

OSIBISA Ghana/Nigeria, male vocal/instrumental group
17 wks

22 May 71	**OSIBISA**	MCA MDKS 8001	**11**	10 wks
5 Feb 72	**WOYAYA**	MCA MDKS 8005	**11**	7 wks

Donny OSMOND US, male vocalist
104 wks

23 Sep 72	● **PORTRAIT OF DONNY**	MGM 2315 108	**5**	43 wks
16 Dec 72	● **TOO YOUNG**	MGM 2315 113	**7**	24 wks
26 May 73	● **ALONE TOGETHER**	MGM 2315 210	**6**	19 wks
15 Dec 73	● **A TIME FOR US**	MGM 2315 273	**4**	13 wks
8 Feb 75	**DONNY**	MGM 2315 314	**16**	4 wks
2 Oct 76	**DISCOTRAIN**	Polydor 2391 226	**59**	1 wk

See also Osmonds; Donny and Marie Osmond.

Donny and Marie OSMOND US, male/female vocal duo
19 wks

2 Nov 74	**I'M LEAVING IT ALL UP TO YOU** MGM 2315 307		**13**	15 wks
26 Jul 75	**MAKE THE WORLD GO AWAY** MGM 2315 343		**30**	3 wks
5 Jun 76	**DEEP PURPLE** Polydor 2391 220		**48**	1 wk

See also Osmonds; Donny Osmond; Marie Osmond.

Little Jimmy OSMOND US, male vocalist
12 wks

17 Feb 73	**KILLER JOE**	MGM 2315 157	**20**	12 wks

See also Osmonds.

Marie OSMOND US, female vocalist
1 wk

9 Feb 74	**PAPER ROSES**	MGM 2315 262	**46**	1 wk

See also Donny and Marie Osmond.

OSMONDS US, male vocal/instrumental group
103 wks

18 Nov 72	**OSMONDS LIVE**	MGM 2315 117	**13**	22 wks
16 Dec 72	● **CRAZY HORSES**	MGM 2315 123	**9**	19 wks
25 Aug 73	● **THE PLAN**	MGM 2315 251	**6**	25 wks
17 Aug 74	● **OUR BEST TO YOU**	MGM 2315 300	**5**	20 wks
7 Dec 74	**LOVE ME FOR A REASON**	MGM 2315 312	**13**	9 wks
14 Jun 75	**I'M STILL GONNA NEED YOU**	MGM 2315 342	**19**	7 wks
10 Jan 76	**AROUND THE WORLD - LIVE IN CONCERT** MGM 2659 044		**41**	1 wk

See also Donny Osmond; Little Jimmy Osmond; Donny and Marie Osmond.

Gilbert O'SULLIVAN UK, male vocalist
191 wks

25 Sep 71	● **HIMSELF**	MAM 501	**5**	82 wks
18 Nov 72	★ **BACK TO FRONT**	MAM 502	**1**	64 wks
6 Oct 73	● **I'M A WRITER NOT A FIGHTER**	MAMS 505	**2**	25 wks
26 Oct 74	● **STRANGER IN MY OWN BACK YARD** MAM MAMS 506		**9**	8 wks
18 Dec 76	**GREATEST HITS**	MAM MAMA 2003	**13**	11 wks
12 Sep 81	**20 GOLDEN GREATS**	K-Tel NE 1133	**98**	1 wk

John OTWAY and Wild Willy BARRETT
UK, male vocal/instrumental duo
1 wk

1 Jul 78	**DEEP AND MEANINGLESS**	Polydor 2383 501	**44**	1 wk

P

PACEMAKERS - *See GERRY and the PACEMAKERS*

Jimmy PAGE UK, male instrumentalist - guitar
4 wks

27 Feb 82	**DEATHWISH II**	Swansong SSK 59415	**40**	4 wks

See also Roy Harper with Jimmy Page

Elaine PAIGE UK, female vocalist
86 wks

1 May 82	**ELAINE PAIGE**	WEA K 58385	**56**	6 wks
5 Nov 83	● **STAGES**	K-Tel NE 1262	**2**	48 wks
20 Oct 84	**CINEMA**	K-Tel NE 1282	**12**	25 wks
16 Nov 85	● **LOVE HURTS**	WEA WX 28	**8†**	7 wks

PALE FOUNTAINS UK, male vocal/instrumental group
3 wks

10 Mar 84	**PACIFIC STREET**	Virgin V 2274	**85**	2 wks
16 Feb 85	**FROM ACROSS THE KITCHEN TABLE** Virgin V 2333		**94**	1 wk

PALLAS UK, male vocal/instrumental group
3 wks

25 Feb 84	**SENTINEL**	Harvest SHSP 2400121	**41**	3 wks

Robert PALMER UK, male vocalist
30 wks

6 Nov 76	**SOME PEOPLE CAN DO WHAT THEY LIKE** Island ILPS 9420		**46**	1 wk
14 Jul 79	**SECRETS**	Island ILPS 9544	**54**	4 wks
6 Sep 80	**CLUES**	Island ILPS 9595	**31**	8 wks
3 Apr 82	**MAYBE IT'S LIVE**	Island ILPS 9665	**32**	6 wks
23 Apr 83	**PRIDE**	Island ILPS 9720	**37**	9 wks
16 Nov 85	**RIPTIDE**	Island ILPS 9801	**69**	2 wks

PAPAS - *See MAMAS and the PAPAS*

Graham PARKER and the RUMOUR UK, male vocal/instrumental group
35 wks

27 Nov 76	**HEAT TREATMENT**	Vertigo 6360 137	**52**	2 wks
12 Nov 77	**STICK TO ME**	Vertigo 9102 017	**19**	4 wks
27 May 78	**PARKERILLA**	Vertigo 6641 797	**14**	5 wks
7 Apr 79	**SQUEEZING OUT SPARKS**	Vertigo 9102 030	**18**	8 wks
7 Jun 80	**THE UP ESCALATOR**	Stiff SEEZ 23	**11**	10 wks
27 Mar 82	**ANOTHER GREY AREA**	RCA RCALP 6029	**40**	6 wks

Another Grey Area credited to Graham Parker.

John PARR UK, male vocalist
2 wks

2 Nov 85	**JOHN PARR**	London LONLP 12	**60**	2 wks

Alan PARSONS PROJECT UK, male vocal/instrumental group
36 wks

28 Aug 76	**TALES OF MYSTERY AND IMAGINATION** Charisma CDS 4003		**56**	1 wk
13 Aug 77	**I ROBOT**	Arista SPARTY 1016	**30**	1 wk
10 Jun 78	**PYRAMID**	Arista SPART 1054	**49**	4 wks
29 Sep 79	**EVE**	Arista SPARTY 1100	**74**	1 wk

PINK FLOYD Pink Floyd in their early days with Syd Barrett. (LFI)

TOM PETTY (below) Wearing the 'Sun' long after dark.

IGGY POP (left) The Idiot with a Lust for Life found Man Power from the New Values as a soldier.

15 Nov 80	THE TURN OF A FRIENDLY CARD			
	Arista DLART 1	38	4 wks
29 May 82	EYE IN THE SKY Arista 204 666	28	11 wks
26 Nov 83	THE BEST OF THE ALAN PARSONS PROJECT			
	Arista APP 1	99	1 wk
3 Mar 84	AMMONIA AVENUE Arista 206 100	24	8 wks
23 Feb 85	VULTURE CULTURE Arista 206 577	40	5 wks

PARTISANS UK, male vocal/instrumental group

1 wk

19 Feb 83	THE PARTISANS No Future PUNK 4	94	1 wk

Dolly PARTON US, female vocalist

13 wks

25 Nov 78	DOLLY PARTON Lotus WH 5006	24	6 wks
6 Jan 79	BOTH SIDES Lotus WH 5006	45	6 wks
7 Sep 85	GREATEST HITS RCA PL 84422	74	1 wk

PARTRIDGE FAMILY US, male/female vocal group

13 wks

8 Jan 72	UP TO DATE Bell SBLL 143	46	2 wks
22 Apr 72	THE PARTRIDGE FAMILY SOUND MAGAZINE			
	Bell BELLS 206	14	7 wks
30 Sep 72	SHOPPING BAG Bell BELLS 212	28	3 wks
9 Dec 72	CHRISTMAS CARD Bell BELLS 214	45	1 wk

PASSIONS UK, male/female vocal/instrumental group

1 wk

3 Oct 81	THIRTY THOUSAND FEET OVER CHINA			
	Polydor POLS 1041	92	1 wk

PAUL - *See PETER, PAUL and MARY*

Luciano PAVAROTTI Italy, male vocalist

1 wk

15 May 82	PAVAROTTI'S GREATEST HITS Decca D 2362	95	1 wk

See also Luciano Pavarotti with the Henry Mancini Orchestra.

Luciano PAVAROTTI with Henry MANCINI ORCHESTRA *Italy, male vocalist with US conductor/ orchestra*

1 wk

30 Jun 84	MAMMA Decca 411959	96	1 wk

See also Luciano Pavarotti;Henry Mancini;James Galway and Henry Mancini.

Tom PAXTON US, male vocalist

10 wks

13 Jun 70	NO.6 Elektra 2469-003	23	5 wks
3 Apr 71	THE COMPLEAT TOM PAXTON			
	Elektra EKD 2003	18	4 wks
1 Jul 72	PEACE WILL COME Reprise K 44182	47	1 wk

PEDDLERS UK, male vocal/instrumental group

16 wks

16 Mar 68	FREE WHEELERS CBS SBPG 63183	27	13 wks
7 Feb 70	BIRTHDAY CBS 63682	16	3 wks

Kevin PEEK UK, male instrumentalist - guitar

2 wks

21 Mar 81	AWAKENING Ariola ARL 5065	52	2 wks

See also Kevin Peek and Rick Wakeman

Kevin PEEK and Rick WAKEMAN UK, male instrumental duo-guitar and keyboards

6 wks

13 Oct 84	BEYOND THE PLANETS Woomera/			
	Telstar STAR 2244	64	6 wks

Beyond the Planets also features Jeff Wayne with narration by Patrick Allen. See also Kevin Peek;Rick Wakeman.

PENETRATION UK, male/female vocal/instrumental group

8 wks

28 Oct 78	MOVING TARGETS Virgin V 2109	22	4 wks
6 Oct 79	COMING UP FOR AIR Virgin V 2131	36	4 wks

PENTANGLE UK, male/female vocal/instrumental group

39 wks

15 Jun 68	THE PENTANGLE Transatlantic TRA 162	21	9 wks
1 Nov 69	● BASKET OF LIGHT Transatlantic TRA 205	5	28 wks
12 Dec 70	CRUEL SISTER Transatlantic TRA 228	51	2 wks

Carl PERKINS US, male vocalist

3 wks

15 Apr 78	OL' BLUE SUEDES IS BACK Jet UATV 30146	38	3 wks

Steve PERRY US, male vocalist

2 wks

14 Jul 84	STREET TALK CBS 25967	59	2 wks

PESTALOZZI CHILDREN'S CHOIR UK, male/female vocal group

2 wks

26 Dec 81	SONGS OF JOY K-Tel NE 1140	65	2 wks

PETER and GORDON UK, male vocal duo

1 wk

20 Jun 64	PETER AND GORDON Columbia 33SX 1630 ...	18	1 wk

PETER, PAUL and MARY US, male/female vocal/ instrumental group

26 wks

4 Jan 64	PETER PAUL & MARY Warner Bros. WM 4064	18	1 wk
21 Mar 64	IN THE WIND Warner Bros. WM 8142	11	19 wks
13 Feb 65	IN CONCERT VOL.1 Warner Bros. WM 8158 ...	20	2 wks
5 Sep 70	TEN YEARS TOGETHER Warner Bros. WS 2552	60	4 wks

PETERS and LEE UK, male/female vocal duo

166 wks

30 Jun 73	★ WE CAN MAKE IT Philips 6308 165	1	55 wks
22 Dec 73	● BY YOUR SIDE Philips 6308 192	9	48 wks
21 Sep 74	● RAINBOW Philips 6308 208	6	27 wks
4 Oct 75	● FAVOURITES Philips 9109 205	2	32 wks
18 Dec 76	INVITATION Philips 9101 027	44	4 wks

Tom PETTY and the HEARTBREAKERS US, male vocal/instrumental group

36 wks

4 Jun 77	TOM PETTY AND THE HEARTBREAKERS			
	Shelter ISA 5014	24	12 wks
1 Jul 78	YOU'RE GONNA GET IT Island ISA 5017	34	5 wks
17 Nov 79	DAMN THE TORPEDOES MCA MCF 3044	57	4 wks
23 May 81	HARD PROMISES MCA MCF 3098	32	5 wks
20 Nov 82	LONG AFTER DARK MCA MCF 3155	45	4 wks

20 Apr 85	**SOUTHERN ACCENTS** *MCA MCF 3260*	**23**	6 wks

Ph.D *UK, male vocal/instrumental duo* *8 wks*

1 May 82	**PH.D** *WEA K 99150*	**33**	8 wks

PHENOMENA *UK, male vocal/instrumental group* *2 wks*

6 Jul 85	**PHENOMENA** *Bronze PM 1*	**63**	2 wks

Arlene PHILLIPS *UK, female exercise instructor* *24 wks*

28 Aug 82	**KEEP IN SHAPE SYSTEM** *Supershape SUP 01* ..	**41**	23 wks
18 Feb 84	**KEEP IN SHAPE SYSTEM VOL.2**		
	Supershape SUP 2	**100**	1 wk

Keep In Shape System *features music by Funk Federation*

PHOTOS *UK, female/male vocal/instrumental group* *9 wks*

21 Jun 80 ●	**THE PHOTOS** *CBS PHOTO 5*	**4**	9 wks

PIGBAG *UK, male instrumental group* *14 wks*

13 Mar 82	**DR HECKLE AND MR JIVE** *Y Y 17*	**18**	14 wks

PILOT *UK, male vocal/instrumental group* *1 wk*

31 May 75	**SECOND FLIGHT** *EMI EMC 3075*	**48**	1 wk

PINK FAIRIES *UK, male vocal/instrumental group* *1 wk*

29 Jul 72	**WHAT A BUNCH OF SWEETIES**		
	Polydor 2383 132	**48**	1 wk

PINK FLOYD *UK, male vocal/instrumental group* *687 wks*

19 Aug 67 ●	**PIPER AT THE GATES OF DAWN**		
	Columbia SCX 6157	**6**	14 wks
13 Jul 68 ●	**SAUCERFUL OF SECRETS** *Columbia SCX 6258*	**9**	11 wks
28 Jun 69 ●	**MORE (film soundtrack)** *Columbia SCX 6346* ...	**9**	5 wks
15 Nov 69 ●	**UMMAGUMMA** *Harvest SHDW 1/2*	**5**	21 wks
24 Oct 70 ★	**ATOM HEART MOTHER** *Harvest SHVL 781* ...	**1**	23 wks
7 Aug 71 ●	**RELICS** *Starline SRS 5071*	**32**	6 wks
20 Nov 71 ●	**MEDDLE** *Harvest SHVL 795*	**3**	82 wks
17 Jun 72 ●	**OBSCURED BY CLOUDS (film soundtrack)**		
	Harvest SHSP 4020	**6**	14 wks
31 Mar 73 ●	**DARK SIDE OF THE MOON** *Harvest SHVL 804*	**2**	294 wks
19 Jan 74	**A NICE PAIR (double re-issue)**		
	Harvest SHDW 403	**21**	20 wks
27 Sep 75 ★	**WISH YOU WERE HERE** *Harvest SHVL 814* ...	**1**	83 wks
19 Feb 77 ●	**ANIMALS** *Harvest SHVL 815*	**2**	33 wks
8 Dec 79 ●	**THE WALL** *Harvest SHDW 411*	**3**	46 wks
5 Dec 81	**A COLLECTION OF GREAT DANCE SONGS**		
	Harvest SHVL 822	**37**	10 wks
2 Apr 83 ★	**THE FINAL CUT** *Harvest SHPF 1983*	**1**	25 wks

A Nice Pair *is a double re-issue of the first two albums.*

PIPS - *See Gladys KNIGHT and the PIPS*

PIRANHAS *UK, male vocal/instrumental group* *3 wks*

20 Sep 80	**PIRANHAS** *Sire SRK 6098*	**69**	3 wks

PIRATES *UK, male vocal/instrumental group* *3 wks*

19 Nov 77	**OUT OF THEIR SKULLS** *Warner Bros. K 56411*	**57**	3 wks

Gene PITNEY *US, male vocalist* *66 wks*

11 Apr 64 ●	**BLUE GENE** *United Artists ULP 1061*	**7**	11 wks
6 Feb 65	**GENE PITNEY'S BIG 16** *Stateside SL 10118*	**12**	6 wks
20 Mar 65	**I'M GONNA BE STRONG** *Stateside SL 10120* ...	**15**	2 wks
20 Nov 65	**LOOKIN' THRU THE EYES OF LOVE**		
	Stateside SL 10148	**15**	5 wks
17 Sep 66	**NOBODY NEEDS YOUR LOVE**		
	Stateside SL 10183	**13**	17 wks
4 Mar 67	**YOUNG WARM AND WONDERFUL**		
	Stateside SSL 10194	**39**	1 wk
22 Apr 67	**GENE PITNEY'S BIG SIXTEEN**		
	Stateside SSL 10199	**40**	1 wk
20 Sep 69 ●	**BEST OF GENE PITNEY** *Stateside SSL 10286*	**8**	9 wks
2 Oct 76 ●	**HIS 20 GREATEST HITS** *Arcade ADEP 22*	**6**	14 wks

Robert PLANT *UK, male vocalist* *33 wks*

10 Jul 82 ●	**PICTURES AT ELEVEN** *Swansong SSK 59418* ..	**2**	15 wks
23 Jul 83 ●	**THE PRINCIPLE OF MOMENTS** *WEA 7901011*	**7**	14 wks
1 Jun 85	**SHAKEN 'N' STIRRED** *Es Paranza 79-0265-1* ...	**19**	4 wks

PLASMATICS *US, female/male vocal/instrumental group* *3 wks*

11 Oct 80	**NEW HOPE FOR THE WRETCHED**		
	Stiff SEEZ 24	**55**	3 wks

PLATTERS *US, male/female vocal group* *13 wks*

8 Apr 78 ●	**20 CLASSIC HITS** *Mercury 9100 049*	**8**	13 wks

PLAYERS ASSOCIATION *US, male/female vocal/instrumental group* *4 wks*

17 Mar 79	**TURN THE MUSIC UP** *Vanguard VSD 79421* ...	**54**	4 wks

PLAYN JAYN *UK, male vocal/instrumental group* *1 wk*

1 Sep 84	**FRIDAY THE 13TH (AT THE MARQUEE CLUB)**		
	A & M JAYN 13	**93**	1 wk

POGUES *Ireland, male vocal/instrumental group* *14 wks*

3 Nov 84	**RED ROSES FOR ME** *Stiff SEEZ 55*	**89**	1 wk
17 Aug 85	**RUM, SODOMY AND THE LASH** *Stiff SEEZ 58*	**13**	13 wks

POINTER SISTERS *US, female vocal group* *78 wks*

29 Aug 81	**BLACK AND WHITE** *Planet K 52300*	**21**	13 wks
5 May 84 ●	**BREAK OUT** *Planet FL 84705*	**9**	58 wks
27 Jul 85	**CONTACT** *Planet PL 85457*	**34**	7 wks

POLECATS UK, male vocal/instrumental group — 2 wks

4 Jul 81	POLECATS	Vertigo 6359 057		28	2 wks

POLICE UK, male vocal/instrumental group — 276 wks

21 Apr 79	● OUTLANDOS D'AMOUR	A & M AMLH 68502		6	96 wks
13 Oct 79	★ REGGATTA DE BLANC	A & M AMLH 64792		1	74 wks
11 Oct 80	★ ZENYATTA MONDATTA	A & M AMLH 64831		1	31 wks
10 Oct 81	★ GHOST IN THE MACHINE	A & M AMLK 63730		1	27 wks
25 Jun 83	★ SYNCHRONICITY	A & M AMLX 63735		1	48 wks

Iggy POP US, male vocalist — 16 wks

9 Apr 77	THE IDIOT	RCA Victor PL 12275		30	3 wks
4 Jun 77	RAW POWER	Embassy 31464		44	2 wks
1 Oct 77	LUST FOR LIFE	RCA PL 12488		28	5 wks
19 May 79	NEW VALUES	Arista SPART 1092		60	4 wks
16 Feb 80	SOLDIER	Arista SPART 1117		62	2 wks

Raw Power *credited to Iggy and the Stooges*

Sandy POSEY US, female vocalist — 1 wk

11 Mar 67	BORN A WOMAN	MGM MGMCS 8035		39	1 wk

Frank POURCEL France, male vocalist — 7 wks

20 Nov 71	● THIS IS POURCEL	Studio Two STWO 7		8	7 wks

Cozy POWELL UK, male instrumentalist - drums — 8 wks

26 Jan 80	OVER THE TOP	Ariola ARL 5038		34	3 wks
19 Sep 81	TILT	Polydor POLD 5047		58	4 wks
28 May 83	OCTOPUSS	Polydor POLD 5093		86	1 wk

Peter POWELL UK, male exercise instructor — 13 wks

20 Mar 82	● KEEP FIT AND DANCE	K-Tel NE 1167		9	13 wks

POWER STATION UK/US, male vocal/instrumental group — 23 wks

6 Apr 85	THE POWER STATION	Parlophone POST 1		12	23 wks

PRAYING MANTIS UK, male vocal/instrumental group — 2 wks

11 Apr 81	TIME TELLS NO LIES	Arista SPART 1153		60	2 wks

PREFAB SPROUT UK, male vocal/instrumental group — 33 wks

17 Mar 84	SWOON	Kitchenware KWLP 1		22	7 wks
22 Jun 85	STEVE McQUEEN	Kitchenware W.KWLP 3		21†	26 wks

Elvis PRESLEY US, male vocalist — 996 wks

8 Nov 58	● ELVIS' GOLDEN RECORDS	RCA RB 16069		3	44 wks
8 Nov 58	● KING CREOLE (film soundtrack) RCA RD 27086			4	14 wks
4 Apr 59	● ELVIS (ROCK 'N' ROLL NO.1) HMV CLP 1093			4	9 wks
8 Aug 59	● A DATE WITH ELVIS	RCA RD 27128		4	15 wks
18 Jun 60	★ ELVIS IS BACK	RCA RD 27171		1	27 wks
18 Jun 60	● ELVIS' GOLDEN RECORDS VOL.2 RCA RD 27159			4	20 wks
10 Dec 60	★ G.I. BLUES (film soundtrack) RCA RD 27192			1	55 wks
20 May 61	● HIS HAND IN MINE	RCA RD 27211		3	25 wks
4 Nov 61	● SOMETHING FOR EVERYBODY RCA RD 27224			2	18 wks
9 Dec 61	★ BLUE HAWAII (film soundtrack) RCA RD 27238			1	65 wks
7 Jul 62	★ POT LUCK	RCA RD 27265		1	25 wks
8 Dec 62	● ROCK 'N' ROLL NO.2	RCA RD 7528		3	17 wks
26 Jan 63	● GIRLS! GIRLS! GIRLS! (film soundtrack) RCA RD 7534			2	21 wks
11 May 63	● IT HAPPENED AT THE WORLD'S FAIR (film soundtrack) RCA RD 7565			4	21 wks
28 Dec 63	● FUN IN ACAPULCO (film soundtrack) RCA RD 7609			9	14 wks
11 Apr 64	● ELVIS' GOLDEN RECORDS VOL.3 RCA RD 7630			6	13 wks
4 Jul 64	● KISSIN' COUSINS (film soundtrack) RCA RD 7645			5	17 wks
9 Jan 65	ROUSTABOUT (film soundtrack) RCA RD 7678			12	4 wks
1 May 65	● GIRL HAPPY (film soundtrack) RCA RD 7714			8	18 wks
25 Sep 65	FLAMING STAR AND SUMMER KISSES RCA RD 7723			11	4 wks
4 Dec 65	● ELVIS FOR EVERYBODY	RCA RD 7782		8	8 wks
15 Jan 66	HAREM HOLIDAY (film soundtrack) RCA RD 7767			11	5 wks
30 Apr 66	FRANKIE AND JOHNNY (film soundtrack) RCA RD 7793			11	5 wks
6 Aug 66	● PARADISE HAWAIIAN STYLE (film soundtrack) RCA Victor RD 7810			7	9 wks
26 Nov 66	CALIFORNIA HOLIDAY (film soundtrack) RCA Victor RD 7820			17	6 wks
8 Apr 67	HOW GREAT THOU ART RCA Victor SF 7867			11	14 wks
2 Sep 67	DOUBLE TROUBLE (film soundtrack) RCA Victor SF 7892			34	1 wk
20 Apr 68	CLAMBAKE (film soundtrack) RCA Victor SD 7917			39	1 wk
3 May 69	● ELVIS - NBC TV SPECIAL RCA RD 8011			2	26 wks
5 Jul 69	● FLAMING STAR	RCA International INTS 1012		2	14 wks
23 Aug 69	★ FROM ELVIS IN MEMPHIS RCA SF 8029			1	13 wks
28 Feb 70	PORTRAIT IN MUSIC (import) RCA 558			36	1 wk
14 Mar 70	FROM MEMPHIS TO VEGAS - FROM VEGAS TO MEMPHIS RCA SF 8080/1			3	16 wks
1 Aug 70	● ON STAGE	RCA SF 8128		2	18 wks
5 Dec 70	ELVIS' GOLDEN RECORDS VOL.1 (re-issue) RCA SF 8129			21	11 wks
12 Dec 70	WORLDWIDE 50 GOLD AWARD HITS VOL 1 RCA LPM 6401			49	2 wks
30 Jan 71	THAT'S THE WAY IT IS RCA SF 8162			12	41 wks
10 Apr 71	● ELVIS COUNTRY	RCA SF 8172		6	9 wks
24 Jul 71	● LOVE LETTERS FROM ELVIS RCA SF 8202			7	5 wks
7 Aug 71	● C'MON EVERYBODY RCA International INTS 1286			5	21 wks
7 Aug 71	YOU'LL NEVER WALK ALONE RCA Camden CDM 1088			20	4 wks
25 Sep 71	ALMOST IN LOVE RCA International INTS 1206			38	2 wks
4 Dec 71	● ELVIS' CHRISTMAS ALBUM RCA International INTS 1126			7	5 wks
18 Dec 71	I GOT LUCKY RCA International INTS 1322			26	3 wks
27 May 72	ELVIS NOW RCA Victor SF 8266			12	8 wks
3 Jun 72	ROCK AND ROLL (RE-ISSUE OF ROCK 'N' ROLL NO.1) RCA Victor SF 8233			34	4 wks
3 Jun 72	ELVIS FOR EVERYONE RCA Victor SF 8232			48	1 wk
15 Jul 72	● ELVIS AT MADISON SQUARE GARDEN RCA Victor SF 8296			3	20 wks
12 Aug 72	HE TOUCHED ME RCA Victor SF 8275			38	3 wks
24 Feb 73	ALOHA FROM HAWAII VIA SATELLITE RCA Victor DPS 2040			11	10 wks
15 Sep 73	ELVIS RCA Victor SF 8378			16	4 wks
2 Mar 74	A LEGENDARY PERFORMER VOL.1 RCA Victor CPLI 0341			20	3 wks
25 May 74	GOOD TIMES RCA Victor APLI 0475			42	1 wk
7 Sep 74	ELVIS PRESLEY LIVE ON STAGE IN MEMPHIS RCA Victor APLI 0606			44	1 wk
22 Feb 75	PROMISED LAND RCA Victor APLI 0873			21	4 wks

Hospital drama of King of Rock

ELVIS IS DEAD

Requiem for a star: His story—Page 14

Elvis at one of his last shows . . . he had been a legend for 20 years

Brian Vine in New York

ELVIS PRESLEY, the King of Rock, died in hospital last night hours after being taken ill at home.

The 42-year-old star was found unconscious at his Graceland mansion in Memphis, Tennessee.

He was driven to the Baptist Hospital in a fire brigade ambulance and doctors fought for 30 minutes in a vain attempt to save him.

The first bulletin said he had breath-

ing difficulties. Then came the stunning police announcement: "Presley is dead."

The hospital said later: "Mr Presley's physician Dr Gorge Nichopoulos indicated that a heart attack was a possible cause of death. This could not be known for sure until a post mortem is completed."

Detectives from Memphis police department said they were investigating the "strong possibility that death was a result of a overdose of drugs."

Sobbing

Back at the Presley mansion his cousin a secretary Patsy Gambill sobbed over the phone to a friend : "Yes it's true. Elvis is dead." Crowds held back by the Police gathered outside and at the hospital as the news swept across the town.

It was his road manager Joe Esposito who found Presley slumped in an upstairs back bedroom of the old colonial style house with its white columns and big gates.

The legendary star showed no signs of breathing and there was no apparent heart beat. Mr Esposito tried desperately to revive him. Then came a seven-mile dash in the ambulance with a doctor at his side still fighting to get Presley's heart going again.

The hospital said: "Mr Presley arrived in the emergency department at about 3 pm. The emergency resuscitation team began working with Mr Presley and continued their effort until approximately 3.30 pm, at which time Mr Presley's personal physician discontinued all efforts.

Sickness had plagued the singer's life for many years and drove him to short cut his career at one point. He spent several spells in hospital.

Elvis's love for . . junk food was well known. The star who could afford the best, liked to eat hamburgers, peanut butter sandwiches, icecream and sweets.

Two years ago there was talk of his . . bulging waistlines, his . . lacklustre performances, and his mysterious trips to hospital.

Presley, who did not smoke or drink, never came to Britain. He had a fear of flying.

His vast fortune is likely to be inherited by his only child, daughter Lisa-Marie . . now nine—and his wife Priscilla who parted from him in 1973. After six years of marriage.

£ and shares surge

By Patrick Lay

SHARE prices soared to a record high for 1977 yesterday, following a massive injection of foreign cash.

An estimated £400 million was added to prices as the financial Times Index rose 11 points to 190.1, its highest level for four-and-a-half years.

Rumour

And the £ jumped points on the foreign exchange markets at $1.7485, its best September 1976.

Behind the . . rumour is a . . the Bank of England soon give the . . plenty free rein against the dollar.

And the devaluation . . from the . . kept flowing into the Continent.

In an effort the . . in the rise, the ceiling on buying dollars financial . .

Take that, bully!

By Walter Partington

THE law is to be toughened up to stamp out street rioting.

That is a Government climb-down, for up to now it has been said that the police already have adequate powers. It means—

FINES of £1,000-plus for

political bully boys of the streets.

POWERS to ban any public meetings as well as marches—which are likely to spark off violence.

The question of banning public meetings and demonstrations Monday drove from Birmingham riot . . by-election . . political bully boys that will have to be decided by the Commons in the autumn.

Two Acts already in force are likely to be used to aid the police.

The Criminal Law Act, which is new, could provide for imprisonment on committal for the Public Order Act of 1936 could be amended to . .

He would use . . powers under the Public At present under the Public Order Act . . . . . the time to make Black Shirt . . . . . the Home Secretary and

police can stop only processions and marches not meetings or demos.

But said the Home Office last night such demonstrations or meetings can lead to violence that marches are by less than marches . . events surrounding the . . election meetings at Lady . .

Yet have shown at . . word have . . this can be self-

Page 2, Column 3

14 Jun 75	TODAY *RCA Victor RS 1011*	**48**	3 wks
5 Jul 75	★ 40 GREATEST HITS *Arcade ADEP 12*	**1**	38 wks
6 Sep 75	THE ELVIS PRESLEY SUN COLLECTION *RCA Starcall HY 1001*	**16**	13 wks
19 Jun 76	FROM ELVIS PRESLEY BOULEVARD, MEMPHIS, TENNESSEE *RCA Victor RS 1060*	**29**	5 wks
19 Feb 77	ELVIS IN DEMAND *RCA Victor PL 42003*	**12**	11 wks
27 Aug 77	● MOODY BLUE *RCA PL 12428*	**3**	15 wks
3 Sep 77	● WELCOME TO MY WORLD *RCA PL 12274*	**7**	9 wks
3 Sep 77	G.I.BLUES (re-issue) *RCA SF5078*	**14**	10 wks
10 Sep 77	ELVIS GOLDEN RECORDS VOL.2 (re-issue) *RCA SF 8151*	**27**	4 wks
10 Sep 77	HITS OF THE 70'S *RCA LPL1 7527*	**30**	4 wks
10 Sep 77	BLUE HAWAII (re-issue) *RCA SF 8145*	**26**	6 wks
10 Sep 77	ELVIS' GOLDEN RECORDS VOL 3 (re-issue) *RCA SF 7630*	**49**	2 wks
10 Sep 77	PICTURES OF ELVIS *RCA Starcall HY 1023*	**52**	1 wk
8 Oct 77	THE SUN YEARS *Charly Sun 1001*	**31**	2 wks
15 Oct 77	LOVING YOU *RCA PL 42358*	**24**	3 wks
19 Nov 77	ELVIS IN CONCERT *RCA PL 02578*	**13**	11 wks
22 Apr 78	HE WALKS BESIDE ME *RCA PL 12772*	**37**	1 wk
3 Jun 78	THE '56 SESSIONS VOL 1 *RCA PL 42101*	**47**	4 wks
2 Sep 78	TV SPECIAL *RCA PL 42370*	**50**	2 wks
11 Nov 78	40 GREATEST (re-issue) *RCA PL 42691*	**40**	14 wks
3 Feb 79	A LEGENDARY PERFORMER VOL 3 *RCA PL 13082*	**43**	3 wks
5 May 79	OUR MEMORIES OF ELVIS *RCA PL 13279*	**72**	1 wk
24 Nov 79	● LOVE SONGS *K-Tel NE 1062*	**4**	13 wks
21 Jun 80	ELVIS PRESLEY SINGS LIEBER AND STOLLER *RCA International INTS 5031*	**32**	5 wks
23 Aug 80	ELVIS ARON PRESLEY *RCA ELVIS 25*	**21**	4 wks
23 Aug 80	PARADISE HAWAIIAN STYLE (re-issue) *RCA International INTS 5037*	**53**	2 wks
29 Nov 80	● INSPIRATION *K-Tel NE 1101*	**6**	8 wks
14 Mar 81	GUITAR MAN *RCA RCALP 5010*	**33**	5 wks
9 May 81	THIS IS ELVIS PRESLEY *RCA RCALP 5029*	**47**	4 wks
28 Nov 81	THE ULTIMATE PERFORMANCE *K-Tel NE 1141*	**45**	6 wks
13 Feb 82	THE SOUND OF YOUR CRY *RCA RCALP 3060*	**31**	12 wks
6 Mar 82	ELVIS PRESLEY EP PACK *RCA EPI*	**97**	1 wk
21 Aug 82	ROMANTIC ELVIS/ROCKIN' ELVIS *RCA RCALP 1000/1*	**62**	5 wks
18 Dec 82	IT WON'T SEEM LIKE CHRISTMAS WITHOUT YOU *RCA INTS 5235*	**80**	1 wk
30 Apr 83	JAILHOUSE ROCK/LOVE IN LAS VEGAS *RCA RCALP 9020*	**40**	2 wks
20 Aug 83	I WAS THE ONE *RCA RCALP 3105*	**83**	1 wk
3 Dec 83	A LEGENDARY PERFORMER VOL. 4 *RCA PL 84848*	**91**	1 wk
7 Apr 84	I CAN HELP *RCA PL 89287*	**71**	3 wks
21 Jul 84	THE FIRST LIVE RECORDINGS *RCA International PG 89387*	**69**	2 wks
26 Jan 85	20 GREATEST HITS VOLUME 2 *RCA International NL 89168*	**98**	1 wk
25 May 85	RECONSIDER BABY *RCA PL 85418*	**92**	1 wk
12 Oct 85	BALLADS *Telstar STAR 2264*	**23†**	12 wks

PRETENDERS UK/US, male/female vocal/instrumental group
78 wks

19 Jan 80	★ PRETENDERS *Real RAL 3*	**1**	35 wks
15 Aug 81	● PRETENDERS II *Real SRK 3572*	**7**	27 wks
21 Jan 84	LEARNING TO CRAWL *Real WX 2*	**11**	16 wks

PRETTY THINGS UK, male vocal/instrumental group
13 wks

27 Mar 65	● PRETTY THINGS *Fontana TL 5239*	**6**	10 wks
27 Jun 70	PARACHUTE *Harvest SHVL 774*	**43**	3 wks

Alan PRICE UK, male vocalist/instrumentalist – keyboards
10 wks

8 Jun 74	● BETWEEN TODAY AND YESTERDAY *Warner Bros. K 56032*	**9**	10 wks

Charley PRIDE US, male vocalist
17 wks

10 Apr 71	CHARLEY PRIDE SPECIAL *RCA SF 8171*	**29**	1 wk
28 May 77	SHE'S JUST AN OLD LOVE TURNED MEMORY *RCA Victor PL 12261*	**34**	2 wks
3 Jun 78	SOMEONE LOVES YOU HONEY *RCA PL 12478*	**48**	2 wks
26 Jan 80	● GOLDEN COLLECTION *K-Tel NE 1056*	**6**	12 wks

PRINCE and the REVOLUTION US, male/female vocal/instrumental group
104 wks

21 Jul 84	● PURPLE RAIN-MUSIC FROM THE MOTION PICTURE *Warner Bros 925110*	**7**	63 wks
8 Sep 84	1999 *Warner Bros 923720*	**30**	21 wks
4 May 85	● AROUND THE WORLD IN A DAY *Warner Bros 92-5286-1*	**5**	20 wks

The second album was just credited to Prince

PRINCE CHARLES & the CITY BEAT BAND US, male vocalist with US male vocal/instrumental group
1 wk

30 Apr 83	STONE KILLERS *Virgin V 2271*	**84**	1 wk

P.J. PROBY US, male vocalist
3 wks

27 Feb 65	I'M P.J. PROBY *Liberty LBY 1235*	**16**	3 wks

PROCOL HARUM UK, male vocal/instrumental group
11 wks

19 Jul 69	A SALTY DOG *Regal Zonophone SLRZ 1009*	**27**	2 wks
27 Jun 70	HOME *Regal Zonophone SLRZ 1014*	**49**	1 wk
3 Jul 71	BROKEN BARRICADES *Island ILPS 9158*	**42**	1 wk
6 May 72	A WHITER SHADE OF PALE/A SALTY DOG (double re-issue) *Fly Double Back TOOFA 7/8*	**26**	4 wks
6 May 72	PROCOL HARUM IN CONCERT WITH THE EDMONTON SYMPHONY ORCHESTRA *Chrysalis CHR 1004*	**48**	1 wk
30 Aug 75	PROCOL'S NINTH *Chrysalis CHR 1080*	**41**	2 wks

A Whiter Shade Of Pale/A Salty Dog *is a double re-issue although* A Whiter Shade Of Pale *was not previously a hit. The Edmonton Symphony Orchestra is a Canadian orchestra.*

PROPAGANDA Germany, male/female vocal/instrumental group
14 wks

13 Jul 85	A SECRET WISH *ZTT ZTTIQ 3*	**16**	12 wks
23 Nov 85	WISHFUL THINKING *ZTT ZTTIQ 20*	**82**	2 wks

Dorothy PROVINE US, female vocalist
49 wks

2 Dec 61	● THE ROARING TWENTIES SONGS FROM THE TV SERIES *Warner Bros. WM 4035*	**3**	42 wks
10 Feb 62	● VAMP OF THE ROARING TWENTIES *Warner Bros. WM 4053*	**9**	7 wks

P. J. PROBY
demonstrates the 'Osteopath's
Delight' position.

GARY PUCKETT AND THE
UNION GAP Gary Puckett, is
second from right.

PSYCHEDELIC FURS UK, male vocal/instrumental
group   30 wks

15 Mar 80	PSYCHEDELIC FURS CBS 84084	18	6 wks
23 May 81	TALK TALK TALK CBS 84892	30	9 wks
2 Oct 82	FOREVER NOW CBS 85909	20	8 wks
19 May 84	MIRROR MOVES CBS 25950	15	9 wks

PUBLIC IMAGE LTD. UK, male vocal/instrumental
group   36 wks

23 Dec 78	PUBLIC IMAGE Virgin V 2114	22	11 wks
8 Dec 79	METAL BOX Virgin METAL 1	18	8 wks
8 Mar 80	SECOND EDITION OF PIL Virgin VD 2512 ...	46	2 wks
22 Nov 80	PARIS IN THE SPRING Virgin V 2183	61	2 wks
18 Apr 81	FLOWERS OF ROMANCE Virgin V 2189	11	5 wks
8 Oct 83	LIVE IN TOKYO Virgin VGD 3508	28	6 wks
21 Jul 84	THIS IS WHAT YOU WANT...THIS IS WHAT YOU GET Virgin V 2309	56	2 wks

Gary PUCKETT and the UNION GAP US,
male vocalist, male vocal/instrumental backing group   4 wks

29 Jun 68	UNION GAP CBS 63342	24	4 wks

Q

Q-TIPS UK, male vocal/instrumental group   1 wk

30 Aug 80	Q-TIPS CHR 1255	50	1 wk

Suzi QUATRO US, female vocalist/instrumentalist - guitar
13 wks

13 Oct 73	SUZI QUATRO RAK SRAK 505	32	4 wks
26 Apr 80	● SUZI QUATRO'S GREATEST HITS RAK EMTV 24	4	9 wks

QUEEN UK, male vocal/instrumental group   572 wks

23 Mar 74	● QUEEN 2 EMI EMA 767	5	29 wks
30 Mar 74	QUEEN EMI EMC 3006	24	18 wks
23 Nov 74	● SHEER HEART ATTACK EMI EMC 3061	2	42 wks
13 Dec 75	★ A NIGHT AT THE OPERA EMI EMTC 103 ...	1	50 wks
25 Dec 76	★ A DAY AT THE RACES EMI EMTC 104 ...	1	24 wks
12 Nov 77	● NEWS OF THE WORLD EMI EMA 784	4	20 wks
25 Nov 78	● JAZZ EMI EMA 788	2	27 wks
7 Jul 79	● LIVE KILLERS EMI EMSP 330	3	27 wks
12 Jul 80	☆ THE GAME EMI EMA 795	1	18 wks
20 Dec 80	● FLASH GORDON (film soundtrack) EMI EMC 3351	10	15 wks
7 Nov 81	★ GREATEST HITS EMI EMTV 30	1†	213 wks
15 May 82	● HOT SPACE EMI EMA 797	4	19 wks
10 Mar 84	● THE WORKS EMI EMC 240014	2	70 wks

QUEENSRHYCHE UK, male vocal/instrumental group
1 wk

29 Sep 84	THE WARNING EMI America EJ 2402201	100	1 wk

QUIET RIOT US, male vocal/instrumental group
1 wk

4 Aug 84	CONDITION CRITICAL Epic EPC 26075	71	1 wk

QUINTESSENCE UK/Australia, male vocal/instrumental
group   6 wks

27 Jun 70	QUINTESSENCE Island ILPS 9128	22	4 wks
3 Apr 71	DIVE DEEP Island ILPS 9143	43	1 wk
27 May 72	SELF RCA Victor SF 8273	50	1 wk

QUIVER - See SUTHERLAND BROTHERS and QUIVER

R

RACING CARS UK, male vocal/instrumental group
6 wks

19 Feb 77	DOWNTOWN TONIGHT Chrysalis CHR 1099 ..	39	6 wks

Gerry RAFFERTY UK, male vocalist   74 wks

25 Feb 78	● CITY TO CITY United Artists UAS 30104	6	37 wks
2 Jun 79	● NIGHT OWL United Artists UAK 30238	9	24 wks
26 Apr 80	SNAKES AND LADDERS United Artists UAK 30298	15	9 wks
25 Sep 82	SLEEPWALKING Liberty LBG 30352	39	4 wks

RAH BAND UK, male/female group under control of
Richard A. Hewson   6 wks

6 Apr 85	MYSTERY RCA PL 70640	60	6 wks

RAINBOW UK, male vocal/instrumental group   159 wks

13 Sep 75	RITCHIE BLACKMORE'S RAINBOW Oyster OYA 2001	11	6 wks
5 Jun 76	RAINBOW RISING Polydor 2490 137	11	33 wks
30 Jul 77	● ON STAGE Poly 2657 016	7	10 wks
6 May 78	● LONG LIVE RC 'N' ROLL Polydor POLD 5002	7	12 wks
18 Aug 79	● DOWN TO EARTH Polydor POLD 5023 ──......	6	37 wks
21 Feb 81	● DIFFICULT TO CURE Polydor POLD 5036	3	22 wks
8 Aug 81	RITCHIE BLACKMORE'S RAINBOW (re-issue) Polydor 2490 141	91	2 wks
21 Nov 81	BEST OF RAINBOW Polydor POLDV 2	14	17 wks
24 Apr 82	● STRAIGHT BETWEEN THE EYES Polydor POLD 5056	5	14 wks
17 Sep 83	BENT OUT OF SHAPE Polydor POLD 5116	11	6 wks

First two albums and re-issue of first album credited to Ritchie Blackmore's Rainbow.

RAIN PARADE US, male vocal/instrumental group
1 wk

29 Jun 85	BEYOND THE SUNSET Island IMA 17	78	1 wk

RAMONES US, male vocal/instrumental group   24 wks

23 Apr 77	LEAVE HOME Philips 9103 254	45	1 wk
24 Dec 77	ROCKET TO RUSSIA Sire 9103 255	60	2 wks
7 Oct 78	ROAD TO RUIN Sire SRK 6063	32	2 wks

QUEEN (above) Twelve weeks at number one, four chart topping albums and twelve Top Ten albums.

RAMONES (left) The group (Joey shown) did best with a Phil Spector production.

RAINBOW (below) Founder and guitarist Ritchie Blackmore constantly changed the group's personnel over the years. The line up at the time of the album depicted here included Ronnie James Dio on vocals and Cozy Powell on drums.

16 Jun 79	IT'S ALIVE *Sire SRK 26074*	27	8 wks
19 Jan 80	END OF THE CENTURY *Sire SRK 6077*	14	8 wks
26 Jan 85	TOO TOUGH TO DIE *Beggars Banquet BEGA 59*	63	3 wks

RATT US, *male vocal/instrumental group* 2 *wks*

13 Jul 85	INVASION OF YOUR PRIVACY *Atlantic 78-1257-1*	50	2 wks

RAVEN UK, *male vocal/instrumental group* 3 *wks*

17 Oct 81	ROCK UNTIL YOU DROP *Neat NEAT 1001* ...	63	3 wks

Chris REA UK, *male vocalist* 31 *wks*

28 Apr 79	DELTICS *Magnet MAG 5028*	54	3 wks
12 Apr 80	TENNIS *Magnet MAG 5032*	60	1 wk
3 Apr 82	CHRIS REA *Magnet MAGL 5040*	52	4 wks
18 Jun 83	WATER SIGN *Magnet MAGL 5048*	64	4 wks
21 Apr 84	WIRED TO THE MOON *Magnet MAGL 5057* ..	35	7 wks
25 May 85	SHAMROCK DIARIES *Magnet MAGL*	15	14 wks

REAL THING UK, *male vocal/instrumental group*
6 *wks*

6 Nov 76	REAL THING *Pye NSPL 18507*	34	3 wks
7 Apr 79	CAN YOU FEEL THE FORCE *Pye NSPH 18601*	73	1 wk
10 May 80	20 GREATEST HITS *K-Tel NE 1073*	56	2 wks

REBEL ROUSERS - *See Cliff BENNETT and the REBEL ROUSERS*

RED NOISE - *See Bill NELSON'S RED NOISE*

Sharon REDD US, *female vocalist* 5 *wks*

23 Oct 82	REDD HOTT *Prelude PRL 25056*	59	5 wks

Otis REDDING US, *male vocalist* 192 *wks*

19 Feb 66	● OTIS BLUE *Atlantic ATL 5041*	6	21 wks
23 Apr 66	SOUL BALLADS *Atlantic ATL 5029*	30	1 wk
23 Jul 66	SOUL ALBUM *Atlantic 587-011*	22	9 wks
21 Jan 67	OTIS REDDING'S DICTIONARY OF SOUL *Atlantic 588-050*	23	16 wks
21 Jan 67	● OTIS BLUE (re-issue) *Atlantic 587-036*	7	54 wks
29 Apr 67	PAIN IN MY HEART *Atlantic 587-042*	28	9 wks
10 Feb 68	● HISTORY OF OTIS REDDING *Volt S 418*	2	43 wks
30 Mar 68	OTIS REDDING IN EUROPE *Stax 589-016* ...	14	16 wks
1 Jun 68	★ DOCK OF THE BAY *Stax 231-001*	1	15 wks
12 Oct 68	IMMORTAL OTIS REDDING *Atlantic 588-113* ..	19	8 wks

See also Otis Redding and Carla Thomas.

Otis REDDING and Carla THOMAS US, *male/female vocal duo* 17 *wks*

1 Jul 67	KING AND QUEEN *Atlantic 589-007*	18	17 wks

See also Otis Redding.

Helen REDDY Australia, *female vocalist* 27 *wks*

8 Feb 75	FREE AND EASY *Capitol E-ST 11348*	17	9 wks
14 Feb 76	● THE BEST OF HELEN REDDY *Capitol E-ST 11467*	5	18 wks

Lou REED US, *male vocalist* 35 *wks*

21 Apr 73	TRANSFORMER *RCA Victor LSP 4807*	13	25 wks
20 Oct 73	● BERLIN *RCA Victor RS 1002*	7	5 wks
16 Mar 74	ROCK 'N' ROLL ANIMAL *RCA Victor APLI 0472*	26	1 wk
14 Feb 76	CONEY ISLAND BABY *RCA Victor RS 1035* ..	52	1 wk
3 Jul 82	TRANSFORMER (re-issue) *RCA INTS 5061*	91	2 wks
9 Jun 84	NEW SENSATIONS *RCA PL 84998*	92	1 wk

Don REEDMAN - *See Jeff JARRATT and Don REEDMAN*

Jim REEVES US, *male vocalist* 381 *wks*

28 Mar 64	● GOOD 'N' COUNTRY *RCA Camden CDN 5114*	10	35 wks
9 May 64	● GENTLEMAN JIM *RCA RD 7541*	3	23 wks
15 Aug 64	● A TOUCH OF VELVET *RCA RD 7521*	8	9 wks
15 Aug 64	INTERNATIONAL JIM REEVES *RCA RD 7577*	11	15 wks
22 Aug 64	HE'LL HAVE TO GO *RCA RD 27176*	16	4 wks
29 Aug 64	THE INTIMATE JIM REEVES *RCA RD 27193*	12	4 wks
29 Aug 64	● GOD BE WITH YOU *RCA RD 7636*	10	10 wks
5 Sep 64	MOONLIGHT AND ROSES *RCA RD 7639*	2	52 wks
19 Sep 64	COUNTRY SIDE OF JIM REEVES *RCA Camden CDN 5100*	12	5 wks
26 Sep 64	WE THANK THEE *RCA RD 7637*	17	3 wks
28 Nov 64	● TWELVE SONGS OF CHRISTMAS *RCA RD 7663*	3	17 wks
30 Jan 65	● BEST OF JIM REEVES *RCA RD 7666*	3	47 wks
10 Apr 65	HAVE I TOLD YOU LATELY THAT I LOVE YOU *RCA Camden CDN 5122*	12	5 wks
22 May 65	THE JIM REEVES WAY *RCA RD 7694* ...	16	4 wks
5 Nov 66	● DISTANT DRUMS *RCA Victor RD 7814*	2	34 wks
18 Jan 69	A TOUCH OF SADNESS *RCA SF 7978*	15	5 wks
5 Jul 69	★ ACCORDING TO MY HEART *RCA International INTS 1013*	1	14 wks
23 Aug 69	JIM REEVES AND SOME FRIENDS *RCA SF 8022*	24	4 wks
29 Nov 69	ON STAGE *RCA SF 8047*	13	4 wks
26 Dec 70	MY CATHEDRAL *RCA SF 8146*	48	2 wks
3 Jul 71	JIM REEVES WRITES YOU A RECORD *RCA SF 8176*	47	2 wks
7 Aug 71	● JIM REEVES' GOLDEN RECORDS *RCA International INTS 1070*	9	21 wks
14 Aug 71	● THE INTIMATE JIM REEVES (re-issue) *RCA International INTS 1256*	8	15 wks
21 Aug 71	GIRLS I HAVE KNOWN *RCA International INTS 1140*	35	5 wks
27 Nov 71	● TWELVE SONGS OF CHRISTMAS (re-issue) *RCA International INTS 1188*	3	6 wks
27 Nov 71	A TOUCH OF VELVET (re-issue) *RCA International INTS 1089*	49	2 wks
15 Apr 72	MY FRIEND *RCA SF 8258*	32	5 wks
20 Sep 75	★ 40 GOLDEN GREATS *Arcade ADEP 16*	1	25 wks
6 Sep 80	COUNTRY GENTLEMAN *K-Tel NE 1088*	53	4 wks

Neil REID UK, *male vocalist* 18 *wks*

5 Feb 72	★ NEIL REID *Decca SKL 5122*	1	16 wks
2 Sep 72	SMILE *Decca SKL 5136*	47	2 wks

R.E.M. US, *male vocal/instrumental group* 5 *wks*

28 Apr 84	RECKONING *IRS A 7045*	91	2 wks
29 Jun 85	FABLES OF THE RECONSTRUCTION *IRS MIRF 1003*	35	3 wks

RENAISSANCE UK, *male/female vocal instrumental group* 10 *wks*

21 Feb 70	RENAISSANCE *Island ILPS 9114*	60	1 wk
19 Aug 78	A SONG FOR ALL SEASONS *Warner Bros. K 56460*	35	8 wks

2 Jun 79	AZUR D'OR	Warner Bros. K 56633	73	1 wk

RENATO *Italy, male vocalist* · 14 wks

25 Dec 82	SAVE YOUR LOVE	Lifestyle LEG 9	26	14 wks

REO SPEEDWAGON *US, male vocal/instrumental group* · 36 wks

25 Apr 81 ●	HI INFIDELITY	Epic EPC 84700	6	29 wks
17 Jul 82	GOOD TROUBLE	Epic EPC 85789	29	7 wks

REZILLOS *UK, male/female vocal/instrumental group* · 15 wks

5 Aug 78	CAN'T STAND THE REZILLOS			
	Sire WEA K 56530		16	10 wks
28 Apr 79	MISSION ACCOMPLISHED BUT THE BEAT			
	GOES ON Sire SRK 6069		30	5 wks

Charlie RICH *US, male vocalist* · 28 wks

23 Mar 74 ●	BEHIND CLOSED DOORS	Epic 65716	4	26 wks
13 Jul 74	VERY SPECIAL LOVE SONGS	Epic 80031	34	2 wks

RICH KIDS *UK, male vocal/instrumental group* · 1 wk

7 Oct 78	GHOST OF PRINCES IN TOWERS			
	EMI EMC 3263		51	1 wk

Cliff RICHARD *UK, male vocalist* · 624 wks

18 Apr 59 ●	CLIFF Columbia 33SX 1147		4	31 wks
14 Nov 59 ●	CLIFF SINGS Columbia 33SX 1192		2	36 wks
15 Oct 60 ●	ME AND MY SHADOWS Columbia 33SX 1261 ..		2	33 wks
22 Apr 61 ●	LISTEN TO CLIFF Columbia 33SX 1320		2	28 wks
21 Oct 61 ★	21 TODAY Columbia 33SX 1368		1	16 wks
23 Dec 61 ●	THE YOUNG ONES (film soundtrack)			
	Columbia 33SX 1384		1	42 wks
29 Sep 62 ●	32 MINUTES AND 17 SECONDS			
	Columbia 33SX 1431		3	21 wks
26 Jan 63 ★	SUMMER HOLIDAY (film soundrack)			
	Columbia 33SX 1472		1	36 wks
13 Jul 63 ●	CLIFF'S HIT ALBUM Columbia 33SX 1512		2	19 wks
28 Sep 63 ●	WHEN IN SPAIN Columbia 33SX 1541		8	10 wks
11 Jul 64 ●	WONDERFUL LIFE (film soundtrack)			
	Columbia 33SX 1628		2	23 wks
9 Jan 65	ALADDIN (pantomime) Columbia 33SX 1676 ...		13	5 wks
17 Apr 65 ●	CLIFF RICHARD Columbia 33SX 1709 ...		9	5 wks
14 Aug 65	MORE HITS BY CLIFF Columbia 33SX 1737		20	1 wk
8 Jan 66	LOVE IS FOREVER Columbia 33SX 1769 ...		19	1 wk
21 May 66 ●	KINDA LATIN Columbia SX 6039		9	12 wks
17 Dec 66 ●	FINDERS KEEPERS (film soundtrack)			
	Columbia SX 6079		6	18 wks
7 Jan 67	CINDERELLA (pantomime)			
	Columbia 33SCX 6103		30	6 wks
15 Apr 67	DON'T STOP ME NOW... Columbia SCX 6133		23	9 wks
11 Nov 67	GOOD NEWS Columbia SCX 6167		37	1 wk
1 Jun 68	CLIFF IN JAPAN Columbia SCX 6244		29	2 wks
16 Nov 68	ESTABLISHED 1958 Columbia SCX 6282 ...		30	4 wks
12 Jul 69 ●	BEST OF CLIFF Columbia SCX 6343		5	17 wks
27 Sep 69	SINCERELY Columbia SCX 6357		24	3 wks
12 Dec 70	TRACKS 'N' GROOVES Columbia SCX 6435		37	2 wks
23 Dec 72	BEST OF CLIFF VOL.2 Columbia SCX 6519		49	2 wks
19 Jan 74	TAKE ME HIGH (film soundtrack)			
	EMI EMC 3016		41	4 wks
29 May 76 ●	I'M NEARLY FAMOUS EMI EMC 3122		5	21 wks
26 Mar 77 ●	EVERY FACE TELLS A STORY EMI EMC 3172 ..		8	10 wks
22 Oct 77 ★	40 GOLDEN GREATS EMI EMTV 6		1	19 wks
4 Mar 78	SMALL CORNERS EMI EMC 3219		33	5 wks

21 Oct 78	GREEN LIGHT EMI EMC 3231		25	3 wks
17 Feb 79 ●	THANK YOU VERY MUCH - REUNION			
	CONCERT AT THE LONDON PALLADIUM			
	EMI EMTV 15		5	12 wks
15 Sep 79 ●	ROCK 'N' ROLL JUVENILE EMI EMC 3307 ...		3	22 wks
13 Sep 80 ●	I'M NO HERO EMI EMA 796		4	11 wks
4 Jul 81 ★	LOVE SONGS EMI EMTV 27		1	43 wks
26 Sep 81 ●	WIRED FOR SOUND EMI EMC 3377		4	25 wks
4 Sep 82 ●	NOW YOU SEE ME, NOW YOU DON'T			
	EMI EMC 3415		4	14 wks
21 May 83 ●	DRESSED FOR THE OCCASION			
	EMI EMC 3432		7	17 wks
15 Oct 83 ●	SILVER EMI EMC 1077871		7	24 wks
14 Jul 84	20 ORIGINAL GREATS EMI CRS 1		43	6 wks
1 Dec 84	THE ROCK CONNECTION EMI CLIF 2		43	5 wks

The Shadows featured on all or some of the tracks of all albums up to and including Aladdin *and the following subsequent albums;* More Hits By Cliff, Love Is Forever, Finders Keepers, Cinderella, Established 1958, Best Of Cliff, Best Of Cliff Vol.2, 40 Golden Greats, Thank You Very Much, Love Songs *and* 20 Original Greats. Cliff *credited to* Cliff Richard and the Drifters. *See also the Shadows.*

Lionel RICHIE *US, male vocalist* · 200 wks

27 Nov 82 ●	LIONEL RICHIE Motown STMA 8037		9	86 wks
29 Oct 83 ★	CAN'T SLOW DOWN Motown STMA 8041		1†	114 wks

Jonathan RICHMAN and the MODERN LOVERS *US, male vocal/instrumental group* · 3 wks

27 Aug 77	ROCK 'N' ROLL WITH THE MODERN LOVERS			
	Beserkeley BSERK 9		50	3 wks

RICHMOND STRINGS/MIKE SAMMES SINGERS *UK, orchestra/male/female vocal group* · 7 wks

19 Jan 76	MUSIC OF AMERICA Ronco TRD 2016		18	7 wks

RIP RIG and PANIC *UK, male/female vocal/instrumental group* · 3 wks

26 Jun 82	I AM GOLD Virgin V 2228		67	3 wks

Minnie RIPERTON *US, female vocalist* · 3 wks

17 May 75	PERFECT ANGEL Epic EPC 80426		33	3 wks

Angela RIPPON *UK, female exercise instructor* · 26 wks

17 Apr 82 ●	SHAPE UP AND DANCE (VOL. II)			
	Lifestyle LEG 2		8	26 wks

David ROACH *UK, male vocalist/instrumentalist - saxophone* · 1 wk

14 Apr 84	I LOVE SAX Nouveau Music NML 1006		73	1 wk

Marty ROBBINS *US, male vocalist* · 15 wks

13 Aug 60	GUNFIGHTER BALLADS Fontana TFL 5063		20	1 wk
10 Feb 79 ●	MARTY ROBBINS COLLECTION			
	Lotus WH 5009		5	14 wks

Paddy ROBERTS *South Africa, male vocalist* · 6 wks

26 Sep 59 ●	STRICTLY FOR GROWN-UPS Decca LF 1322 ..		8	5 wks

HELEN REDDY As a nun in the film 'Airport '75'.

CLIFF RICHARD (below) David Bowie is the only British male solo star with more weeks on chart. (LFI)

JIM REEVES (above) Two months after his death eight of the top twenty albums were his.

LOU REED (below) Looking like he has been walking on the wild side.

17 Sep 60	**PADDY ROBERTS TRIES AGAIN**			
	Decca LK 4358		**16**	1 wk

B.A. ROBERTSON *UK, male vocalist* · 10 wks

29 Mar 80	**INITIAL SUCCESS** *Asylum K 52216*		**32**	8 wks
4 Apr 81	**BULLY FOR YOU** *Asylum K 52275*		**61**	2 wks

Smokey ROBINSON *US, male vocalist* · 10 wks

20 Jun 81	**BEING WITH YOU** *Motown STML 12151*		**17**	10 wks

Tom ROBINSON BAND *UK, male vocal/instrumental group* · 23 wks

3 Jun 78 ●	**POWER IN THE DARKNESS** *EMI EMC 3226*		**4**	12 wks
24 Mar 79	**TRB2** *EMI EMC 3296*		**18**	6 wks
29 Sep 84	**HOPE AND GLORY** *Castaway ZL 70483*		**21**	5 wks

ROCK GODDESS *UK, female vocal/instrumental group* · 3 wks

12 Mar 83	**ROCK GODDESS** *A & M AMLH 68554*		**65**	2 wks
29 Oct 83	**HELL HATH NO FURY** *A & M AMLX 68560*		**84**	1 wk

ROCKIN' BERRIES *UK, male vocal/instrumental group* · 1 wk

19 Jun 65	**IN TOWN** *Pye NPL 38013*		**15**	1 wk

ROCKPILE *UK, male vocal/instrumental group* · 5 wks

18 Oct 80	**SECONDS OF PLEASURE** *F-Beat XXLP 7*		**34**	5 wks

ROCKSTEADY CREW *US, male/female vocal group* · 1 wk

16 Jun 84	**READY FOR BATTLE** *Charisma RSC LP1*		**73**	1 wk

ROCKWELL *US, male vocalist* · 5 wks

25 Feb 84	**SOMEBODY'S WATCHING ME**			
	Motown ZL 72147		**52**	5 wks

Clodagh RODGERS *Ireland, female vocalist* · 1 wk

13 Sep 69	**CLODAGH RODGERS** *RCA SF 8033*		**27**	1 wk

RODS *US, male vocal/instrumental group* · 4 wks

24 Jul 82	**WILD DOGS** *Arista SPART 1196*		**75**	4 wks

Kenny ROGERS *US, male vocalist* · 87 wks

18 Jun 77	**KENNY ROGERS** *United Artists UAS 30046*		**14**	7 wks
6 Oct 79	**THE KENNY ROGERS SINGLES ALBUM**			
	United Artists UAK 30263		**12**	22 wks
9 Feb 80 ●	**KENNY** *United Artists UAG 30273*		**7**	10 wks
31 Jan 81	**LADY** *Liberty LBG 30334*		**40**	5 wks
1 Oct 83	**EYES THAT SEE IN THE DARK**			
	RCA RCALP 6088		**53**	19 wks

27 Oct 84	**WHAT ABOUT ME?** *RCA PL 85043*		**97**	1 wk
27 Jul 85 ●	**THE KENNY ROGERS STORY**			
	Liberty EMTV 39		**4†**	23 wks

ROLAND RAT SUPERSTAR *UK, male rat vocalist* · 3 wks

15 Dec 84	**THE CASSETTE OF THE ALBUM**			
	Rodent RATL 1001		**67**	3 wks

ROLLING STONES *UK, male vocal/instrumental group* · 632 wks

25 Apr 64 ★	**ROLLING STONES** *Decca LK 4805*		**1**	51 wks
23 Jan 65 ★	**ROLLING STONES NO.2** *Decca LK 4661*		**1**	37 wks
2 Oct 65 ●	**OUT OF OUR HEADS** *Decca LK 4733*		**2**	24 wks
23 Apr 66 ★	**AFTERMATH** *Decca LK 4786*		**1**	28 wks
12 Nov 66 ●	**BIG HITS (HIGH TIDE AND GREEN GRASS)**			
	Decca TXS 101		**4**	43 wks
28 Jan 67 ●	**BETWEEN THE BUTTONS** *Decca SKL 4852* ...		**3**	22 wks
23 Dec 67 ●	**THEIR SATANIC MAJESTIES REQUEST**			
	Decca TXS 103		**3**	13 wks
21 Dec 68 ●	**BEGGARS BANQUET** *Decca SKL 4955*		**3**	12 wks
27 Sep 69 ●	**THROUGH THE PAST DARKLY (BIG HITS VOL.2)** *Decca SKL 5019*		**2**	37 wks
20 Dec 69 ●	**LET IT BLEED** *Decca SKL 5025*		**1**	29 wks
19 Sep 70 ★	**GET YOUR YA-YAS OUT** *Decca SKL 5065*		**1**	15 wks
3 Apr 71 ●	**STONE AGE** *Decca SKL 5084*		**4**	7 wks
8 May 71 ★	**STICKY FINGERS** *Rolling Stones COC 59100* ...		**1**	25 wks
18 Sep 71	**GIMME SHELTER** *Decca SKL 5101*		**19**	5 wks
11 Mar 72	**MILESTONES** *Decca SKL 5098*		**14**	8 wks
10 Jun 72 ★	**EXILE ON MAIN STREET**			
	Rolling Stones COC 69100		**1**	16 wks
11 Nov 72	**ROCK 'N' ROLLING STONES** *Decca SKL 5149* ...		**41**	1 wk
22 Sep 73 ★	**GOAT'S HEAD SOUP** *Rolling Stones COC 59101*		**1**	14 wks
2 Nov 74 ●	**IT'S ONLY ROCK 'N' ROLL**			
	Rolling Stones COC 59103		**2**	9 wks
28 Jun 75	**MADE IN THE SHADE**			
	Rolling Stones COC 59104		**14**	12 wks
28 Jun 75	**METAMORPHOSIS** *Decca SKL 5212*		**45**	1 wk
29 Nov 75 ●	**ROLLED GOLD – THE VERY BEST OF THE ROLLING STONES** *Decca ROST 1/2*		**7**	50 wks
8 May 76 ●	**BLACK & BLUE** *Rolling Stones COC 59106* ...		**2**	14 wks
8 Oct 77 ●	**LOVE YOU LIVE** *Rolling Stones COC 89101* ...		**3**	8 wks
5 Nov 77	**GET STONED** *Arcade ADEP 32*		**13**	15 wks
24 Jun 78 ●	**SOME GIRLS** *Rolling Stones CUN 39108*		**2**	25 wks
5 Jul 80 ★	**EMOTIONAL RESCUE** *Rolling Stones CUN 39111*		**1**	18 wks
12 Sep 81 ●	**TATTOO YOU** *Rolling Stones CUNS 39114*		**2**	29 wks
12 Jun 82 ●	**STILL LIFE (AMERICAN CONCERTS 1981)**			
	Rolling Stones CUN 39115		**4**	18 wks
31 Jul 82	**IN CONCERT (import)** *Decca (Holland) 6640 037*		**94**	3 wks
11 Dec 82	**STORY OF THE STONES** *K-Tel NE 1200*		**24**	12 wks
19 Nov 83 ●	**UNDERCOVER** *Rolling Stones CUN 1654361* ...		**3**	18 wks
7 Jul 84	**REWIND 1971-1984 (THE BEST OF THE ROLLING STONES)** *Rolling Stones CUN 1* ...		**23**	13 wks

ROMAN HOLIDAY *UK, male vocal/instrumental group* · 3 wks

22 Oct 83	**COOKIN' ON THE ROOF** *Jive HIP 9*		**31**	3 wks

RONDO VENEZIANO *UK, male/female orchestral group* · 26 wks

5 Nov 83	**VENICE IN PERIL** *Ferroway RON 1*		**39**	13 wks
10 Nov 84	**THE GENIUS OF VENICE** *Ferroway RON 2* ...		**60**	13 wks

ROLLING STONES (above) One solo hit album by Mick Jagger, three misses by Ronnie Wood, and Keith Richard has yet to try. (LFI)

B. A. ROBERTSON and HANK MARVIN (left) Two guys who've both had initial success, Hank B. Marvin and B. A. Robertson.

Mick RONSON *UK, male vocalist/instrumentalist – guitar*

10 wks

16 Mar 74 ●	SLAUGHTER ON TENTH AVENUE				
	RCA Victor APL1 0353		9	7 wks	
8 Mar 75	PLAY DON'T WORRY	*RCA Victor APL1 0681*	29	3 wks	

Linda RONSTADT *US, female vocalist*

31 wks

4 Sep 76	HASTEN DOWN THE WIND	*Asylum K 53045*	32	8 wks
25 Dec 76	GREATEST HITS	*Asylum K 53055*	37	9 wks
1 Oct 77	SIMPLE DREAMS	*Asylum K 53065*	15	5 wks
14 Oct 78	LIVING IN THE USA	*Asylum K 53085*	39	2 wks
8 Mar 80	MAD LOVE	*Asylum K 52210*	65	1 wk
28 Jan 84	WHAT'S NEW	*Asylum 96 0260*	31	5 wks
19 Jan 85	LUSH LIFE	*Asylum 96-0387-1*	100	1 wk

Last two albums credited to Linda Ronstadt with the Nelson Riddle Orchestra.

ROSE MARIE *UK, female vocalist*

13 wks

13 Apr 85	ROSE MARIE SINGS JUST FOR YOU			
	AI RMTV 1		30	13 wks

ROSE ROYCE *US, male/female vocal/instrumental group*

62 wks

22 Oct 77	IN FULL BLOOM	*Warner Bros. K 56394*	18	13 wks
30 Sep 78 ●	STRIKES AGAIN	*Whitfield K 56257*	7	11 wks
22 Sep 79	RAINBOW CONNECTION IV	*Atlantic K 56714*	72	2 wks
1 Mar 80 ★	GREATEST HITS	*Whitfield K RRTV 1*	1	34 wks
13 Oct 84	MUSIC MAGIC	*Streetwave MKL 2*	69	2 wks

ROSE TATTOO *Australia, male vocal/instrumental group*

4 wks

26 Sep 81	ASSAULT AND BATTERY	*Carrere CAL 127*	40	4 wks

Diana ROSS *US, female vocalist*

334 wks

24 Oct 70	DIANA ROSS	*Tamla Motown SFTML 11159*	14	5 wks
19 Jun 71	EVERYTHING IS EVERYTHING			
	Tamla Motown STML 11178		31	3 wks
9 Oct 71 ●	I'M STILL WAITING	*Tamla Motown STML 11193*	10	11 wks
9 Oct 71	DIANA	*Tamla Motown STMA 8001*	43	1 wk
11 Nov 72	GREATEST HITS	*Tamla Motown STMA 8006*	34	10 wks
1 Sep 73 ●	TOUCH ME IN THE MORNING			
	Tamla Motown STML 11239		7	35 wks
27 Oct 73	LADY SINGS THE BLUES			
	Tamla Motown TMSP 1131		50	1 wk
2 Mar 74	LAST TIME I SAW HIM			
	Tamla Motown STML 11255		41	1 wk
8 Jun 74	LIVE	*Tamla Motown STML 11248*	21	8 wks
27 Mar 76 ●	DIANA ROSS	*Tamla Motown STML 12022*	4	26 wks
7 Aug 76 ●	GREATEST HITS 2	*Tamla Motown STML 12036*	2	29 wks
19 Mar 77	AN EVENING WITH DIANA ROSS			
	Motown TMSP 6005		52	1 wk
4 Aug 79	THE BOSS	*Motown STML 12118*	52	2 wks
17 Nov 79 ●	20 GOLDEN GREATS	*Motown EMTV 21*	2	29 wks
21 Jun 80	DIANA	*Motown STMA 8033*	12	32 wks
28 Mar 81	TO LOVE AGAIN	*Motown STML 12152*	26	10 wks
7 Nov 81	WHY DO FOOLS FALL IN LOVE			
	Capitol EST 26733		17	24 wks
21 Nov 81	ALL THE GREATEST HITS			
	Motown STMA 8036		21	31 wks
13 Feb 82	DIANA ROSS	*Motown STML 12163*	43	6 wks
23 Oct 82	SILK ELECTRIC	*Capitol EAST 27313*	33	12 wks
4 Dec 82 ●	LOVE SONGS	*K-Tel NE 1200*	5	17 wks
19 Jul 83	ROSS	*Capitol EST 1867051*	44	5 wks
24 Dec 83 ●	PORTRAIT	*Telstar STAR 2238*	8	26 wks
6 Oct 84	SWEPT AWAY	*Capitol ROSS 1*	40	5 wks
28 Sep 85	EATEN ALIVE	*Capitol ROSS 2*	41	4 wks

See also Diana Ross and Marvin Gaye; Diana Ross and the Supremes with the Temptations.

Diana ROSS and Marvin GAYE *US, female/male vocal duo*

45 wks

19 Jan 74 ●	DIANA AND MARVIN			
	Tamla Motown STMA 8015		6	43 wks
29 Aug 81	DIANA AND MARVIN (re-issue)			
	Motown STMS 5001		78	2 wks

See also Marvin Gaye; Marvin Gaye and Tammi Terrell; Diana Ross; Diana Ross and the Supremes with the Temptations.

Diana ROSS and the SUPREMES with the TEMPTATIONS *US, male/female vocal group*

31 wks

25 Jan 69 ★	DIANA ROSS AND THE SUPREMES JOIN THE TEMPTATIONS	*Tamla Motown STML 11096*	1	15 wks
28 Jun 69	TCB	*Tamla Motown STML 11110*	11	12 wks
14 Feb 70	TOGETHER	*Tamla Motown STML 11122*	28	4 wks

See also Supremes; Supremes and the Four Tops; Temptations.

ROSTAL and SCHAEFER *UK, male instrumental duo*

2 wks

14 Jul 79	BEATLES CONCERTO	*Parlophone PAS 10014*	61	2 wks

David Lee ROTH *US, male vocalist*

2 wks

2 Mar 85	CRAZY FROM THE HEAT			
	Warner Bros 92-5222-1		91	2 wks

Uli Jon ROTH *Germany, male vocalist*

2 wks

23 Feb 85	BEYOND THE ASTRAL SKIES	*EMI ROTH 1*	64	2 wks

The musicians and contributors to this album are collectively referred to as Electric Sun.

Thomas ROUND – *See June BRONHILL and Thomas ROUND*

Demis ROUSSOS *Greece, male vocalist*

143 wks

22 Jun 74 ●	FOREVER AND EVER	*Philips 6325 021*	2	68 wks
19 Apr 75	SOUVENIRS	*Philips 6325 201*	25	18 wks
24 Apr 76 ●	HAPPY TO BE	*Philips 9101 027*	4	34 wks
3 Jul 76	MY ONLY FASCINATION	*Philips 6325 094*	39	6 wks
16 Apr 77	THE MAGIC OF DEMIS ROUSSOS			
	Philips 9101 131		29	6 wks
28 Oct 78	LIFE AND LOVE	*Philips 9199 873*	36	11 wks

ROXY MUSIC *UK, male vocal/instrumental group*

293 wks

29 Jul 72 ●	ROXY MUSIC	*Island ILPS 9200*	10	16 wks
7 Apr 73 ●	FOR YOUR PLEASURE	*Island ILPS 9232*	4	27 wks
1 Dec 73 ★	STRANDED	*Island ILPS 9252*	1	17 wks
30 Nov 74 ●	COUNTRY LIFE	*Island ILPS 9303*	3	10 wks
8 Nov 75 ●	SIREN	*Island ILPS 9344*	4	17 wks
31 Jul 76 ●	VIVA ROXY MUSIC	*Island ILPS 9400*	6	12 wks
19 Nov 77	GREATEST HITS	*Polydor 2302 073*	20	11 wks
24 Mar 79 ●	MANIFESTO	*Polydor POLH 001*	7	34 wks
31 May 80 ★	FLESH AND BLOOD	*Polydor POLH 002*	1	60 wks
5 Jun 82 ★	AVALON	*EG EGHP 50*	1	57 wks
19 Mar 83	THE HIGH ROAD	*E.G.(Import) EGMLP 1*	26	7 wks
12 Nov 83	ATLANTIC YEARS 1973-1980	*E.G. EGLP 54*	23	25 wks

ROYAL CHORAL SOCIETY – *See LONDON SYMPHONY ORCHESTRA*

ROYAL PHILHARMONIC ORCHESTRA
UK, orchestra — *16 wks*

23 Dec 78	CLASSIC GOLD VOL.2	*Ronco RTD 42032*	.....	31	4 wks
13 Jan 79	CLASSICAL GOLD	*Ronco RTV 42020*	....	65	1 wk
8 Oct 83	LOVE CLASSICS	*Nouveau Music NML 1003*	....	30	9 wks
26 May 84	AS TIME GOES BY	*Telstar STAR 2240*	....	95	2 wks

Love Classics was conducted by Nick Portlock and As Time Goes By was conducted by Harry Rabinovitz. See also Louis Clark/Royal Philharmonic Orchestra.

RUBETTES *UK, male vocal/instrumental group* — *1 wk*

10 May 75	WE CAN DO IT	*State ETAT 001*	....	41	1 wk

Jimmy RUFFIN *US, male vocalist* — *10 wks*

13 May 67	JIMMY RUFFIN WAY	*Tamla Motown STML 11048*	....	32	6 wks
1 Jun 74	GREATEST HITS	*Tamla Motown STML 11259*	..	41	4 wks

RUFUS and Chaka KHAN *US, male instrumental group with US female vocalist* — *7 wks*

12 Apr 75	RUFUSIZED	*ABC ABCL 5063*	....	48	2 wks
21 Apr 84	STOMPIN' AT THE SAVOY	*Warner Bros 923679*	...	64	5 wks

The first album gave Chaka Khan no separate billing. See also Chaka Khan.

RUMOUR - *See Graham PARKER and the RUMOUR*

Todd RUNDGREN *US, male vocalist* — *9 wks*

29 Jan 77	RA	*Bearsville K 55514*	....	27	6 wks
6 May 78	HERMIT OF MINK HOLLOW	*Bearsville K 55521*	...	42	3 wks

RUSH *Canada, male vocal/instrumental group* — *76 wks*

8 Oct 77	FAREWELL TO KINGS	*Mercury 9100 042*	......	22	4 wks
25 Nov 78	HEMISPHERES	*Mercury 9100 059*	....	14	6 wks
26 Jan 80 ●	PERMANENT WAVES	*Mercury 9100 071*	....	3	16 wks
21 Feb 81 ●	MOVING PICTURES	*Mercury 6337 160*	....	3	11 wks
7 Nov 81 ●	EXIT STAGE LEFT	*Mercury 6619 053*	....	6	14 wks
18 Sep 82 ●	SIGNALS	*Mercury 6337 243*	....	3	9 wks
28 Apr 84 ●	GRACE UNDER PRESSURE	*Vertigo VERH 12*	...	5	12 wks
9 Nov 85 ●	POWER WINDOWS	*Vertigo VERH 31*	....	9	4 wks

Jennifer RUSH *US, female vocalist* — *7 wks*

16 Nov 85 ●	JENNIFER RUSH	*CBS 26488*	....	7†	7 wks

Patrice RUSHEN *US, female vocalist* — *17 wks*

1 May 82	STRAIGHT FROM THE HEART	*Elektra K 52532*	..	24	14 wks
16 Jun 84	NOW	*Elektra 9603060*	....	73	3 wks

Leon RUSSELL *US, male vocalist* — *1 wk*

3 Jul 71	LEON RUSSELL AND THE SHELTER PEOPLE				
		A & M AMLS 65003	....	29	1 wk

Mike RUTHERFORD *UK, male vocalist/instrumentalist - guitar* — *11 wks*

23 Feb 80	SMALLCREEP'S DAY	*Charisma CAS 1149*	.....	13	7 wks
18 Sep 82	ACTING VERY STRANGE	*WEA K 99249*	.....	23	4 wks

RUTLES *UK, male vocal/instrumental group* — *11 wks*

15 Apr 78	THE RUTLES	*Warner Bros. K 56459*	....	12	11 wks

RUTS *UK, male vocal/instrumental group* — *10 wks*

13 Oct 79	THE CRACK	*Virgin V 2132*	....	16	6 wks
18 Oct 80	GRIN AND BEAR IT	*Virgin V 2188*	....	28	4 wks

Second album credited to Ruts D.C.

S

SAD CAFE *UK, male vocal/instrumental group* — *36 wks*

1 Oct 77	FANX TA RA	*RCA PL 25101*	....	56	1 wk
29 Apr 78	MISPLACED IDEALS	*RCA PL 25133*	......	50	1 wk
29 Sep 79 ●	FACADES	*RCA PL 25249*	....	8	23 wks
25 Oct 80	SAD CAFE	*RCA SADLP 4*	....	46	5 wks
21 Mar 81	LIVE	*RCA SAD LP 5*	....	37	4 wks
24 Oct 81	OLE	*Polydor POLD 5045*	....	72	2 wks

SADE *UK, female/male vocal/instrumental group* — *82 wks*

28 Jul 84 ●	DIAMOND LIFE	*Epic EPC 26044*	....	2†	75 wks
16 Nov 85 ★	PROMISE	*Epic EPC 86318*	....	1†	7 wks

SAILOR *UK, male vocal/instrumental group* — *8 wks*

7 Feb 76	TROUBLE	*Epic EPC 69192*	....	45	8 wks

ST. PAUL'S BOYS' CHOIR *UK, choir* — *8 wks*

29 Nov 80	REJOICE	*K-Tel NE 1064*	....	36	8 wks

Ryuichi SAKAMOTO *Japan, male composer/ multi-instrumentalist* — *9 wks*

3 Sep 83	MERRY CHRISTMAS MR LAWRENCE				
		Virgin V 2276	....	36	9 wks

SALVATION ARMY *UK, Brass Band* — *5 wks*

24 Dec 77	BY REQUEST	*Warwick WW 5038*	....	16	5 wks

SAM and DAVE *US, male vocal duo* — *20 wks*

21 Jan 67	HOLD ON I'M A COMIN'	*Atlantic 588-045*	.....	35	7 wks
22 Apr 67	DOUBLE DYNAMITE	*Stax 589-003*	....	28	5 wks
23 Mar 68	SOUL MAN	*Stax 589-015*	....	32	8 wks

Mike SAMMES SINGERS - *See RICHMOND STRINGS/Mike SAMMES SINGERS*

SAMSON *UK, male vocal/instrumental group* — *6 wks*

26 Jul 80	HEAD ON	*Gem GEMLP 108*	....	34	6 wks

SANTANA *US, male vocal/instrumental group* — *197 wks*

2 May 70	SANTANA	*CBS 63815*	....	26	11 wks
28 Nov 70 ●	ABRAXAS	*CBS 64807*	....	7	52 wks

13 Nov 71 ●	**SANTANA 3** CBS 69015			**6**	14 wks
29 Nov 72 ●	**CARAVANSERAI** CBS 65299			**6**	11 wks
8 Dec 73 ●	**WELCOME** CBS 69040			**8**	6 wks
21 Sep 74	**GREATEST HITS** CBS 69081			**14**	15 wks
30 Nov 74	**BARBOLETTA** CBS 69084			**18**	5 wks
10 Apr 76	**AMIGOS** CBS 86005			**21**	9 wks
8 Jan 77	**FESTIVAL** CBS 86020			**27**	3 wks
5 Nov 77 ●	**MOONFLOWER** CBS 88272			**7**	27 wks
11 Nov 78	**INNER SECRETS** CBS 86075			**17**	16 wks
24 Mar 79	**ONENESS - SILVER DREAMS GOLDEN REALITY** CBS 86037			**55**	4 wks
27 Oct 79	**MARATHON** CBS 86098			**28**	5 wks
20 Sep 80	**THE SWING OF DELIGHT** CBS 22057			**74**	2 wks
18 Apr 81	**ZE BOP** CBS 84946			**33**	4 wks
14 Aug 82	**SHANGO** CBS 85914			**35**	7 wks
30 Apr 83	**HAVANA MOON** CBS 25350			**84**	3 wks
23 Mar 85	**BEYOND APPEARANCES** CBS 86307			**58**	3 wks

Oneness-Silver Dreams Golden Reality, The Swing Of Delight *and* Havana Moon *are all credited to Carlos Santana,US, male instrumentalist - guitar. See also Carlos Santana; Carlos Santana and Alice Coltrane; Carlos Santana and Mahavishnu John McLaughlin; Carlos Santana and Buddy Miles.*

Carlos SANTANA and Alice COLTRANE
US, male/female instrumental duo   *1 wk*

2 Nov 74	**ILLUMINATIONS** CBS 69063			**40**	1 wk

See also Santana; Carlos Santana and Mahavishnu John McLaughlin; Carlos Santana and Buddy Miles.

Carlos SANTANA and Mahavishnu John McLAUGHLIN *US, male instrumental duo*   *9 wks*

28 Jul 73 ●	**LOVE DEVOTION SURRENDER** CBS 69037 ..			**7**	9 wks

See also Mahavishnu Orchestra; Santana; Carlos Santana and Alice Coltrane; Carlos Santana and Buddy Miles.

Carlos SANTANA and Buddy MILES *US, male instrumental duo*   *4 wks*

26 Aug 72	**CARLOS SANTANA AND BUDDY MILES LIVE** CBS 65142			**29**	4 wks

See also Santana; Carlos Santana and Alice Coltrane; Carlos Santana and Mahavishnu John McLaughlin.

Peter SARSTEDT *UK, male vocalist*   *4 wks*

15 Mar 69 ●	**PETER SARSTEDT** United Artists SULP 1219 ...			**8**	4 wks

Telly SAVALAS *US, male vocalist*   *10 wks*

22 Mar 75	**TELLY** MCA MCF 2699			**12**	10 wks

SAVOY BROWN *UK, male vocal/instrumental group*   *1 wk*

28 Nov 70	**LOOKIN' IN** Decca SKL 5066			**50**	1 wk

SAXON *UK, male vocal/instrumental group*   *71 wks*

12 Apr 80 ●	**WHEELS OF STEEL** Carrere CAL 115			**5**	29 wks
15 Nov 80	**STRONG ARM OF THE LAW** Carrere CAL 120			**11**	11 wks
3 Oct 81 ●	**DENIM AND LEATHER** Carrere CAL 128			**9**	11 wks
26 Mar 83	**POWER AND THE GLORY** Carrere CAL 147			**15**	9 wks
11 Feb 84	**CRUSADER** Carrere CAL 200			**18**	7 wks
14 Sep 85	**INNOCENCE IS NO EXCUSE** Parlophone SAXON 2			**36**	4 wks

Leo SAYER *UK, male vocalist*   *232 wks*

5 Jan 74 ●	**SILVER BIRD** Chrysalis CHR 1050			**2**	22 wks
26 Oct 74 ●	**JUST A BOY** Chrysalis CHR 1068			**4**	14 wks
20 Sep 75 ●	**ANOTHER YEAR** Chrysalis CHR 1087			**8**	9 wks
27 Nov 76 ●	**ENDLESS FLIGHT** Chrysalis CHR 1125			**4**	66 wks
22 Oct 77	**THUNDER IN MY HEART** Chrysalis CDL 1154			**8**	16 wks
2 Sep 78	**LEO SAYER** Chrysalis CDL 1198			**15**	25 wks
31 Mar 79 ★	**THE VERY BEST OF LEO SAYER** Chrysalis CDL 1222			**1**	37 wks
13 Oct 79	**HERE** Chrysalis CDL 1240			**44**	4 wks
23 Aug 80	**LIVING IN A FANTASY** Chrysalis CDL 1297			**15**	9 wks
8 May 82	**WORLD RADIO** Chrysalis CDL 1345			**30**	12 wks
12 Nov 83	**HAVE YOU EVER BEEN IN LOVE** Chrysalis LEOTV 1			**15**	18 wks

Alexei SAYLE *UK, male comedian*   *5 wks*

17 Mar 84	**THE FISH PEOPLE TAPES** Island IMA 9			**62**	5 wks

Boz SCAGGS *US, male vocalist*   *29 wks*

12 Mar 77	**SILK DEGREES** CBS 81193			**37**	24 wks
17 Dec 77	**DOWN TWO, THEN LEFT** CBS 86036			**55**	1 wk
3 May 80	**MIDDLE MAN** CBS 86094			**52**	4 wks

SCARS *UK, male vocal/instrumental group*   *3 wks*

18 Apr 81	**AUTHOR AUTHOR** Pre PREX 5			**67**	3 wks

SCHAEFER - *See ROSTAL and SCHAEFER*

Michael SCHENKER GROUP *Germany/UK, male vocal/instrumental group*   *42 wks*

6 Sep 80 ●	**MICHAEL SCHENKER GROUP** Chrysalis CHR 1302			**8**	8 wks
19 Sep 81	**MICHAEL SCHENKER GROUP** (re-issue) Chrysalis CHR 1336			**14**	8 wks
13 Mar 82 ●	**ONE NIGHT AT BUDOKAN** Chrysalis CTY 1375			**5**	11 wks
23 Oct 82	**ASSAULT ATTACK** Chrysalis CHR 1393			**19**	5 wks
10 Sep 83	**BUILT TO DESTROY** Chrysalis CHR 1441			**23**	5 wks
23 Jun 84	**ROCK WILL NEVER DIE** Chrysalis CUX 1470 ..			**24**	5 wks

SCORPIONS *Germany, male vocal/instrumental group*   *42 wks*

21 Apr 79	**LOVE DRIVE** Harvest SHSP 4097			**36**	11 wks
3 May 80	**ANIMAL MAGNETISM** Harvest SHSP 4113			**23**	6 wks
10 Apr 82	**BLACKOUT** Harvest SHVL 823			**11**	11 wks
24 Mar 84	**LOVE AT FIRST STING** Harvest SHSP 2400071			**17**	6 wks
29 Jun 85	**WORLD WIDE LIVE** Harvest SCORP 1			**18**	8 wks

SCOTLAND FOOTBALL WORLD CUP SQUAD 1974 *UK, male football team vocalists*   *9 wks*

25 May 74 ●	**EASY EASY** Polydor 2383 282			**3**	9 wks

Band Of The SCOTS GUARDS *UK, military band*   *2 wks*

28 Jun 69	**BAND OF THE SCOTS GUARDS** Fontana SFXL 54			**25**	2 wks

THE SEARCHERS (below) John McNally, Mike Pender, Tony Jackson and Chris Curtis took their name from a John Wayne film.

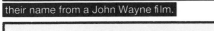

SADE (above) The jewel of 1984. (Toshi Yajima)

SHADOWS (left) Four chart topping albums and more weeks in the chart than any other instrumental act.

Jack SCOTT *Canada, male vocalist* *12 wks*

7 May 60	●	**I REMEMBER HANK WILLIAMS**			
		Top Rank BUY 034	**7**	11 wks
3 Sep 60		**WHAT IN THE WORLD'S COME OVER YOU**			
		Top Rank 25/024	**11**	1 wk

SCRITTI POLITTI *UK, male vocal/instrumental group* *26 wks*

11 Sep 82		**SONGS TO REMEMBER**			
		Rough Trade ROUGH 20	**12**	7 wks
22 Jun 85	●	**CUPID AND PSYCHE 85** *Virgin V 2350*	**5**	19 wks

SEARCHERS *UK, male vocal/instrumental group* *87 wks*

10 Aug 63	●	**MEET THE SEARCHERS** *Pye NPL 18086*	**2**	44 wks
16 Nov 63	●	**SUGAR AND SPICE** *Pye NPL 18089*	**5**	21 wks
30 May 64	●	**IT'S THE SEARCHERS** *Pye NPL 18092* ...	**4**	17 wks
27 Mar 65	●	**SOUNDS LIKE THE SEARCHERS**			
		Pye NPL 18111	**8**	5 wks

Harry SECOMBE *UK, male vocalist* *46 wks*

31 Mar 62		**SACRED SONGS** *Philips RBL 7501*	**16**	1 wk
22 Apr 67	●	**SECOMBE'S PERSONAL CHOICE**			
		Philips BETS 707	**6**	13 wks
7 Aug 71		**IF I RULED THE WORLD** *Contour 6870 501* ...	**17**	20 wks
16 Dec 78	●	**20 SONGS OF JOY** *Warwick WW 5052*	**8**	12 wks

See also Harry Secombe and Moira Anderson; Harry Secombe, Peter Sellers and Spike Milligan.

Harry SECOMBE and Moira ANDERSON *UK, male/female vocal duo* *5 wks*

5 Dec 81		**GOLDEN MEMORIES** *Warwick WW 5107*	**46**	5 wks

See also Harry Secombe; Harry Secombe, Peter Sellers and Spike Milligan.

Harry SECOMBE, Peter SELLERS and Spike MILLIGAN *UK, male vocal group* *1 wk*

18 Apr 64		**HOW TO WIN AN ELECTION** *Philips AL 3464*	**20**	1 wk

See also Harry Secombe; Harry Secombe and Moira Anderson; Peter Sellers; Peter Sellers and Sophia Loren; Anthony Newley, Peter Sellers, Joan Collins; Spike Milligan.

SECOND IMAGE *UK, male vocal/instrumental group* *1 wk*

30 Mar 85		**STRANGE REFLECTIONS** *MCA MCF 3255* ...	**100**	1 wk

SECRET AFFAIR *UK, male vocal/instrumental group* *15 wks*

1 Dec 79		**GLORY BOYS** *I-Spy 1*	**41**	8 wks
20 Sep 80		**BEHIND CLOSED DOORS** *I-Spy 2*	**48**	4 wks
13 Mar 82		**BUSINESS AS USUAL** *I-Spy 3*	**84**	3 wks

Neil SEDAKA *US, male vocalist* *52 wks*

1 Sep 73		**THE TRA-LA DAYS ARE OVER**		
		MGM 2315 248	**13**	10 wks
22 Jun 74		**LAUGHTER IN THE RAIN** *Polydor 2383 265* ...	**17**	10 wks
23 Nov 74		**LIVE AT THE ROYAL FESTIVAL HALL**		
		Polydor 2383 299	**48**	1 wk
1 Mar 75		**OVERNIGHT SUCCESS** *Polydor 2442 131*	**31**	6 wks
10 Jul 76	●	**LAUGHTER AND TEARS - THE BEST OF NEIL SEDAKA TODAY** *Polydor 2383 399*	**2**	25 wks

SEEKERS *Australia, male/female vocal group* *268 wks*

3 Jul 65	●	**A WORLD OF OUR OWN** *Columbia 33SX 1722*	**5**	36 wks
3 Jul 65		**THE SEEKERS** *Decca LK 4694*	**16**	1 wk
19 Nov 66	●	**COME THE DAY** *Columbia SX 6093*	**3**	67 wks
25 Nov 67		**SEEKERS - SEEN IN GREEN**		
		Columbia SCX 6193	**15**	10 wks
14 Sep 68	●	**LIVE AT THE TALK OF THE TOWN**		
		Columbia SCX 6278	**2**	29 wks
16 Nov 68	★	**BEST OF THE SEEKERS** *Columbia SCX 6268* ..	**1**	125 wks

Bob SEGER and the SILVER BULLET BAND *US, male vocal/instrumental group* *32 wks*

3 Jun 78		**STRANGER IN TOWN** *Capitol EAST 11698*	**31**	6 wks
15 Mar 80		**AGAINST THE WIND** *Capitol EA-ST 12041* ...	**26**	6 wks
26 Sep 81		**NINE TONIGHT** *Capitol ESTSP 23*	**24**	10 wks
8 Jan 83		**THE DISTANCE** *Capitol EST 12254*	**45**	10 wks

The SELECTER *UK, male/female vocal/instrumental group* *17 wks*

23 Feb 80	●	**TOO MUCH PRESSURE**		
		Two Tone CDL TT 5002	**5**	13 wks
7 Mar 81		**CELEBRATE THE BULLET** *Chrysalis CHR 1306*	**41**	4 wks

Peter SELLERS *UK, male vocalist* *84 wks*

14 Feb 59	●	**THE BEST OF SELLERS** *Parlophone PMD 1069*	**3**	47 wks
12 Dec 59	●	**SONGS FOR SWINGING SELLERS**		
		Parlophone PMC 1111	**3**	37 wks

See also Peter Sellers; Peter Sellers and Sophia Loren; Harry Secombe, Peter Sellers and Spike Milligan; Anthony Newley, Peter Sellers, Joan Collins.

Peter SELLERS and Sophia LOREN *UK/Italy, male/female vocal duo* *18 wks*

3 Dec 60	●	**PETER AND SOPHIA** *Parlophone PMC 1131*	**5**	18 wks

See also Peter Sellers; Harry Secombe, Peter Sellers and Spike Milligan; Anthony Newley, Peter Sellers, Joan Collins.

Captain SENSIBLE *UK, male vocalist* *3 wks*

11 Sep 82		**WOMEN AND CAPTAIN FIRST**		
		A&M AMLH 68548	**64**	3 wks

SEX PISTOLS *UK, male vocal/instrumental group* *97 wks*

12 Nov 77	★	**NEVER MIND THE BOLLOCKS HERE'S THE SEX PISTOLS** *Virgin V 2086*	**1**	48 wks
10 Mar 79	●	**THE GREAT ROCK 'N' ROLL SWINDLE**		
		Virgin VD 2410	**7**	33 wks
11 Aug 79	●	**SOME PRODUCT - CARRI ON SEX PISTOLS**		
		Virgin VR 2	**6**	10 wks
16 Feb 80		**FLOGGING A DEAD HORSE** *Virgin V 2142* ...	**23**	6 wks

SHADOWS *UK, male instrumental group* *366 wks*

16 Sep 61	★	**THE SHADOWS** *Columbia 33SX 1374*	**1**	57 wks

13 Oct 62 ★	OUT OF THE SHADOWS	Columbia 33SX 1458	1	38 wks
22 Jun 63 ●	GREATEST HITS	Columbia 33SX 1522	2	49 wks
9 May 64 ●	DANCE WITH THE SHADOWS	Columbia 33SX 1619	2	27 wks
17 Jul 65 ●	SOUND OF THE SHADOWS	Columbia 33SX 1736	4	17 wks
21 May 66 ●	SHADOW MUSIC	Columbia SX 6041	5	17 wks
15 Jul 67 ●	JIGSAW	Columbia SCX 6148	8	16 wks
24 Oct 70	SHADES OF ROCK	Columbia SCX 6420	30	4 wks
13 Apr 74	ROCKIN' WITH CURLY LEADS	EMI EMA 762	45	1 wk
11 May 74	GREATEST HITS (re-issue)	Columbia SCX 1522	48	6 wks
29 Mar 75	SPECS APPEAL	EMI EMC 3066	30	5 wks
12 Feb 77 ★	20 GOLDEN GREATS	EMI EMTV 3	1	38 wks
15 Sep 79 ★	STRING OF HITS	EMI EMC 3310	1	48 wks
26 Jul 80	ANOTHER STRING OF HITS	EMI EMC 3339	16	8 wks
13 Sep 80	CHANGE OF ADDRESS	Polydor 2442 179	17	6 wks
19 Sep 81	HITS RIGHT UP YOUR STREET	Polydor POLD 5046	15	16 wks
25 Sep 82	LIFE IN THE JUNGLE/LIVE AT ABBEY ROAD	Polydor SHADS 1	24	6 wks
22 Oct 83	XXV	Polydor POLD 5120	34	6 wks
17 Nov 84	GUARDIAN ANGEL	Polydor POLD 5169	98	1 wk

See also Cliff Richard.

SHAKATAK *UK, male/female vocal/instrumental group*

72 wks

30 Jan 82	DRIVIN' HARD	Polydor POLS 1030	35	17 wks
15 May 82 ●	NIGHT BIRDS	Polydor POLD 1059	4	28 wks
27 Nov 82	INVITATIONS	Polydor POLD 5068	30	11 wks
22 Oct 83	OUT OF THIS WORLD	Polydor POLD 5115	30	4 wks
25 Aug 84	DOWN ON THE STREET	Polydor POLD 5148 ..	17	9 wks
23 Feb 85	LIVE!	Polydor POLH 21	82	3 wks

SHAKIN' PYRAMIDS *UK, male vocal/instrumental group*

4 wks

4 Apr 81	SKIN 'EM UP	Cuba/Libra V 2199	48	4 wks

SHALAMAR *US, male/female vocal/instrumental group*

97 wks

27 Mar 82 ●	FRIENDS	Solar K 52345	6	72 wks
11 Sep 82	GREATEST HITS	Solar SOLA 3001	71	5 wks
30 Jul 83 ●	THE LOOK	Solar 960239	7	20 wks

SHAM 69 *UK, male vocal/instrumental group*

27 wks

11 Mar 78	TELL US THE TRUTH	Polydor 2383 491	25	8 wks
2 Dec 78	THAT'S LIFE	Polydor POLD 5010	27	11 wks
29 Sep 79 ●	THE ADVENTURES OF THE HERSHAM BOYS	Polydor POLD 5025	8	8 wks

Jimmy SHAND, his band and guests *UK, male instrumentalist - accordian, with male/female vocal/instrumental dance band*

2 wks

24 Dec 83	FIFTY YEARS ON WITH JIMMY SHAND	Ross WGR 062	97	2 wks

SHANNON *US, female vocalist*

12 wks

10 Mar 84	LET THE MUSIC PLAY	Club JABL 1	52	12 wks

Del SHANNON *US, male vocalist*

23 wks

11 May 63 ●	HATS OFF TO DEL SHANNON	London HAX 8071	9	17 wks
2 Nov 63	LITTLE TOWN FLIRT	London HAX 8091	15	6 wks

Helen SHAPIRO *UK, female vocalist*

25 wks

10 Mar 62 ●	TOPS WITH ME	Columbia 33SX 1397	2	25 wks

Feargal SHARKEY *UK, male vocalist*

6 wks

23 Nov 85	FEARGAL SHARKEY	Virgin V 2360	12†	6 wks

Sandie SHAW *UK, female vocalist*

13 wks

6 Mar 65 ●	SANDIE	Pye NPL 18110	3	13 wks

Pete SHELLEY *US, male vocalist*

4 wks

2 Jul 83	XL-1	Genetic XL 1	42	4 wks

Brendon SHINE *Ireland, male vocalist*

22 wks

12 Nov 83	THE BRENDON SHINE COLLECTION	Play PLAYTV 1	51	12 wks
3 Nov 84	WITH LOVE	Play PLAYTV 2	74	4 wks
16 Nov 85	MEMORIES	Play PLAY TV 3	81†	6 wks

SHOWADDYWADDY *UK, male vocal/instrumental group*

125 wks

7 Dec 74 ●	SHOWADDYWADDY	Bell BELLS 248	9	19 wks
12 Jul 75 ●	STEP TWO	Bell BELLS 256	7	17 wks
29 May 76	TROCADERO	Bell SYBEL 8003	41	3 wks
25 Dec 76 ●	GREATEST HITS	Arista ARTY 145	4	26 wks
3 Dec 77	RED STAR	Arista SPARTY 1023	20	10 wks
9 Dec 78 ★	GREATEST HITS	Arista ARTV 1	1	17 wks
10 Nov 79 ●	CREPES AND DRAPES	Arista ARTV 3	8	14 wks
20 Dec 80	BRIGHT LIGHTS	Arista SPART 1142	54	8 wks
7 Nov 81	THE VERY BEST OF	Arista SPART 1178	33	11 wks

SHRIEKBACK *UK, male vocal/instrumental group*

1 wk

11 Aug 84	JAM SCIENCE	Arista 206 416	85	1 wk

Labi SIFFRE *UK, male vocalist*

2 wks

24 Jul 71	SINGER AND THE SONG	Pye NSPL 28147	47	1 wk
14 Oct 72	CRYING, LAUGHING, LOVING, LYING	Pye NSPL 28163	46	1 wk

SILVER BULLET BAND - *See Bob SEGER and the SILVER BULLET BAND*

SILVER CONVENTION *Germany/US, female vocal group*

3 wks

25 Jun 77	SILVER CONVENTION: GREATEST HITS	Magnet MAG 6001	34	3 wks

SIMPLE MINDS (left) Surely after two number one albums Jim Kerr and group could afford better accommodation than this?

SLADE Three number ones in 14 months.

FRANK SINATRA (right) On the very first chart but had to wait nineteen years to hit number one.

SIMON and GARFUNKEL US, male vocal duo

1017 wks

16 Apr	66		**SOUNDS OF SILENCE** *CBS 62690*		13	104 wks
3 Aug	68	★	**BOOKENDS** *CBS 63101*		1	77 wks
31 Aug	68		**PARSLEY, SAGE, ROSEMARY & THYME** *CBS 62860*		13	66 wks
26 Oct	68	●	**THE GRADUATE** (film soundtrack) *CBS 70042*		3	71 wks
9 Nov	68		**WEDNESDAY MORNING 3 A.M.** *CBS 63370*		24	6 wks
21 Feb	70	★	**BRIDGE OVER TROUBLED WATER** *CBS 63699*		1	303 wks
22 Jul	72	●	**GREATEST HITS** *CBS 69003*		2	283 wks
4 Apr	81		**SOUNDS OF SILENCE** (re-issue) *CBS 32020*		68	1 wk
21 Nov	81	●	**THE SIMON AND GARFUNKEL COLLECTION** *CBS 10029*		4	63 wks
20 Mar	82	●	**THE CONCERT IN CENTRAL PARK** *Geffen 96008*		6	43 wks

See also Paul Simon; Art Garfunkel.

Carly SIMON US, female vocalist

35 wks

20 Jan	73	●	**NO SECRETS** *Elektra K 42127*		3	26 wks
16 Mar	74		**HOT CAKES** *Elektra K 52005*		19	9 wks

Paul SIMON US, male vocalist

114 wks

26 Feb	72	★	**PAUL SIMON** *CBS 69007*		1	26 wks
2 Jun	73	●	**THERE GOES RHYMIN' SIMON** *CBS 69035*		4	22 wks
1 Nov	75	●	**STILL CRAZY AFTER ALL THESE YEARS** *CBS 86001*		6	31 wks
3 Dec	77	●	**GREATEST HITS, ETC.** *CBS 10007*		6	15 wks
30 Aug	80		**ONE-TRICK PONY** *Warner Bros. K 56846*		17	12 wks
12 Nov	83		**HEARTS AND BONES** *Warner Bros 92-3942-1*		34	8 wks

See also Simon and Garfunkel.

Nina SIMONE US, female vocalist

4 wks

24 Jul	65		**I PUT A SPELL ON YOU** *Philips BL 7671*		18	3 wks
15 Feb	69		**'NUFF SAID** *RCA SF 7979*		11	1 wk

SIMPLE MINDS UK, male vocal/instrumental group

97 wks

5 May	79		**A LIFE IN THE DAY** *Zoom ZULP 1*		30	6 wks
27 Sep	80		**EMPIRES AND DANCE** *Arista SPART 1140*		41	3 wks
12 Sep	81		**SONS AND FASCINATIONS/SISTERS FEELINGS CALL** *Virgin V 2207*		11	7 wks
27 Feb	82		**CELEBRATION** *Arista SPART 1183*		45	7 wks
25 Sep	82	●	**NEW GOLD DREAM (81,82,83,84)** *Virgin V 2230*		3	37 wks
18 Feb	84	★	**SPARKLE IN THE RAIN** *Virgin V 2300*		1	28 wks
2 Nov	85	★	**ONCE UPON A TIME** *Virgin V 2364*		1†	9 wks

SIMPLY RED UK, male vocal/instrumental group

8 wks

26 Oct	85		**PICTURE BOOK** *Elektra EKT 27*		34	8 wks

Frank SINATRA US, male vocalist

596 wks

8 Nov	58	●	**COME FLY WITH ME** *Capitol LCT 6154*		2	18 wks
15 Nov	58	●	**SONGS FOR SWINGING LOVERS** *Capitol LCT 6106*		8	8 wks
29 Nov	58	●	**FRANK SINATRA STORY** *Fontana TFL 5030*		8	1 wk
13 Dec	58	●	**FRANK SINATRA SINGS FOR ONLY THE LONELY** *Capitol LCT 6168*		5	13 wks
16 May	59	●	**COME DANCE WITH ME** *Capitol LCT 6179*		2	30 wks
22 Aug	59	●	**LOOK TO YOUR HEART** *Capitol LCT 6181*		5	8 wks
11 Jun	60	●	**COME BACK TO SORRENTO** *Fontana TFL 5082*		6	9 wks
29 Oct	60	●	**SWING EASY** *Capitol W 587*		5	17 wks
21 Jan	61	●	**NICE 'N EASY** *Capitol W 1417*		4	27 wks
15 Jul	61		**SINATRA SOUVENIR** *Fontana TFL 5138*		18	1 wk
19 Aug	61	●	**WHEN YOUR LOVER HAS GONE** *Encore ENC 101*		6	10 wks
23 Sep	61	●	**SINATRA'S SWINGING SESSION** *Capitol W 1491*		6	8 wks
28 Oct	61	●	**SINATRA SWINGS** *Reprise R 1002*		8	8 wks
25 Nov	61	●	**SINATRA PLUS** *Fontana SET 303*		7	9 wks
16 Dec	61	●	**RING-A-DING-DING** *Reprise R 1001*		8	9 wks
17 Feb	62	●	**COME SWING WITH ME** *Capitol W 1594*		13	4 wks
7 Apr	62	●	**I REMEMBER TOMMY** *Reprise R 1003*		10	12 wks
9 Jun	62	●	**SINATRA AND STRINGS** *Reprise R 1004*		6	20 wks
27 Oct	62		**GREAT SONGS FROM GREAT BRITAIN** *Reprise R 1006*		12	9 wks
29 Dec	62		**SINATRA WITH SWINGING BRASS** *Reprise R 1005*		14	11 wks
27 Jul	63	●	**CONCERT SINATRA** *Reprise R 1009*		8	18 wks
5 Oct	63	●	**SINATRA'S SINATRA** *Reprise R 1010*		9	24 wks
19 Sep	64		**IT MIGHT AS WELL BE SWING** *Reprise R 1012*		17	4 wks
20 Mar	65		**SOFTLY AS I LEAVE YOU** *Reprise R 1013*		20	1 wk
22 Jan	66	●	**A MAN AND HIS MUSIC** *Reprise R 1016*		9	19 wks
21 May	66		**MOONLIGHT SINATRA** *Reprise R 1018*		18	8 wks
2 Jul	66	●	**STRANGERS IN THE NIGHT** *Reprise R 1017*		4	18 wks
1 Oct	66	●	**SINATRA AT THE SANDS** *Reprise RLP 1019*		7	18 wks
3 Dec	66		**FRANK SINATRA SINGS SONGS FOR PLEASURE** *MFP 1120*		26	2 wks
25 Feb	67		**THAT'S LIFE** *Reprise RSLP 1020*		22	12 wks
7 Oct	67		**FRANK SINATRA** *Reprise R 1022*		28	5 wks
19 Oct	68	●	**GREATEST HITS** *Reprise RSLP 1025*		8	38 wks
7 Dec	68		**BEST OF FRANK SINATRA** *Capitol ST 21140*		17	10 wks
7 Jun	69	●	**MY WAY** *Reprise RSLP 1029*		2	59 wks
4 Oct	69		**A MAN ALONE** *Reprise RSLP 1030*		18	7 wks
9 May	70		**WATERTOWN** *Reprise RSLP 1031*		14	9 wks
12 Dec	70	●	**GREATEST HITS VOL.2** *Reprise RSLP 1032*		6	40 wks
5 Jun	71	●	**SINATRA AND COMPANY** *Reprise RSLP 1033*		9	9 wks
27 Nov	71		**FRANK SINATRA SINGS RODGERS AND HART** *Starline SRS 5083*		35	1 wk
8 Jan	72		**MY WAY** (re-issue) *Reprise K 44015*		35	1 wk
8 Jan	72		**GREATEST HITS VOL.2** *Reprise K 44018*		29	3 wks
1 Dec	73		**OL' BLUE EYES IS BACK** *Warner Bros. K 44249*		12	13 wks
17 Aug	74		**SOME NICE THINGS I'VE MISSED** *Reprise K 54020*		35	3 wks
15 Feb	75		**THE MAIN EVENT** (tv soundtrack) *Reprise K 54031*		30	2 wks
14 Jun	75		**THE BEST OF OL' BLUE EYES** *Reprise K 54042*		30	3 wks
19 Mar	77	★	**PORTRAIT OF SINATRA** *Reprise K 64039*		1	18 wks
13 May	78	●	**20 GOLDEN GREATS** *Capitol EMTV 10*		4	11 wks
18 Aug	84		**L.A. IS MY LADY** *Qwest 925145*		41	8 wks

See also Frank Sinatra and Count Basie.

Frank SINATRA and Count BASIE US, male vocalist and male orchestra leader/instrumentalist - piano

23 wks

23 Feb	63	●	**SINATRA - BASIE** *Reprise R 1008*		2	23 wks

See also Count Basie; Frank Sinatra.

Nancy SINATRA US, female vocalist

15 wks

16 Apr	66		**BOOTS** *Reprise R 6202*		12	9 wks
18 Jun	66		**HOW DOES THAT GRAB YOU** *Reprise R 6207*		12	3 wks
10 Oct	70		**NANCY'S GREATEST HITS** *Reprise RSLP 6409*		39	3 wks

See also Nancy Sinatra and Lee Hazlewood.

Nancy SINATRA and Lee HAZLEWOOD US, female/male vocal duo

17 wks

29 Jun	68		**NANCY AND LEE** *Reprise RSLP 6273*		17	12 wks
25 Sep	71		**NANCY AND LEE** (re-issue) *Reprise K 44126*		42	1 wk
29 Jan	72		**DID YOU EVER** *RCA Victor SF 8240*		31	4 wks

See also Nancy Sinatra.

SIOUXSIE and the BANSHEES UK, male/female
vocal/instrumental group — 92 wks

2 Dec 78	**THE SCREAM** *Polydor POLD 5009*	12	11 wks
22 Sep 79	**JOIN HANDS** *Polydor POLD 5024*	13	5 wks
16 Aug 80	● **KALEIDOSCOPE** *Polydor 2442 177*	5	6 wks
27 Jun 81	● **JU JU** *Polydor POLS 1034*	7	17 wks
12 Dec 81	**ONCE UPON A TIME** *Polydor POLS 1056*	21	26 wks
13 Nov 82	**A KISS IN THE DREAMHOUSE** *Polydor POLD 5064*	11	11 wks
3 Dec 83	**NOCTURNE** *Wonderland SHAH 1*	29	10 wks
16 Jun 84	**HYENA** *Wonderful SHEHP 1*	15	6 wks

SISTER SLEDGE US, female vocal group — 50 wks

12 May 79	● **WE ARE FAMILY** *Atlantic K 50587*	7	39 wks
22 Jun 85	**WHEN THE BOYS MEET THE GIRLS** *Atlantic 78-1255-1*	19	11 wks

SISTERS of MERCY UK, male vocal/instrumental
group — 8 wks

23 Mar 85	**FIRST AND LAST AND ALWAYS** *Merciful Release MR 337 L*	14	8 wks

Peter SKELLERN UK, male vocalist — 28 wks

9 Sep 78	**SKELLERN** *Mercury 9109 701*	48	3 wks
8 Dec 79	**ASTAIRE** *Mercury 9102 702*	23	20 wks
4 Dec 82	**A STRING OF PEARLS** *Mercury MERL 10*	67	5 wks

SKID ROW UK, male vocal/instrumental group — 3 wks

17 Oct 70	**SKID** *CBS 63965*	30	3 wks

SKIDS UK, male vocal/instrumental group — 20 wks

17 Mar 79	**SCARED TO DANCE** *Virgin V 2116*	19	10 wks
27 Oct 79	**DAYS IN EUROPE** *Virgin V 2138*	32	5 wks
27 Sep 80	● **THE ABSOLUTE GAME** *Virgin V 2174*	9	5 wks

SKY UK/Australia, male instrumental group — 202 wks

2 Jun 79	● **SKY** *Ariola ARLH 5022*	9	56 wks
26 Apr 80	★ **SKY 2** *Ariola ADSKY 2*	1	53 wks
28 Mar 81	● **SKY 3** *Ariola ASKY 3*	3	23 wks
3 Apr 82	● **SKY 4-FORTHCOMING** *Ariola ASKY 4*	7	22 wks
22 Jan 83	**SKY FIVE LIVE** *Ariola 302 171*	14	14 wks
3 Dec 83	**CADMIUM** *Ariola 205 885*	44	10 wks
12 May 84	**MASTERPIECES-THE VERY BEST OF SKY** *Telstar STAR 2241*	15	18 wks
13 Apr 85	**THE GREAT BALLOON RACE** *Epic EPC 26419*	63	6 wks

SLADE UK, male vocal/instrumental group — 199 wks

8 Apr 72	● **SLADE ALIVE** *Polydor 2383 101*	2	58 wks
9 Dec 72	★ **SLAYED?** *Polydor 2383 163*	1	34 wks
6 Oct 73	★ **SLADEST** *Polydor 2442 119*	1	24 wks
23 Feb 74	★ **OLD NEW BORROWED AND BLUE** *Polydor 2383 261*	1	16 wks
14 Dec 74	● **SLADE IN FLAME** *Polydor 2442 126*	6	18 wks
27 Mar 76	**NOBODY'S FOOL** *Polydor 2383 377*	14	4 wks
22 Nov 80	**SLADE SMASHES** *Polydor POLTV 13*	21	15 wks
21 Mar 81	**WE'LL BRING THE HOUSE DOWN** *Cheapskate SKATE 1*	25	4 wks
28 Nov 81	**TILL DEAF US DO PART** *RCA RCALP 6021*	68	2 wks
18 Dec 82	**SLADE ON STAGE** *RCA RCALP 3107*	58	3 wks
24 Dec 83	**THE AMAZING KAMIKAZE SYNDROME** *RCA PL 70116*	49	13 wks
9 Jun 84	**SLADE'S GREATS** *Polydor SLAD 1*	89	1 wk
6 Apr 85	**ROGUES GALLERY** *RCA PL 70604*	60	2 wks
30 Nov 85	**CRACKERS- THE SLADE CHRISTMAS PARTY ALBUM** *Telstar STAR 2271*	34†	5 wks

SLEIGHRIDERS UK, male vocal/instrumental group — 1 wk

17 Dec	**A VERY MERRY DISCO** *Warwick WW 5136*	100	1 wk

Grace SLICK US, female vocalist — 6 wks

31 May 80	**DREAMS** *RCA PL 13544*	28	6 wks

SLIK UK, male vocal/instrumental group — 1 wk

12 Jun 76	**SLIK** *Bell SYBEL 8004*	58	1 wk

SLITS UK, female vocal/instrumental group — 5 wks

22 Sep 79	**CUT** *Island ILPS 9573*	30	5 wks

SLY and the FAMILY STONE US, male/female
vocal/instrumental group — 2 wks

5 Feb 72	**THERE'S A RIOT GOIN' ON** *Epic EPC 64613*	31	2 wks

SMALL FACES UK, male vocal/instrumental group — 66 wks

14 May 66	● **SMALL FACES** *Decca LK 4790*	3	25 wks
17 Jun 67	**FROM THE BEGINNING** *Decca LK 4879*	17	5 wks
1 Jul 67	**SMALL FACES** *Immediate IMSP 008*	12	17 wks
15 Jun 68	★ **OGDEN'S NUT GONE FLAKE** *Immediate IMLP 012*	1	19 wks

Brian SMITH and his HAPPY PIANO UK,
male instrumentalist - piano — 1 wk

19 Sep 81	**PLAY IT AGAIN** *Deram DS 047*	97	1 wk

Jimmy SMITH US, male instrumentalist - organ — 3 wks

18 Jun 66	**GOT MY MOJO WORKING** *Verve VLP 912*	19	3 wks

Keely SMITH US, female vocalist — 9 wks

16 Jan 65	**LENNON-McCARTNEY SONGBOOK** *Reprise R 6142*	12	9 wks

O.C. SMITH US, male vocalist — 1 wk

17 Aug 68	**HICKORY HOLLER REVISITED** *CBS 63362*	40	1 wk

Steven SMITH and FATHER UK, male instrumental
duo — 3 wks

13 May 72	**STEVEN SMITH AND FATHER AND 16 GREAT SONGS** *Decca SKL 5128*	17	3 wks

SHAM 69 (above) Jimmy Pursey makes a victory speech after winning the 1978 Andy Capp lookalike award.

SISTER SLEDGE (right) 'We Are Family' entered the chart in May 1979. It made the Top Ten some 284 weeks later in October 1984. This is the longest time any album has taken to make the Top Ten.

GRACE SLICK (below) Grace Slick dreaming about her six weeks of solo success. (Retna Pictures Int)

Patti SMITH GROUP US, female vocalist and male
instrumental backing group   20 wks

	Date		Title	Label	Pos	Wks
1	Apr 78		EASTER	Arista SPART 1043	16	14 wks
19	May 79		WAVE	Arista SPART 1086	41	6 wks

SMITHS UK, male vocal instrumental band   83 wks

Date		Title	Label	Pos	Wks
3 Mar 84	●	THE SMITHS	Rough Trade ROUGH 61	2	33 wks
24 Nov 84	●	HATFUL OF HOLLOW	Rough Trade ROUGH 76	7	37 wks
23 Feb 85	★	MEAT IS MURDER	Rough Trade ROUGH 81	1	13 wks

SMOKIE UK, male vocal/instrumental group   42 wks

Date		Title	Label	Pos	Wks
1 Nov 75		SMOKIE/CHANGING ALL THE TIME RAK SRAK 517		18	5 wks
30 Apr 77	●	GREATEST HITS RAK SRAK 526		6	22 wks
4 Nov 78		THE MONTREUX ALBUM RAK SRAK 6757		52	2 wks
11 Oct 80		SMOKIE'S HITS RAK SRAK 540		23	13 wks

SOFT CELL UK, male vocal/instrumental duo   78 wks

Date		Title	Label	Pos	Wks
12 Dec 81	●	NON-STOP EROTIC CABARET Some Bizzare BZLP 2		5	46 wks
26 Jun 82	●	NON-STOP ECSTATIC DANCING Some Bizzare BZX 1012		6	18 wks
22 Jan 83	●	THE ART OF FALLING APART Some Bizzare BIZL 3		5	9 wks
31 Mar 84		THIS LAST NIGHT IN SODOM Some Bizzare BIZL 6		12	5 wks

SOFT MACHINE UK, male vocal/instrumental group   8 wks

Date		Title	Label	Pos	Wks
4 Jul 70		THIRD CBS 66246		18	6 wks
3 Apr 71		FOURTH CBS 64280		32	2 wks

SOLID SENDERS UK, male vocal/instrumental group   3 wks

Date		Title	Label	Pos	Wks
23 Sep 78		SOLID SENDERS Virgin V 2105		42	3 wks

Diane SOLOMON UK, female vocalist   6 wks

Date		Title	Label	Pos	Wks
9 Aug 75		TAKE TWO Philips 6308 236		26	6 wks

SONNY and CHER US, male/female vocal duo   20 wks

Date		Title	Label	Pos	Wks
16 Oct 65	●	LOOK AT US Atlantic ATL 5036		7	13 wks
14 May 66		THE WONDROUS WORLD OF SONNY & CHER Atlantic 587-006		15	7 wks

See also Cher.

S.O.S BAND US, male/female vocal/instrumental group   10 wks

Date		Title	Label	Pos	Wks
1 Sep 84		JUST THE WAY YOU LIKE IT Tabu TBU 26058		29	10 wks

David SOUL US, male vocalist   51 wks

Date		Title	Label	Pos	Wks
27 Nov 76	●	DAVID SOUL Private Stock PVLP 1012		2	28 wks
17 Sep 77	●	PLAYING TO AN AUDIENCE OF ONE Private Stock PVLP 1026		8	23 wks

---

SOUL CITY SYMPHONY - See Van McCOY and the SOUL CITY SYMPHONY

SOUNDS ORCHESTRAL UK, orchestra   1 wk

Date		Title	Label	Pos	Wks
12 Jun 65		CAST YOUR FATE TO THE WIND Piccadilly NPL 38041		17	1 wk

SOUNDTRACKS (films, tv etc) - See VARIOUS ARTISTS

SOUTH BANK ORCHESTRA UK, orchestra   6 wks

Date		Title	Label	Pos	Wks
2 Dec 78		LILLIE Sounds MOR 516		47	6 wks

This album was conducted by Joseph Morovitz and Laurie Holloway.

SPACE France, male instrumental group   9 wks

Date		Title	Label	Pos	Wks
17 Sep 77		MAGIC FLY Pye NSPL 28232		11	9 wks

SPANDAU BALLET UK, male vocal/instrumental group   183 wks

Date		Title	Label	Pos	Wks
14 Mar 81	●	JOURNEY TO GLORY Reformation CHR 1331		5	29 wks
20 Mar 82	●	DIAMOND Reformation CDL 1353		15	18 wks
12 Mar 83	★	TRUE Reformation CDL 1403		1	90 wks
7 Jul 84	●	PARADE Reformation CDL 1473		2	39 wks
16 Nov 85	●	THE SINGLES COLLECTION Chrysalis SBTV 1		3†	7 wks

SPARKS US/UK, male vocal/instrumental group   42 wks

Date		Title	Label	Pos	Wks
1 Jun 74	●	KIMONO MY HOUSE Island ILPS 9272		4	24 wks
23 Nov 74	●	PROPAGANDA Island ILPS 9312		9	13 wks
18 Oct 75		INDISCREET Island ILPS 9345		18	4 wks
8 Sep 79		NUMBER ONE IN HEAVEN Virgin V 2115		73	1 wk

SPEAR OF DESTINY UK, male vocal/instrumental group   16 wks

Date		Title	Label	Pos	Wks
23 Apr 83		GRAPES OF WRATH Epic EPC 25318		62	2 wks
28 Apr 84		ONE EYED JACKS Burning Rome EPC 25836		22	7 wks
7 Sep 85		WORLD SERVICE Burning Rome EPC 26514		11	7 wks

Billie Jo SPEARS US, female vocalist   28 wks

Date		Title	Label	Pos	Wks
11 Sep 76		WHAT I'VE GOT IN MIND United Artists UAS 29955		47	2 wks
19 May 79	●	THE BILLIE JO SPEARS SINGLES ALBUM United Artists UAK 30231		7	17 wks
21 Nov 81		COUNTRY GIRL Warwick WW 5109		17	9 wks

SPECIAL A.K.A. UK, male/female vocal/instrumental group   6 wks

Date		Title	Label	Pos	Wks
23 Jun 84		IN THE STUDIO 2-Tone CHR TT 5008		34	6 wks

SPECIALS UK, male vocal/instrumental group   64 wks

Date		Title	Label	Pos	Wks
3 Nov 79	●	SPECIALS Two-Tone CDL TT 5001		4	45 wks
4 Oct 80	●	MORE SPECIALS Two-Tone CHR TT 5003		5	19 wks

Phil SPECTOR US, male producer 23 wks

23 Dec 72	PHIL SPECTOR'S CHRISTMAS ALBUM Apple SAPCOR 24	21	3 wks
15 Oct 77	PHIL SPECTOR'S ECHOES OF THE 60'S Phil Spector International 2307 013	21	10 wks
25 Dec 82	PHIL SPECTOR'S CHRISTMAS ALBUM (re-issue) Phil Spec.Int/Polydor 2307 005	96	2 wks
10 Dec 83	PHIL SPECTOR'S GREATEST HITS/PHIL SPECTOR'S CHRISTMAS ALBUM (2nd re-issue) Impression PSLP 1/2	19	8 wks

SPIDER UK, male vocal/instrumental group 2 wks

23 Oct 82	ROCK 'N' ROLL GYPSIES RCA RCALP 3101	75	1 wk
7 Apr 84	ROUGH JUSTICE A & M AMLX 68563	96	1 wk

SPINNERS UK, male vocal group 24 wks

5 Sep 70	THE SPINNERS ARE IN TOWN Fontana 6309 014	40	5 wks
7 Aug 71	SPINNERS LIVE PERFORMANCE Contour 6870 502	14	12 wks
13 Nov 71	THE SWINGING CITY Philips 6382 002	20	3 wks
8 Apr 72	LOVE IS TEASING Columbia SCX 6493	33	4 wks

SPIRIT US, male vocal/instrumental duo 2 wks

18 Apr 81	POTATO LAND Beggars Banquet BEGA 23	40	2 wks

SPLIT ENZ New Zealand/UK, male vocal/instrumental group 9 wks

30 Aug 80	TRUE COLOURS A & M AMLH 64822	42	8 wks
8 May 82	TIME AND TIDE A&M AMLH 64894	71	1 wk

SPOTNICKS Sweden, male instrumental group 1 wk

9 Feb 63	OUT-A-SPACE Oriole PS 40036	20	1 wk

Dusty SPRINGFIELD UK, female vocalist 82 wks

25 Apr 64	● A GIRL CALLED DUSTY Philips BL 7594	6	23 wks
23 Oct 65	● EVERYTHING COMES UP DUSTY Philips RBL 1002	6	12 wks
22 Oct 66	● GOLDEN HITS Philips BL 7737	2	36 wks
11 Nov 67	WHERE AM I GOING Philips SBL 7820	40	1 wk
21 Dec 68	DUSTY...DEFINITELY Philips SBL 7864	30	6 wks
2 May 70	FROM DUSTY WITH LOVE Philips SBL 7927	35	2 wks
4 Mar 78	IT BEGINS AGAIN Mercury 9109 607	41	2 wks

Rick SPRINGFIELD Australia, male vocalist 7 wks

11 Feb 84	LIVING IN OZ RCA PL 84660	41	4 wks
25 May 85	TAO RCA PL 85370	68	3 wks

Bruce SPRINGSTEEN US, male vocalist 300 wks

1 Nov 75	BORN TO RUN CBS 69170	17	50 wks
17 Jun 78	DARKNESS ON THE EDGE OF TOWN CBS 86061	16	40 wks
25 Oct 80	● THE RIVER CBS 88510	2	88 wks
2 Oct 82	● NEBRASKA CBS 25100	3	19 wks
16 Jun 84	★ BORN IN THE USA CBS 86304	1†	81 wks
15 Jun 85	THE WILD THE INNOCENT AND THE E STREET SHUFFLE CBS 32363	33	12 wks
15 Jun 85	GREETINGS FROM ASBURY PARK, N.J. CBS 32210	41	10 wks

SPYRO GYRA US, male instrumental group 22 wks

14 Jul 79	MORNING DANCE Infinity INS 2003	11	16 wks
23 Feb 80	CATCHING THE SUN MCA MCG 4009	31	6 wks

SQUEEZE UK, male vocal/instrumental group 92 wks

28 Apr 79	COOL FOR CATS A & M AMLH 68503	45	11 wks
16 Feb 80	ARGY BARGY A & M AMLH 64802	32	15 wks
23 May 81	EAST SIDE STORY A & M AMLH 64854	19	26 wks
15 May 82	SWEETS FROM A STRANGER A&M AMLH 64899	37	10 wks
6 Nov 82	● SINGLES-45'S AND UNDER A&M AMLH 68522	3	23 wks
7 Sep 85	COSI FAN TUTTI FRUTTI A & M AMA 5085	31	7 wks

Chris SQUIRE UK, male vocalist/instrumentalist - bass 7 wks

6 Dec 75	FISH OUT OF WATER Atlantic K 50203	25	7 wks

STAGE CAST RECORDINGS - See VARIOUS ARTISTS

Alvin STARDUST UK, male vocalist 17 wks

16 Mar 74	● THE UNTOUCHABLE Magnet MAG 5001	4	12 wks
21 Dec 74	ALVIN STARDUST Magnet MAG 5004	37	3 wks
4 Oct 75	ROCK WITH ALVIN Magnet MAG 5007	52	2 wks

Kay STARR US, female vocalist 1 wk

26 Mar 60	MOVIN' Capitol T 1254	16	1 wk

Ringo STARR UK, male vocalist 28 wks

18 Apr 70	● SENTIMENTAL JOURNEY Apple PCS 7101	7	6 wks
8 Dec 73	● RINGO Apple PCTC 252	7	20 wks
7 Dec 74	GOODNIGHT VIENNA Apple PMC 7168	30	2 wks

STARSOUND Holland, disco aggregation 28 wks

16 May 81	★ STARS ON 45 CBS 86132	1	21 wks
19 Sep 81	STARS ON 45 VOL.2 CBS 85181	18	6 wks
3 Apr 82	STARS MEDLEY CBS 85651	94	1 wk

STARTRAX UK, disco aggregation 7 wks

1 Aug 81	STARTRAX CLUB DISCO Picksy KSYA 1001	26	7 wks

Candi STATON US, female vocalist 3 wks

24 Jul 76	YOUNG HEARTS RUN FREE Warner Bros. K 56259	34	3 wks

STATUS QUO UK, male vocal/instrumental group 369 wks

20 Jan 73	● PILEDRIVER Vertigo 6360 082	5	37 wks
9 Jun 73	THE BEST OF STATUS QUO Pye NSPL 18402	32	7 wks
6 Oct 73	★ HELLO Vertigo 6360 098	1	28 wks
18 May 74	● QUO Vertigo 9102 001	2	16 wks
1 Mar 75	★ ON THE LEVEL Vertigo 9102 002	1	27 wks
8 Nov 75	DOWN THE DUSTPIPE Golden Hour CH 604	20	6 wks
20 Mar 76	★ BLUE FOR YOU Vertigo 9102 006	1	30 wks
12 Mar 77	● LIVE Vertigo 6641 580	3	14 wks

SPECIALS (above) Their debut album hit the charts the same month as the first album from Two-Tone stable mates, Madness.

SIMON AND GARFUNKEL (above) Paul Simon proves not only did he write the duo's hits, he can also balance his head on a pencil. (LFI)

BRUCE SPRINGSTEEN (below) On 20 July 1985, Bruce Springsteen placed all seven of his albums in the Top Fifty. (LFI)

THE SMITHS (below) Topping the chart was murder. (Paul Slattery)

26 Nov 77	● ROCKIN' ALL OVER THE WORLD			
	Vertigo 9102 014		5	15 wks
11 Nov 78	● CAN'T STAND THE HEAT	Vertigo 9102 027	3	14 wks
20 Oct 79	● WHATEVER YOU WANT	Vertigo 9102 037	3	14 wks
22 Mar 80	● 12 GOLD BARS	Vertigo QUO TV 1	3	48 wks
25 Oct 80	● JUST SUPPOSIN'	Vertigo 6302 057	4	18 wks
28 Mar 81	● NEVER TOO LATE	Vertigo 6302 104	2	13 wks
10 Oct 81	FRESH QUOTA	PRT DOW 2	74	1 wk
24 Apr 82	★ 1982	Vertigo/Phonogram 6302 169	1	20 wks
13 Nov 82	● FROM THE MAKERS OF...	Vertigo/Phonogram PROLP 1	4	18 wks
3 Dec 83	● BACK TO BACK	Vertigo VERH 10	9	22 wks
4 Aug 84	STATUS QUO LIVE AT THE NEC	Vertigo (Holland) 8189 471	83	3 wks
1 Dec 84	12 GOLD BARS VOLUME 2 (AND 1)	Vertigo QUO TV 2	12	18 wks

STEEL PULSE UK, *male vocal/instrumental group*
18 wks

5 Aug 78	● HANDSWORTH REVOLUTION	Island EMI ILPS 9502	9	12 wks
14 Jul 79	TRIBUTE TO MARTYRS	Island ILPS 9568	42	6 wks

STEELEYE SPAN UK, *male/female vocal instrumental group*
48 wks

10 Apr 71	PLEASE TO SEE THE KING	B & C CAS 1029	45	2 wks
14 Oct 72	BELOW THE SALT	Chrysalis CHR 1008	43	1 wk
28 Apr 73	PARCEL OF ROGUES	Chrysalis CHR 1046	26	5 wks
23 Mar 74	NOW WE ARE SIX	Chrysalis CHR 1053	13	13 wks
15 Feb 75	COMMONER'S CROWN	Chrysalis CHR 1071	21	4 wks
25 Oct 75	● ALL AROUND MY HAT	Chrysalis CHR 1091	7	20 wks
16 Oct 76	ROCKET COTTAGE	Chrysalis CHR 1123	41	3 wks

STEELY DAN US, *male vocal/instrumental group*
73 wks

30 Mar 74	PRETZEL LOGIC	Probe SPBA 6282	37	2 wks
3 May 75	KATY LIED	ABC ABCL 5094	13	6 wks
20 Sep 75	CAN'T BUY A THRILL	ABC ABCL 5024	38	1 wk
22 May 76	ROYAL SCAM	ABC ABCL 5161	11	13 wks
8 Oct 77	● AJA	ABC ABCL 5225	5	10 wks
2 Dec 78	GREATEST HITS	ABC BLD 616	41	18 wks
29 Nov 80	GAUCHO	MCA MCF 3090	27	12 wks
3 Jul 82	GOLD	MCA MCF 3145	44	6 wks
26 Oct 85	REELIN' IN THE YEARS-THE VERY BEST OF STEELY DAN	MCA DANTV 1	43	5 wks

Wout STEENHUIS Holland, *male instrumentalist - guitar*
7 wks

21 Nov 81	HAWAIIAN PARADISE/CHRISTMAS	Warwick WW 5106	28	7 wks

Jim STEINMAN US, *male vocalist*
24 wks

9 May 81	● BAD FOR GOOD	Epic EPC 84361	7	24 wks

STEPPENWOLF US, *male vocal/instrumental group*
20 wks

28 Feb 70	MONSTER	Stateside SSL 5021	43	4 wks
25 Apr 70	STEPPENWOLF	Stateside SSL 5020	59	2 wks
4 Jul 70	STEPPENWOLF LIVE	Stateside SSL 5029	16	14 wks

Little STEVEN and the DISCIPLES of SOUL
US, *male vocal/instrumental group*
2 wks

6 Nov 82	MEN WITHOUT WOMEN	EMI America AML 3027	73	2 wks

Cat STEVENS UK, *male vocalist*
243 wks

25 Mar 67	● MATTHEW AND SON	Deram SML 1004	7	16 wks
11 Jul 70	MONA BONE JAKON	Island ILPS 9118	63	4 wks
28 Nov 70	TEA FOR THE TILLERMAN	Island ILPS 9135	20	39 wks
2 Oct 71	● TEASER AND THE FIRECAT	Island ILPS 9154	3	93 wks
7 Oct 72	● CATCH BULL AT FOUR	Island ILPS 9206	2	27 wks
21 Jul 73	● FOREIGNER	Island ILPS 9240	3	10 wks
6 Apr 74	● BUDDAH AND THE CHOCOLATE BOX	Island ILPS 9274	3	15 wks
19 Jul 75	● GREATEST HITS	Island ILPS 9310	2	24 wks
14 May 77	IZITSO	Island ILPS 9451	18	15 wks

Ray STEVENS US, *male vocalist*
8 wks

26 Sep 70	EVERYTHING IS BEAUTIFUL	CBS 64074	62	1 wk
13 Sep 75	MISTY	Janus 9109 401	23	7 wks

Shakin' STEVENS UK, *male vocalist*
137 wks

15 Mar 80	TAKE ONE	Epic EPC 83978	62	2 wks
4 Apr 81	● THIS OLE HOUSE	Epic EPC 84985	2	28 wks
8 Aug 81	SHAKIN' STEVENS	Hallmark/Pickwick SHM 3065	34	5 wks
19 Sep 81	★ SHAKY	Epic EPC 10027	1	28 wks
9 Oct 82	● GIVE ME YOUR HEART TONIGHT	Epic EPC 10035	3	18 wks
26 Nov 83	THE BOP WON'T STOP	Epic EPC 86301	21	27 wks
17 Nov 84	● GREATEST HITS	Epic EPC 10047	8	22 wks
16 Nov 85	LIPSTICK POWDER AND PAINT	Epic EPC 26646	37†	7 wks

Al STEWART UK, *male vocalist*
20 wks

11 Apr 70	ZERO SHE FLIES	CBS 63848	40	4 wks
5 Feb 77	YEAR OF THE CAT	RCA RS 1082	38	7 wks
21 Oct 78	TIME PASSAGES	RCA PL 25173	39	1 wk
6 Sep 80	24 CARAT	RCA PL 25306	55	6 wks
9 Jun 84	RUSSIANS AND AMERICANS	RCA PL 70307	83	2 wks

Andy STEWART UK, *male vocalist*
2 wks

3 Feb 62	ANDY STEWART	Top Rank 35-116	13	2 wks

Rod STEWART UK, *male vocalist*
530 wks

3 Oct 70	GASOLINE ALLEY	Vertigo 6360 500	62	1 wk
24 Jul 71	★ EVERY PICTURE TELLS A STORY	Mercury 6338 063	1	81 wks
5 Aug 72	★ NEVER A DULL MOMENT	Philips 6499 153	1	36 wks
25 Aug 73	★ SING IT AGAIN ROD	Mercury 6499 484	1	30 wks
19 Oct 74	★ SMILER	Mercury 9104 011	1	20 wks
30 Aug 75	★ ATLANTIC CROSSING	Warner Bros. K 56151	1	88 wks
3 Jul 76	★ A NIGHT ON THE TOWN	Riva RVLP 1	1	47 wks
16 Jul 77	BEST OF ROD STEWART	Mercury 6643 030	18	22 wks
19 Nov 77	● FOOT LOOSE AND FANCY FREE	Riva RVLP 5	3	26 wks
21 Jan 78	ATLANTIC CROSSING (re-issue)	Riva RVLP 4	60	1 wk
9 Dec 78	● BLONDES HAVE MORE FUN	Riva RVLP 8	3	31 wks
10 Nov 79	★ GREATEST HITS	Riva ROD TV 1	1	64 wks
22 Nov 80	● FOOLISH BEHAVIOUR	Riva RVLP 11	4	13 wks
14 Nov 81	● TONIGHT I'M YOURS	Riva RVLP 14	8	21 wks
13 Nov 82	ABSOLUTELY LIVE	Riva RVLP 17	35	5 wks
18 Jun 83	● BODY WISHES	Warner Bros K 923 8771	5	27 wks

SQUEEZE (above) Squeeze outside the Plaza Hotel, New York.

ROD STEWART (above) 1985 was the first year that Rod Stewart failed to chart since his debut in 1970.

SHAKIN' STEVENS (left) Though thought of as a singles artist, Shaky was one of the leading male album stars of the early eighties. (Alan Ballard)

BARBRA STREISAND (below) The most successful female soloist of all. (LFI)

STING (below) Dreaming of solo success.

| 23 Jun 84 | ● **CAMOUFLAGE** *Warner Brothers 925095* | 8 | 17 wks |

See also Rod Stewart and the Faces. Greatest Hits changed label/number to Warner Bros K 56744 during its chart run.

STIFF LITTLE FINGERS *UK, male vocal/instrumental group*

57 wks

3 Mar 79	**INFLAMMABLE MATERIAL** *Rough Trade ROUGH 1*	14	19 wks
15 Mar 80	● **NOBODY'S HEROES** *Chrysalis CHR 1270*	8	10 wks
20 Sep 80	● **HANX** *Chrysalis CHR 1300*	9	5 wks
25 Apr 81	**GO FOR IT** *Chrysalis CHX 1339*	14	8 wks
2 Oct 82	**NOW THEN** *Chrysalis CHR 1400*	24	6 wks
12 Feb 83	**ALL THE BEST** *Chrysalis CTY 1414*	19	9 wks

Stephen STILLS *US, male vocalist*

7 wks

19 Dec 70	**STEPHEN STILLS** *Atlantic 2401 004*	30	1 wk
14 Aug 71	**STEPHEN STILLS 2** *Atlantic 2401 013*	22	3 wks
26 Jul 75	**STILLS** *CBS 69146*	31	1 wk
29 May 76	**ILLEGAL STILLS** *CBS 81330*	54	2 wks

See also Crosby, Stills and Nash; Crosby, Stills, Nash and Young; Stills-Young Band; Stephen Stills' Manassas.

STILLS – YOUNG BAND *US/Canada male vocal/instrumental group*

5 wks

9 Oct 76	**LONG MAY YOU RUN** *Reprise K 54081*	12	5 wks

See also Crosby, Stills and Nash; Crosby, Stills, Nash and Young; Stephen Stills; Stephen Stills' Manassas; Neil Young.

Stephen STILLS' MANASSAS *US, male vocal/instrumental group*

7 wks

20 May 72	**MANASSAS** *Atlantic K 60021*	30	5 wks
19 May 73	**DOWN THE ROAD** *Atlantic K 40440*	33	2 wks

See also Crosby, Stills and Nash; Crosby, Stills, Nash and Young; Stephen Stills; Stills-Young Band.

STING *UK, male vocalist*

27 wks

29 Jun 85	● **THE DREAM OF THE BLUE TURTLES** *A & M DREAM 1*	3†	27 wks

STONE THE CROWS *UK, female/male vocal/instrumental group*

3 wks

7 Oct 72	**ONTINUOUS PERFORMANCE** *Polydor 2391 043*	33	3 wks

STORYVILLE JAZZMEN - *See Bob WALLIS and his STORYVILLE JAZZMEN*

STRANGLERS *UK, male vocal/instrumental group*

149 wks

30 Apr 77	● **STRANGLERS IV (RATTUS NORVEGICUS)** *United Artists UAG 30045*	4	34 wks
8 Oct 77	● **NO MORE HEROES** *United Artists UAG 30200*	2	19 wks
3 Jun 78	● **BLACK AND WHITE** *United Artists UAK 30222*	2	18 wks
10 Mar 79	● **LIVE (X CERT)** *United Artists UAG 30224*	7	10 wks
6 Oct 79	● **THE RAVEN** *United Artists UAG 30262*	4	8 wks
21 Feb 81	● **THEMENINBLACK** *Liberty LBG 30313*	8	5 wks
21 Nov 81	**LA FOLIE** *Liberty LBG 30342*	11	18 wks
25 Sep 82	**THE COLLECTION 1977-1982** *Liberty LBS 30353*	12	16 wks
22 Jan 83	● **FELINE** *Epic EPC 25237*	4	11 wks
17 Nov 84	**AURAL SCULPTURE** *Epic EPC 26220*	14	10 wks

STRAWBERRY SWITCHBLADE *UK, female vocal duo*

4 wks

13 Apr 85	**STRAWBERRY SWITCHBLADE** *Korova KODE 11*	25	4 wks

STRAWBS *UK, male vocal/instrumental group*

31 wks

21 Nov 70	**JUST A COLLECTION OF ANTIQUES AND CURIOS** *A & M AMLS 994*	27	2 wks
17 Jul 71	**FROM THE WITCHWOOD** *A & M AMLH 64304*	39	2 wks
26 Feb 72	**GRAVE NEW WORLD** *A & M AMLH 68078*	11	12 wks
24 Feb 73	● **BURSTING AT THE SEAMS** *A & M AMLH 68144*	2	12 wks
27 Apr 74	**HERO AND HEROINE** *A & M AMLH 63607*	35	3 wks

STRAY CATS *US, male vocal/instrumental group*

31 wks

28 Feb 81	● **STRAY CATS** *Arista STRAY 1*	6	22 wks
21 Nov 81	**GONNA BALL** *Arista STRAY 2*	48	4 wks
3 Sep 83	**RANT 'N' RAVE WITH THE STRAY CATS** *Arista STRAY 3*	51	5 wks

STREETWALKERS *UK, male vocal/instrumental group*

6 wks

12 Jun 76	**RED CARD** *Vertigo 9102 010*	16	6 wks

Barbra STREISAND *US, female vocalist*

338 wks

22 Jan 66	● **MY NAME IS BARBRA, TWO** *CBS BPG 62603*	6	22 wks
4 Apr 70	**GREATEST HITS** *CBS 63921*	44	2 wks
17 Apr 71	**STONEY END** *CBS 64269*	28	2 wks
15 Jun 74	**THE WAY WE WERE** *CBS 69057*	49	1 wk
23 Jul 77	**STREISAND SUPERMAN** *CBS 86030*	32	9 wks
15 Jul 78	**SONGBIRD** *CBS 86060*	50	1 wk
17 Mar 79	★ **BARBRA STREISAND HITS VOL.2** *CBS 10012*	1	30 wks
17 Nov 79	**WET** *CBS 86104*	25	13 wks
11 Oct 80	★ **GUILTY** *CBS 86122*	1	82 wks
16 Jan 82	★ **LOVE SONGS** *CBS 10031*	1	129 wks
19 Nov 83	**YENTL - (original soundtrack)** *CBS 86302*	21	35 wks
27 Oct 84	**EMOTION** *CBS 86309*	15	12 wks

STRINGS FOR PLEASURE *UK, orchestra*

1 wk

4 Dec 71	**BEST OF BACHARACH** *MFP 1334*	49	1 wk

STYLE COUNCIL *UK, male vocal/instrumental duo*

60 wks

24 Mar 84	● **CAFE BLEU** *Polydor TSCLP*	2	38 wks
8 Jun 85	★ **OUR FAVOURITE SHOP** *Polydor TSCLP 2*	1	22 wks

STYLISTICS *US, male vocal group*

139 wks

24 Aug 74	**ROCKIN' ROLL BABY** *Avco 6466 012*	42	3 wks
21 Sep 74	**LET'S PUT IT ALL TOGETHER** *Avoc 6466 013*	26	14 wks
1 Mar 75	**FROM THE MOUNTAIN** *Avco 9109 002*	36	1 wk
5 Apr 75	★ **THE BEST OF THE STYLISTICS** *Avco 9109 003*	1	63 wks
5 Jul 75	● **THANK YOU BABY** *Avco 9109 005*	5	23 wks
6 Dec 75	**YOU ARE BEAUTIFUL** *Avco 9109 006*	26	9 wks
12 Jun 76	**FABULOUS** *Avco 9109 008*	21	5 wks
18 Sep 76	★ **BEST OF THE STYLISTICS VOL.2** *H & L 9109 010*	1	21 wks

STYLE COUNCIL (above) Mick Talbot watches bemused as Paul Weller applies his mascara. TALKING HEADS (below) Heads not speaking. From left to right, David Byrne, Chris Frantz, Tina Weymouth and Jerry Harrison.

STYX US, male vocal/instrumental group — 24 wks

3 Nov 79	CORNERSTONE A & M AMLK 63711	36	8 wks
24 Jan 81 ●	PARADISE THEATER A & M AMLH 63719	8	8 wks
12 Mar 83	KILROY WAS HERE A&M AMLX 63734	67	6 wks
5 May 84	CAUGHT IN THE ACT A & M AMLM 66704	44	2 wks

Donna SUMMER US, female vocalist — 159 wks

31 Jan 76	LOVE TO LOVE YOU BABY GTO GTLP 008	16	9 wks
22 May 76	A LOVE TRILOGY GTO GTLP 010	41	10 wks
25 Jun 77 ●	I REMEMBER YESTERDAY GTO GTLP 025	3	23 wks
26 Nov 77	ONCE UPON A TIME Casablanca CALD 5003	24	13 wks
7 Jan 78 ●	GREATEST HITS GTO GTLP 028	4	18 wks
21 Oct 78	LIVE AND MORE Casablanca CALD 5006	16	16 wks
2 Jun 79	BAD GIRLS Casablanca CALD 5007	23	23 wks
10 Nov 79	ON THE RADIO - GREATEST HITS VOLS. 1 & 2 Casablanca CALD 5008	24	22 wks
1 Nov 80	THE WANDERER Geffen K 99124	55	2 wks
31 Jul 82	DONNA SUMMER Warner Bros. K 99163	13	16 wks
16 Jul 83	SHE WORKS HARD FOR THE MONEY Mercury MERL 21	28	5 wks
15 Sep 84	CATS WITHOUT CLAWS Warner Brothers 250806	69	2 wks

SUNSHINE BAND - See KC and the SUNSHINE BAND

SUPERTRAMP UK/US, male vocal/instrumental group — 150 wks

23 Nov 74 ●	CRIME OF THE CENTURY A & M AMLS 68258	4	22 wks
6 Dec 75	CRISIS? WHAT CRISIS? A & M AMLH 68347	20	15 wks
23 Apr 77	EVEN IN THE QUIETEST MOMENTS A & M AMLK 64634	12	22 wks
31 Mar 79 ●	BREAKFAST IN AMERICA A & M AMLK 63708	3	53 wks
4 Oct 80 ●	PARIS A & M AMLM 66702	7	17 wks
6 Nov 82 ●	FAMOUS LAST WORDS A&M AMLK 63732	6	16 wks
25 May 85	BROTHER WHERE YOU BOUND A & M AMA 5014	20	5 wks

SUPREMES US, female vocal group — 171 wks

5 Dec 64 ●	MEET THE SUPREMES Stateside SL 10109	8	6 wks
17 Dec 66	SUPREMES A GO-GO Tamla Motown STML 11039	15	21 wks
13 May 67	SUPREMES SING MOTOWN Tamla Motown STML 11047	15	16 wks
30 Sep 67	SUPREMES SING RODGERS AND HART Tamla Motown STML 11054	25	7 wks
20 Jan 68 ★	GREATEST HITS Tamla Motown STML 11063	1	60 wks
30 Mar 68 ●	LIVE AT THE TALK OF THE TOWN Tamla Motown STML 11070	6	18 wks
20 Jul 68	REFLECTIONS Tamla Motown STML 11073	30	2 wks
1 Feb 69	LOVE CHILD Tamla Motown STML 11095	8	6 wks
25 Sep 71	TOUCH Tamla Motown STML 11189	40	1 wk
17 Sep 77 ★	20 GOLDEN GREATS Motown EMTV 5	1	34 wks

See also Diana Ross and the Supremes with the Temptations; Supremes and the Four Tops.
20 Golden Greats is credited to Diana Ross and the Supremes.

SUPREMES and the FOUR TOPS US, female and male vocal groups — 11 wks

29 May 71 ●	MAGNIFICENT SEVEN Tamla Motown STML 11179	6	11 wks

See also Diana Ross and the Supremes with the Temptations; Supremes; Four Tops

SURVIVOR US, male vocal/instrumental group — 10 wks

21 Aug 82	EYE OF THE TIGER Scotti Bros SCT 85845	12	10 wks

SUTHERLAND BROTHERS and QUIVER UK, male vocal/instrumental group — 11 wks

15 May 76	REACH FOR THE SKY CBS 69191	26	8 wks
9 Oct 76	SLIPSTREAM CBS 81593	49	3 wks

SWANS WAY UK, male/female vocal/instrumental group — 1 wk

3 Nov 84	THE FUGITIVE KIND Balgier SWAN 1	88	1 wk

SWEET UK, male/vocal/instrumental group — 8 wks

18 May 74	SWEET FANNY ADAMS RCA LPI 5038	27	2 wks
22 Sep 84	SWEET 16-IT'S...IT'S...SWEET'S HITS Anagram GRAM 16	49	6 wks

SWINGLE SINGERS US/France, male/female vocal group — 18 wks

1 Feb 64	JAZZ SEBASTIAN BACH Philips BL 7572	13	18 wks

SYLVESTER US, male vocalist — 3 wks

23 Jun 79	MIGHTY REAL Fantasy FTA 3009	62	3 wks

David SYLVIAN UK, male vocalist — 14 wks

7 Jul 84 ●	BRILLIANT TREES Virign V 2290	4	14 wks

T

T. REX UK, male vocal/instrumental group — 200 wks

13 Jul 68	MY PEOPLE WERE FAIR AND HAD SKY IN THEIR HAIR BUT NOW THEY'RE CONTENT TO WEAR STARS ON THEIR BROWS Regal Zonophone SLRZ 1003	15	9 wks
7 Jun 69	UNICORN Regal Zonophone S 1007	12	3 wks
14 Mar 70	A BEARD OF STARS Regal Zonophone SLRZ 1013	21	6 wks
16 Jan 71	T. REX Fly HIFLY 2	13	24 wks
7 Aug 71	THE BEST OF T. REX Flyback TON 2	21	7 wks
9 Oct 71 ★	ELECTRIC WARRIOR Fly HIFLY 6	1	44 wks
29 Mar 72 ★	PROPHETS, SEERS AND SAGES THE ANGELS OF THE AGES/MY PEOPLE WERE FAIR..... Fly Doubleback 0037 TOOFA 3/4	1	12 wks
20 May 72 ★	BOLAN BOOGIE Fly HIFLY 8	1	19 wks
5 Aug 72 ●	THE SLIDER EMI BLN 5001	4	18 wks
9 Dec 72	A BEARD OF STARS/UNICORN Cube TOOFA 9/10	44	2 wks
31 Mar 73 ●	TANX EMI BLN 5002	4	12 wks
10 Nov 73	GREAT HITS EMI BLN 5003	32	3 wks
16 Mar 74	ZINC ALLOY AND THE HIDDEN RIDERS OF TOMORROW EMI BLNA 7751	12	3 wks
21 Feb 76	FUTURISTIC DRAGON EMI BLN 5004	50	1 wk
9 Apr 77	DANDY IN THE UNDERWORLD EMI BLN 5005	26	3 wks
30 Jun 79	SOLID GOLD EMI NUT 5	51	3 wks
12 Sep 81	T. REX IN CONCERT Marc ABOLAN 1	35	6 wks
7 Nov 81	YOU SCARE ME TO DEATH Cherry Red ERED 20	88	1 wk
24 Sep 83	DANCE IN THE MIDNIGHT Marc On Wax MARCL 501	83	3 wks

4 May 85	● BEST OF THE 20TH CENTURY BOY		
	K-Tel NE 1297	**5**	21 wks

*Prophets .../My People ... is a double re-issue although Prophets had not previously been a
hit. Beard Of Stars/Unicorn is a double re-issue. The first three albums and the two double
re-issues are credited to Tyrannosaurus Rex. Zinc Alloy ... and Best Of The 20th Century
Boy are credited to Marc Bolan and T.Rex. You Scare Me To Death and Dance In The
Midnight are credited to Marc Bolan.*

TALK TALK UK, male vocal/instrumental group

			32 wks
24 Jul 82	THE PARTY'S OVER EMI EMC 3431	**21**	24 wks
25 Feb 84	IT'S MY LIFE EMI EMC 2400021	**35**	8 wks

TALKING HEADS US, male/female vocal/instrumental group

			117 wks
25 Feb 78	TALKING HEADS '77 Sire 9103 328	**60**	1 wk
29 Jul 78	MORE SONGS ABOUT FOOD AND BUILDINGS		
	Sire K 56531	**21**	3 wks
15 Sep 79	FEAR OF MUSIC Sire SRK 6076	**33**	5 wks
1 Nov 80	REMAIN IN LIGHT Sire SRK 6095	**21**	17 wks
10 Apr 82	THE NAME OF THIS BAND IS TALKING		
	HEADS Sire SRK 23590	**22**	5 wks
18 Jun 83	SPEAKING IN TONGUES Sire K 923 8831	**21**	8 wks
27 Oct 84	STOP MAKING SENSE EMI TAH 1	**37**	51 wks
29 Jun 85	● LITTLE CREATURES EMI TAH 2	**10†**	27 wks

TANGERINE DREAM Germany, male instrumental group

			75 wks
20 Apr 74	PHAEDRA Virgin V 2010	**15**	15 wks
5 Apr 75	RUBYCON Virgin V 2025	**12**	14 wks
20 Dec 75	RICOCHET Virgin V 2044	**40**	2 wks
13 Nov 76	STRATOSFEAR Virgin V 2068	**39**	4 wks
23 Jul 77	SORCERER (film soundtrack) MCA MCF 2806	**25**	7 wks
19 Nov 77	ENCORE Virgin VD 2506	**55**	1 wk
1 Apr 78	CYCLONE Virgin V 2097	**37**	4 wks
17 Feb 79	FORCE MAJEURE Virgin V 2111	**26**	7 wks
7 Jun 80	TANGRAM Virgin V 2147	**36**	5 wks
18 Apr 81	THIEF Virgin V 2198	**43**	3 wks
19 Sep 81	EXIT Virgin V 2212	**43**	5 wks
10 Apr 82	WHITE EAGLE Virgin V 2226	**57**	5 wks
5 Nov 83	HYPERBOREA Virgin V 2292	**45**	2 wks
10 Nov 84	POLAND Jive Electro HIP 22	**90**	1 wk

TANK UK, male vocal/instrumental group

			5 wks
13 Mar 82	FILTH HOUNDS OF HADES		
	Kamaflage KAMLP 1	**33**	5 wks

TASTE Ireland, male vocal/instrumental group

			12 wks
7 Feb 70	ON THE BOARDS Polydor 583-083	**18**	11 wks
9 Sep 72	TASTE LIVE AT THE ISLE OF WIGHT		
	Polydor 2383 120	**41**	1 wk

TAVARES US, male vocal group

			15 wks
21 Aug 76	SKY HIGH Capitol EST 11533	**22**	13 wks
1 Apr 78	THE BEST OF TAVARES Capitol EST 11701	**39**	2 wks

James TAYLOR US, male vocalist

			106 wks
21 Nov 70	● SWEET BABY JAMES Warner Bros. ES 1843	**7**	53 wks
29 May 71	● MUD SLIDE SLIM AND THE BLUE HORIZON		
	Warner Bros. WS 2561	**4**	41 wks

8 Jan 72	SWEET BABY JAMES (re-issue)		
	Warner Bros K 46043	**34**	6 wks
18 Mar 72	MUD SLIDE SLIM AND THE BLUE HORIZON		
	(re-issue) Warner Bros. K 46085	**49**	1 wk
9 Dec 72	ONE MAN DOG Warner Bros. K 46185	**27**	5 wks

Roger TAYLOR UK, male vocalist/instrumentalist - drums

			9 wks
18 Apr 81	FUN IN SPACE EMI EMC 3369	**18**	5 wks
7 Jul 84	STRANGE FRONTIER EMI RTA 1	**30**	4 wks

Kiri TE KANAWA New Zealand, female vocalist

			11 wks
2 Apr 83	CHANTS D'AUVERGNE VOL.1		
	Decca SXDL 7604	**57**	1 wk
26 Oct 85	BLUE SKIES London KTKT 1	**41†**	10 wks

*Chants d'Auvergne Vol.1 credits the English Chamber Orchestra. Blue Skies credits the
Nelson Riddle Orchestra.*

The TEARDROP EXPLODES UK, male vocal/instrumental group

			41 wks
18 Oct 80	KILIMANJARO Mercury 6359 035	**24**	35 wks
5 Dec 81	WILDER Mercury 6359 056	**29**	6 wks

TEARS FOR FEARS UK, male vocal/instrumental duo

			108 wks
19 Mar 83	★ THE HURTING Mercury MERS 17	**1**	65 wks
9 Mar 85	● SONGS FROM THE BIG CHAIR		
	Mercury MERH 58	**2†**	43 wks

TELEVISION US, male vocal/instrumental group

			17 wks
26 Mar 77	MARQUEE MOON Elektra K 52046	**28**	13 wks
29 Apr 78	● ADVENTURE Elektra K 52072	**7**	4 wks

TEMPERANCE SEVEN UK, male vocal/instrumental group

			10 wks
13 May 61	TEMPERANCE SEVEN PLUS ONE Argo RG 11	**19**	1 wk
25 Nov 61	TEMPERANCE SEVEN 1961		
	Parlophone PMC 1152	**11**	9 wks

TEMPLE CHURCH CHOIR UK, male vocal/instrumental group

			3 wks
16 Dec 61	● CHRISTMAS CAROLS HMV CLP 1309	**8**	3 wks

TEMPTATIONS US, male vocal group

			99 wks
24 Dec 66	GETTING READY Tamla Motown STML 11035	**40**	2 wks
11 Feb 67	TEMPTATIONS GREATEST HITS		
	Tamla Motown STML 11042	**26**	40 wks
22 Jul 67	TEMPTATIONS LIVE		
	Tamla Motown STML 11053	**20**	4 wks
18 Nov 67	TEMPTATIONS WITH A LOT OF SOUL		
	Tamla Motown STML 11057	**19**	18 wks
20 Sep 69	CLOUD NINE Tamla Motown STML 11109	**32**	1 wk
14 Feb 70	PUZZLE PEOPLE Tamla Motown STML 11133	**20**	4 wks
11 Jul 70	PSYCHEDELIC SHACK		
	Tamla Motown STML 11147	**56**	1 wk

26 Dec 70	**GREATEST HITS VOL.2**			
	Tamla Motown STML 11170	**35**	12 wks	
29 Apr 72	**SOLID ROCK** *Tamla Motown STML 11202*	**34**	2 wks	
20 Jan 73	**ALL DIRECTIONS** *Tamla Motown STML 11218*	**19**	7 wks	
7 Jul 73	**MASTERPIECE** *Tamla Motown STML 11229*	**28**	3 wks	
8 Dec 84	**TRULY FOR YOU** *Motown ZL 72342*	**75**	5 wks	

See also Diana Ross and the Supremes with the Temptations.

10 C.C. *UK, male vocal/instrumental group* 197 wks

1 Sep 73	**10 C.C.** *UK UKAL 1005*	**36**	5 wks
15 Jun 74	● **SHEET MUSIC** *UK UKAL 1007*	**9**	24 wks
22 Mar 75	● **THE ORIGINAL SOUNDTRACK**		
	Mercury 9102 50Q	**4**	40 wks
7 Jun 75	● **GREATEST HITS OF 10 C.C.** *Decca UKAL 1012*	**9**	18 wks
31 Jan 76	● **HOW DARE YOU?** *Mercury 9102 501*	**5**	31 wks
14 May 77	● **DECEPTIVE BENDS** *Mercury 9102 502*	**3**	21 wks
10 Dec 77	**LIVE AND LET LIVE** *Mercury 6641 698*	**14**	15 wks
23 Sep 78	● **BLOODY TOURISTS** *Mercury 9102 503*	**3**	15 wks
6 Oct 79	● **GREATEST HITS 1972-1978** *Mercury 9102 504* ...	**5**	21 wks
5 Apr 80	**LOOK HERE** *Mercury 9102 505*	**35**	5 wks
15 Oct 83	**WINDOW IN THE JUNGLE** *Mercury MERL28* ..	**70**	2 wks

TEN POLE TUDOR *UK, male vocal/instrumental group* 8 wks

9 May 81	● **EDDIE, OLD BOB, DICK & GARRY**		
	Stiff SEEZ 31	**4**	8 wks

TEN YEARS AFTER *UK, male vocal/instrumental group* 73 wks

21 Sep 68	**UNDEAD** *Deram SML 1023*	**26**	7 wks
22 Feb 69	● **STONEDHENGE** *Deram SML 1029*	**6**	5 wks
4 Oct 69	● **SSSSH** *Deram SML 1052*	**4**	18 wks
2 May 70	● **CRICKLEWOOD GREEN** *Deram SML 1065*	**4**	27 wks
9 Jan 71	● **WATT** *Deram SML 1078*	**5**	12 wks
13 Nov 71	**SPACE IN TIME** *Chrysalis CHR 1001*	**36**	1 wk
7 Oct 72	**ROCK AND ROLL** *Chrysalis CHR 1009*	**27**	1 wk
28 Jul 73	**RECORDED LIVE** *Chrysalis CHR 1049*	**36**	2 wks

TENNILLE - *See CAPTAIN and TENNILLE*

The THE *UK, male vocal/instrumental group* 5 wks

29 Oct 83	**SOUL MINING** *Some Bizarre EPC25525*	**27**	5 wks

Matt Johnson leads The The which is an informal group of his studio guests and friends.

THEATRE OF HATE *UK, male vocal/instrumental group* 9 wks

13 Mar 82	**WESTWORLD** *Burning Rome ROME TOH 1*	**17**	6 wks
18 Aug 84	**REVOLUTION** *Burning Rome TOH 2*	**67**	3 wks

THIN LIZZY *Ireland/UK/US, male vocal/instrumental group* 212 wks

27 Sep 75	**FIGHTING** *Vertigo 6360 121*	**60**	1 wk
10 Apr 76	● **JAILBREAK** *Vertigo 9102 008*	**10**	50 wks
6 Nov 76	**JOHNNY THE FOX** *Vertigo 9102 012*	**11**	24 wks
1 Oct 77	● **BAD REPUTATION** *Vertigo 9102 016*	**4**	9 wks
17 Jun 78	● **LIVE AND DANGEROUS** *Vertigo 6641 807* ...	**2**	62 wks
5 May 79	● **BLACK ROSE (A ROCK LEGEND)**		
	Vertigo 9102 032 ...	**2**	21 wks
18 Oct 80	● **CHINA TOWN** *Vertigo 6359 030*	**7**	7 wks
11 Apr 81	● **ADVENTURES OF THIN LIZZY**		
	Vertigo LIZTV 1 ...	**6**	13 wks
5 Dec 81	**RENEGADE** *Vertigo 6359 083*	**38**	8 wks

12 Mar 83	● **THUNDER AND LIGHTNING** *Vertigo VERL 3*	**4**	11 wks
26 Nov 83	**LIFE** *Vertigo VERD 6*	**29**	6 wks

THIRD EAR BAND *UK, male instrumental group* 2 wks

27 Jun 70	**AIR, EARTH, FIRE, WATER** *Harvest SHVL 773*	**49**	2 wks

THIRD WORLD *Jamaica, male vocal/instrumental group* 18 wks

21 Oct 78	**JOURNEY TO ADDIS** *Island ILPS 9554*	**30**	6 wks
11 Jul 81	**ROCKS THE WORLD** *CBS 85027*	**37**	9 wks
15 May 82	**YOU'VE GOT THE POWER** *CBS 85563*	**87**	3 wks

THIS MORTAL COIL *UK, male/female vocal/instrumental group* 4 wks

20 Oct 84	**IT'LL END IN TEARS** *4AD CAD 411*	**38**	4 wks

Carla THOMAS - *See Otis REDDING and Carla THOMAS*

Ray THOMAS *UK, male vocalist* 3 wks

26 Jul 75	**FROM MIGHTY OAKS** *Threshold THS 16*	**23**	3 wks

Richard THOMPSON *UK, male vocalist/instrumentalist-guitar* 2 wks

27 Apr 85	**ACROSS A CROWDED ROOM**		
	Polydor POLD 5175	**80**	2 wks

THOMPSON TWINS *UK, male/female vocal instrumental group* 119 wks

13 Mar 82	**SET** *Tee TELP 2*	**48**	3 wks
26 Feb 83	● **QUICK STEP AND SIDE KICK** *Arista 204 924*	**2**	56 wks
25 Feb 84	★ **INTO THE GAP** *Arista 205 971*	**1**	51 wks
28 Sep 85	● **HERE'S TO FUTURE DAYS** *Arista 207 164*	**5**	9 wks

George THOROGOOD and the DESTROYERS *US, male vocal/instrumental group* 1 wk

2 Dec 78	**GEORGE THOROGOOD AND THE**		
	DESTROYERS *Sonet SNTF 781*	**67**	1 wk

THREE DEGREES *US, female vocal group* 91 wks

10 Aug 74	**THREE DEGREES** *Philadelphia International 65858*	**12**	22 wks
17 May 75	● **TAKE GOOD CARE OF YOURSELF**		
	Philadelphia Int. PIR 69137	**6**	16 wks
24 Feb 79	**NEW DIMENSIONS** *Ariola ARLH 5012*	**34**	13 wks
3 Mar 79	● **A COLLECTION OF THEIR 20 GREATEST HITS**		
	Epic EPC 10013	**8**	18 wks
15 Dec 79	**3D** *Ariola 3D1*	**61**	7 wks
27 Sep 80	● **GOLD** *Ariola 3D 2*	**9**	15 wks

TICH - *See Dave DEE, DOZY, BEAKY, MICK and TICH*

TIGHT FIT *UK, male/female vocal group* 6 wks

26 Sep 81	**BACK TO THE SIXTIES** *Jive HIP 1*	**38**	4 wks

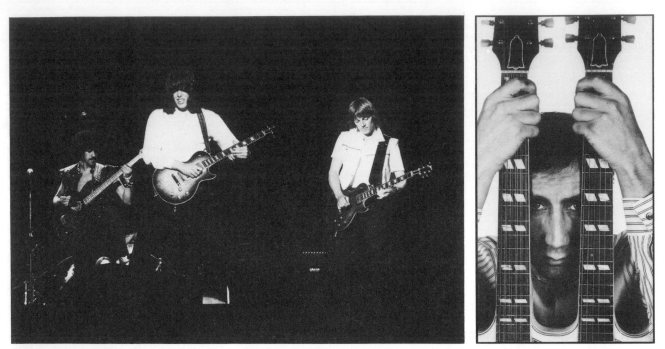

THIN LIZZY (above) The first major Irish albums act, led by the late Phil Lynott. (LFI)

PETE TOWNSHEND (top right) Pete practices his skiing grip. (Davies/Starr)

THOMPSON TWINS (left) Thompson Twins got set for their breakthrough with a set called 'Set'.

TOYAH (below) Voted top UK female singer in major 1982 and 1983 polls. (Geved Mankowitz)

4 Sep 82	**TIGHT FIT**	*Jive HIP 2*	**87**	2 wks

TIK and TOK *UK, male vocal/instrumental duo* 2 wks

4 Aug 84	**INTOLERANCE**	*Survival SUR LP 008*	**89**	2 wks

TOM TOM CLUB *US, female/male vocal/instrumental group* 1 wk

24 Oct 81	**TOM TOM CLUB**	*Island ILPS 9686*	**78**	1 wk

TOMITA *Japan, male instrumentalist – synthesiser* 33 wks

7 Jun 75	**SNOWFLAKES ARE DANCING** *RCA Red Seal ARL 1 0488*		**17**	20 wks
16 Aug 75	**PICTURES AT AN EXHIBITION** *RCA Red Seal ARL 1 0838*		**42**	5 wks
7 May 77	**HOLST: THE PLANETS**	*RCA Red Seal RL 11919*	**41**	6 wks
9 Feb 80	**TOMITA'S GREATEST HITS** *RCA Red Seal RL 43076*		**66**	2 wks

TOPOL *Israel, male vocalist* 1 wk

11 May 85	**TOPOL'S ISRAEL**	*BBC REH 529*	**80**	1 wk

Bernie TORME *UK, male vocalist/instrumentalist – guitar* 3 wks

3 Jul 82	**TURN OUT THE LIGHTS**	*Kamaflage KAMLP 2*	**50**	3 wks

Peter TOSH *Jamaica, male vocalist* 1 wk

25 Sep 76	**LEGALIZE IT**	*Virgin V 2061*	**54**	1 wk

TOTO *US, male vocal/instrumental group* 37 wks

31 Mar 79	**TOTO**	*CBS 83148*	**37**	5 wks
26 Feb 83	● **TOTO IV**	*CBS 85529*	**4**	30 wks
17 Nov 84	**ISOLATION**	*CBS 86305*	**67**	2 wks

TOURISTS *UK, male/female vocal/instrumental group* 18 wks

14 Jul 79	**THE TOURISTS**	*Logo GO 1018*	**72**	1 wk
3 Nov 79	**REALITY EFFECT**	*Logo GO 1019*	**23**	16 wks
22 Nov 80	**LUMINOUS BASEMENT**	*RCA RCALP 5001* ...	**75**	1 wk

Pete TOWNSHEND *UK, male vocalist/instrumentalist – guitar* 25 wks

21 Oct 72	**WHO CAME FIRST**	*Track 2408 201*	**30**	2 wks
3 May 80	**EMPTY GLASS**	*Atco K 50699*	**11**	14 wks
3 Jul 82	**ALL THE BEST COWBOYS HAVE CHINESE EYES** *Atco K 50889*		**32**	8 wks
30 Nov 85	**WHITE CITY**	*Atco 25-2392-1*	**70**	1 wk

See also Pete Townshend and Ronnie Lane.

Pete TOWNSHEND and Ronnie LANE *UK, male vocal/instrumental duo* 3 wks

15 Oct 77	**ROUGH MIX**	*Polydor 2442 147*	**44**	3 wks

See also Pete Townshend; Ronnie Lane and the Band Slim Chance.

TOYAH *UK, female vocalist* 97 wks

14 Jun 80	**THE BLUE MEANING**	*Safari IEYA 666*	**40**	4 wks
17 Jan 81	**TOYAH TOYAH TOYAH**	*Safari LIVE 2*	**22**	14 wks
30 May 81	● **ANTHEM**	*Safari VOOR 1*	**2**	46 wks
19 Jun 82	● **THE CHANGELING**	*Safari VOOR 9*	**6**	12 wks
13 Nov 82	**WARRIOR ROCK-TOYAH ON TOUR** *Safari TNT 1*		**20**	6 wks
5 Nov 83	**LOVE IS THE LAW**	*Safari VOOR 10*	**28**	7 wks
25 Feb 84	**TOYAH! TOYAH! TOYAH!**	*K-Tel NE 1268*	**43**	4 wks
3 Aug 85	**MINX**	*Portrait PRT 26415*	**24**	4 wks

TOY DOLLS *UK, male vocal/instrumental group* 1 wk

25 May 85	**A FAR OUT DISC**	*Volume VOLP 2*	**71**	1 wk

TRACIE *UK, female vocalist* 2 wks

30 Jun 84	**FAR FROM THE HURTING KIND** *Respond RRL 502*		**64**	2 wks

TRAFFIC *UK, male vocal/instrumental group* 37 wks

30 Dec 67	● **MR. FANTASY**	*Island ILP 9061*	**8**	16 wks
26 Oct 68	● **TRAFFIC**	*Island ILPS 9081 T*	**9**	8 wks
8 Aug 70	**JOHN BARLEYCORN MUST DIE** *Island ILPS 9116*		**11**	9 wks
24 Nov 73	**ON THE ROAD**	*Island ISLD 2*	**40**	3 wks
28 Sep 74	**WHEN THE EAGLE FLIES**	*Island ILPS 9273* ..	**31**	1 wk

Pat TRAVERS *US, male instrumentalist – guitar* 3 wks

2 Apr 77	**MAKIN' MAGIC**	*Polydor 2383 436*	**40**	3 wks

John TRAVOLTA *US, male vocalist* 6 wks

23 Dec 78	**SANDY**	*Polydor POLD 5014*	**40**	6 wks

TREMELOES *UK, male vocal/instrumental group* 7 wks

3 Jun 67	**HERE COME THE TREMELOES** *CBS SBPG 63017*		**15**	7 wks

TRIUMPH *Canada, male vocal/instrumental group* 8 wks

10 May 80	**PROGRESSIONS OF POWER**	*RCA PL 13524* ..	**61**	5 wks
3 Oct 81	**ALLIED FORCES**	*RCA RCALP 6002*	**64**	3 wks

TROGGS *UK, male vocal/instrumental group* 32 wks

30 Jul 66	● **FROM NOWHERE...THE TROGGS** *Fontana TL 5355*		**6**	16 wks
25 Feb 67	● **TROGGLODYNAMITE**	*Page One POL 001*	**10**	11 wks
5 Aug 67	**BEST OF THE TROGGS**	*Page One FOR 001* ...	**24**	5 wks

TROUBADOURS DU ROI BAUDOUIN *Zaire, male/female vocal group* 1 wk

22 May 76	**MISSA LUBA**	*Philips SBL 7952*	**59**	1 wk

TRACEY ULLMAN (left) Only broke the chart once.

BONNIE TYLER (right) The only female soloist to reach number one in 1983.

U2 (below)
U2 have had more hits than official releases – a US import EP also charted. (Anton Corbiju)

UB40 (below inset) Their first two albums peaked at number two.

Robin TROWER UK, male instrumentalist - guitar

16 wks

1 Mar 75	FOR EARTH BELOW	Chrysalis CHR 1073	.....	26	4 wks
13 Mar 76	LIVE	Chrysalis CHR 1089	....	15	6 wks
30 Oct 76	LONG MISTY DAYS	Chrysalis CHR 1107	......	31	1 wk
29 Oct 77	IN CITY DREAMS	Chrysalis CHR 1148	....	58	1 wk
16 Feb 80	VICTIMS OF THE FURY	Chrysalis CHR 1215	..	61	4 wks

TUBES US, male vocal/instrumental group

7 wks

4 Mar 78	WHAT DO YOU WANT FROM LIFE				
	A & M AMS 68460	....	38	1 wk	
2 Jun 79	REMOTE CONTROL A & M AMLH 64751	...	40	5 wks	
4 Jun 83	OUTSIDE INSIDE Capitol EST 12260	....	77	1 wk	

TUBEWAY ARMY - *See Gary Numan*

Ike and Tina TURNER US, male instrumentalist - guitar and female vocalist

1 wk

1 Oct 66	RIVER DEEP - MOUNTAIN HIGH				
	London HAU 8298	....	27	1 wk	

See also Tina Turner

Tina TURNER US, female vocalist

79 wks

30 Jun 84 ●	PRIVATE DANCER Capitol TINA 1	....	2†	79 wks	

See also Ike and Tina Turner

TURTLES US, male vocal/instrumental group

9 wks

22 Jul 67	HAPPY TOGETHER London HAU 8330	....	18	9 wks	

TWELFTH NIGHT UK, male vocal/instrumental group

2 wks

27 Oct 84	ART AND ILLUSION Music For Nations MFN 36		83	2 wks	

TWIGGY UK, female vocalist

11 wks

21 Aug 76	TWIGGY Mercury 9102 600	....	33	8 wks	
30 Apr 77	PLEASE GET MY NAME RIGHT				
	Mercury 9102 601	....	35	3 wks	

TWISTED SISTER US, male vocal/instrumental group

18 wks

25 Sep 82	UNDER THE BLADE Secret SECX 9	....	70	3 wks	
7 May 83	YOU CAN'T STOP ROCK 'N' ROLL				
	Atlantic A 0074	....	14	9 wks	
16 Jun 84	STAY HUNGRY Atlantic 780156	....	34	5 wks	
14 Dec 85	COME OUT AND PLAY Atlantic 78-1275-1	.....	95	1 wk	

TYGERS OF PAN TANG UK, male vocal/instrumental group

20 wks

30 Aug 80	WILD CAT MCA MCF 3075	....	18	5 wks	
18 Apr 81	SPELLBOUND MCA MCF 3104	....	33	4 wks	
21 Nov 81	CRAZY NIGHTS MCA MCF 3123	....	51	3 wks	
28 Aug 82	THE CAGE MCA MCF 3150	....	13	8 wks	

Bonnie TYLER UK, female vocalist

45 wks

16 Apr 83 ★	FASTER THAN THE SPEED OF LIGHT				
	CBS 25304	....	1	45 wks	

Judie TZUKE UK, female vocalist

60 wks

4 Aug 79	WELCOME TO THE CRUISE Rocket TRAIN 7		14	17 wks	
10 May 80 ●	SPORTS CAR Rocket TRAIN 9	....	7	11 wks	
16 May 81	I AM PHOENIX Rocket TRAIN 15	....	17	10 wks	
17 Apr 82	SHOOT THE MOON Chrysalis CDL 1382	......	19	10 wks	
30 Oct 82	ROAD NOISE-THE OFFICIAL BOOTLEG				
	Chrysalis CTY 1405	....	39	4 wks	
1 Oct 83	RITMO Chrysalis CDL 1442	....	26	5 wks	
15 Jun 85	THE CAT IS OUT Legacy LLP 102	....	35	3 wks	

U

U 2 Ireland, male vocal/instrumental group

375 wks

29 Aug 81	BOY Island ILPS 9646	....	52	31 wks	
24 Oct 81	OCTOBER Island ILPS 9680	....	11	41 wks	
12 Mar 83 ★	WAR Island ILPS 9733	....	1	115 wks	
3 Dec 83 ●	UNDER A BLOOD RED SKY Island IMA 3	...	2†	109 wks	
13 Oct 84 ★	THE UNFORGETTABLE FIRE Island U 25	....	1†	64 wks	
27 Jul 85	WIDE AWAKE IN AMERICA				
	Island (Import) 902791	....	11	15 wks	

UB 40 UK, male vocal/instrumental group

242 wks

6 Sep 80 ●	SIGNING OFF Graduate GRAD LP 2	....	2	71 wks	
6 Jun 81 ●	PRESENT ARMS DEP International LP DEP 1	...	2	38 wks	
10 Oct 81	PRESENT ARMS IN DUB				
	DEP International LPS DEP 2	....	38	7 wks	
28 Aug 82	THE SINGLES ALBUM Graduate GRADLSP 3	..	17	8 wks	
9 Oct 82 ●	UB 44 Dep International LP DEP 3	....	4	8 wks	
26 Feb 83	UB 40 LIVE DEP International LP DEP 4	.....	44	5 wks	
24 Sep 83 ★	LABOUR OF LOVE DEP International LP DEP 5	..	1	75 wks	
20 Oct 84 ●	GEFFREY MORGAN DEP International DEP 6	..	3	14 wks	
14 Sep 85	BAGGARADDIM DEP International LP DEP 10	..	14†	16 wks	

UFO UK, male vocal/instrumental group

48 wks

4 Jun 77	LIGHTS OUT Chrysalis CHR 1127	....	54	2 wks	
15 Jul 78	OBSESSION Chrysalis CDL 1182	....	26	7 wks	
10 Feb 79 ●	STRANGERS IN THE NIGHT Chrysalis CJT 5		8	11 wks	
19 Jan 80	NO PLACE TO RUN Chrysalis CDL 1239	....	11	7 wks	
24 Jan 81	THE WILD THE WILLING AND THE				
	INNOCENT Chrysalis CHR 1307	.....	19	5 wks	
20 Feb 82 ●	MECHANIX Chrysalis CHR 1360	.....	8	6 wks	
12 Feb 83	MAKING CONTACT Chrysalis CHR 1402	....	32	4 wks	
3 Sep 83	HEADSTONE - THE BEST OF UFO				
	Chrysalis CTY 1437	....	39	4 wks	
16 Nov 85	MISDEMEANOUR Chrysalis CHR 1518	....	74	2 wks	

U.K. UK, male vocal/instrumental group

3 wks

27 May 78	U.K. Polydor 2302 080	....	43	3 wks	

U.K. SUBS UK, male vocal/instrumental group

26 wks

13 Oct 79	ANOTHER KIND OF BLUES Gem GEMLP 100	....	21	6 wks	
19 Apr 80	BRAND NEW AGE Gem GEMLP 106	.....	18	9 wks	
27 Sep 80 ●	CRASH COURSE Gem GEMLP 111	....	8	6 wks	
21 Feb 81	DIMINISHED RESPONSIBILITY				
	Gem GEMLP 112	....	18	5 wks	

VAN DER GRAAF GENERATOR Van der Graaf Generator and dog, not even waving to each other. MIDGE URE (below) Midge Ure, Phil Lynott and Paula Yates at the party for *Guinness Book of British Hit Singles* Vol 3.

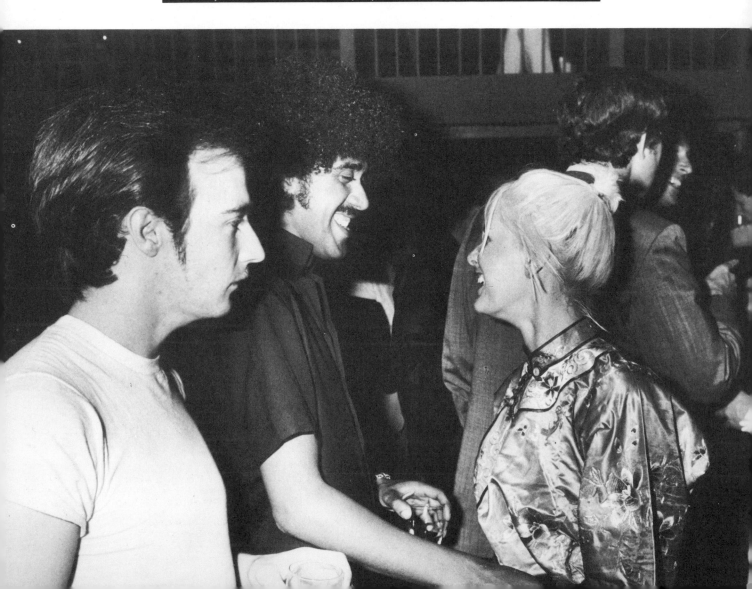

Tracey ULLMAN *UK, female vocalist*   *22 wks*

3 Dec 83	YOU BROKE MY HEART IN 17 PLACES		
	Stiff SEEZ 51	14	20 wks
8 Dec 84	YOU CAUGHT ME OUT *Stiff SEEZ 56*	92	2 wks

ULTRAVOX *UK, male vocal/instrumental group*

218 wks

19 Jul 80	● VIENNA *Chrysalis CHR 1296*	3	72 wks
19 Sep 81	● RAGE IN EDEN *Chrysalis CDL 1338*	4	23 wks
23 Oct 82	● QUARTET *Chrysalis CDL 1394*	6	30 wks
22 Oct 83	● MONUMENT - THE SOUNDTRACK		
	Chrysalis CUX 1452	9	15 wks
14 Apr 84	● LAMENT *Chrysalis CDL 1459*	8	26 wks
10 Nov 84	● THE COLLECTION *Chrysalis UTV 1*	2	52 wks

UNDERTONES *UK, male vocal/instrumental group*

46 wks

19 May 79	THE UNDERTONES *Sire SRK 6071*	13	21 wks
26 Apr 80	● HYPNOTISED *Sire SRK 6088*	6	10 wks
16 May 81	POSITIVE TOUCH *Ardeck ARD 103*	17	6 wks
19 Mar 83	THE SIN OF PRIDE *Ardeck ARD 104*	43	5 wks
10 Dec 83	ALL WRAPPED UP *Ardeck ARD 1654281/3*	67	4 wks

UNION GAP - *See Gary PUCKETT and the UNION GAP*

UNTOUCHABLES *US, male vocal/instrumental group*

7 wks

| 13 Jul 85 | WILD CHILD *Stiff SEEZ 57* .... | 51 | 7 wks |

Midge URE *UK, male vocalist*   *11 wks*

| 19 Oct 85 | ● THE GIFT *Chrysalis CHR 1508* .... | 2† | 11 wks |

URIAH HEEP *UK, male vocal/instrumental group*

51 wks

13 Nov 71	LOOK AT YOURSELF *Island ILPS 9169*	39	1 wk
10 Jun 72	DEMONS AND WIZARDS *Bronze ILPS 9193* ...	20	11 wks
2 Dec 72	THE MAGICIAN'S BIRTHDAY		
	Bronze ILPS 9213	28	3 wks
19 May 73	LIVE *Island ISLD 1*	23	8 wks
29 Sep 73	SWEET FREEDOM *Island ILPS 9245*	18	3 wks
29 Jun 74	WONDERWORLD *Bronze ILPS 9280*	23	3 wks
5 Jul 75	● RETURN TO FANTASY *Bronze ILPS 9335*	7	6 wks
12 Jun 76	HIGH AND MIGHTY *Island ILPS 9384*	55	1 wk
22 Mar 80	CONQUEST *Bronze BRON 524*	37	3 wks
17 Apr 82	ABOMINOG *Bronze BRON 538*	34	6 wks
18 Jun 83	HEAD FIRST *Bronze BRON 545*	46	4 wks
6 Apr 85	EQUATOR *Portrait PRT 2614*	79	2 wks

USA FOR AFRICA *US, male/female vocal/instrumental group*

5 wks

| 25 May 85 | WE ARE THE WORLD *CBS USAID F1* ...... | 31 | 5 wks |

This album contains tracks by various artists in addition to the title track.

U.T.F.O. *US, male vocal group*   *1 wk*

| 16 Mar 85 | ROXANNE ROXANNE (6 track version) | | |
| | *Streetwave 6 TRACK X KHAN 506* .... | 72 | 1 wk |

UTOPIA *UK, male vocal/instrumental group*   *3 wks*

1 Oct 77	OOPS SORRY WRONG PLANET		
	Bearsville K 53517	59	1 wk
16 Feb 80	ADVENTURES IN UTOPIA *Island ILPS 9602* ..	57	2 wks

V

VAN DE GRAAF GENERATOR *UK, male vocal/instrumental group*

2 wks

| 25 Apr 70 | THE LEAST WE CAN DO IS WAVE TO EACH | | |
| | OTHER *Charisma CAS 1007* .... | 47 | 2 wks |

VAN HALEN *US/Holland, male vocal/instrumental group*

57 wks

27 May 78	VAN HALEN *Warner Bros. K 56470*	34	11 wks
14 Apr 79	VAN HALEN II *Warner Bros. K 566116*	23	7 wks
5 Apr 80	WOMEN AND CHILDREN FIRST		
	Warner Bros. K 56793	15	7 wks
23 May 81	FAIR WARNING *Warner Bros. K 56899*	49	4 wks
1 May 82	DIVER DOWN *Warner Bros. K 57003*	36	5 wks
4 Feb 84	1984 *Warner Bros. 92-3985*	15	23 wks

Luther VANDROSS *US, male vocalist*   *17 wks*

| 21 Jan 84 | BUSY BODY *Epic EPC 25608* .... | 42 | 8 wks |
| 6 Apr 85 | THE NIGHT I FELL IN LOVE *Epic EPC 26387* | 19 | 9 wks |

VANGELIS *Greece, male instrumentalist - keyboards*

125 wks

10 Jan 76	HEAVEN AND HELL *RCA Victor RS 1025*	31	7 wks
9 Oct 76	ALBEDO 0.39 *RCA Victor RS 1080*	18	6 wks
18 Apr 81	● CHARIOTS OF FIRE *Polydor POLS 1026*	5	97 wks
5 May 84	CHARIOTS OF FIRE (re-issue)		
	Polydor POLD 5160	39	9 wks
13 Oct 84	SOIL FESTIVITIES *Polydor POLH 11*	55	4 wks
30 Mar 85	MASK *Polydor POLH 19*	69	2 wks

See also Jon and Vangelis.

VANILLA FUDGE *US, male vocal/instrumental group*

3 wks

| 4 Nov 67 | VANILLA FUDGE *Atlantic 588-086* .... | 31 | 3 wks |

VAPORS *UK, male vocal/instrumental group*   *6 wks*

| 7 Jun 80 | NEW CLEAR DAYS *United Artists UAG 30300* .. | 44 | 6 wks |

VARDIS *UK, male vocal/instrumental group*   *1 wk*

| 1 Nov 80 | 100 MPH *Logo MOGO 4012* .... | 52 | 1 wk |

Frankie VAUGHAN *UK, male vocalist*   *20 wks*

5 Sep 59	● FRANKIE VAUGHAN AT THE LONDON		
	PALLADIUM *Philips BDL 7330*	6	2 wks
4 Nov 67	FRANKIE VAUGHAN SONGBOOK		
	Philips DBL 001	40	1 wk
25 Nov 67	THERE MUST BE A WAY *Columbia SCX 6200*	22	8 wks

| 12 Nov 77 | **100 GOLDEN GREATS** | *Ronco RTDX 2021* | ..... | **24** | 9 wks |

Sarah VAUGHAN *US, female vocalist*   *1 wk*

| 26 Mar 60 | **NO COUNT - SARAH** | *Mercury MMC 14021* | .... | **19** | 1 wk |

Bobby VEE *US, male vocalist*   *46 wks*

24 Feb 62	● **TAKE GOOD CARE OF MY BABY**				
	London HAG 2428	....	**7**	8 wks
31 Mar 62	**HITS OF THE ROCKIN' 50'S** *London HAG 2406*		**20**	1 wk
12 Jan 63	● **A BOBBY VEE RECORDING SESSION**			
	Liberty LBY 1084	....	**10**	11 wks
20 Apr 63	● **BOBBY VEE'S GOLDEN GREATS**			
	Liberty LBY 1112	....	**10**	14 wks
5 Oct 63	**THE NIGHT HAS A THOUSAND EYES**			
	Liberty LIB 1139	....	**15**	2 wks
19 Apr 80	● **THE BOBBY VEE SINGLES ALBUM**			
	United Artists UAG 30253	....	**5**	10 wks

See also Bobby Vee and the Crickets.

Bobby VEE and the CRICKETS *US, male vocalist and male vocal/instrumental group*   *27 wks*

| 27 Oct 62 | ● **BOBBY VEE MEETS THE CRICKETS** | | | |
| | *Liberty LBY 1086* | .... | **2** | 27 wks |

See also Bobby Vee; Crickets; Buddy Holly and the Crickets.

Suzanne VEGA *US, female vocalist*   *5 wks*

| 19 Oct 85 | **SUZANNE VEGA** | *A & M AMA 5072* | .... | **63** | 5 wks |

VELVET UNDERGROUND *US, male/female vocal/instrumental group*   *4 wks*

| 23 Feb 85 | **V.U.** | *Polydor POLD 5167* | .... | **47** | 4 wks |

VENOM *UK, male vocal/instrumental group*   *2 wks*

| 21 Apr 84 | **AT WAR WITH SATAN** | *Neat NEAT 1015* | ..... | **64** | 1 wk |
| 13 Apr 85 | **POSSESSED** | *Neat NEAT 1024* | .... | **99** | 1 wk |

Anthony VENTURA ORCHESTRA *Switzerland, orchestra*   *4 wks*

| 20 Jan 79 | **DREAM LOVER** | *Lotus WH 5007* | .... | **44** | 4 wks |

VIBRATORS *UK, male vocal/instrumental group*   *7 wks*

| 25 Jun 77 | **THE VIBRATORS** | *Epic EPC 82907* | .... | **49** | 5 wks |
| 29 Apr 78 | **V2** | *Epic EPC 82495* | .... | **33** | 2 wks |

VICE SQUAD *UK, male/female vocal instrumental group*   *10 wks*

24 Oct 81	**NO CAUSE FOR CONCERN**			
	Zonophone ZEM 103	....	**32**	5 wks
22 May 82	**STAND STRONG STAND PROUD**			
	Zonophone ZEM 104	....	**47**	5 wks

Sid VICIOUS *UK, male vocalist*   *8 wks*

| 15 Dec 79 | **SID SINGS** | *Virgin V 2144* | .... | **30** | 8 wks |

VILLAGE PEOPLE *US, male vocal/instrumental group*   *28 wks*

| 27 Jan 79 | **CRUISIN'** | *Mercury 9109 614* | .... | **24** | 9 wks |
| 12 May 79 | **GO WEST** | *Mercury 9109 621* | .... | **14** | 19 wks |

Gene VINCENT *US, male vocalist*   *2 wks*

| 16 Jul 60 | **CRAZY TIMES** | *Capitol T 1342* | .... | **12** | 2 wks |

VIOLINSKI *UK, male instrumental group*   *1 wk*

| 26 May 79 | **NO CAUSE FOR ALARM** | *Jet JETLU 219* | ...... | **49** | 1 wk |

VISAGE *UK, male vocal/instrumental group*   *49 wks*

24 Jan 81	**VISAGE**	*Polydor 2490 157*	....	**13**	20 wks
3 Apr 82	● **THE ANVIL**	*Polydor POLD 5050*	.....	**6**	16 wks
19 Nov 83	**FADE TO GREY-THE SINGLES COLLECTION**			
	Polydor POLD 5117	....	**38**	11 wks
3 Nov 84	**BEAT BOY**	*Polydor POLH 12*	....	**79**	2 wks

VOYAGE *UK/France, disco aggregation*   *1 wk*

| 9 Sep 78 | **VOYAGE** | *GTO GTLP 030* | .... | **59** | 1 wk |

W

WAH! *UK, male vocal/instrumental group*   *5 wks*

| 18 Jul 81 | **NAH-POO THE ART OF BLUFF** | | | |
| | *Eternal CLASSIC 1* | .... | **33** | 5 wks |

John WAITE *UK, male vocalist*   *3 wks*

| 10 Nov 84 | **NO BREAKS** | *EMI America WAIT 1* | .... | **64** | 3 wks |

TOM WAITS *US, male vocalist*   *8 wks*

| 8 Oct 83 | **SWORDFISHTROMBONE** | *Island ILPS 9762* | ... | **62** | 3 wks |
| 19 Oct 85 | **RAIN DOGS** | *Island ILPS 9803* | .... | **29** | 5 wks |

WAILERS - *See Bob MARLEY and the WAILERS*

Rick WAKEMAN *UK, male instrumentalist - keyboards*   *122 wks*

24 Feb 73	● **THE SIX WIVES OF HENRY VIII**			
	A & M AMLH 64361	....	**7**	22 wks
18 May 74	★ **JOURNEY TO THE CENTRE OF THE EARTH**			
	A & M AMLH 63621	....	**1**	30 wks
12 Apr 75	● **THE MYTHS AND LEGENDS OF KING ARTHUR AND THE KNIGHTS OF THE ROUND TABLE** *A & M AMLH 64515 0022*	..	**2**	28 wks
24 Apr 76	● **NO EARTHLY CONNECTION**			
	A & M AMLK 64583	....	**9**	9 wks
12 Feb 77	**WHITE ROCK** *A & M AMLH 64614*	....	**14**	9 wks
3 Dec 77	**CRIMINAL RECORD** *A & M AMLK 64660*	....	**25**	5 wks

BOBBY VEE Pictured left with Del Shannon. The two enormously popular American stars of the early sixties toured Great Britain with Rick Nelson in 1985. (Bob Celli)

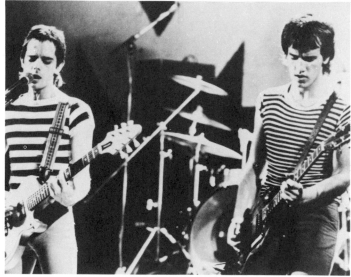

VAPORS (left) They soon evaporated.

FRANKIE VAUGHAN (right) Served in Malta as an army medical corporal.

2 Jun 79	**RHAPSODIES**	A & M AMLX 68508	....	**25**	10 wks
27 Jun 81	**1984**	Charisma CDS 4022	....	**24**	9 wks

See also Kevin Peek and Rick Wakeman.

Scott WALKER *US, male vocalist* 44 *wks*

16 Sep 67 ●	**SCOTT**	Philips SBL 7816	....	**3**	17 wks
20 Apr 68 ★	**SCOTT 2**	Philips SBL 7840	....	**1**	18 wks
5 Apr 69 ●	**SCOTT 3**	Philips S 7882	....	**3**	4 wks
5 Jul 69	**SONGS FROM HIS TV SERIES**	Philips SBL 7900		**7**	3 wks
31 Mar 84	**CLIMATE OF HUNTER**	Virgin V 2303	....	**60**	2 wks

See also Walker Brothers.

WALKER BROTHERS *US, male vocal group*

96 *wks*

18 Dec 65 ●	**TAKE IT EASY**	Philips BL 7691	....	**3**	36 wks
3 Sep 66 ●	**PORTRAIT**	Philips BL 7691	....	**3**	23 wks
18 Mar 67 ●	**IMAGES**	Philips SBL 7770	....	**6**	15 wks
16 Sep 67 ●	**WALKER BROTHERS' STORY**	Philips DBL 002		**9**	19 wks
21 Feb 76	**NO REGRETS**	GTO GTLP 007	....	**49**	3 wks

See also Scott Walker.

Bob WALLIS and his STORYVILLE JAZZMEN *UK, male vocal/instrumental group*

1 *wk*

11 Jun 60	**EVERYBODY LOVES SATURDAY NIGHT**				
	Top Rank BUY 023	....		**20**	1 wk

Joe WALSH *US, male vocalist* 20 *wks*

17 Apr 76	**YOU CAN'T ARGUE WITH A SICK MIND**				
	Anchor ABCL 5156	....		**28**	3 wks
10 Jun 78	**BUT SERIOUSLY FOLKS**	Asylum K 53081	.....	**16**	17 wks

WANG CHUNG *UK, male vocal/instrumental group*

5 *wks*

21 Apr 84	**POINTS ON THE CURVE**	Geffen GEF 25589	...	**34**	5 wks

WAR - *See Eric BURDON and WAR.*

Clifford T. WARD *UK, male vocalist* 5 *wks*

21 Jul 73	**HOME THOUGHTS**	Charisma CAS 1066	....	**40**	3 wks
16 Feb 74	**MANTLE PIECES**	Charisma CAS 1077	....	**42**	2 wks

Michael WARD *UK, male vocalist* 3 *wks*

5 Jan 74	**INTRODUCING MICHAEL WARD**				
	Philips 6308 189	....		**26**	3 wks

Dionne WARWICK *US, female vocalist* '131 *wks*

23 May 64	**PRESENTING DIONNE WARWICK**				
	Pye NPL 28037	....		**14**	10 wks
7 May 66 ●	**BEST OF DIONNE WARWICK**	Pye NPL 28078		**8**	11 wks
4 Feb 67	**HERE WHERE THERE IS LOVE**	Pye NPL 28096		**39**	2 wks
18 May 68 ●	**VALLEY OF THE DOLLS**	Pye NSPL 28114	....	**10**	13 wks
23 May 70	**GREATEST HITS VOL.1**	Wand WNS 1	....	**31**	26 wks
6 Jun 70	**GREATEST HITS VOL.2**	Wand WNS 2	....	**28**	14 wks
30 Oct 82 ●	**HEARTBREAKER**	Arista 204 974	....	**3**	33 wks
21 May 83	**THE COLLECTION**	Arista DIONE 1	.....	**11**	17 wks
29 Oct 83	**SO AMAZING**	Arista 205 755	....	**60**	3 wks
23 Feb 85	**WITHOUT YOUR LOVE**	Arista 206 571	......	**86**	2 wks

Geno WASHINGTON *UK, male vocalist* 51 *wks*

10 Dec 66 ●	**HAND CLAPPIN' – FOOT STOMPIN' – FUNKY BUTT – LIVE!** Piccadilly NPL 38026			**5**	38 wks
23 Sep 67 ●	**HIPSTERS, FLIPSTERS, AND FINGER POPPIN' DADDIES** Piccadilly NSPL 38032	....		**8**	13 wks

Grover WASHINGTON Jr *US, male instrumentalist – saxophone*

10 *wks*

9 May 81	**WINELIGHT**	Elektra K 52262	....	**34**	9 wks
19 Dec 81	**COME MORNING**	Elektra K 52337	....	**98**	1 wk

W.A.S.P. *US, male vocal/instrumental group* 3 *wks*

8 Sep 84	**W.A.S.P.**	Capitol EJ 2401951	....	**51**	2 wks
9 Nov 85	**THE LAST COMMAND**	Capitol WASP 2	......	**48**	1 wk

WATERBOYS *UK, male vocal/instrumental group*

11 *wks*

16 Jun 84	**A PAGAN PLACE**	Ensign ENCL 3	....	**100**	1 wk
28 Sep 85	**THIS IS THE SEA**	Ensign ENCL 5	....	**37**	10 wks

Roger WATERS *UK, male vocalist/instrumentalist – bass*

11 *wks*

12 May 84	**THE PROS AND CONS OF HITCH-HIKING**				
	Harvest SHVL 240105	....		**13**	11 wks

Jeff WAYNE *US/UK orchestra and cast* 226 *wks*

1 Jul 78 ●	**WAR OF THE WORLDS**	CBS 96000	....	**5**	226 wks

This album featured various artists but is commonly credited to Jeff Wayne, its creator and producer.

WAYSTED *UK, male vocal/instrumental group* 5 *wks*

8 Oct 83	**VICES**	Chrysalis CHR 1438	....	**78**	3 wks
22 Sep 84	**WAYSTED**	Music For Nations MFN 31	....	**73**	2 wks

WEATHER REPORT *US, male instrumental group*

12 *wks*

23 Apr 77	**HEAVY WEATHER**	CBS 81775	....	**43**	6 wks
11 Nov 78	**MR. GONE**	CBS 82775	....	**47**	3 wks
27 Feb 82	**WEATHER REPORT**	CBS 85326	....	**88**	2 wks
24 Mar 84	**DOMINO THEORY**	CBS 25839	....	**54**	1 wk

Marti WEBB *UK, female vocalist* 27 *wks*

16 Feb 80 ●	**TELL ME ON A SUNDAY**	Polydor POLD 5031		**2**	23 wks
28 Sep 85	**ENCORE**	Starblend BLEND 1	....	**55**	4 wks

Ben WEBSTER - *See Gerry MULLIGAN and Ben WEBSTER*

Bert WEEDON *UK, male instrumentalist – guitar*

26 *wks*

16 Jul 60	**KING SIZE GUITAR**	Top Rank BUY 026	......	**18**	1 wk
23 Oct 76 ★	**22 GOLDEN GUITAR GREATS**				
	Warwick WW 5019	....		**1**	25 wks

DIONNE WARWICK (above) had her greatest success when produced by the Gibb brothers. (David Vance)

MARTI WEBB (above) 23 sabbaths on the chart.

GENE VINCENT (left) Gene Vincent, John Lennon and Paul McCartney watch Sounds Incorporated on stage at Liverpool's Cavern.

WHAM! UK, male/female vocal/instrumental group

170 wks

9 Jul 83	★	FANTASTIC	Inner Vision IVL 25328	....	1	113 wks
17 Nov 84	★	MAKE IT BIG	Epic EPC 86311	....	1†	57 wks

WHISPERS US, male vocal group

5 wks

14 Mar 81	IMAGINATION	Solar SOLA 7	....	42	5 wks

Alan WHITE UK, male instrumentalist - drums

4 wks

13 Mar 76	RAMSHACKLED	Atlantic K 50217	....	41	4 wks

Barry WHITE US, male vocalist

106 wks

9 Mar 74		STONE GON'	Pye NSPL 28186	....	18	17 wks
6 Apr 74		RHAPSODY IN WHITE	Pye NSPL 28191	......	50	1 wk
2 Nov 74	●	CAN'T GET ENOUGH	20th Century BT 444	....	4	34 wks
26 Apr 75		JUST ANOTHER WAY TO SAY I LOVE YOU 20th Century BT 466			12	15 wks
22 Nov 75		GREATEST HITS	20th Century BTH 8000		18	12 wks
21 Feb 76		LET THE MUSIC PLAY	20th Century BT 502		22	14 wks
9 Apr 77		BARRY WHITE'S GREATEST HITS VOL.2 20th Century BTH 8001			17	7 wks
10 Feb 79		THE MAN	20th Century BT 571	....	46	4 wks
21 Dec 85		HEART AND SOUL	K-Tel NE 1316	.....	36†	2 wks

Snowy WHITE UK, male vocalist/instrumentalist-guitar

5 wks

11 Feb 84	WHITE FLAMES	Towerbell TOWLP 3	....	21	4 wks
9 Feb 85	SNOWY WHITE	Towerbell TOWLP 8	....	88	1 wk

Tony Joe WHITE US, male vocalist

1 wk

26 Sep 70	TONY JOE	CBS 63800	....	63	1 wk

WHITESNAKE UK, male vocal/instrumental group

78 wks

18 Nov 78		TROUBLE	EMI International INS 3022	....	50	2 wks
13 Oct 79		LOVE HUNTER	United Artists UAG 30264	......	29	7 wks
7 Jun 80	●	READY AND WILLING United Artists UAG 30302		....	6	15 wks
8 Nov 80	●	LIVE IN THE HEART OF THE CITY United Artists SNAKE 1		......	5	15 wks
18 Apr 81	●	COME AND GET IT	Liberty LBG 30327	....	2	23 wks
27 Nov 82	●	SAINTS 'N' SINNERS	Liberty LBG 30354	......	9	9 wks
11 Feb 84	●	SLIDE IT IN	Liberty LBG 2400001	......	9	7 wks

Slim WHITMAN US, male vocalist

59 wks

14 Dec 74		HAPPY ANNIVERSARY United Artists UAS 29670		....	44	2 wks
31 Jan 76	★	THE VERY BEST OF SLIM WHITMAN United Artists UAS 29898		......	1	17 wks
15 Jan 77	★	RED RIVER VALLEY	United Artists UAS 29993		1	14 wks
15 Oct 77	●	HOME ON THE RANGE United Artists UATV 30102		......	2	13 wks
13 Jan 79		GHOST RIDERS IN THE SKY United Artists UATV 30202		......	27	6 wks
22 Dec 79		SLIM WHITMAN'S 20 GREATEST LOVE SONGS United Artists UAG 30270		....	18	7 wks

Roger WHITTAKER Kenya, male vocalist

80 wks

27 Jun 70		I DON'T BELIEVE IN IF ANYMORE Columbia SCX 6404		....	23	1 wk
3 Apr 71		NEW WORLD IN THE MORNING Columbia SCX 6456		....	45	2 wks
6 Sep 75	●	THE VERY BEST OF ROGER WHITTAKER Columbia SCX 6560			5	42 wks
15 May 76		THE SECOND ALBUM OF THE VERY BEST OF ROGER WHITTAKER	EMI EMC 3117	......	27	7 wks
9 Dec 78		ROGER WHITTAKER SINGS THE HITS Columbia SCX 6601		......	52	5 wks
4 Aug 79		20 ALL TIME GREATS	Polydor POLTV 8	......	24	9 wks
7 Feb 81		THE ROGER WHITTAKER ALBUM K-Tel NE 1105		....	18	14 wks

WHO UK, male vocal/instrumental group

187 wks

25 Dec 65	●	MY GENERATION	Brunswick LAT 8616	......	5	11 wks
17 Dec 66	●	A QUICK ONE	Reaction 593-002	......	4	17 wks
13 Jan 68		THE WHO SELL OUT	Track 613-002	......	13	11 wks
7 Jun 69	●	TOMMY	Track 613-013/4	......	2	9 wks
6 Jun 70	●	LIVE AT LEEDS	Track 2406-001	......	3	21 wks
11 Sep 71	★	WHO'S NEXT	Track 2408-102	......	1	13 wks
18 Dec 71	●	MEATY, BEATY, BIG & BOUNCY Track 2406-006		......	9	8 wks
17 Nov 73	●	QUADROPHENIA	Track 2657-013	......	2	13 wks
26 Oct 74	●	ODDS AND SODS	Track 2406-116	......	10	4 wks
23 Aug 75		TOMMY (film soundtrack version)	Track 2657-007		30	2 wks
18 Oct 75	●	THE WHO BY NUMBERS	Polydor 2490-129	....	7	6 wks
9 Oct 76	●	THE STORY OF THE WHO	Polydor 2683-069	..	2	18 wks
9 Sep 78	●	WHO ARE YOU	Polydor WHOD 5004	......	6	9 wks
30 Jun 79		THE KIDS ARE ALRIGHT	Polydor 2675 174	....	26	13 wks
25 Oct 80		MY GENERATION (re-issue)	Virgin V 2179	....	20	7 wks
28 Mar 81	●	FACE DANCES	Polydor WHOD 5037	......	2	9 wks
11 Sep 82		IT'S HARD	Polydor WHOD 5066	......	11	6 wks
17 Nov 84		WHO'S LAST	MCA WHO 1	......	48	4 wks
12 Oct 85		THE WHO COLLECTION	Impression IMDP 4	..	44	6 wks

WILD HORSES UK, male vocal/instrumental group

4 wks

26 Apr 80	WILD HORSES	EMI EMC 3324	....	38	4 wks

WILD WILLY BARRETT - See John OTWAY and Wild Willy BARRETT

Eugene WILDE US, male vocalist

4 wks

8 Dec 84	EUGENE WILDE	Fourth And Broadway BRLP 502		67	4 wks

Kim WILDE UK, female vocalist

32 wks

11 Jul 81	●	KIM WILDE	RAK SRAK 544	....	3	14 wks
22 May 82		SELECT	RAK SRAK 548	....	19	11 wks
26 Nov 83		CATCH AS CATCH CAN	RAK SRAK 165408	..	90	1 wk
17 Nov 84		TEASES AND DARES	MCA MCF 3250	......	66	2 wks
18 May 85		THE VERY BEST OF KIM WILDE RAK WILDE 1		....	78	4 wks

Andy WILLIAMS US, male vocalist

439 wks

26 Jun 65	●	ALMOST THERE	CBS BPG 62533	....	4	46 wks
7 Aug 65		CAN'T GET USED TO LOSING YOU CBS BPG 62146		....	16	1 wk
19 Mar 66		MAY EACH DAY	CBS BPG 62658	......	11	6 wks
30 Apr 66		GREAT SONGS FROM MY FAIR LADY CBS BPG 62430		....	30	1 wk
23 Jul 66		SHADOW OF YOUR SMILE	CBS 62633	......	24	4 wks
29 Jul 67		BORN FREE	CBS SBPG 63027	......	22	11 wks
11 May 68	★	LOVE ANDY	CBS 63167	......	1	22 wks
6 Jul 68	●	HONEY	CBS 63311	......	4	17 wks

THE WHO Roger, John, Keith and Pete (left to right) only had one number one but got to the runner-up spot four times. (LFI)

WHAM! Andrew bites his tongue wondering what the Australian press are going to make of the duo's choice of hats Down Under. (Retina Pictures Ltd)

26 Jul 69	HAPPY HEART *CBS 63614*	22	9 wks
27 Dec 69	GET TOGETHER WITH ANDY WILLIAMS *CBS 63800*	13	12 wks
24 Jan 70	ANDY WILLIAMS' SOUND OF MUSIC *CBS 66214*	22	10 wks
11 Apr 70 ★	GREATEST HITS *CBS 63920*	1	116 wks
20 Jun 70 ●	CAN'T HELP FALLING IN LOVE *CBS 64067*	7	48 wks
5 Dec 70 ●	ANDY WILLIAMS SHOW *CBS 64127*	10	6 wks
3 Apr 71 ★	HOME LOVING MAN *CBS 64286*	1	25 wks
31 Jul 71	LOVE STORY *CBS 64467*	11	11 wks
29 Apr 72	THE IMPOSSIBLE DREAM *CBS 67236*	26	3 wks
29 Jul 72	LOVE THEME FROM 'THE GODFATHER' *CBS 64869*	11	16 wks
16 Dec 72	GREATEST HITS VOL.2 *CBS 65151*	23	10 wks
22 Dec 73 ●	SOLITAIRE *CBS 65638*	3	26 wks
15 Jun 74 ●	THE WAY WE WERE *CBS 80152*	7	11 wks
11 Oct 75	THE OTHER SIDE OF ME *CBS 69152*	60	1 wk
28 Jan 78 ●	REFLECTIONS *CBS 10006*	2	17 wks
27 Oct 84	GREATEST LOVE CLASSICS *EMI ANDY 1*	22	10 wks

Greatest Love Classics also credits the Royal Philharmonic Orchestra.

Deniece WILLIAMS *US, female vocalist* *12 wks*

21 May 77	THIS IS NIECEY *CBS 81869*	31	12 wks

See also Johnny Mathis and Deniece Williams.

Don WILLIAMS *US, male vocalist* *136 wks*

10 Jul 76	GREATEST HITS VOL.1 *ABC ABCL 5147*	29	15 wks
19 Feb 77	VISIONS *ABC ABCL 5200*	13	20 wks
15 Oct 77	COUNTRY BOY *ABC ABCL 5233*	27	5 wks
5 Aug 78 ●	IMAGES *K-Tel NE 1033*	2	38 wks
5 Aug 78	YOU'RE MY BEST FRIEND *ABC ABCD 5127*	58	1 wk
4 Nov 78	EXPRESSIONS *ABC ABCL 5253*	28	8 wks
22 Sep 79	NEW HORIZONS *K-Tel NE 1048*	29	12 wks
15 Dec 79	PORTRAIT *MCA MCS 3045*	58	4 wks
6 Sep 80	I BELIEVE IN YOU *MCA MCF 3077*	36	5 wks
18 Jul 81	ESPECIALLY FOR YOU *MCA MCF 3114*	33	7 wks
17 Apr 82	LISTEN TO THE RADIO *MCA MCF 3135*	69	3 wks
23 Apr 83	YELLOW MOON *MCA MCF 3159*	52	1 wk
15 Oct 83	LOVE STORIES *K-Tel NE 1252*	22	13 wks
26 May 84	CAFE CAROLINA *MCA MCF 3225*	65	4 wks

Iris WILLIAMS *UK, female vocalist* *4 wks*

22 Dec 79	HE WAS BEAUTIFUL *Columbia SCX 6627*	69	4 wks

John WILLIAMS *UK, male instrumentalist – guitar* *31 wks*

3 Oct 70	PLAYS SPANISH MUSIC *CBS 72860*	46	1 wk
17 Jun 78	TRAVELLING *Cube HIFLY 27*	23	5 wks
30 Jun 79 ●	BRIDGES *Lotus WH 5015*	5	22 wks
4 Aug 79	CAVATINA *Cube/Electric HIFLY 32*	64	3 wks

See also John Williams with the English Chamber Orchestra conducted by Daniel Barenboim.

John WILLIAMS *US, male conductor* *10 wks*

25 Dec 82	ET-THE EXTRATERRESTRIAL *MCA MCF 3160*	47	10 wks

John WILLIAMS with the ENGLISH CHAMBER ORCHESTRA conducted by Daniel BARENBOIM *UK, male instrumentalist – guitar, UK orchestra and male conductor* *9 wks*

28 Feb 76	RODRIGO: CONCERTO DE ARANJUEZ *CBS 76369*	20	9 wks

See also John Williams (UK)

Wendy O.WILLIAMS *US, female vocalist* *1 wk*

30 Jun 84	W.O.W. *Music For Nations MFN 24*	100	1 wk

Sonny Boy WILLIAMSON *US, male vocalist/ instrumentalist – guitar* *1 wk*

20 Jun 64	DOWN AND OUT BLUES *Pye NPL 28036*	20	1 wk

Mari WILSON *UK, female vocalist* *9 wks*

26 Feb 83	SHOW PEOPLE *Compact COMP 2*	24	9 wks

Show People credits Mari Wilson with the Wilsations .

WINDJAMMER *US, male vocal/instrumental group* *1 wk*

25 Aug 84	WINDJAMMER II *MCA MCF*	82	1 wk

WINGS - *See Paul McCartney*

Johnny WINTER *US, male vocal/instrumental group* *12 wks*

16 May 70	SECOND WINTER *CBS 66321*	59	2 wks
31 Oct 70	JOHNNY WINTER AND... *CBS 64117*	29	4 wks
15 May 71	JOHNNY WINTER AND LIVE *CBS 64289*	20	6 wks

Ruby WINTERS *US, female vocalist* *16 wks*

10 Jun 78	RUBY WINTERS *Creole CRLP 512*	27	7 wks
23 Jun 79	SONGBIRD *K-Tel NE 1045*	31	9 wks

Steve WINWOOD *UK, male vocalist* *42 wks*

9 Jul 77	STEVE WINWOOD *Island ILPS 9494*	12	9 wks
10 Jan 81	ARC OF A DIVER *Island ILPS 9576*	13	20 wks
14 Aug 82 ●	TALKING BACK TO THE NIGHT *Island ILPS 9777*	6	13 wks

WIRE *UK, male vocal/instrumental group* *2 wks*

7 Oct 78	CHAIRS MISSING *Harvest SHSP 4093*	48	1 wk
13 Oct 79	154 *Harvest SHSP 4105*	39	1 wk

WISHBONE ASH *UK, male vocal/instrumental group* *75 wks*

23 Jan 71	WISHBONE ASH *MCA MKPS 2014*	34	2 wks
9 Oct 71	PILGRIMAGE *MCA MDKS 8004*	14	9 wks
20 May 72 ●	ARGUS *MCA MDKS 8006*	3	20 wks
26 May 73	WISHBONE FOUR *MCA MDKS 8011*	12	10 wks
30 Nov 74	THERE'S A RUB *MCA MCF 2585*	16	5 wks

ROY WOOD (above) A moment of tension before his audition for Kiss.

ANDY WILLIAMS (left) Andy Williams getting excited that his 'Greatest Hits' has reached number one after thirty-five weeks on chart.

WRECKLESS ERIC (below) Wreckless Eric Gould almost stiffed with his eponymous debut and was over optimistic with the title of his next hit.

3 Apr 76	**LOCKED IN** MCA MCF 2750		36	2 wks
27 Nov 76	**NEW ENGLAND** MCA MCG 3523		22	3 wks
29 Oct 77	**FRONT PAGE NEWS** MCA MCG 3524		31	4 wks
28 Oct 78	**NO SMOKE WITHOUT FIRE** MCA MCG 3528		43	3 wks
2 Feb 80	**JUST TESTING** MCA MCF 3052		41	4 wks
1 Nov 80	**LIVE DATES II** MCA MCG 4012		40	3 wks
25 Apr 81	**NUMBER THE BRAVE** MCA MCF 3103		61	5 wks
16 Oct 82	**BOTH BARRELS BURNING** AUM ASH 1		22	5 wks

Bill WITHERS *US, male vocalist* *6 wks*

11 Feb 78	**MENAGERIE** CBS 82265		27	5 wks
15 Jun 85	**WATCHING YOU, WATCHING ME** CBS 26200		60	1 wk

WIZZARD *UK, male vocal/instrumental group* *11 wks*

19 May 73	**WIZZARD BREW** Harvest SHSP 4025		29	7 wks
17 Aug 74	**INTRODUCING EDDY AND THE FALCONS** Warner Bros. K 52029		19	4 wks

WOMACK and WOMACK *US, male/female vocal duo* *15 wks*

21 Apr 84	**LOVE WARS** Elektra 960293		45	13 wks
22 Jun 85	**RADIO M.U.S.C. MAN** Elektra EKT 6		56	2 wks

Bobby WOMACK *US, male vocalist* *15 wks*

28 Apr 84	**THE POET 11** Motown ZL 72205		31	8 wks
28 Sep 85	**SO MANY RIVERS** MCA MCF		28	7 wks

WOMBLES *UK, Mike Batt, male vocalist, arranger and producer under group name* *55 wks*

2 Mar 74	**WOMBLING SONGS** CBS 65803		19	17 wks
13 Jul 74	**REMEMBER YOU'RE A WOMBLE** CBS 80191		18	31 wks
21 Dec 74	**KEEP ON WOMBLING** CBS 80526		17	6 wks
8 Jan 77	**20 WOMBLING GREATS** Warwick PR 5022		29	1 wk

Stevie WONDER *US, male vocalist/multi-instrumentalist* *317 wks*

7 Sep 68	**STEVIE WONDER'S GREATEST HITS** Tamla Motown STML 11075		25	10 wks
13 Dec 69	**MY CHERIE AMOUR** Tamla Motown STML 11128		17	2 wks
12 Feb 72	**GREATEST HITS VOL.2** Tamla Motown STML 11196		30	4 wks
3 Feb 73	**TALKING BOOK** Tamla Motown STMA 8007		16	48 wks
1 Sep 73	● **INNERVISIONS** Tamla Motown STMA 8011		8	55 wks
17 Aug 74	● **FULFILLINGNESS' FIRST FINALE** Tamla Motown STMA 8019		5	16 wks
16 Oct 76	● **SONGS IN THE KEY OF LIFE** Tamla Motown TMSP 6002		2	54 wks
10 Nov 79	● **JOURNEY THROUGH THE SECRET LIFE OF PLANTS** Motown TMSP 6009		8	15 wks
8 Nov 80	● **HOTTER THAN JULY** Motown STMA 8035		2	55 wks
22 May 82	● **ORIGINAL MUSIQUARIUM 1** Motown TMSP 6012		8	17 wks
22 Sep 84	● **WOMAN IN RED-SELECTIONS FROM ORIGINAL MOTION PICTURE SOUNDTRACK** Motown ZL 72285		2	19 wks
24 Nov 84	**LOVE SONGS-16 CLASSIC HITS** Telstar STAR 2251		20	10 wks
28 Sep 85	● **IN SQUARE CIRCLE** Motown ZL 72005		5†	12 wks

The Woman In Red also features Dionne Warwick

Roy WOOD *UK, male vocalist/multi-instrumentalist* *14 wks*

18 Aug 73	**BOULDERS** Harvest SHVL 803		15	8 wks
24 Jul 82	**THE SINGLES** Speed SPEED 1000		37	6 wks

Edward WOODWARD *UK, male vocalist* *12 wks*

6 Jun 70	**THIS MAN ALONE** DJM DJLPS 405		53	2 wks
19 Aug 72	**THE EDWARD WOODWARD ALBUM** Jam JAL 103		20	10 wks

WORKING WEEK *UK, male/female vocal/instrumental group* *9 wks*

6 Apr 85	**WORKING NIGHTS** Virgin V 2343		23	9 wks

WRECKLESS ERIC *UK, male vocalist* *5 wks*

1 Apr 78	**WRECKLESS ERIC** Stiff SEEZ 6		46	1 wk
8 Mar 80	**BIG SMASH** Stiff SEEZ 21		30	4 wks

Klaus WUNDERLICH *Germany, male instrumentalist - organ* *19 wks*

30 Aug 75	**THE HIT WORLD OF KLAUS WUNDERLICH** Decca SPA 434		27	8 wks
20 May 78	**THE UNIQUE KLAUS WUNDERLICH SOUND** Decca DBC 5/6		28	4 wks
26 May 79	**THE FANTASTIC SOUND OF KLAUS WUNDERLICH** Lotus LH 5013		43	5 wks
17 Mar 84	**ON THE SUNNY SIDE OF THE STREET** Polydor POLD 5133		81	2 wks

WURZELS *UK, male vocal/instrumental group* *25 wks*

3 Jul 76	**COMBINE HARVESTER** One-Up OU 2138		15	20 wks
2 Apr 77	**GOLDEN DELICIOUS** EMI Note NTS 122		32	5 wks

See also Adge Cutler and the Wurzels.

Bill WYMAN *UK, male vocalist/instrumentalist - bass* *7 wks*

8 Jun 74	**MONKEY GRIP** Rolling Stones COC 59102		39	1 wk
10 Apr 82	**BILL WYMAN** A&M AMLH 68540		55	6 wks

Tammy WYNETTE *US, female vocalist* *44 wks*

17 May 75	● **THE BEST OF TAMMY WYNETTE** Epic EPC 63578		4	23 wks
21 Jun 75	**STAND BY YOUR MAN** Epic EPC 69141		13	7 wks
17 Dec 77	● **20 COUNTRY CLASSICS** CBS PR 5040		3	11 wks
4 Feb 78	**COUNTRY GIRL MEETS COUNTRY BOY** Warwick PR 5039		43	3 wks

X

X MAL DEUTSCHLAND *UK/Germany male/female vocal/instrumental group* *1 wk*

7 Jul 84	**TOCSIN** 4AD CAD 407		86	1 wk

X-RAY SPEX (above) Spex vocalist Poly Styrene in the heady days before driver-only buses.

XTC (top right) Their 'best of' album had the worst of their chart placings. (Justin Thomas)

BRYN YEMM (right) The British artist with the most new albums in the chart in 1984.

X-RAY SPEX *UK, male/female vocal/instrumental group*
14 wks

9 Dec 78	**GERM FREE ADOLESCENTS**				
	EMI International INS 3023			30	14 wks

XTC *UK, male vocal/instrumental group*
41 wks

11 Feb 78	**WHITE MUSIC**	*Virgin V 2095*		38	4 wks
28 Oct 78	**GO 2**	*Virgin V 2108*		21	3 wks
1 Sep 79	**DRUMS AND WIRES**	*Virgin V 2129*		34	7 wks
20 Sep 80	**BLACK SEA**	*Virgin V 2173*		16	7 wks
20 Feb 82 ●	**ENGLISH SETTLEMENT**	*Virgin V2223*		5	11 wks
13 Nov 82	**WAXWORKS—SOME SINGLES (1977-82)**				
	Virgin V 2251			54	3 wks
10 Sep 83	**MUMMER**	*Virgin V 2264*		51	4 wks
27 Oct 84	**THE BIG EXPRESS**	*Virgin V 2325*		38	2 wks

Y

YARDBIRDS *UK, male vocal/instrumental group*
8 wks

23 Jul 66	**YARDBIRDS**	*Columbia SX 6063*		20	8 wks

YAZOO *UK, female/male vocal/instrumental duo*
83 wks

4 Sep 82 ●	**UPSTAIRS AT ERIC'S**	*Mute STUMM 7*		2	63 wks
16 Jul 83 ★	**YOU AND ME BOTH**	*Mute STUMM 12*		1	20 wks

YELLO *Switzerland, male vocal/instrumental group*
3 wks

21 May 83	**YOU GOTTA SAY YES TO ANOTHER EXCESS**				
	Stiff SEEZ			65	2 wks
6 Apr 85	**STELLA**	*Elektra EKT 1*		92	1 wk

Bryn YEMM *UK, male vocalist*
14 wks

9 Jun 84	**HOW DO I LOVE THEE**	*Lifestyle LEG 17*		57	2 wks
7 Jul 84	**HOW GREAT THOU ART**	*Lifestyle LEG 15*		67	8 wks
22 Dec 84	**THE BRYN YEMM CHRISTMAS COLLECTION**				
	Bay BAY 104			95	2 wks
26 Oct 85	**MY TRIBUTE- BRYN YEMM INSPIRATIONAL**				
	ALBUM *Word WSTR 9665*			85	2 wks

My Tribute... also credits the Gwent Chorale

YES *UK, male vocal/instrumental group*
192 wks

1 Aug 70	**TIME AND A WORD**	*Atlantic 2400-006*		45	3 wks
3 Apr 71 ●	**THE YES ALBUM**	*Atlantic 2400-101*		7	29 wks
4 Dec 71 ●	**FRAGILE**	*Atlantic 2409-019*		7	17 wks
23 Sep 72 ●	**CLOSE TO THE EDGE**	*Atlantic K 50012*		4	13 wks
26 May 73 ●	**YESSONGS**	*Atlantic K 60045*		7	13 wks
22 Dec 73 ★	**TALES FROM TOPOGRAPHIC OCEAN**				
	Atlantic K 80001			1	15 wks
21 Dec 74 ●	**RELAYER**	*Atlantic K 50096*		4	11 wks
29 Mar 75	**YESTERDAYS**	*Atlantic K 50048*		27	7 wks
30 Jul 77 ★	**GOING FOR THE ONE**	*Atlantic K 50379*		1	28 wks
7 Oct 78 ●	**TORMATO**	*Atlantic K 50518*		8	11 wks
30 Aug 80 ●	**DRAMA**	*Atlantic K 50736*		2	8 wks
10 Jan 81	**YESSHOWS**	*Atlantic K 60142*		22	9 wks
26 Nov 83	**90125**	*Atco 790125*		16	28 wks

Faron YOUNG *US, male vocalist*
5 wks

28 Oct 72	**IT'S FOUR IN THE MORNING**	*Mercury 6338 095*		27	5 wks

Neil YOUNG *Canada, male vocalist*
156 wks

31 Oct 70 ●	**AFTER THE GOLDRUSH**	*Reprise RSLP 6383*	...	7	68 wks
4 Mar 72 ★	**HARVEST**	*Reprise K 54005*		1	33 wks
27 Oct 73	**TIME FADES AWAY**	*Warner Bros. K 54010*		20	2 wks
10 Aug 74	**ON THE BEACH**	*Reprise K 54014*		42	2 wks
5 Jul 75	**TONIGHT'S THE NIGHT**	*Reprise K 54040*		48	1 wk
27 Dec 75	**ZUMA**	*Reprise K 54057*		44	2 wks
9 Jul 77	**AMERICAN STARS 'N' BARS**	*Reprise K 54088*		17	8 wks
17 Dec 77	**DECADE**	*Reprise K 64037*		46	4 wks
28 Oct 78	**COMES A TIME**	*Reprise K 54099*		42	3 wks
14 Jul 79	**RUST NEVER SLEEPS**	*Reprise K 54105*		13	13 wks
1 Dec 79	**LIVE RUST**	*Reprise K 64041*		55	3 wks
15 Nov 80	**HAWKS AND DOVES**	*Reprise K 54109*		34	3 wks
14 Nov 81	**RE-AC-TOR**	*Reprise K 54116*		69	3 wks
5 Feb 83	**TRANS**	*Geffen GEF 25019*		29	5 wks
3 Sep 83	**EVERYBODY'S ROCKIN'**	*Geffen GEF 25590*	...	50	3 wks
14 Sep 85	**OLD WAYS**	*Geffen GEF 26377*		39	3 wks

Rust Never Sleeps, Live Rust and Re-ac-tor credited to Neil Young and Crazy Horse. Everybody's Rockin' credited to Neil Young and the Shocking Pinks. See also Stills-Young Band; and Crosby, Stills, Nash and Young

PAUL YOUNG *UK, male vocalist*
153 wks

30 Jul 83 ★	**NO PARLEZ**	*CBS 25521*		1	115 wks
6 Apr 85 ★	**THE SECRET OF ASSOCIATION**	*CBS 26234*		1†	38 wks

Y&T *US, male vocal/instrumental group*
15 wks

11 Sep 82	**BLACK TIGER**	*A & M AMLH 64910*		53	8 wks
10 Sep 83	**MEAN STREAK**	*A & M AMLX 64960*		35	4 wks
18 Aug 84	**IN ROCK WE TRUST**	*A & M AMLX 65007*	...	33	3 wks

Z

Frank ZAPPA *US, male vocalist/multi-instrumentalist*
53 wks

28 Feb 70 ●	**HOT RATS**	*Reprise RSLP 6356*		9	27 wks
19 Dec 70	**CHUNGA'S REVENGE**	*Reprise RSLP 2030*		43	1 wk
6 May 78	**ZAPPA IN NEW YORK**	*Discreet K 69204*		55	1 wk
10 Mar 79	**SHEIK YERBOUTI**	*CBS 88339*		32	7 wks
13 Oct 79	**JOE'S GARAGE ACT 1**	*CBS 86101*		62	3 wks
19 Jan 80	**JOE'S GARAGE ACTS 2 & 3**	*CBS 88475*		75	1 wk
16 May 81	**TINSEL TOWN REBELLION**	*CBS 88516*		55	4 wks
24 Oct 81	**YOU ARE WHAT YOU IS**	*CBS 88560*		51	2 wks
19 Jun 82	**SHIP ARRIVING TOO LATE TO SAVE A**				
	DROWNING WITCH *CBS 85804*			61	4 wks
18 Jun 83	**THE MAN FROM UTOPIA**	*CBS 25251*		87	1 wk
27 Oct 84	**THEM OR US**	*EMI FZD 1*		53	2 wks

See also Mothers of Invention.

Lena ZAVARONI *UK, female vocalist*
5 wks

23 Mar 74 ●	**MA**	*Philips 6308 201*		8	5 wks

Z.Z.TOP *US, male vocal/instrumental group*
110 wks

12 Jul 75	**FANDANGO**	*London SHU 8482*		60	1 wk
8 Aug 81	**EL LOCO**	*Warner Bros. K 56929*		88	2 wks
30 Apr 83 ●	**ELIMINATOR**	*Warner Bros. W 3774*		3	99 wks
9 Noc 85 ●	**AFTERBURNER**	*Warner Bros WX 27*		2†	8 wks

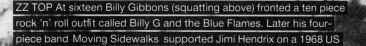

ZZ TOP At sixteen Billy Gibbons (squatting above) fronted a ten piece rock 'n' roll outfit called Billy G and the Blue Flames. Later his four-piece band Moving Sidewalks supported Jimi Hendrix on a 1968 US tour.

SOUTH PACIFIC The album that spent 115 weeks at number one also spent 36 weeks at number two.

VARIOUS ARTISTS

ANONYMOUS COVER VERSIONS

29 Feb 64		**BEATLEMANIA** *Top Six TSL 1*	19	1 wk
7 Aug 71		**HOT HITS 5** *MFP 5208*	48	1 wk
7 Aug 71	★	**HOT HITS 6** *MFP 5214*	1	7 wks
7 Aug 71		**TOP OF THE POPS VOL.17** *Hallmark SHM 740*	16	3 wks
7 Aug 71	★	**TOP OF THE POPS VOL. 18** *Hallmark SHM 745*	1	12 wks
7 Aug 71		**MILLION SELLER HITS** *MFP 5203*	46	2 wks
21 Aug 71		**SMASH HIT SUPREMES STYLE** *MFP 5184*	36	3 wks
2 Oct 71	●	**TOP OF THE POPS VOL.19** *Hallmark SHM 750*	3	9 wks
23 Oct 71	●	**HOT HITS 7** *MFP 5236*	3	9 wks
6 Nov 71		**SMASH HITS COUNTRY STYLE** *MFP 5228*	38	1 wk
13 Nov 71	★	**TOP OF THE POPS VOL.20** *Hallmark SHM 739*	1	8 wks
27 Nov 71		**NON STOP VOL.4** *Plexium PXMS 1006*	35	2 wks
4 Dec 71		**SMASH HITS 71** *MFP 5229*	21	3 wks
11 Dec 71	●	**HOT HITS 8** *MFP 5243*	2	4 wks
27 Sep 75		**40 SINGALONG PUB SONGS** *K-Tel NE 509*	21	7 wks
6 Nov 76		**FORTY MANIA** *Ronco RDT 2018*	21	6 wks

COMPILATIONS

Arcade

29 Jul 72	★	**20 FANTASTIC HITS** *Arcade 2891 001*	1	24 wks
29 Nov 72	●	**20 FANTASTIC HITS VOL.2** *Arcade 2891 002*	2	14 wks
7 Apr 73	●	**40 FANTASTIC HITS FROM THE 50'S AND 60'S** *Arcade ADEP 3/4*	2	15 wks
26 May 73	●	**20 FANTASTIC HITS VOL.3** *Arcade ADEP 5*	3	8 wks
15 Nov 75	●	**DISCO HITS '75** *Arcade ADEP 18*	5	11 wks
26 Mar 77		**ROCK ON** *Arcade ADEP 27*	16	10 wks
2 Jun 77		**RULE BRITANNIA** *Arcade ADEP 29*	56	1 wk
23 Feb 80		**FIRST LOVE** *Arcade ADEP 41*	58	2 wks

Atlantic

2 Apr 66		**SOLID GOLD SOUL** *Atlantic ATL 5048*	12	27 wks
5 Nov 66		**MIDNIGHT SOUL** *Atlantic 587-021*	22	19 wks
14 Jun 69		**THIS IS SOUL** *Atlantic 643-301*	16	15 wks
25 Mar 72		**THE NEW AGE OF ATLANTIC** *Atlantic K 20024*	25	1 wk
22 Jun 74		**ATLANTIC BLACK GOLD** *Atlantic K 40550*	23	7 wks
3 Apr 76		**BY INVITATION ONLY** *Atlantic K 60112*	17	6 wks
11 Apr 81		**CONCERTS FOR THE PEOPLE OF KAMPUCHEA** *Atlantic K 60153*	39	2 wks
2 Feb 85		**THIS IS SOUL** *Atlantic SOUL 1*	78	7 wks

CBS

20 May 67		**THRILL TO THE SENSATIONAL SOUNDS OF SUPER STEREO** *CBS PR 5*	20	30 wks
28 Jun 69		**THE ROCK MACHINE TURNS YOU ON** *CBS SPR 22*	18	7 wks
28 Jun 69		**ROCK MACHINE I LOVE YOU** *CBS SPR 26*	15	5 wks
20 May 72	●	**THE MUSIC PEOPLE** *CBS 66315*	10	9 wks
21 Oct 78	●	**SATIN CITY** *CBS 10010*	10	11 wks
2 Jun 79		**THIS IS IT** *CBS 10014*	6	12 wks
19 Apr 80		**FIRST LADIES OF COUNTRY** *CBS 10018*	37	6 wks
21 Jun 80		**KILLER WATTS** *CBS KW1*	27	6 wks
4 Apr 81		**BITTER SUITE** *CBS 22082*	55	3 wks
16 Oct 82	●	**REFLECTIONS** *CBS 10034*	4	91 wks
22 Oct 83		**IMAGINATIONS** *CBS 10044*	15	21 wks
20 Apr 85		**CLUB CLASSICS VOLUME 2** *CBS VAULT 2*	90	2 wks

Decca

8 Feb 64		**READY STEADY GO** *Decca LK 4577*	20	1 wk
16 May 64		**OUT CAME THE BLUES** *Ace Of Hearts AH 72*	19	1 wk
28 Jun 69		**THE WORLD OF BLUES POWER** *Decca SPA 14*	24	6 wks
5 Jul 69		**THE WORLD OF BRASS BANDS** *Decca SPA 20*	13	11 wks
6 Sep 69	●	**THE WORLD OF HITS VOL.2** *Decca SPA 35*	7	5 wks
20 Sep 69		**THE WORLD OF PROGRESSIVE MUSIC (WOWIE ZOWIE)** *Decca SPA 34*	17	2 wks
20 Sep 69		**THE WORLD OF PHASE 4 STEREO** *Decca SPA 32*	29	2 wks
7 Aug 71	●	**THE WORLD OF YOUR 100 BEST TUNES** *Decca SPA 112*	10	22 wks
9 Oct 71	●	**THE WORLD OF YOUR 100 BEST TUNES VOL.2** *Decca SPA 155*	9	13 wks
27 Sep 75		**THE WORLD OF YOUR 100 BEST TUNES VOL.10** *Decca SPA 400*	41	4 wks
13 Dec 75		**THE TOP 25 FROM YOUR 100 BEST TUNES** *Decca HBT 1112*	21	5 wks
26 Nov 83	●	**FORMULA 30** *Decca PROLP 4*	6	17 wks

EMI

21 Jun 69		**IMPACT** *EMI STWO 2*	15	14 wks
2 Jun 73	★	**PURE GOLD** *EMI EMK 251*	1	11 wks
18 Nov 78	★	**DON'T WALK BOOGIE** *EMI EMTV 13*	1	23 wks
21 Apr 79	●	**COUNTRY LIFE** *EMI EMTV 16*	2	14 wks
2 Jun 79		**KNUCKLE SANDWICH** *EMI International EMYV 18*	19	6 wks
15 Dec 79		**ALL ABOARD** *EMI EMTX 101*	13	8 wks
23 Feb 80		**METAL FOR MUTHAS** *EMI EMC 3318*	16	7 wks
14 Jun 80		**METAL FOR MUTHAS VOL.2** *EMI EMC 3337*	58	1 wk
13 Mar 82		**20 WITH A BULLET** *EMI EMTV 32*	11	8 wks
26 May 84	●	**THEN CAME ROCK 'N' ROLL** *EMI THEN 1*	5	15 wks

EMI/Virgin

10 Dec 83	★	**NOW THAT'S WHAT I CALL MUSIC** *EMI/Virgin NOW 1*	1	50 wks
7 Apr 84	★	**NOW THAT'S WHAT I CALL MUSIC 2** *EMI/Virgin NOW 2*	1	38 wks
11 Aug 84	★	**NOW THAT'S WHAT I CALL MUSIC 3** *EMI/Virgin NOW 3*	1	30 wks
8 Dec 84	●	**NOW THAT'S WHAT I CALL MUSIC 4** *EMI/Virgin NOW 4*	2	41 wks
1 Jun 85	●	**NOW DANCE** *EMI/Virgin NOD 1*	3	14 wks
13 Jul 85		**KERRANG! KOMPILATION** *EMI/Virgin KER 1*	84	2 wks
17 Aug 85	★	**NOW THAT'S WHAT I CALL MUSIC 5** *EMI/Virgin NOW 5*	1†	20 wks
30 Nov 85	★	**NOW - THE CHRISTMAS ALBUM** *EMI/Virgin NOX 1*	1†	5 wks
7 Dec 85	★	**NOW THAT'S WHAT I CALL MUSIC 6** *EMI/Virgin NOW 6*	1†	5 wks

Epic

2 Jul 83		**DANCE MIX-DANCE HITS VOL.1** *Epic EPC 25564*	85	2 wks
24 Sep 83		**DANCE MIX-DANCE HITS VOL.2** *Epic DM 2*	51	3 wks
3 Mar 84		**DANCE MIX-DANCE HITS VOL.3** *Epic DM 3*	70	1 wk
3 Mar 84		**ELECTRO SHOCK VOLTAGE** *Epic VOLT 1*	73	1 wk
16 Jun 84	●	**AMERICAN HEARTBEAT** *Epic EPC 10045*	4	22 wks
16 Jun 84		**DANCE MIX- DANCE HITS VOLUME 4** *Epic DM*	99	1 wk

Impression

Date	Title	Catalogue	Pos	Wks
16 Oct 82	BEST FRIENDS *Impression LP IMP 1*		28	21 wks
3 Sep 83	SUNNY AFTERNOON *Impression LP IMP 2*		13	8 wks
26 Nov 83	PRECIOUS MOMENTS *Impression LP IMP 3*		77	5 wks
7 Apr 84	ALWAYS AND FOREVER-THE COLLECTION *Impression LP IMP 4*		24	12 wks
21 Jul 84	WIPEOUT-20 INSTRUMENTAL GREATS *Impression LPIMP 5*		37	3 wks
28 Jul 84	SUNNY AFTERNOON VOLUME TWO *Impression LPIMP 7*		90	1 wk
22 Dec 84	FRIENDS AGAIN *Impression LP IMP 8*		91	1 wk

Island

Date	Title	Catalogue	Pos	Wks
26 Aug 67	CLUB SKA '67 *Island ILP 956*		37	19 wks
14 Jun 69	YOU CAN ALL JOIN IN *Island IWPS 2*		18	10 wks
29 Mar 80	CLUB SKA '67 (re-issue) *Island IRSP 4*		53	6 wks
16 Jun 84	CREW CUTS *Island IMA 11*		71	4 wks
27 Oct 84	CREW CUTS-LESSON 2 *Island IMA 14*		95	2 wks

K-Tel

Date	Title	Catalogue	Pos	Wks
10 Jun 72	★ 20 DYNAMIC HITS *K-Tel TE 292*		1	28 wks
7 Oct 72	★ 20 ALL TIME HITS OF THE 50'S *K-Tel NE 490*		1	22 wks
29 Nov 72	● 25 DYNAMIC HITS VOL.2 *K-Tel TE 291*		2	12 wks
2 Dec 72	★ 25 ROCKIN' & ROLLIN' GREATS *K-Tel NE 493*		1	18 wks
31 Mar 73	★ 20 FLASHBACK GREATS OF THE SIXTIES *K-Tel NE 494*		1	11 wks
21 Apr 73	● BELIEVE IN MUSIC *K-Tel TE 294*		2	8 wks
8 Nov 75	GOOFY GREATS *K-Tel NE 707*		19	7 wks
13 Dec 75	● 40 SUPER GREATS *K-Tel NE 708*		9	8 wks
31 Jan 76	● MUSIC EXPRESS *K-Tel TE 702*		3	10 wks
10 Apr 76	● JUKE BOX JIVE *K-Tel NE 709*		3	13 wks
17 Apr 76	GREAT ITALIAN LOVE SONGS *K-Tel NE 303*		17	14 wks
15 May 76	● HIT MACHINE *K-Tel TE 713*		4	10 wks
5 Jun 76	EUROVISION FAVOURITES *K-Tel NE 712*		44	1 wk
2 Oct 76	SUMMER CRUISING *K-Tel NE 918*		30	1 wk
16 Oct 76	COUNTRY COMFORT *K-Tel NE 294*		8	12 wks
16 Oct 76	★ SOUL MOTION *K-Tel NE 930*		1	14 wks
4 Dec 76	● DISCO ROCKET *K-Tel NE 948*		3	14 wks
11 Dec 76	44 SUPERSTARS *K-Tel NE 939*		14	10 wks
12 Feb 77	● HEARTBREAKERS *K-Tel NE 954*		2	18 wks
19 Feb 77	DANCE TO THE MUSIC *K-Tel NE 957*		5	9 wks
7 May 77	HIT ACTION *K-Tel NE 993*		15	9 wks
29 Oct 77	SOUL CITY *K-Tel NE 1003*		12	7 wks
12 Nov 77	FEELINGS *K-Tel NE 1006*		3	24 wks
26 Nov 77	★ DISCO FEVER *K-Tel NE 1014*		1	20 wks
21 Jan 78	40 NUMBER ONE HITS *K-Tel NE 1008*		15	7 wks
4 Mar 78	● DISCO STARS *K-Tel NE 1022*		6	8 wks
10 Jun 78	● DISCO DOUBLE *K-Tel NE 1024*		10	6 wks
8 Jul 78	ROCK RULES *K-Tel RL 001*		12	11 wks
19 Aug 78	● STAR PARTY *K-Tel NE 1034*		4	9 wks
4 Nov 78	● EMOTIONS *K-Tel NE 1035*		2	17 wks
25 Nov 78	● MIDNIGHT HUSTLE *K-Tel NE 1037*		2	13 wks
20 Jan 79	★ ACTION REPLAY *K-Tel NE 1040*		1	14 wks
7 Apr 79	DISCO INFERNO *K-Tel NE 1043*		11	9 wks
5 May 79	HI ENERGY *K-Tel NE 1044*		17	7 wks
22 Sep 79	HOT TRACKS *K-Tel NE 1049*		31	8 wks
24 Nov 79	NIGHT MOVES *K-Tel NE 1065*		10	10 wks
24 Nov 79	TOGETHER *K-Tel NE 1053*		35	8 wks
12 Jan 80	● VIDEO STARS *K-Tel NE 1066*		5	10 wks
26 Jan 80	THE SUMMIT *K-Tel NE 1067*		17	5 wks
29 Mar 80	● STAR TRACKS *K-Tel NE 1070*		6	8 wks
26 Apr 80	GOOD MORNING AMERICA *K-Tel NE 1072*		15	12 wks
17 May 80	HAPPY DAYS *K-Tel ONE 1076*		32	6 wks
17 May 80	● MAGIC REGGAE *K-Tel NE 1074*		9	17 wks
14 Jun 80	HOT WAX *K-Tel NE 1082*		3	10 wks
27 Sep 80	● MOUNTING EXCITEMENT *K-Tel NE 1091*		2	8 wks
11 Oct 80	● THE LOVE ALBUM *K-Tel NE 1062*		6	16 wks
25 Oct 80	AXE ATTACK *K-Tel NE 1100*		15	14 wks
15 Nov 80	● CHART EXPLOSION *K-Tel NE 1103*		6	17 wks
3 Jan 81	NIGHTLIFE *K-Tel NE 1107*		25	9 wks
14 Feb 81	HIT MACHINE *K-Tel NE 1113*		17	6 wks
21 Mar 81	RHYTHM 'N' REGGAE *K-Tel NE 1115*		42	4 wks
25 Apr 81	● CHARTBUSTERS 81 *K-Tel NE 1118*		3	9 wks
2 May 81	AXE ATTACK 2 *K-Tel NE -120*		31	6 wks
23 May 81	THEMES *K-Tel NE 1122*		6	15 wks
29 Aug 81	CALIFORNIA DREAMING *K-Tel NE 1126*		27	11 wks
19 Sep 81	DANCE DANCE DANCE *K-Tel NE 1143*		29	4 wks
3 Oct 81	THE PLATINUM ALBUM *K-Tel NE 1134*		32	11 wks
10 Oct 81	● LOVE IS... *K-Tel NE 1129*		10	15 wks
21 Nov 81	★ CHART HITS 81 *K-Tel NE 1142*		1	17 wks
26 Dec 81	MINI POPS *K-Tel NE 1102*		63	7 wks
9 Jan 82	● MODERN DANCE *K-Tel NE 1156*		6	10 wks
6 Feb 82	● DREAMING *K-Tel NE 1159*		2	12 wks
6 Mar 82	● ACTION TRAX *K-Tel NE 1162*		2	12 wks
1 May 82	MIDNIGHT HOUR *K-Tel NE 1157*		98	1 wk
3 Jul 82	TURBO TRAX *K-Tel NE 1176*		17	7 wks
4 Sep 82	THE NO 1 SOUNDS OF THE SEVENTIES *K-Tel NE 1172*		83	1 wk
11 Sep 82	● CHARTBEAT/CHARTHEAT *K-Tel NE 1180*		2	14 wks
30 Oct 82	THE LOVE SONGS ALBUM *K-Tel NE 1179*		28	8 wks
6 Nov 82	CHART HITS '82 *K-Tel NE 1195*		11	17 wks
6 Nov 82	DISCO DANCER *K-Tel NE 1190*		26	8 wks
18 Dec 82	STREETSCENE *K-Tel NE 1183*		42	6 wks
15 Jan 83	● VISIONS *T-Tel ONE 1199*		5	21 wks
12 Feb 83	HEAVY *K-Tel NE 1203*		46	12 wks
5 Mar 83	● HOTLINE *K-Tel NE 1207*		3	9 wks
11 Jun 83	● CHART STARS *K-Tel NE 1225*		7	9 wks
20 Aug 83	COOL HEAT *K-Tel NE 1231*		79	3 wks
10 Sep 83	HEADLINE HITS *K-Tel NE 1253*		5	6 wks
8 Oct 83	● THE TWO OF US *K-Tel NE 1222*		3	16 wks
8 Oct 83	IMAGES *K-Tel ONE 1254*		33	6 wks
12 Nov 83	● CHART HITS '83 VOLS 1 AND 2 *K-Tel NE 1256*		6	11 wks
24 Mar 84	NIGHT MOVES *K-Tel NE 1255*		15	11 wks
26 May 84	● HUNGRY FOR HITS *K-Tel NE 1272*		4	11 wks
23 Jun 84	THE THEMES ALBUM *K-Tel ONE 1257*		43	3 wks
28 Jul 84	BREAKDANCE, YOU CAN DO IT *K-Tel ONE 1276*		18	12 wks
22 Sep 84	● ALL BY MYSELF *K-Tel NE 1273*		7	16 wks
1 Dec 84	HOOKED ON NUMBER ONES-100 NON-STOP HITS *K-Tel ONE*		25	12 wks
2 Feb 85	FOUR STAR COUNTRY *K-Tel NE 1278*		52	6 wks
2 Mar 85	MODERN LOVE *K-Tel NE 1286*		13	7 wks
5 Oct 85	EXPRESSIONS *K-Tel NE 1307*		11	8 wks
9 Nov 85	● ROCK ANTHEMS *K-Tel NE 1309*		10†	8 wks
9 Nov 85	OVATION - THE BEST OF ANDREW LLOYD WEBBER *K-Tel ONE 1311*		34†	8 wks

Polydor

Date	Title	Catalogue	Pos	Wks
10 Dec 66	STEREO MUSICALE SHOWCASE *Polydor 104-450*		26	2 wks
9 Oct 71	THE A-Z OF EASY LISTENING *Polydor 2661-005*		24	4 wks
24 Feb 79	20 OF ANOTHER KIND *Polydor POLS 1006*		45	3 wks
9 Feb 80	CAPTAIN BEAKY AND HIS BAND *Polydor 238 3462*		28	12 wks
3 May 80	● CHAMPAGNE AND ROSES *Polydor ROSTV 1*		7	14 wks
30 Aug 80	I AM WOMAN *Polydor WOMTV 1*		11	13 wks
11 Oct 80	COUNTRY ROUND UP *Polydor KOWTV 1*		64	3 wks
18 Oct 80	MONSTERS OF ROCK *Polydor 2488 810*		16	5 wks
6 Dec 80	THE HITMAKERS *Polydor HOPTV 1*		45	10 wks
12 Jan 85	BREAKDANCE 2- ELECTRIC BOOGALOO *Polydor POLD 5168*		34	20 wks

Pye

Date	Title	Catalogue	Pos	Wks
9 May 59	● CURTAIN UP *Pye Nixa BRTH 0059*		4	13 wks
23 Jun 62	HONEY HIT PARADE *Pye Golden Guinea GGL 0129*		13	7 wks
30 Nov 62	ALL THE HITS BY ALL THE STARS *Pye Golden Guinea GGL 0162*		19	2 wks
7 Sep 63	HITSVILLE *Pye Golden Guinea GGL 0202*		11	6 wks
14 Sep 63	THE BEST OF RADIO LUXEMBOURG *Pye Golden Guinea GGL 0208*		14	2 wks
23 Nov 63	HITSVILLE VOL.2 *Pye Golden Guinea GGL 0233*		20	1 wk
4 Jan 64	THE BLUES VOL.1 *Pye NPL 28030*		15	3 wks
22 Feb 64	FOLK FESTIVAL OF THE BLUES (LIVE RECORDING) *Pye NPL 28033*		16	4 wks
30 May 64	THE BLUES VOL.2 *Pye NPL 28035*		16	3 wks
10 Feb 68	STARS OF '68 *Marble Arch MAL 762*		23	3 wks
16 Oct 71	PYE CHARTBUSTERS *Pye PCB 15000*		36	1 wk
18 Dec 71	PYE CHARTBUSTERS VOL.2 *Pye PCB 15001*		29	3 wks

Ronco

Date	Title	Catalogue	Pos	Wks
21 Oct 72	● 20 STAR TRACKS *Ronco PP 2001*		2	13 wks
23 Jun 73	★ THAT'LL BE THE DAY *Ronco MR 2002/3*		1	8 wks

8 Nov 75		**BLAZING BULLETS** *Ronco RTI 2012*	**17**	8 wks
6 Dec 75		**GREATEST HITS OF WALT DISNEY**		
		Ronco RTD 2013	**11**	12 wks
13 Dec 75		**A CHRISTMAS GIFT** *Ronco P 12430*	**39**	5 wks
24 Jan 76	●	**STAR TRACKIN' 76** *Ronco RTL 2014*	**9**	5 wks
8 Jan 77		**CLASSICAL GOLD** *Ronco RTD 42020*	**24**	12 wks
16 Jul 77		**SUPERGROUPS** *Ronco RTL 2023*	**57**	1 wk
26 Nov 77		**BLACK JOY** *Ronco RTL 2025*	**26**	13 wks
18 Mar 78	●	**BOOGIE NIGHTS** *Ronco RTL 2027*	**5**	7 wks
18 Nov 78		**BOOGIE FEVER** *Ronco RTL 2034*	**15**	11 wks
9 Jun 79		**ROCK LEGENDS** *Ronco RTL 2037*	**54**	3 wks
3 Nov 79	●	**ROCK 'N' ROLLER DISCO** *Ronco RTL 2040*	**3**	11 wks
8 Dec 79		**PEACE IN THE VALLEY** *Ronco RTL 2043*	**6**	18 wks
22 Dec 79		**MILITARY GOLD** *Ronco RTD 42042*	**62**	3 wks
25 Oct 80		**STREET LEVEL** *Ronco RTL 2048*	**29**	5 wks
8 Nov 80		**COUNTRY LEGENDS** *Ronco RTL 2050*	**9**	12 wks
15 Nov 80		**RADIOACTIVE** *Ronco RTL 2049*	**13**	9 wks
29 Nov 80		**SPACE INVADERS** *Ronco RTL 2051*	**47**	3 wks
6 Dec 80		**THE LEGENDARY BIG BANDS**		
		Ronco RTL 2047	**24**	6 wks
9 May 81	★	**DISCO DAZE AND DISCO NITES**		
		Ronco RTL 2056 A/B	**1**	23 wks
19 Sep 81	●	**SUPER HITS 1 & 2** *Ronco RTL 2058 A/B*	**2**	17 wks
24 Oct 81		**COUNTRY SUNRISE/COUNTRY SUNSET**		
		Ronco RTL 2059 A/B	**27**	11 wks
14 Nov 81		**ROCK HOUSE** *Ronco RTL 2061*	**44**	4 wks
12 Dec 81		**MISTY MORNINGS** *Ronco RTL 2066*	**44**	5 wks
12 Dec 81		**MEMORIES ARE MADE OF THIS**		
		Ronco RTL 2062	**84**	4 wks
26 Dec 81	●	**HITS HITS HITS** *Ronco RTL 2063*	**2**	10 wks
24 Apr 82	●	**DISCO UK & DISCO USA** *Ronco RTL 2073*	**7**	10 wks
15 May 82	●	**CHARTBUSTERS** *Ronco RTL 2074*	**3**	10 wks
3 Jul 82	●	**OVERLOAD** *Ronco RTL 2074*	**10**	8 wks
28 Aug 82		**SOUL DAZE/SOUL NITES** *Ronco RTL 2080*	**25**	8 wks
11 Sep 82	●	**BREAKOUT** *Ronco RTL 2081*	**4**	8 wks
30 Oct 82		**MUSIC FOR THE SEASONS** *Ronco RTL 2075* ..	**41**	8 wks
27 Nov 82		**CHART WARS** *Ronco RTL 2086*	**30**	7 wks
27 Nov 82		**THE GREAT COUNTRY MUSIC SHOW**		
		Ronco RTD 2083	**38**	7 wks
18 Dec 82		**THE BEST OF BEETHOVEN/STRAUSS/**		
		TCHAIKOWSKY/MOZART (4 lp's)		
		Ronco RTL 2084	**49**	10 wks
25 Dec 82	★	**RAIDERS OF THE POP CHARTS**		
		Ronco RTL 2088	**1**	17 wks
19 Mar 83	●	**CHART RUNNERS** *Ronco RTL 2090*	**4**	13 wks
21 May 83	●	**CHART ENCOUNTERS OF THE HIT KIND**		
		Ronco RTL 2091	**5**	10 wks
4 Jun 83		**MUSIC FOR THE SEASONS** *Ronco RTL 2075* ..	**74**	2 wks
18 Jun 83		**LOVERS ONLY** *Ronco RTL 2093*	**12**	13 wks
16 Jul 83		**HITS ON FIRE** *Ronco RTL 2095*	**11**	10 wks
17 Sep 83	●	**THE HIT SQUAD - CHART TRACKING**		
		Ronco RON LP 1	**4**	9 wks
17 Sep 83		**THE HIT SQUAD - NIGHT CLUBBING**		
		Ronco RON LP 2	**28**	7 wks
12 Nov 83		**HIT SQUAD-HITS OF '83** *Ronco RON LP 4*	**12**	11 wks
17 Dec 83	●	**GREEN VELVET** *Ronco RON LP 6*	**6**	17 wks
7 Jan 84		**CHART TREK VOLS.1 & 2** *Ronco RON LP 8* ..	**20**	9 wks
21 Jan 84	●	**SOMETIMES WHEN WE TOUCH**		
		Ronco RON LP 9	**8**	14 wks
24 Mar 84		**BABY LOVE** *Ronco RON LP 11*	**47**	6 wks
7 Apr 84		**DREAMS AND THEMES** *Ronco RONLP 10*	**75**	2 wks

Starblend

12 Nov 83	**IN TOUCH** *Starblend STD 9*	**89**	2 wks
23 Jun 84	**BROKEN DREAMS** *Starblend SLTD 1*	**48**	7 wks
27 Apr 85	**12 X 12 MEGA MIXES** *Starblend INCH 1*	**77**	2 wks
3 Aug 85	**AMERICAN DREAMS** *Starblend SLTD 12*	**43**	7 wks
21 Dec 85	**CHRISTMAS AT THE COUNTRY STORE**		
	Starblend NOEL 1	**94**	1 wk

Street Sounds

19 Feb 83	**STREET SOUNDS EDITION 2**		
	Street Sounds STSND 002	**35**	6 wks
23 Apr 83	**STREET SOUNDS EDITION 3**		
	Street Sounds STSND 003	**21**	5 wks
25 Jun 83	**STREET SOUNDS EDITION 4**		
	Street Sounds STSND 004	**14**	8 wks

13 Aug 83	**STREET SOUNDS EDITION 5**		
	Street Sounds STSND 005	**16**	8 wks
8 Oct 83	**STREET SOUNDS EDITION 6**		
	Street Sounds STSND 006	**23**	5 wks
22 Oct 83	**STREET SOUNDS ELECTRO 1**		
	Street Sounds ELCST 1	**18**	8 wks
17 Dec 83	**STREET SOUNDS EDITION 7**		
	Street Sounds STSND 007	**48**	4 wks
7 Jan 84	**STREET SOUNDS ELECTRO 2**		
	Street Sounds ELCST 2	**49**	7 wks
3 Mar 84	**STREET SOUNDS HI-ENERGY**		
	Street Sounds HINRG 16	**71**	1 wk
10 Mar 84	**STREET SOUNDS CRUCIAL ELECTRO**		
	Street Sounds Electro ELCST 999	**24**	10 wks
10 Mar 84	**STREET SOUNDS EDITION 8**		
	Street Sounds STSND 008	**22**	7 wks
7 Apr 84	**STREET SOUNDS ELECTRO 3**		
	Street Sounds ELCST 3	**25**	9 wks
12 May 84	**STREET SOUNDS EDITION 9**		
	Street Sounds STSND 009	**22**	5 wks
9 Jun 84	**STREET SOUNDS ELECTRO 4**		
	Street Sounds ELCST 4	**25**	9 wks
30 Jun 84	**STREET SOUNDS UK ELECTRO**		
	Street Sounds ELCST 1984	**60**	4 wks
21 Jul 84	**LET THE MUSIC SCRATCH**		
	Street Sounds MKL 1	**91**	3 wks
11 Aug 84	**STREET SOUNDS CRUCIAL ELECTRO 2**		
	Street Sounds ELCST 1000	**35**	6 wks
18 Aug 84	**STREET SOUNDS EDITION 10**		
	Street Sounds STSND 010	**24**	6 wks
6 Oct 84	**STREET SOUNDS ELECTRO 5**		
	Street Sounds Electro ELCST 5	**17**	6 wks
10 Nov 84	**STREET SOUNDS EDITION 11**		
	Street Sounds STSND 011	**48**	4 wks
9 Mar 85	**STREET SOUNDS ELECTRO 6**		
	Street Sounds ELCST 6	**24**	10 wks
9 Mar 85	**THE ARTISTS VOLUME 1**		
	Street Sounds ARTIS 1	**65**	4 wks
18 May 85	**STREET SOUNDS ELECTRO 7**		
	Street Sounds ELCST 7	**12**	7 wks
18 May 85	**STREET SOUNDS EDITION 12**		
	Street Sounds STSND 12	**23**	4 wks
13 Jul 85	**STREET SOUNDS ELECTRO 8**		
	Street Sounds ELCST 8	**23**	5 wks
13 Jul 85	**THE ARTISTS VOLUME 2**		
	Street Sounds ARTIS 2	**45**	4 wks
17 Aug 85	**STREET SOUNDS EDITION 13**		
	Street Sounds STSND 13	**19**	9 wks
17 Aug 85	**STREET SOUNDS N.Y. VS. L.A.BEATS**		
	Street Sounds ELCST 1001	**65**	4 wks
5 Oct 85	**STREET SOUNDS ELECTRO 9**		
	Street Sounds ELCST 9	**18**	6 wks
12 Oct 85	**THE ARTISTS VOLUME 3**		
	Street Sounds ARTIS 3	**87**	2 wks
16 Nov 85	**STREET SOUNDS EDITION 14**		
	Street Sounds STSND 14	**43**	3 wks
21 Dec 85	**STREET SOUNDS ELECTRO 10**		
	Street Sounds ELCST 10	**76†**	2 wks
21 Dec 85	**STREET SOUNDS EDITION 15**		
	Street Sounds STSND 15	**83†**	2 wks

Stylus

3 Aug 85	**THE MAGIC OF TORVILL AND DEAN**		
	Stylus SMR 8502	**35**	9 wks
17 Aug 85	**NIGHT BEAT** *Stylus SMR 8501*	**15**	8 wks
24 Aug 85	**DISCO BEACH PARTY** *Stylus SMR 8503*	**29**	6 wks
23 Nov 85	**TELLYHITS-16 TOP TV THEMES** *Stylus/*		
	BBC BBSR 508	**34†**	6 wks
14 Dec 85	**VELVET WATERS** *Stylus SMR 8507*	**54†**	3 wks
28 Dec 85	**CHOICES OF THE HEART** *Stylus SMR 8511* ...	**87†**	1 wk

Tamla Motown

3 Apr 65	**A COLLECTION OF TAMLA MOTOWN HITS**		
	Tamla Motown TML 11001	**16**	4 wks
4 Mar 67	**16 ORIGINAL BIG HITS - VOL.4**		
	Tamla Motown TML 11043	**33**	3 wks
17 Jun 67	**TAMLA MOTOWN HITS VOL.5**		
	Tamla Motown TML 11050	**11**	40 wks

Date	Title	Label / Cat. No.	Pos	Weeks
21 Oct 67	● BRITISH MOTOWN CHARTBUSTERS	Tamla Motown TML 11055	2	54 wks
10 Feb 68	MOTOWN MEMORIES	Tamla Motown TML 11064	21	13 wks
24 Aug 68	TAMLA MOTOWN HITS VOL.6	Tamla Motown STML 11074	32	2 wks
30 Nov 68	● BRITISH MOTOWN CHARTBUSTERS VOL.2	Tamla Motown STML 11082	8	11 wks
25 Oct 69	★ BRITISH MOTOWN CHARTBUSTERS VOL.3	Tamla Motown STML 11121	1	93 wks
21 Feb 70	COLLECTION OF BIG HITS VOL.8	Tamla Motown STML 11130	56	1 wk
24 Oct 70	★ MOTOWN CHARTBUSTERS VOL.4	Tamla Motown STML 11162	1	40 wks
17 Apr 71	★ MOTOWN CHARTBUSTERS VOL.5	Tamla Motown STML 11181	1	36 wks
23 Oct 71	● MOTOWN CHARTBUSTERS VOL.6	Tamla Motown STML 11191	2	36 wks
26 Feb 72	MOTOWN MEMORIES	Tamla Motown STML 11200	22	4 wks
18 Mar 72	MOTOWN STORY	Tamla Motown TMSP 1130	21	8 wks
29 Nov 72	● MOTOWN CHARTBUSTERS VOL.7	Tamla Motown STML 11215	9	16 wks
3 Nov 73	● MOTOWN CHARTBUSTERS VOL.8	Tamla Motown STML 11246	9	15 wks
26 Oct 74	MOTOWN CHARTBUSTERS VOL.9	Tamla Motown STML 11270	14	15 wks
1 Nov 75	● MOTOWN GOLD	Tamla Motown STML 12003	8	35 wks
5 Nov 77	MOTOWN GOLD VOL.2	Motown STML 12070	28	4 wks
7 Oct 78	BIG WHEELS OF MOTOWN	Motown EMTV 12	2	18 wks
2 Feb 80	★ THE LAST DANCE	Motown EMTV 20	1	23 wks
2 Aug 80	THE 20TH ANNIVERSARY ALBUM	Motown TMSP 6010	53	2 wks

Telstar

Date	Title	Label / Cat. No.	Pos	Weeks
16 Oct 82	● CHART ATTACK	Telstar STAR 2221	7	6 wks
6 Nov 82	MIDNIGHT IN MOTOWN	Telstar STAR 2224	34	16 wks
18 Dec 82	DIRECT HITS	Telstar STAR 2224	41	2 wks
8 Jan 83	DANCIN'-20 ORIGINAL MOTOWN MOVERS	Telstar STAR 2225	97	1 wk
5 Feb 83	INSTRUMENTAL MAGIC	Telstar STAR 2227	68	5 wks
30 Apr 83	20 GREAT ITALIAN LOVE SONGS	Telstar STAR 2230	28	6 wks
4 Jun 83	IN THE GROOVE-THE 12 INCH DISCO PARTY	Telstar STAR 2228	20	12 wks
12 Nov 83	ROOTS REGGAE/REGGAE ROCK	Telstar STAR 2233	34	6 wks
19 Nov 83	SUPERCHART '83	Telstar STAR 2236	22	9 wks
4 Feb 84	● THE VERY BEST OF MOTOWN LOVE SONGS	Telstar STAR 2239	10	22 wks
26 May 84	DON'T STOP DANCING	Telstar STAR 2242	11	12 wks
13 Oct 84	● HITS HITS HITS-18 SMASH ORIGINALS	Telstar STAR 2243	6	9 wks
8 Dec 84	LOVE SONGS-16 CLASSIC LOVE SONGS	Telstar STAR 2246	22	12 wks
15 Dec 84	● GREEN VELVET (re-issue) Telstar STAR 2252		10	10 wks
7 Sep 85	OPEN TOP CARS AND GIRLS IN T-SHIRTS	Telstar STAR 2257	13	9 wks
16 Nov 85	● THE LOVE ALBUM Telstar STAR 2268		7†	7 wks
16 Nov 85	★ GREATEST HITS OF 1985 Telstar STAR 2269		1†	7 wks
30 Nov 85	THE PRINCE'S TRUST COLLECTION	Telstar STAR 2275	64†	5 wks
7 Dec 85	PERFORMANCE-THE VERY BEST OF TIM RICE AND ANDREW LLOYD WEBBER	Telstar STAR 2262	33†	4 wks
7 Dec 85	MORE GREEN VELVET Telstar STAR 2267		42†	4 wks

Warwick

Date	Title	Label / Cat. No.	Pos	Weeks
29 Nov 75	ALL-TIME PARTY HITS Warwick WW 5001		21	8 wks
17 Apr 76	● INSTRUMENTAL GOLD Warwick WW 5012		3	24 wks
29 May 76	HAMILTON'S HOT SHOTS Warwick WW 5014		15	5 wks
8 Jan 77	SONGS OF PRAISE Warwick WW 5020		31	2 wks
29 Jan 77	HIT SCENE Warwick PR 5023		19	5 wks
11 Mar 78	● FONZIE'S FAVOURITES Warwick WW 5037		8	16 wks
25 Nov 78	LOVE SONGS Warwick WW 5046		47	7 wks
2 Dec 78	BLACK VELVET Warwick WW 5047		72	3 wks
31 Mar 79	LEMON POPSICLE Warwick WW 5050		42	6 wks
7 Apr 79	COUNTRY PORTRAITS Warwick WW 5057		14	10 wks
10 Nov 79	20 SMASH DISCO HITS (THE BITCH) Warwick WW 5061		42	5 wks
16 Feb 80	COUNTRY GUITAR Warwick WW 5070		46	3 wks
14 Nov 81	DISCO EROTICA Warwick WW 5108		35	8 wks
10 Apr 82	PS I LOVE YOU Warwick WW 5121		68	3 wks
6 Nov 82	HITS OF THE SCREAMING 60'S Warwick WW 5124		24	10 wks
22 Dec 84	MERRY CHRISTMAS TO YOU Warwick WW 5141		64	2 wks

Other Compilation Albums

Date	Title	Label / Cat. No.	Pos	Weeks
10 Mar 62	GREAT MOTION PICTURE THEMES	HMV CLP 1508	19	1 wk
9 Mar 63	● ALL STAR FESTIVAL Philips DL 99500		4	19 wks
24 Aug 63	THE MERSEY BEAT VOL.1 Oriole PS 40047		17	5 wks
11 Sep 66	● STARS CHARITY FANTASIA SAVE THE CHILDREN FUND SCF PL 145		6	16 wks
8 Apr 67	● HIT THE ROAD STAX Stax 589-005		10	16 wks
21 Oct 67	● BREAKTHROUGH Studio Two STWO 1		2	11 wks
11 May 68	BLUES ANYTIME Immediate IMLP 014		40	1 wk
7 Aug 71	TIGHTEN UP VOL.4 Trojan TBL 163		20	7 wks
21 Aug 71	CLUB REGGAE Trojan TBL 159		25	4 wks
4 Sep 71	TOTAL SOUND Studio Two STWO 4		39	4 wks
30 Oct 71	STUDIO TWO CLASSICS Studio Two STWO 6		16	4 wks
4 Dec 71	BREAKTHROUGH MFP 1334		49	1 wk
22 Jan 72	★ CONCERT FOR BANGLADESH (recorded live) Apple STCX 3385		1	13 wks
2 Jun 73	● 20 ORIGINAL CHART HITS Philips TV 1		9	11 wks
2 Jun 73	NICE 'N' EASY Philips 6441 076		36	1 wk
27 Apr 74	AMERICAN GRAFFITI MCA MCSP 253		37	1 wk
4 Jan 75	BBC TV'S BEST OF TOP OF THE POPS Super Beeb BELP 001		21	5 wks
15 Mar 75	SOLID SOUL SENSATIONS Disco Demand DDLP 5001		30	1 wk
16 Aug 75	NEVER TOO YOUNG TO ROCK GTO GTLP 004		30	5 wks
6 Dec 75	SUPERSONIC Stallion SSM 001		21	6 wks
31 Jan 76	REGGAE CHARTBUSTERS 75 Cactus CTLP 114		53	1 wk
22 May 76	● A TOUCH OF COUNTRY Topaz TOC 1976		7	7 wks
3 Jul 76	GOLDEN FIDDLE AWARDS 1976 Mountain TOPC 5002		45	2 wks
3 Jul 76	A TOUCH OF CLASS Topaz TOC 1976		57	1 wk
27 Nov 76	ALL THIS AND WORLD WAR II Riva RVLP 2		23	7 wks
16 Jul 77	THE ROXY LONDON WC2 Harvest SHSP 4069		24	5 wks
6 Aug 77	NEW WAVE Philips 6300 902		11	12 wks
22 Oct 77	10 YEARS OF HITS-RADIO ONE Super Beeb BEDP 002		39	3 wks
11 Mar 78	STIFF'S LIVE STIFFS Stiff GET 1		28	7 wks
25 Mar 78	HOPE AND ANCHOR FRONT ROW FESTIVAL Warner Bros. K 66077		28	3 wks
17 Jun 78	WHITE MANSIONS A & M AMLX 64691		51	3 wks
8 Jul 78	THE WORLD'S WORST RECORD SHOW Yuk/K-Tel NE 1023		47	2 wks
28 Oct 78	ECSTACY Lotus WH 5003		24	6 wks
9 Dec 78	STARS ON SUNDAY BY REQUEST Curzon Sounds CSL 0081		65	3 wks
19 May 79	BOOGIE BUS Polystar 9198 174		23	11 wks
26 May 79	A MONUMENT TO BRITISH ROCK Harvest EMTV 17		13	12 wks
9 Jun 79	THAT SUMMER Arista SPART 1088		36	8 wks
21 Jul 79	★ THE BEST DISCO ALBUM IN THE WORLD Warner Bros. K 58062		1	17 wks
3 Nov 79	MODS MAYDAY 79 Arista FOUR 1		75	1 wk
8 Mar 80	THE WANDERERS Gem GEMLP 103		48	7 wks
24 May 80	PRECIOUS METAL MCA MCF 3069		60	2 wks
22 Nov 80	CASH COWS Virgin MILK 1		49	1 wk
14 Mar 81	SOME BIZARRE ALBUM Some Bizarre BZLP 1		58	1 wk
4 Apr 81	● ROLL ON Polystar REDTV 1		3	13 wks
4 Apr 81	REMIXTURE Champagne CHAMP 1		32	5 wks
30 May 81	STRENGTH THROUGH OI SKIN 1		51	5 wks
8 Aug 81	ROYAL ROMANCE Windsor WIN 001		84	1 wk
17 Oct 81	MONSTER TRACKS Polystar HOPTV 2		20	8 wks
31 Oct 81	CARRY ON OI Secret SEC 2		60	4 wks
21 Nov 81	SLIP STREAM Beggars Banquet BEGA 31		72	3 wks
12 Dec 81	THE SECRET POLICEMAN'S OTHER BALL Springtime HAHA 6003		69	4 wks
12 Dec 81	LIVE AND HEAVY Nems NEL 6020		100	2 wks
19 Dec 81	WE ARE MOST AMUSED Ronco/Charisma 2067		30	9 wks

SECRET POLICEMAN'S OTHER BALL Rowan Atkinson and John Cleese were just two of the performers on this charity album. (LFI)

FIDDLER ON THE ROOF (left) More Britons bought the stage recording than the movie soundtrack. (Theo Cowan)

Date	Title	Label/Cat. No.	Pos	Weeks
27 Mar 82	● JAMES BOND'S GREATEST HITS *Liberty EMTV 007*		4	13 wks
27 Mar 82	PUNK AND DISORDERLY *Abstract AABT 100*		48	8 wks
17 Apr 82	MUSIC OF QUALITY AND DISTINCTION VOL 1 *Virgin V 2219*		25	5 wks
15 May 82	SEX SWEAT AND BLOOD *Beggars Banquet BEGA 34*		88	1 wk
14 Aug 82	SONETO *Rough Trade ROUGH 37*		66	3 wks
4 Sep 82	PUNK AND DISORDERLY (FURTHER CHARGES) *Anagram GRAM 001*		91	2 wks
11 Sep 82	THE BEST OF BRITISH JAZZ FUNK VOL 2 *Beggars Banquet BEGA 41*		44	4 wks
25 Sep 82	OI OI THAT'S YER LOT *Secret SEC 5*		54	4 wks
2 Oct 82	MODERN HEROES *TV Records TVA 1*		24	7 wks
9 Oct 82	ENDLESS LOVE *TV Records TVA 2*		26	8 wks
23 Oct 82	STREETPOISE VOL I *Epic/Streetware STR 32234*		51	4 wks
23 Oct 82	ON THE AIR - 60 YEARS OF BBC THEME MUSIC *BBC REF 454*		85	3 wks
6 Nov 82	FLASH TRACKS *Records PTVL 1*		19	7 wks
25 Dec 82	PARTY FEVER/DISCO MANIA *TV Records TVA 5*		71	3 wks
14 May 83	THE LAUGHTER AND TEARS COLLECTION *WEA LTC*		19	16 wks
28 May 83	GET ON UP *RCA BSLP 5001*		35	5 wks
18 Jun 83	TEARDROPS *Ritz RITZ SP 399*		37	6 wks
2 Jul 83	WIRED FOR CLUBS (CLUB TRACKS VOL.1) *Mercury CLUBL 001*		58	4 wks
3 Sep 83	COME WITH CLUB (CLUB TRACKS VOL.2) *Club CLUBL 002*		55	2 wks
24 Sep 83	CLASSIC THEMES *Nouveau Music NML 1001*		61	2 wks
15 Oct 83	LOVE THE REASON *Respond RRL 501*		50	3 wks
26 Nov 83	THIS ARE TWO TONE *Two Tone CHR TT 5007*		51	9 wks
26 Nov 83	TWELVE INCHES OF PLEASURE *Proto PROTO 1*		100	1 wk
2 Jun 84	ESSENTIAL DISCO AND DANCE *Nouveau Music NML 1010*		96	1 wk
16 Jun 84	EMERALD CLASSICS *Stoic SRTV 1*		35	13 wks
16 Jun 84	20 REGGAE CLASSICS *Trojan TRLS 222*		89	1 wk
21 Jul 84	ROCKABILLY PSYCHOS AND THE GARAGE DISEASE *Big Beat WIK 18*		88	3 wks
11 Aug 84	CHUNKS OF FUN *Loose End CHUNK 1*		46	5 wks
8 Sep 84	RECORD SHACK PRESENTS-VOLUME 1 *Record Shack RSTV 1*		41	4 wks
1 Dec 84	★ THE HITS ALBUM *CBS/WEA HITS 1*		1	36 wks
8 Dec 84	THE CHRISTMAS CAROL COLLECTION *Fame WHS 413000*		75	2 wks
16 Feb 85	STARGAZERS *Kasino KTV 1*		69	3 wks
30 Mar 85	REGGAE HITS VOLUME 1 *Jetstar JETLP 1001*		32	11 wks
30 Mar 85	DREAM MELODIES *Nouveau Music NML 1013*		91	1 wk
6 Apr 85	TOMMY BOY GREATEST BEATS *Tommy Boy ILPS 9825*		44	6 wks
13 Apr 85	★ THE HITS ALBUM 2 *CBS/WEA HITS 2*		1†	21 wks
4 May 85	EMERALD CLASSICS *Stoic SRTV*		87	1 wk
25 May 85	● OUT NOW! *Chrysalis/MCA OUTV 1*		2	16 wks
1 Jun 85	MASSIVE *Virgin V 2346*		61	3 wks
24 Aug 85	20 HOLIDAY HITS *Creole CTV 1*		48	6 wks
28 Sep 85	THE TV HITS ALBUM *Towerbell TVLP 3*		26	12 wks
19 Oct 85	IQ6:ZANG TUMB TUUM SAMPLED *ZTT IQ6*		40	3 wks
26 Oct 85	● OUT NOW! 2 *Chrysalis/MCA OUTV 2*		3	9 wks
26 Oct 85	REGGAE HITS VOLUME 2 *Jetstar JELP 1002*		86	2 wks
7 Dec 85	● THE HITS ALBUM 3 *CBS/WEA HITS 3*		2†	4 wks
21 Dec 85	THE CHRISTMAS CAROL COLLECTION *Fame WHS 41-3000-1*		90	1 wk

FILM SOUNDTRACKS

Date	Title	Label/Cat. No.	Pos	Weeks
8 Nov 58	★ SOUTH PACIFIC *RCA RB 16065*		1	286 wks
8 Nov 58	● THE KING AND I *Capitol LCT 6108*		4	103 wks
8 Nov 58	● OKLAHOMA *Capitol LCT 6100*		4	90 wks
6 Dec 58	● CAROUSEL *Capitol LCT 6105*		8	15 wks
31 Jan 59	● GIGI *MGM C 770*		2	88 wks
10 Oct 59	● PORGY AND BESS *Philips ABL 3282*		7	5 wks
23 Jan 60	● THE FIVE PENNIES *London HAU 2189*		2	15 wks
7 May 60	● CAN CAN *Capitol W 1301*		2	31 wks
28 May 60	● PAL JOEY *Capitol LCT 6148*		20	1 wk
23 Jul 60	HIGH SOCIETY *Capitol LCT 6116*		16	1 wk
5 Nov 60	BEN-HUR *MGM C 802*		15	3 wks
21 Jan 61	NEVER ON SUNDAY *London HAT 2309*		17	1 wk
18 Feb 61	● SONG WITHOUT END *Pye GGL 30169*		9	10 wks
29 Apr 61	● SEVEN BRIDES FOR SEVEN BROTHERS *MGM C 853*		6	22 wks
3 Jun 61	EXODUS *RCA RD 27210*		17	1 wk
11 Nov 61	GLENN MILLER STORY *Ace Of Hearts AH 12*		12	7 wks
24 Mar 62	★ WEST SIDE STORY *Philips BBL 7530*		1	175 wks
28 Apr 62	● IT'S TRAD DAD *Columbia 33SX 1412*		3	21 wks
22 Sep 62	THE MUSIC MAN *Warner Bros. WB 4066*		14	9 wks
3 Nov 62	PORGY AND BESS *CBS APG 60002*		14	7 wks
15 Jun 63	JUST FOR FUN *Decca LK 4524*		20	2 wks
31 Oct 64	● MY FAIR LADY *CBS BPG 72237*		9	51 wks
31 Oct 64	● GOLDFINGER *United Artists ULP 1076*		14	5 wks
16 Jan 65	● MARY POPPINS *HMV CLP 1794*		2	82 wks
10 Apr 65	★ SOUND OF MUSIC *RCA RB 6616*		1	381 wks
30 Apr 66	FUNNY GIRL *Capitol W 2059*		19	3 wks
11 Sep 66	● DR ZHIVAGO *MGM C 8007*		3	106 wks
22 Jul 67	CASINO ROYALE *RCA Victor SF 7874*		35	1 wk
29 Jul 67	A MAN AND A WOMAN *United Artists SULP 1155*		31	11 wks
28 Oct 67	● THOROUGHLY MODERN MILLIE *Brunswick STA 8685*		9	19 wks
9 Mar 68	● THE JUNGLE BOOK *Disney ST 3948*		5	51 wks
21 Sep 68	STAR *Stateside SSL 10233*		36	1 wk
12 Oct 68	● THE GOOD, THE BAD AND THE UGLY *United Artists SULP 1197*		2	18 wks
23 Nov 68	● OLIVER *RCA Victor SB 6777*		4	107 wks
23 Nov 68	CAMELOT *Warner Bros. WS 1712*		37	1 wk
8 Feb 69	● CHITTY CHITTY BANG BANG *United Artists SULP 1200*		10	4 wks
10 May 69	FUNNY GIRL *CBS 70044*		11	22 wks
14 Jun 69	● 2001 - A SPACE ODYSSEY *MGMCS 8078*		3	67 wks
20 Dec 69	● EASY RIDER *Stateside SSL 5018*		2	67 wks
24 Jan 70	JUNGLE BOOK (re-issue) *Disney BVS 4041*		25	26 wks
7 Feb 70	● PAINT YOUR WAGON *Paramount SPFL 257*		2	102 wks
14 Mar 70	HELLO DOLLY *Stateside SSL 10292*		45	2 wks
18 Jul 70	WOODSTOCK *Atlantic 2662 001*		35	19 wks
24 Apr 71	● LOVE STORY *Paramount SPFL 267*		10	33 wks
12 Feb 72	● CLOCKWORK ORANGE *Warner Bros. K 46127*		4	46 wks
8 Apr 72	FIDDLER ON THE ROOF *United Artists UAD 60011/2*		26	2 wks
13 May 72	2001 - A SPACE ODYSSEY (re-issue) *MGM 2315 034*		20	2 wks
29 Nov 72	SOUTH PACIFIC (re-issue) *RCA Victor SB 2011*		25	2 wks
31 Mar 73	CABARET *Probe SPB 1052*		13	22 wks
14 Apr 73	LOST HORIZON *Bell SYBEL 8000*		36	3 wks
22 Sep 73	JESUS CHRIST SUPERSTAR *MCA MDKS 8012/3*		23	18 wks
23 Mar 74	● THE STING *MCA MCF 2537*		7	35 wks
8 Jun 74	A TOUCH OF CLASS *Philips 6612 040*		32	1 wk
5 Oct 74	SUNSHINE *MCA MCF 2566*		47	3 wks
5 Apr 75	TOMMY *Polydor 2657 014*		21	9 wks
31 Jan 76	JAWS *MCA MCF 2716*		55	1 wk
5 Mar 77	MOSES *Pye 28503*		43	2 wks
9 Apr 77	★ A STAR IS BORN *CBS 86021*		1	54 wks
2 Jul 77	THE BEST OF CAR WASH *MCA MCF 2799*		59	1 wk
11 Mar 78	★ SATURDAY NIGHT FEVER *RSO 2658 123*		1	65 wks
22 Apr 78	● THE STUD *Ronco RTD 2029*		2	19 wks
29 Apr 78	CLOSE ENCOUNTERS OF THE THIRD KIND *Arista DLART 2001*		40	6 wks
6 May 78	THE LAST WALTZ *Warner Brothers K 66076*		39	4 wks
20 May 78	THANK GOD IT'S FRIDAY *Casablanca TGIF 100*		40	5 wks
27 May 78	FM *MCA MCSP 284*		37	7 wks
8 Jul 78	★ GREASE *RSO RSD 2001*		1	47 wks
12 Aug 78	SGT PEPPER'S LONELY HEARTS CLUB BAND *A & M AMLZ 66600*		38	2 wks
7 Oct 78	CONVOY *Capitol EST 24590*		52	1 wk
30 Jun 79	THE WORLD IS FULL OF MARRIED MEN *Ronco RTD 2038*		25	9 wks
14 Jul 79	THE WARRIORS *A & M AMLH 64761*		53	7 wks
6 Oct 79	QUADROPHENIA *Polydor 2625 037*		23	16 wks
5 Jan 80	THE SECRET POLICEMAN'S BALL *Island ILPS 9601*		33	6 wks
9 Feb 80	SUNBURN *Warwick RTL 2044*		45	7 wks
16 Feb 80	GOING STEADY *Warwick WW 5078*		25	10 wks
8 Mar 80	THE ROSE *Atlantic K 50681*		68	1 wk

7 Jun 80	THE GREAT ROCK 'N' ROLL SWINDLE		
	Virgin V 2168	16	11 wks
19 Jul 80	● XANADU *Jet JET LX 526*	2	17 wks
16 Aug 80	● CAN'T STOP THE MUSIC *Mercury 6399 051*	9	8 wks
14 Feb 81	● DANCE CRAZE *2-Tone CHRTT 5004*	5	15 wks
12 Dec 81	THE SECRET POLICEMAN'S OTHER BALL		
	Springtime HAHA 6003	69	4 wks
6 Sep 80	★ FAME *RSO 2479 253*	1	25 wks
20 Mar 82	THE SECRET POLICEMAN'S OTHER BALL		
	(THE MUSIC) *Springtime HA-HA 6004*	29	5 wks
17 Jul 82	THE SOUND OF MUSIC (re-issue)		
	RCA Ints 5134	98	1 wk
4 Sep 82	ROCKY III *Liberty LBG 30351*	42	7 wks
4 Sep 82	ANNIE *CBS 70219*	83	2 wks
11 Sep 82	BRIMSTONE AND TREACLE		
	A & M AMLH 64915	67	3 wks
12 Feb 83	AN OFFICER AND A GENTLEMAN		
	Island ISTA 3	40	14 wks
25 Jun 83	RETURN OF THE JEDI *RSO RSD 5023*	85	5 wks
2 Jul 83	● FLASHDANCE *Casablanca CANH 5*	9	30 wks
1 Oct 83	STAYING ALIVE *RSO RSBG 3*	14	8 wks
21 Apr 84	● FOOTLOOSE *CBS 70246*	7	25 wks
21 Apr 84	AGAINST ALL ODDS *Virgin V 2313*	29	10 wks
16 Jun 84	● BREAKDANCE *Polydor POLD 5147*	6	29 wks
7 Jul 84	BEAT STREET *Atlantic 780154*	30	13 wks
18 Aug 84	ELECTRIC DREAMS *Virgin V 2318*	46	7 wks
29 Sep 84	GHOSTBUSTERS *Arista 206 559*	24	25 wks
16 Feb 85	BEVERLY HILLS COP *MCA MCF 3253*	24	32 wks
22 Jun 85	A VIEW TO A KILL *Parlophone BOND 1*	81	1 wk

The West Side Story album on Phillips BBL 7530 during its chart run changed label and number to CBS BPG 62058.

STAGE CAST RECORDINGS

8 Nov 58	● MY FAIR LADY (BROADWAY)		
	Philips RBL 1000	2	129 wks
24 Jan 59	● WEST SIDE STORY (BROADWAY)		
	Philips BBL 7277	3	27 wks
26 Mar 60	● AT THE DROP OF A HAT (LONDON)		
	Parlophone PMC 1033	9	1 wk
26 Mar 60	● FINGS AIN'T WOT THEY USED TO BE		
	(LONDON) *Decca LK 4346*	5	11 wks
2 Apr 60	● FLOWER DRUM SONG (BROADWAY)		
	Philips ABL 3302	2	27 wks
7 May 60	● FOLLOW THAT GIRL (LONDON)		
	HMV CLP 1366	5	9 wks
21 May 60	● MOST HAPPY FELLA (BROADWAY)		
	Philips BBL 7374	6	13 wks
21 May 60	MAKE ME AN OFFER (LONDON)		
	HMV CLP 1333	18	1 wk
28 May 60	FLOWER DRUM SONG (LONDON)		
	HMV CLP 1359	10	3 wks
9 Jul 60	MOST HAPPY FELLA (LONDON)		
	HMV CLP 1365	19	1 wk
30 Jul 60	WEST SIDE STORY (BROADWAY)		
	Philips SBBL 504	14	1 wk
10 Sep 60	● OLIVER (LONDON) *Decca LK 4359*	4	91 wks
11 Mar 61	KING KONG (SOUTH AFRICA) *Decca LK 4392*	12	8 wks
6 May 61	● MUSIC MAN (LONDON) *HMV CLP 1444*	8	13 wks
24 Jun 61	● SOUND OF MUSIC (BROADWAY)		
	Philips ABL 3370	4	19 wks
22 Jul 61	BYE-BYE BIRDIE (LONDON) *Philips ABL 3385*	17	3 wks
22 Jul 61	BEYOND THE FRINGE (LONDON)		
	Parlophone PMC 1145	13	17 wks
29 Jul 61	● SOUND OF MUSIC (LONDON) *HMV CLP 1453*	4	68 wks
9 Sep 61	● STOP THE WORLD I WANT TO GET OFF		
	(LONDON) *Decca LK 4408*	8	14 wks
14 Jul 62	● BLITZ (LONDON) *HMV CLP 1569*	7	21 wks
18 May 63	HALF A SIXPENCE (LONDON) *Decca LK 4521*	20	2 wks
3 Aug 63	PICKWICK (LONDON) *Philips AL 3431*	12	10 wks
4 Jan 64	MY FAIR LADY (BROADWAY)		
	CBS BPG 68001	19	1 wk
22 Feb 64	AT THE DROP OF ANOTHER HAT (LONDON)		
	Parlophone PMC 1216	12	11 wks

3 Oct 64	● CAMELOT (BROADWAY) *CBS APG 60001*	10	12 wks
16 Jan 65	CAMELOT (LONDON) *HMV CLP 1756*	19	1 wk
11 Mar 67	● FIDDLER ON THE ROOF (LONDON)		
	CBS SBPG 70030	4	50 wks
28 Dec 68	● HAIR (LONDON) *Polydor 583-043*	3	94 wks
30 Aug 69	THE WORLD OF OLIVER (orig. london cast		
	album) (re-issue) *Decca SPA 30*	23	4 wks
6 Sep 69	HAIR (BROADWAY) *RCA SF 7959*	29	3 wks
19 Feb 72	● GODSPELL (LONDON) *Bell BELLS 203*	25	17 wks
18 Nov 78	● EVITA (LONDON) *MCA MCF 3257*	24	18 wks
1 Aug 81	● CATS (LONDON) *Polydor CATX 001*	6	26 wks
6 Nov 82	MACK AND MABEL (BROADWAY)		
	MCA MCL 1728	38	7 wks
7 Aug 84	STARLIGHT EXPRESS (LONDON) *Starlight/*		
	Polydor LNER 1	21	9 wks

STUDIO CAST RECORDINGS

25 Jun 60	SHOWBOAT *HMV CLP 1310*	12	1 wk
8 Feb 72	● JESUS CHRIST SUPERSTAR *MCA MKPS 2011/*		
	2	6	20 wks
22 Jan 77	● EVITA *MCA MCX 503*	4	35 wks
10 Nov 84	● CHESS *RCA PL 70500*	10	16 wks
18 May 85	WEST SIDE STORY *Deutsche Grammophon 41523-1*	11†	24 wks
2 Nov 85	CHESS PIECES *Telstar STAR 2274*	87	3 wks

TV and RADIO SOUNDTRACKS and SPIN-OFFS

13 Dec 58	● OH BOY! *Parlophone PMC 1072*	9	14 wks
4 Mar 61	● HUCKLEBERRY HOUND *Pye GGL 004*	10	12 wks
30 Feb 63	THAT WAS THE WEEK THAT WAS		
	Parlophone PMC 1197	11	9 wks
28 Mar 64	STARS FROM STARS AND GARTERS		
	Pye GGL 0252	17	2 wks
10 Apr 76	★ ROCK FOLLIES *Island ILPS 9362*	1	15 wks
8 Apr 78	● PENNIES FROM HEAVEN *World Records SH 266*	10	17 wks
1 Jul 78	MORE PENNIES FROM HEAVEN		
	World Records SH 267	31	4 wks
15 Dec 79	FAWLTY TOWERS *BBC REB 377*	25	10 wks
14 Feb 81	HITCHHIKERS GUIDE TO THE GALAXY VOL.2		
	Original ORA 54	47	4 wks
1 Aug 81	THE MUSIC OF COSMOS *RCA RCALP 5032*	43	10 wks
21 Nov 81	BRIDESHEAD REVISITED *Chrysalis CDL 1367*	50	12 wks
26 Nov 83	REILLY ACE OF THEMES *Red Bus BUSLP 1004*	54	6 wks
4 Feb 84	AUF WIEDERSEHEN PET *Towerbell AUF 1*	21	6 wks
18 Feb 84	THE TUBE *K-Tel NE 1261*	30	6 wks
8 Sep 84	SONG AND DANCE *RCA BL 70480*	46	4 wks
26 Oct 85	MIAMI VICE *BBC REMV 584*	11	7 wks
16 Nov 85	EASTENDERS SING-ALONG *BBC REB 586*	33†	7 wks

MISCELLANEOUS

12 Sep 70	EDINBURGH MILITARY TATTOO 1970		
	Waverley SZLP 2121	34	4 wks
18 Sep 71	EDINBURGH MILITARY TATTOO 1971		
	Waverley SZLP 2128	44	1 wk
11 Dec 71	ELECTRONIC ORGANS TODAY		
	Ad-Rhythm ADBS 1	48	1 wk
4 Nov 72	THE BBC 1922-1972 (TV AND RADIO		
	EXTRACTS) *BBC 50*	16	7 wks
8 Dec 73	● MUSIC FOR A ROYAL WEDDING		
	BBC REW 163	7	6 wks
27 Dec 75	STRINGS OF SCOTLAND *Philips 6382 108*	50	1 wk
8 Aug 81	★ THE ROYAL WEDDING *BBC REP 413*	1	11 wks
18 May 85	VICTORY IN EUROPE - BROADCASTS AND		
	REPORTS FROM BBC CORRESPONDENTS		
	BBC REC 562	61	1 wk

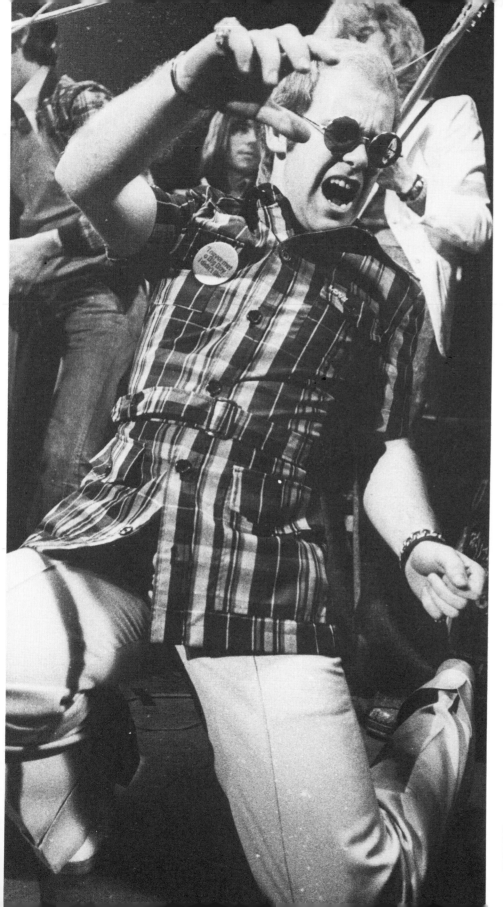

HIT ALBUMS

FACTS AND FEATS

MOST WEEKS ON CHART
in a year
in each chart year
in 1983, 1984 and 1985
by an album in total
least successful chart act

MOST HIT ALBUMS
most Top Ten hit albums

MOST ALBUMS ON CHART IN ONE WEEK

THE NUMBER ONE ALBUMS
from 8 November 1958 to
28 December 1985
most number one hit albums
most weeks at number one: by artist
most weeks at number one by
one album: consecutive
most weeks at number one by
one album: total
longest climb to number one
most hits without a number one

Elton John performing a rock 'n' roll medley
with friends at the launch of Rocket Records in
Moreton-on-Marsh, 1973. (LFI)

MOST WEEKS ON CHART

The following table lists all the recording acts that have spent 100 weeks or more on the British albums chart from the first chart on 8 November 1958 up to and including the chart of 28 December 1985. It is of course possible for an act to be credited with two or more chart weeks in the same week if the act has more than one album on the chart in any one week.

Weeks

BEATLES............................**1021**
SIMON AND GARFUNKEL..**1017**
(Paul Simon a further 114 weeks solo, Art Garfunkel a further 58 weeks solo)
ELVIS PRESLEY.....................**996**
DAVID BOWIE.......................**813**
PINK FLOYD **687**
ROLLING STONES...............**632**

CLIFF RICHARD....................**624**
DIRE STRAITS **599**
FRANK SINATRA.................**596**
(plus 23 weeks with Count Basie)
QUEEN **572**
ELTON JOHN **570**
BOB DYLAN.........................**536**
ROD STEWART **530**
(plus 56 weeks with The Faces)
BEACH BOYS **524**
ABBA **499**
MEAT LOAF **499**
FLEETWOOD MAC **484**
CARPENTERS.....................**470**
PAUL McCARTNEY/WINGS .**454**
(Wings 305 weeks, Paul McCartney 149 weeks)
MIKE OLDFIELD **449**
ANDY WILLIAMS **439**
NEIL DIAMOND **429**
LED ZEPPELIN.....................**411**
TOM JONES **392**
THE SOUND OF MUSIC
(Original Soundtrack) **382**

JIM REEVES **381**
U2 ....**375**
STATUS QUO......................**369**
SHADOWS...........................**366**
PHIL COLLINS **350**
MICHAEL JACKSON **349**
(plus a further 55 weeks with Jackson Five)
BARBRA STREISAND...........**338**
JAMES LAST **334**
DIANA ROSS **334**
(plus 45 weeks with Marvin Gaye)
ELECTRIC LIGHT
ORCHESTRA **333**
STEVIE WONDER **317**
BUDDY HOLLY **308**
HERB ALPERT **306**
DURAN DURAN.................**305**

The Beatles spent 79 out of 91 weeks at the top between May 1963 and February 1965

Deep Purple in 1972, the year that 'Machine Head' became their second consecutive chart topping album

Commiserations with Marillion, for whom the first week of 1986 was their 100th on the albums chart.

The Temptations have scored 99 weeks, plus a further 31 weeks with Diana Ross and the Supremes. The Jacksons have scored 79 weeks on the chart (32 as the Jackson Five and 47 as the Jacksons) as well as a further 55 weeks with Michael Jackson. John Mayall has scored 97 chart weeks, plus 17 more with Eric Clapton. Peter Sellers has clocked up 84 weeks, plus 18 with Sophia Loren, 10 with Anthony Newley and Joan Collins, and 1 more with Harry Secombe and Spike Milligan, a total of 113 weeks. The London Symphony Orchestra is also credited on various albums featuring different soloists and conductors.

MOST WEEKS ON CHART IN A YEAR

Simon and Garfunkel have scored 100 chart weeks in a year 5 times. The Beatles, David Bowie and Dire Straits have topped the century in three years, while Abba and U2 have done it twice.

MOST WEEKS ON CHART IN EACH CHART YEAR

Elvis Presley and David Bowie have each been the year's chart champions 3 times. No other act has been chart champion more than once.

MOST WEEKS ON CHART
1983

198	David Bowie
107	Dire Straits
105	Duran Duran
97	Michael Jackson (plus 26 more with Jackson Five)
87	U2
83	Kids from Fame
78	Phil Collins
76	Meat Loaf
69	Men At Work
66	Richard Clayderman

David Bowie's total of 198 weeks (in other words, the equivalent of four albums on the chart every week) established a new record for most chart weeks in one year. The previous record was set in 1973 – by David Bowie.

The Thin White Duke in Red Square (LFI)

MOST WEEKS ON CHART
1984

116	Dire Straits
107	Michael Jackson (plus 29 more with Jackson Five)
100	U2
97	Queen
87	Lionel Richie
69	Duran Duran
	Spandau Ballet
67	Eurythmics
	Barbra Streisand
66	Billy Joel
	Elton John

Phil Collins scored 65 weeks as a solo artist, and a further 35 with Genesis. Dire Straits matched the achievement of David Bowie in 1973 and 1974 by recording two consecutive years with more than 100 chart weeks.

Duran Duran accumulated over four years on chart with just their first two releases (Brian Avis)

MOST WEEKS ON CHART
1985

177	Bruce Springsteen
168	U2
158	Dire Straits
131	Phil Collins
86	Wham!
79	Queen
78	Paul Young
77	Madonna
73	Prince
72	Tears For Fears

1985 was the first year in which four different acts scored over 100 weeks since 1974. It was also the first year in which three acts scored over 150 weeks, the equivalent of at least 3 albums in the chart each week throughout the year. Dire Straits, by clocking up 100 weeks for the third straight year, equalled Simon and Garfunkel's record set in 1973, 74 and 75.

Michael Jackson's 'Thriller', the biggest selling album of all time, was one of five albums to stay on the chart for the whole of 1983

MOST WEEKS ON CHART BY AN ALBUM IN TOTAL

This is a list of all the albums that have spent a total of 100 weeks or more on the chart. Re-releases and re-issues are counted provided that the re-issue is identical to the original release.

Three albums by Simon and Garfunkel, Beatles and Dire Straits have each spent over 100 weeks on the chart. Two albums each by David Bowie, Phil Collins, Duran Duran, Electric Light Orchestra, Michael Jackson and U2 have also hit the three-figure mark.

'Bat Out Of Hell' enjoyed its 383rd week on chart on 8 February 1986.

LEAST SUCCESSFUL CHART ACT

Since 8 August 1981, when the chart was extended from a Top 75 to a Top 100, eight acts have achieved the minor distinction of a chart career consisting of only one week at number 100. These acts, in chronological order, are:

17 Oct 81	RONNIE LAWS	Solid Ground
17 Dec 83	SLEIGHRIDERS	A Very Merry Disco
11 Feb 84	EUROPEANS	Live
30 June 84	WENDY O. WILLIAMS	W.O.W.
29 Sept 84	QUEENSRHYCHE	The Warning
30 Mar 85	SECOND IMAGE	Strange Reflections
12 Oct 85	ALIEN SEX FIEND	Maximum Security
16 Nov 85	*BIG AUDIO DYNAMITE	This Is Big Audio Dynamite

There is also one compilation album which took the number 100 slot for just one week:

26 NOV 83   VARIOUS ARTISTS .... Twelve Inches Of Pleasure

*Re-entered the charts in early 1986.

MOST HIT ALBUMS

An album is a hit if it spends only one week at number 100. Double, treble and quadruple albums count as only one hit. Re-issues do not count as a new hit.

90   ELVIS PRESLEY
51   JAMES LAST
47   FRANK SINATRA (plus one with Count Basie)
42   CLIFF RICHARD
33   ROLLING STONES
29   BOB DYLAN
28   SHIRLEY BASSEY
26   JIM REEVES
25   BEACH BOYS
25   DAVID BOWIE
25   ELTON JOHN
25   DIANA ROSS (plus 2 with Marvin Gaye)
24   JOHNNY MATHIS (plus 1 with Natalie Cole and 1 with Deniece Williams)
24   ANDY WILLIAMS
23   BEATLES
22   NEIL DIAMOND
20   STATUS QUO
19   JETHRO TULL
19   SHADOWS
18   HAWKWIND
18   TOM JONES
18   SANTANA (Carlos Santana 3 more with various other partners)
18   WHO
17   DEEP PURPLE
17   JIMI HENDRIX (plus 1 with Curtis Knight)
16   JOHNNY CASH
16   PAUL McCARTNEY/ WINGS (9 Wings, 7 Paul McCartney)
16   ROD STEWART (plus 1 with The Faces)
16   MARC BOLAN/T. REX/ TYRANNOSAURUS REX
16   NEIL YOUNG (plus 1 with Stills-Young Band and 3 with Crosby, Stills, Nash and Young)
15   GARY NUMAN/ TUBEWAY ARMY
14   HERB ALPERT
14   BLACK SABBATH
14   CARPENTERS
14   ERIC CLAPTON
14   GENESIS
14   MIKE OLDFIELD
14   PINK FLOYD
14   SLADE
14   DON WILLIAMS
13   JOHN DENVER (plus 1 with Placido Domingo)
13   DAVID ESSEX
13   ROY ORBISON
13   QUEEN
13   TANGERINE DREAM
13   TEMPTATIONS (plus 3 with Diana Ross and the Supremes)
13   WISHBONE ASH
13   STEVIE WONDER
13   YES
12   ALICE COOPER
12   MANTOVANI
12   JOHN MAYALL
12   MOODY BLUES
12   ROXY MUSIC
12   BARBRA STREISAND
12   DONNA SUMMER
12   URIAH HEEP
11   ABBA
11   RAY CONNIFF
11   EVERLY BROTHERS (Phil Everly 1 more solo)

11 FLEETWOOD MAC
11 HOLLIES
11 BUDDY HOLLY
11 KISS
11 BARRY MANILOW
11 BOB MARLEY AND THE WAILERS
11 JONI MITCHELL
11 VAN MORRISON
11 LEO SAYER
11 10 C.C.
11 THIN LIZZY
11 FRANK ZAPPA
10 MAX BYGRAVES
10 BYRDS
10 ELVIS COSTELLO
10 VAL DOONICAN
10 RORY GALLAGHER
10 JACKSONS (4 as Jackson Five, 6 as Jacksons, plus 1 more with Michael Jackson)
10 BERT KAEMPFERT
10 KING CRIMSON
10 KINKS
10 LED ZEPPELIN
10 JOHN LENNON/PLASTIC ONO BAND
10 GEORGE MITCHELL MINSTRELS
10 RAINBOW
10 STRANGLERS
10 DIONNE WARWICK

Simon and Garfunkel have had 9 hit albums. Both Paul Simon and Art Garfunkel have had 6 more solo album hits.

MOST TOP TEN HIT ALBUMS

The rules for this category are the same as for Most Hit Albums, except that the album must have made the Top Ten for at least one week.

35 ELVIS PRESLEY
27 FRANK SINATRA (plus 1 with Count Basie)
26 CLIFF RICHARD
24 ROLLING STONES
23 BOB DYLAN
18 BEATLES

17 DAVID BOWIE
15 ELTON JOHN
15 STATUS QUO
14 PAUL McCARTNEY/WINGS (Wings 8, Paul McCartney 6)
13 BEACH BOYS
13 JIM REEVES
13 ROD STEWART (plus 1 with The Faces)
12 PINK FLOYD
12 QUEEN
12 WHO
11 GENESIS
11 TOM JONES
10 LED ZEPPELIN
10 ANDY WILLIAMS
9 BLACK SABBATH
9 ELVIS COSTELLO
9 ROXY MUSIC
9 SHADOWS
9 YES
8 ABBA
8 CREAM
8 DEEP PURPLE
8 JIMI HENDRIX
8 JOHNNY MATHIS (plus 1 with Natalie Cole)
8 MOODY BLUES
8 STEVIE WONDER
7 CARPENTERS
7 EMERSON, LAKE AND PALMER
7 BUDDY HOLLY
7 JOHN LENNON/PLASTIC ONO BAND
7 STRANGLERS
7 10 C.C.
7 THIN LIZZY
6 SHIRLEY BASSEY
6 BEE GEES
6 BLONDIE
6 MARC BOLAN/T. REX/ TYRANNOSAURUS REX
6 RUSS CONWAY
6 DIRE STRAITS
6 ELECTRIC LIGHT ORCHESTRA
6 FLEETWOOD MAC
6 HOLLIES
6 ENGELBERT HUMPERDINCK
6 JAM
6 JETHRO TULL
6 MADNESS

6 BARRY MANILOW
6 MANTOVANI
6 GEORGE MITCHELL MINSTRELS
6 GARY NUMAN/TUBEWAY ARMY
6 DIANA ROSS (plus 1 with Marvin Gaye)
6 RUSH
6 LEO SAYER
6 SIMON AND GARFUNKEL (Paul Simon 4 more solo, Art Garfunkel 2 more solo)
6 CAT STEVENS
6 ULTRAVOX
5 AC/DC
5 HERB ALPERT
5 KATE BUSH
5 JOHNNY CASH
5 JOHN DENVER
5 NEIL DIAMOND
5 VAL DOONICAN
5 EAGLES
5 DUANE EDDY
5 EVERLY BROTHERS
5 FREE
5 PETER GABRIEL
5 IRON MAIDEN
5 KINKS
5 BOB MARLEY AND THE WAILERS
5 MEAT LOAF
5 MIKE OLDFIELD
5 POLICE
5 RAINBOW
5 SANTANA (plus 1 more with Mahavishnu John McLaughlin)
5 SHOWADDYWADDY
5 SLADE
5 SUPREMES (plus 1 with Four Tops, and 1 with Diana Ross and Temptations)
5 UB40
5 WHITESNAKE

Bryan Ferry has scored four solo Top Ten hit albums and nine with Roxy Music. The only album act to have hit the chart ten times or more and to take every hit into the Top Ten is Led Zeppelin, who have scored ten Top Ten hits out of ten chart entries. James Last has hit the Top Ten only four times in 51 chart albums.

MOST ALBUMS ON CHART IN ONE WEEK

Only four artists in the history of the chart have charted seven albums in one week as follows:

14 albums in a chart of 60	Elvis Presley	10 Sep 1977
12 albums in a chart of 60	Elvis Presley	17 Sep 1977
11 albums in a chart of 60	Elvis Presley	1 Oct 1977
	Elvis Presley	8 Oct 1977
10 albums in a chart of 100	David Bowie	16 Jul 1983
9 albums in a chart of 60	Elvis Presley	24 Sep 1977
9 albums in a chart of 100	David Bowie	11 Jun 1983
	David Bowie	9 Jul 1983
8 albums in a chart of 20	Jim Reeves	26 Sep 1964
8 albums in a chart of 100	David Bowie	27 Aug 1983
7 albums in a chart of 20	Jim Reeves	29 Aug 1964
	Jim Reeves	5 Sep 1964
	Jim Reeves	3 Oct 1964
	Jim Reeves	10 Oct 1964
7 albums in a chart of 60	Elvis Presley	15 Oct 1977
7 albums in a chart of 100	David Bowie	14 May 1983
	David Bowie	21 May 1983
	David Bowie	28 May 1983
	David Bowie	4 Jun 1983
	David Bowie	18 June 1983
	David Bowie	30 Jul 1983
	David Bowie	20 Aug 1983
	Bruce Springsteen	15 Jun 1985
	(nine consecutive weeks) to	10 Aug 1985

Of all these instances, only Elvis Presley on 10 Sep 1977 and Bruce Springsteen for four weeks from 6 Jul 1985 held the top spot. The most complete chart domination was by Jim Reeves on 26 Sep 1964, when he accounted for 40% of the albums chart. Bruce Springsteen is the only example of an artist charting *all* his albums and getting as many as seven on the chart at once. Only Jim Reeves on 3 Oct 1964 and Elvis Presley on 10 Sep 1977 placed three albums in the Top Ten.

THE NUMBER ONE ALBUMS 8 NOV 1958
TO 28 DEC 1985

Weeks

8 Nov 58 SOUTH PACIFIC Film Soundtrack (RCA)..70

12 Mar 60 THE EXPLOSIVE FREDDY CANNON Freddy Cannon (Top Rank).. 1
19 Mar 60 SOUTH PACIFIC Film Soundtrack (RCA)..19
30 Jul 60 ELVIS IS BACK Elvis Presley (RCA)..... 1
6 Aug 60 SOUTH PACIFIC Film Soundtrack (RCA).. 5
10 Sep 60 DOWN DRURY LANE TO MEMORY LANE 101 Strings (Pye)...................... 5
15 Oct 60 SOUTH PACIFIC Film Soundtrack (RCA)..13

14 Jan 61 GI BLUES Elvis Presley (RCA)............ 7
4 Mar 61 SOUTH PACIFIC Film Soundtrack (RCA).. 1
11 Mar 61 GI BLUES Elvis Presley (RCA)............ 3
1 Apr 61 SOUTH PACIFIC Film Soundtrack (RCA).. 1
8 Apr 61 GI BLUES Elvis Presley (RCA)............12
1 Jul 61 SOUTH PACIFIC Film Soundtrack (RCA).. 4
29 Jul 61 BLACK AND WHITE MINSTREL SHOW George Mitchell Minstrels (HMV)4
26 Aug 61 SOUTH PACIFIC Film Soundtrack (RCA).. 1
2 Sep 61 BLACK AND WHITE MINSTREL SHOW George Mitchell Minstrels (HMV)1
9 Sep 61 SOUTH PACIFIC Film Soundtrack (RCA).. 1
16 Sep 61 BLACK AND WHITE MINSTREL SHOW George Mitchell Minstrels (HMV)1
23 Sep 61 THE SHADOWS Shadows (Columbia) .. 4
21 Oct 61 BLACK AND WHITE MINSTREL SHOW George Mitchell Minstrels (HMV)1
28 Oct 61 THE SHADOWS Shadows (Columbia) .. 1
4 Nov 61 21 TODAY Cliff Richard (Columbia)..... 1
11 Nov 61 ANOTHER BLACK AND WHITE MINSTREL SHOW George Mitchell Minstrels (HMV)................................ 8

6 Jan 62 BLUE HAWAII Elvis Presley (RCA)...... 1
13 Jan 62 THE YOUNG ONES Cliff Richard (Columbia).. 6
24 Feb 62 BLUE HAWAII Elvis Presley (RCA).....17
23 Jun 62 WEST SIDE STORY Film Soundtrack (Philips/CBS) 5

Weeks

28 Jul 62 POT LUCK Elvis Presley (RCA)........... 5
1 Sep 62 WEST SIDE STORY Film Soundtrack (CBS) 1
8 Sep 62 POT LUCK Elvis Presley (RCA)........... 1
15 Sep 62 WEST SIDE STORY Film Soundtrack (CBS) 1
22 Sep 62 THE BEST OF BALL, BARBER AND BILK Kenny Ball, Chris Barber and Acker Bilk (Pye)................................ 1
29 Sep 62 WEST SIDE STORY Film Soundtrack (CBS) 3
20 Oct 62 THE BEST OF BALL, BARBER AND BILK Kenny Ball, Chris Barber, Acker Bilk (Pye) 1
27 Oct 62 OUT OF THE SHADOWS Shadows (Columbia)... 3
17 Nov 62 WEST SIDE STORY Film Soundtrack (CBS) 1
24 Nov 62 OUT OF THE SHADOWS Shadows (Columbia)... 1
1 Dec 62 ON STAGE WITH THE BLACK AND WHITE MINSTRELS George Mitchell Minstrels (HMV).............................. 2
15 Dec 62 WEST SIDE STORY Film Soundtrack (CBS) 1
22 Dec 62 OUT OF THE SHADOWS Shadows (Columbia)... 1
29 Dec 62 BLACK AND WHITE MINSTREL SHOW George Mitchell Minstrels (HMV)2

12 Jan 63 WEST SIDE STORY Film Soundtrack (CBS) 1
19 Jan 63 OUT OF THE SHADOWS Shadows (Columbia)... 2
2 Feb 63 SUMMER HOLIDAY Cliff Richard and the Shadows (Columbia)...................14
11 May 63 PLEASE PLEASE ME Beatles (Parlophone)..30
7 Dec 63 WITH THE BEATLES Beatles (Parlophone)..21

2 May 64 ROLLING STONES Rolling Stones (Decca)..12
25 Jul 64 A HARD DAY'S NIGHT Beatles (Parlophone)..21
19 Dec 64 BEATLES FOR SALE Beatles (Parlophone).. 7

6 Feb 65 ROLLING STONES No. 2 Rolling Stones (Decca).. 3

27 Feb 65 BEATLES FOR SALE Beatles (Parlophone).................... 1

6 Mar 65 ROLLING STONES No. 2 Rolling Stones (Decca)...................... 6

17 Apr 65 FREEWHEELIN' BOB DYLAN Bob Dylan (CBS).................... 1

24 Apr 65 ROLLING STONES No. 2 Rolling Stones (Decca)...................... 1

1 May 65 BEATLES FOR SALE Beatles (Parlophone).................... 3

22 May 65 FREEWHEELIN' BOB DYLAN Bob Dylan (CBS).................... 1

29 May 65 BRINGING IT ALL BACK HOME Bob Dylan (CBS).................... 1

5 Jun 65 SOUND OF MUSIC Soundtrack (RCA)10

14 Aug 65 HELP Beatles (Parlophone).................... 9

16 Oct 65 SOUND OF MUSIC Soundtrack (RCA)10

25 Dec 65 RUBBER SOUL Beatles (Parlophone).... 9

19 Feb 66 SOUND OF MUSIC Soundtrack (RCA)10

30 Apr 66 AFTERMATH Rolling Stones (Decca).... 8

25 Jun 66 SOUND OF MUSIC Soundtrack (RCA) 7

13 Aug 66 REVOLVER Beatles (Parlophone) 7

1 Oct 66 SOUND OF MUSIC Soundtrack (RCA)18

4 Feb 67 MONKEES Monkees (RCA)................. 7

25 Mar 67 SOUND OF MUSIC Soundtrack (RCA) 7

13 May 67 MORE OF THE MONKEES Monkees (RCA)..................................... 1

20 May 67 SOUND OF MUSIC Soundtrack (RCA) 1

27 May 67 MORE OF THE MONKEES Monkees (RCA)..................................... 1

3 Jun 67 SOUND OF MUSIC Soundtrack (RCA) 1

10 Jun 67 SERGEANT PEPPER'S LONELY HEARTS CLUB BAND Beatles (Parlophone)............................23

18 Nov 67 SOUND OF MUSIC Soundtrack (RCA) 1

25 Nov 67 SERGEANT PEPPER'S LONELY HEARTS CLUB BAND Beatles (Parlophone)..................................... 1

2 Dec 67 SOUND OF MUSIC Soundtrack (RCA) 3

23 Dec 67 SERGEANT PEPPER'S LONELY HEARTS CLUB BAND Beatles (Parlophone)..................................... 2

6 Jan 68 VAL DOONICAN ROCKS BUT GENTLY Val Doonican (Pye)............... 3

27 Jan 68 SOUND OF MUSIC Soundtrack (RCA) 1

3 Feb 68 SERGEANT PEPPER'S LONELY HEARTS CLUB BAND Beatles (Parlophone)..................................... 1

10 Feb 68 GREATEST HITS Four Tops (Tamla Motown)..................................... 1

17 Feb 68 GREATEST HITS Diana Ross and the Supremes (Tamla Motown) 3

9 Mar 68 JOHN WESLEY HARDING Bob Dylan (CBS) 10

18 May 68 SCOTT 2 Scott Walker (Philips)............ 1

25 May 68 JOHN WESLEY HARDING Bob Dylan (CBS) 3

15 Jun 68 LOVE ANDY Andy Williams (CBS) 1

22 Jun 68 DOCK OF THE BAY Otis Redding (Stax) 1

29 Jun 68 OGDEN'S NUT GONE FLAKE Small Faces (Immediate) 6

10 Aug 68 DELILAH Tom Jones (Decca)............... 1

17 Aug 68 BOOKENDS Simon and Garfunkel (CBS) 5

21 Sep 68 DELILAH Tom Jones (Decca)............... 1

28 Sep 68 BOOKENDS Simon and Garfunkel (CBS) 2

12 Oct 68 GREATEST HITS Hollies (Parlophone).. 6

23 Nov 68 SOUND OF MUSIC Soundtrack (RCA) 1

30 Nov 68 GREATEST HITS Hollies (Parlophone).. 1

7 Dec 68 THE BEATLES Beatles (Apple) 7

25 Jan 69 BEST OF THE SEEKERS Seekers (Columbia)..................................... 1

1 Feb 69 THE BEATLES Beatles (Apple) 1

8 Feb 69 BEST OF THE SEEKERS Seekers (Columbia)..................................... 1

15 Feb 69 DIANA ROSS AND THE SUPREMES JOIN THE TEMPTATIONS Diana Ross/Supremes/Temptations (Tamla Motown) 4

15 Mar 69 GOODBYE Cream (Polydor)............... 2

29 Mar 69 BEST OF THE SEEKERS Seekers (Columbia)..................................... 2

12 Apr 69 GOODBYE Cream (Polydor)............... 1

19 Apr 69 BEST OF THE SEEKERS Seekers (Columbia)..................................... 1

26 Apr 69 GOODBYE Cream (Polydor)............... 1

3 May 69 BEST OF THE SEEKERS Seekers (Columbia)..................................... 1

10 May 69 ON THE THRESHOLD OF A DREAM Moody Blues (Deram) 2

24 May 69 NASHVILLE SKYLINE Bob Dylan (CBS) 4

21 Jun 69 HIS ORCHESTRA, HIS CHORUS, HIS SINGERS, HIS SOUND Ray Conniff (CBS) 3

12 Jul 69 ACCORDING TO MY HEART Jim Reeves (RCA International)................. 4

9 Aug 69 STAND UP Jethro Tull (Island) 3

30 Aug 69 FROM ELVIS IN MEMPHIS Elvis Presley (RCA)..................................... 1

6 Sep 69 STAND UP Jethro Tull (Island) 2

20 Sep 69 BLIND FAITH Blind Faith (Polydor) 2

4 Oct 69 ABBEY ROAD Beatles (Apple) 11

20 Dec 69 LET IT BLEED Rolling Stones (Decca)... 1
27 Dec 69 ABBEY ROAD Beatles (Apple) 6

7 Feb 70 LED ZEPPELIN 2 Led Zeppelin (Atlantic) 1
14 Feb 70 MOTOWN CHARTBUSTERS VOL. 3
Various (Tamla Motown) 1
21 Feb 70 BRIDGE OVER TROUBLED WATER
Simon and Garfunkel (CBS) 13
23 May 70 LET IT BE Beatles (Parlophone) 3
13 Jun 70 BRIDGE OVER TROUBLED WATER
Simon and Garfunkel (CBS) 4
11 Jul 70 SELF PORTRAIT Bob Dylan (CBS) 1
18 Jul 70 BRIDGE OVER TROUBLED WATER
Simon and Garfunkel (CBS) 5
22 Aug 70 QUESTION OF BALANCE Moody Blues
(Threshold) 3
12 Sep 70 COSMO'S FACTORY Creedence
Clearwater Revival (Liberty) 1
19 Sep 70 GET YOUR YA YAS OUT Rolling Stones
(Decca) 2
3 Oct 70 BRIDGE OVER TROUBLED WATER
Simon and Garfunkel (CBS) 1
10 Oct 70 PARANOID Black Sabbath (Vertigo) 1
17 Oct 70 BRIDGE OVER TROUBLED WATER
Simon and Garfunkel (CBS) 1
24 Oct 70 ATOM HEART MOTHER Pink Floyd
(Harvest) 1
31 Oct 70 MOTOWN CHARTBUSTERS VOL. 4
Various (Tamla Motown) 1
7 Nov 70 LED ZEPPELIN 3 Led Zeppelin (Atlantic) 3
28 Nov 70 NEW MORNING Bob Dylan (CBS) 1
5 Dec 70 GREATEST HITS Andy Williams (CBS) 1
12 Dec 70 LED ZEPPELIN 3 Led Zeppelin (Atlantic) 1
19 Dec 70 GREATEST HITS Andy Williams
(CBS) 4

16 Jan 71★ BRIDGE OVER TROUBLED WATER
Simon and Garfunkel (CBS) 11
3 Apr 71 HOME LOVING MAN Andy Williams
(CBS) 2
17 Apr 71 MOTOWN CHARTBUSTERS VOL. 5
Various (Tamla Motown) 3
8 May 71 STICKY FINGERS Rolling Stones
(Rolling Stones) 4
5 Jun 71 RAM Paul and Linda McCartney (Apple) 2
19 Jun 71 STICKY FINGERS Rolling Stones
(Rolling Stones) 1
26 Jun 71 TARKUS Emerson, Lake and Palmer
(Island) 1
3 Jul 71 BRIDGE OVER TROUBLED WATER
Simon and Garfunkel (CBS) 5

*This includes 8 weeks at number one when charts were not
published due to a postal strike.

7 Aug 71 HOT HITS 6 Various (MFP) 1
14 Aug 71 EVERY GOOD BOY DESERVES
FAVOUR Moody Blues (Threshold) 1
21 Aug 71 TOP OF THE POPS VOL. 18 Various
(Hallmark) 3
11 Sep 71 BRIDGE OVER TROUBLED WATER
Simon and Garfunkel (CBS) 1
18 Sep 71 WHO'S NEXT Who (Track) 1
25 Sep 71 FIREBALL Deep Purple (Harvest) 1
2 Oct 71 EVERY PICTURE TELLS A STORY
Rod Stewart (Mercury) 4
30 Oct 71 IMAGINE John Lennon/Plastic Ono Band
(Apple) 2
13 Nov 71 EVERY PICTURE TELLS A STORY
Rod Stewart (Mercury) 2
27 Nov 71 TOP OF THE POPS VOL. 20 Various
(Hallmark) 1
4 Dec 71 FOUR SYMBOLS Led Zeppelin
(Atlantic) 2
18 Dec 71 ELECTRIC WARRIOR T. Rex (Fly) 6

29 Jan 72 CONCERT FOR BANGLADESH
Various (Apple) 1
5 Feb 72 ELECTRIC WARRIOR T. Rex (Fly) 2
19 Feb 72 NEIL REID Neil Reid (Decca) 3
11 Mar 72 HARVEST Neil Young (Reprise) 1
18 Mar 72 PAUL SIMON Paul Simon (CBS) 1
25 Mar 72 FOG ON THE TYNE Lindisfarne
(Charisma) 4
22 Apr 72 MACHINE HEAD Deep Purple (Purple) 2
6 May 72 PROPHETS, SEERS AND SAGES
AND THE ANGELS OF THE
AGES/MY PEOPLE WERE FAIR AND
HAD SKY IN THEIR HAIR . . . BUT
NOW THEY'RE CONTENT TO
WEAR STARS ON THEIR BROWS
Tyrannosaurus Rex (Fly Double Back) 1
13 May 72 MACHINE HEAD Deep Purple (Purple) 1
20 May 72 BOLAN BOOGIE T. Rex (Fly) 3
10 Jun 72 EXILE ON MAIN STREET Rolling
Stones (Rolling Stones) 1
17 Jun 72 20 DYNAMIC HITS Various (K-Tel) 8
12 Aug 72 20 FANTASTIC HITS Various (Arcade) . 5
16 Sep 72 NEVER A DULL MOMENT
Rod Stewart (Philips) 2
30 Sep 72 20 FANTASTIC HITS Various (Arcade) . 1
7 Oct 72 20 ALLTIME HITS OF THE FIFTIES
Various (K-Tel) 8
2 Dec 72 25 ROCKIN' AND ROLLIN' GREATS
Various (K-Tel) 3
23 Dec 72 20 ALLTIME HITS OF THE FIFTIES
Various (K-Tel) 3

13 Jan 73 SLAYED Slade (Polydor) 1

20 Jan 73 BACK TO FRONT Gilbert O'Sullivan (MAM) 1

27 Jan 73 SLAYED Slade (Polydor) 2

10 Feb 73 DON'T SHOOT ME, I'M ONLY THE PIANO PLAYER Elton John (DJM) 6

24 Mar 73 BILLION DOLLAR BABIES Alice Cooper (Warner Bros.) 1

31 Mar 73 20 FLASHBACK GREAT HITS OF THE SIXTIES Various (K-Tel) 2

14 Apr 73 HOUSES OF THE HOLY Led Zeppelin (Atlantic) 2

28 Apr 73 OOH LA LA Faces (Warner Bros.) 1

5 May 73 ALADDIN SANE David Bowie (RCA Victor) 5

9 Jun 73 PURE GOLD Various (EMI) 3

30 Jun 73 THAT'LL BE THE DAY Various (Ronco) 7

18 Aug 73 WE CAN MAKE IT Peters and Lee (Philips) 2

1 Sep 73 SING IT AGAIN Rod Stewart (Mercury) 3

22 Sep 73 GOAT'S HEAD SOUP Rolling Stones (Rolling Stones) 2

6 Oct 73 SLADEST Slade (Polydor) 3

27 Oct 73 HELLO Status Quo (Vertigo) 1

3 Nov 73 PIN UPS David Bowie (RCA) 5

8 Dec 73 STRANDED Roxy Music (Island) 1

15 Dec 73 DREAMS ARE NOTHIN' MORE THAN WISHES David Cassidy (Bell) 1

22 Dec 73 GOODBYE YELLOW BRICK ROAD Elton John (DJM) 2

5 Jan 74 TALES FROM TOPOGRAPHIC OCEAN Yes (Atlantic) 2

19 Jan 74 SLADEST Slade (Polydor) 1

26 Jan 74 AND I LOVE YOU SO Perry Como (RCA) 1

2 Feb 74 THE SINGLES 1969–73 Carpenters (A&M) 4

2 Mar 74 OLD, NEW, BORROWED AND BLUE Slade (Polydor) 1

9 Mar 74 THE SINGLES 1969–73 Carpenters (A&M) 11

25 May 74 JOURNEY TO THE CENTRE OF THE EARTH Rick Wakeman (A&M) 1

1 Jun 74 THE SINGLES 1969–73 Carpenters (A&M) 1

8 Jun 74 DIAMOND DOGS David Bowie (RCA) 4

6 Jul 74 THE SINGLES 1969–73 Carpenters (A&M) 1

13 Jul 74 CARIBOU Elton John (DJM) 2

27 Jul 74 BAND ON THE RUN Wings (Apple) ... 7

14 Sep 74 HERGEST RIDGE Mike Oldfield (Virgin) 3

5 Oct 74 TUBULAR BELLS Mike Oldfield (Virgin) 1

12 Oct 74 ROLLIN' Bay City Rollers (Bell) 1

19 Oct 74 SMILER Rod Stewart (Mercury) 1

26 Oct 74 ROLLIN' Bay City Rollers (Bell) 1

2 Nov 74 SMILER Rod Stewart (Mercury) 1

9 Nov 74 ROLLIN' Bay City Rollers (Bell) 2

23 Nov 74 ELTON JOHN'S GREATEST HITS Elton John (DJM) 11

8 Feb 75 HIS GREATEST HITS Engelbert Humperdinck (Decca) 3

1 Mar 75 ON THE LEVEL Status Quo (Vertigo) .. 2

15 Mar 75 PHYSICAL GRAFFITI Led Zeppelin (Swansong) 1

22 Mar 75 20 GREATEST HITS Tom Jones (Decca) 4

19 Apr 75 THE BEST OF THE STYLISTICS Stylistics (Avco) 2

3 May 75 ONCE UPON A STAR Bay City Rollers (Bell) 3

24 May 75 THE BEST OF THE STYLISTICS Stylistics (Avco) 5

28 Jun 75 VENUS AND MARS Wings (Apple) 1

5 Jul 75 HORIZON Carpenters (A&M) 2

19 Jul 75 VENUS AND MARS Wings (Apple) 1

26 Jul 75 HORIZON Carpenters (A&M) 3

16 Aug 75 THE BEST OF THE STYLISTICS Stylistics (Avco) 2

30 Aug 75 ATLANTIC CROSSING Rod Stewart (Warner Bros.) 5

4 Oct 75 WISH YOU WERE HERE Pink Floyd (Harvest) 1

11 Oct 75 ATLANTIC CROSSING Rod Stewart (Warner Bros.) 2

25 Oct 75 40 GOLDEN GREATS Jim Reeves (Arcade) 3

15 Nov 75 WE ALL HAD DOCTORS' PAPERS Max Boyce (EMI) 1

22 Nov 75 40 GREATEST HITS Perry Como (K-Tel) 5

27 Dec 75 A NIGHT AT THE OPERA Queen (EMI) 2

10 Jan 76 40 GREATEST HITS Perry Como (K-Tel) 1

17 Jan 76 A NIGHT AT THE OPERA Queen (EMI) 2

31 Jan 76 THE BEST OF ROY ORBISON Roy Orbison (Arcade) 1

7 Feb 76 THE VERY BEST OF SLIM WHITMAN Slim Whitman (United Artists) 6

20 Mar 76 BLUE FOR YOU Status Quo (Vertigo) .. 3

10 Apr 76 ROCK FOLLIES TV Soundtrack (Island) 2

24 Apr 76 PRESENCE Led Zeppelin (Swansong).... 1
1 May 76 ROCK FOLLIES TV Soundtrack (Island) 1
8 May 76 GREATEST HITS Abba (Epic) 9
10 Jul 76 A NIGHT ON THE TOWN
Rod Stewart (Riva) 2
24 Jul 76 20 GOLDEN GREATS Beach Boys
(Capitol)............................... 10
2 Oct 76 BEST OF THE STYLISTICS VOL. 2
Stylistics (H&L).......................... 1
9 Oct 76 STUPIDITY Dr Feelgood (United Artists) 1
16 Oct 76 GREATEST HITS Abba (Epic) 2
30 Oct 76 SOUL MOTION Various (K-Tel) 2
13 Nov 76 THE SONG REMAINS THE SAME Led
Zeppelin (Swansong) 1
20 Nov 76 22 GOLDEN GUITAR GREATS Bert
Weedon (Warwick) 1
27 Nov 76 20 GOLDEN GREATS Glen Campbell
(Capitol)............................... 6

8 Jan 77 DAY AT THE RACES Queen (EMI)..... 1
15 Jan 77 ARRIVAL Abba (Epic)................... 1
22 Jan 77 RED RIVER VALLEY Slim Whitman
(United Artists) 4
19 Feb 77 20 GOLDEN GREATS Shadows (EMI).. 6
2 Apr 77 PORTRAIT Frank Sinatra (Reprise) 2
16 Apr 77 ARRIVAL Abba (Epic)................... 9
18 Jun 77 LIVE AT THE HOLLYWOOD BOWL
Beatles (Parlophone)..................... 1
25 Jun 77 THE MUPPET SHOW Muppets (Pye)... 1
2 Jul 77 A STAR IS BORN Soundtrack (CBS) 2
16 Jul 77 JOHNNY MATHIS COLLECTION
Johnny Mathis (CBS) 4
13 Aug 77 GOING FOR THE ONE Yes (Atlantic).. 2
27 Aug 77 20 ALL TIME GREATS Connie Francis
(Polydor) 2
10 Sep 77 ELVIS PRESLEY'S 40 GREATEST
HITS Elvis Presley (Arcade)............. 1
17 Sep 77 20 GOLDEN GREATS Diana Ross and
the Sumpremes (Tamla Motown).......... 7
5 Nov 77 40 GOLDEN GREATS Cliff Richard
(EMI) 1
12 Nov 77 NEVER MIND THE BOLLOCKS
HERE'S THE SEX PISTOLS Sex Pistols
(Virgin) 2
26 Nov 77 SOUND OF BREAD Bread (Elektra) 2
10 Dec 77 DISCO FEVER Various (K-Tel)........... 6

21 Jan 78 THE SOUND OF BREAD Bread
(Elektra) 1
28 Jan 78 RUMOURS Fleetwood Mac
(Warner Bros.) 1
4 Feb 78 THE ALBUM Abba (Epic) 7
25 Mar 78 20 GOLDEN GREATS Buddy
Holly/Crickets (MCA).................... 3

15 Apr 78 20 GOLDEN GREATS Nat King Cole
(Capitol)............................... 3
6 May 78 SATURDAY NIGHT FEVER Various
(RSO) 18
9 Sep 78 NIGHT FLIGHT TO VENUS Boney M
(Atlantic/Hansa) 4
7 Oct 78 GREASE Soundtrack (RSO) 13

6 Jan 79 GREATEST HITS Showaddywaddy
(Arista) 2
26 Jan 79 DON'T WALK–BOOGIE Various
(EMI) 3
10 Feb 79 ACTION REPLAY Various (K-Tel) 1
17 Feb 79 PARALLEL LINES Blondie (Chrysalis) .. 4
17 Mar 79 SPIRITS HAVING FLOWN Bee Gees
(RSO) 2
31 Mar 79 GREATEST HITS VOL. 2
Barbra Streisand (CBS) 4
28 Apr 79 THE VERY BEST OF LEO SAYER
Leo Sayer (Chrysalis) 3
19 May 79 VOULEZ–VOUS Abba (Epic) 4
16 Jun 79 DISCOVERY Electric Light Orchestra
(Jet) 5
21 Jul 79 REPLICAS Tubeway Army (Beggars
Banquet) 1
28 Jul 79 THE BEST DISCO ALBUM IN THE
WORLD Various (Warner Bros.).......... 6
8 Sep 79 IN THROUGH THE OUT DOOR
Led Zeppelin (Swansong) 2
22 Sep 79 THE PLEASURE PRINCIPLE Gary
Numan (Beggars Banquet)................ 1
29 Sep 79 OCEANS OF FANTASY Boney M
(Atlantic/Hansa) 1
6 Oct 79 THE PLEASURE PRINCIPLE Gary
Numan (Beggars Banquet)................ 1
13 Oct 79* EAT TO THE BEAT Blondie (Chrysalis) 1
13 Oct 79* REGGATTA DE BLANC Police (A&M) 4
10 Nov 79 TUSK Fleetwood Mac (Warner Bros.) 1
17 Nov 79 GREATEST HITS VOL 2 Abba (Epic) ... 3
8 Dec 79 GREATEST HITS Rod Stewart (Riva) ... 5

12 Jan 80 GREATEST HITS VOL. 2 Abba (Epic) .. 1
19 Jan 80 PRETENDERS Pretenders (Real) 4
16 Feb 80 THE LAST DANCE Various (Motown) . 2
1 Mar 80 STRING OF HITS Shadows (EMI)........ 3
22 Mar 80 TEARS AND LAUGHTER
Johnny Mathis (CBS) 2
5 Apr 80 DUKE Genesis (Charisma) 2
19 Apr 80 GREATEST HITS Rose Royce
(Whitfield)............................. 2
3 May 80 SKY 2 Sky (Ariola) 2

*Two charts published this week because of a change in chart
collation.

173

17 May 80 THE MAGIC OF BONEY M Boney M
(Atlantic/Hansa) 2

31 May 80 McCARTNEY II Paul McCartney
(Parlophone) 2

14 Jun 80 PETER GABRIEL Peter Gabriel
(Charisma) 2

28 Jun 80 FLESH AND BLOOD Roxy Music
(Polydor) 1

5 Jul 80 EMOTIONAL RESCUE Rolling Stones
(Rolling Stones).............................. 2

19 Jul 80 THE GAME Queen (EMI) 2

2 Aug 80 DEEPEST PURPLE Deep Purple
(Harvest) 1

9 Aug 80 BACK IN BLACK AC/DC (Atlantic) 2

23 Aug 80 FLESH AND BLOOD Roxy Music
(Polydor) 3

13 Sep 80 TELEKON Gary Numan
(Beggars Banquet) 1

20 Sep 80 NEVER FOR EVER Kate Bush (EMI) ... 1

27 Sep 80 SCAREY MONSTERS AND
SUPERCREEPS David Bowie (RCA) 2

11 Oct 80 ZENYATTA MONDATTA Police
(A&M)....................................... 4

8 Nov 80 GUILTY Barbra Streisand (CBS)........... 2

22 Nov 80 SUPER TROUPER Abba (Epic) 9

24 Jan 81 KINGS OF THE WILD FRONTIER
Adam and the Ants (CBS) 2

7 Feb 81 DOUBLE FANTASY John Lennon
(Geffen)..................................... 2

21 Feb 81 FACE VALUE Phil Collins (Virgin)....... 3

14 Mar 81 KINGS OF THE WILD FRONTIER
Adam and the Ants (CBS) 10

23 May 81 STARS ON 45 Starsound (CBS)........... 5

27 Jun 81 NO SLEEP TIL HAMMERSMITH
Motorhead (Bronze) 1

4 Jul 81 DISCO DAZE & DISCO NITES Various
(Ronco) 1

11 Jul 81 LOVE SONGS Cliff Richard (EMI) 5

15 Aug 81 THE OFFICIAL BBC ALBUM OF THE
ROYAL WEDDING Soundtrack (BBC) . 2

29 Aug 81 TIME Electric Light Orchestra (Jet)........ 2

12 Sep 81 DEAD RINGER Meat Loaf (Epic) 2

26 Sep 81 ABACAB Genesis (Charisma)............... 2

10 Oct 81 GHOST IN THE MACHINE Police
(A&M)....................................... 3

31 Oct 81 DARE Human League (Virgin) 1

7 Nov 81 SHAKY Shakin' Stevens (Epic) 1

14 Nov 81 GREATEST HITS Queen (EMI) 4

12 Dec 81 CHART HITS '81 Various (K-Tel) 1

19 Dec 81 THE VISITORS Abba (Epic)................ 3

9 Jan 82 DARE Human League (Virgin) 3

30 Jan 82 LOVE SONGS Barbra Streisand (CBS) .. 7

20 Mar 82 THE GIFT Jam (Polydor).................... 1

27 Mar 82 LOVE SONGS Barbra Streisand (CBS) .. 2

10 Apr 82 THE NUMBER OF THE BEAST Iron
Maiden (EMI) 2

24 Apr 82 1982 Status Quo (Vertigo) 1

1 May 82 TUG OF WAR Paul McCartney
(Parlophone) 2

22 May 82 COMPLETE MADNESS Madness (Stiff) 2

5 Jun 82 AVALON Roxy Music (Polydor) 1

12 Jun 82 COMPLETE MADNESS Madness (Stiff) 1

19 Jun 82 AVALON Roxy Music (Polydor) 2

3 Jul 82 THE LEXICON OF LOVE ABC
(Neutron) 3

24 Jul 82 =THE LEXICON OF LOVE ABC
(Neutron) 1
=FAME Original Soundtrack (RSO) 1

31 Jul 82 FAME Original Soundtrack (RSO)......... 1

7 Aug 82 KIDS FROM FAME Kids from Fame
(BBC).. 8

2 Oct 82 LOVE OVER GOLD Dire Straits
(Vertigo) 4

30 Oct 82 KIDS FROM FAME Kids from Fame
(BBC).. 4

27 Nov 82 THE SINGLES, THE FIRST TEN
YEARS Abba (Epic).......................... 1

4 Dec 82 THE JOHN LENNON COLLECTION
John Lennon (Parlophone) 6

15 Jan 83 RAIDERS OF THE POP CHARTS
Various Artists (Ronco)...................... 2

29 Jan 83 BUSINESS AS USUAL Men At Work
(Epic).. 5

5 Mar 83 THRILLER Michael Jackson (Epic) 1

12 Mar 83 WAR U2 (Island) 1

19 Mar 83 THRILLER Michael Jackson (Epic) 1

26 Mar 83 THE HURTING Tears For Fears
(Mercury) 1

2 Apr 83 THE FINAL CUT Pink Floyd (Harvest) . 2

16 Apr 83 FASTER THAN THE SPEED OF
NIGHT Bonnie Tyler (CBS)................. 1

23 Apr 83 LET'S DANCE David Bowie (EMI
America)..................................... 3

14 May 83 TRUE Spandau Ballet (Reformation)...... 1

21 May 83 THRILLER Michael Jackson (Epic) 5

25 Jun 83 SYNCHRONICITY Police (A&M) 2

9 Jul 83 FANTASTIC! Wham! (InnerVision)....... 2

23 Jul 83 YOU AND ME BOTH Yazoo (Mute) ... 2

6 Aug 83 THE VERY BEST OF THE BEACH
BOYS Beach Boys (Capitol) 2

20 Aug 83 18 GREATEST HITS Michael Jackson
plus the Jackson Five (Telstar) 3

10 Sep 83 THE VERY BEST OF THE BEACH
BOYS Beach Boys (Capitol) 1

17 Sep 83 NO PARLEZ Paul Young (CBS)........... 1

24 Sep 83 LABOUR OF LOVE UB 40 (DEP International) 1

1 Oct 83 NO PARLEZ Paul Young (CBS).......... 2

15 Oct 83 GENESIS Genesis (Charisma/Virgin) 1

22 Oct 83 COLOUR BY NUMBERS Culture Club (Virgin)..................... 3

12 Nov 83 CAN'T SLOW DOWN Lionel Richie (Motown) 1

19 Nov 83 COLOUR BY NUMBERS Culture Club (Virgin)..................... 2

3 Dec 83 SEVEN AND THE RAGGED TIGER Duran Duran (EMI) 1

10 Dec 83 NO PARLEZ Paul Young (CBS).......... 1

17 Dec 83 NOW THAT'S WHAT I CALL MUSIC Various Artists (EMI/Virgin) 4

14 Jan 84 NO PARLEZ Paul Young (CBS).......... 1

21 Jan 84 NOW THAT'S WHAT I CALL MUSIC Various Artists (EMI/Virgin) 1

28 Jan 84 THRILLER Michael Jackson (Epic) 1

4 Feb 84 TOUCH Eurythmics (RCA) 2

18 Feb 84 SPARKLE IN THE RAIN Simple Minds (Virgin)..................... 1

25 Feb 84 INTO THE GAP Thompson Twins (Arista)..................... 3

17 Mar 84 HUMAN'S LIB Howard Jones (WEA) ... 2

31 Mar 84 CAN'T SLOW DOWN Lionel Richie (Motown) 2

14 Apr 84 NOW THAT'S WHAT I CALL MUSIC 2 Various Artists (EMI/Virgin) 5

19 May 84 LEGEND Bob Marley and the Wailers (Island) 12

11 Aug 84 NOW THAT'S WHAT I CALL MUSIC 3 Various Artists (EMI/Virgin) 8

6 Oct 84 TONIGHT David Bowie (EMI America) 1

13 Oct 84 THE UNFORGETTABLE FIRE U2 (Island) 2

27 Oct 84 STEELTOWN Big Country (Mercury)... 1

3 Nov 84 GIVE MY REGARDS TO BROAD STREET Paul McCartney (Parlophone)... 1

10 Nov 84 WELCOME TO THE PLEASURE DOME Frankie Goes To Hollywood (ZTT) 1

17 Nov 84 MAKE IT BIG Wham! (Epic) 2

1 Dec 84 THE HITS ALBUM/THE HITS TAPE Various Artists (CBS/WEA) 7

19 Jan 85 ALF Alison Moyet (CBS).................... 1

26 Jan 85 AGENT PROVOCATEUR Foreigner (Atlantic) 3

16 Feb 85 BORN IN THE U.S.A. Bruce Springsteen (CBS) 1

23 Feb 85 MEAT IS MURDER Smiths (Rough Trade) 1

2 Mar 85 NO JACKET REQUIRED Phil Collins (Virgin) 5

6 Apr 85 THE SECRET OF ASSOCIATION Paul Young (CBS) 1

13 Apr 85 THE HITS ALBUM 2/THE HITS TAPE 2 Various Artists (CBS/WEA)............... 6

25 May 85 BROTHERS IN ARMS Dire Straits (Vertigo)..................... 2

8 Jun 85 OUR FAVOURITE SHOP Style Council (Polydor)..................... 1

15 Jun 85 BOYS AND GIRLS Bryan Ferry (EG).... 2

29 Jun 85 MISPLACED CHILDHOOD Marillion (EMI)..................... 1

6 Jul 85 BORN IN THE U.S.A. Bruce Springsteen (CBS)..................... 4

3 Aug 85 BROTHERS IN ARMS Dire Straits (Vertigo)..................... 2

17 Aug 85 NOW THAT'S WHAT I CALL MUSIC 5 Various Artists (EMI/Virgin) 5

21 Sep 85 LIKE A VIRGIN Madonna (Sire).......... 1

28 Sep 85 HOUNDS OF LOVE Kate Bush (EMI).. 2

12 Oct 85 LIKE A VIRGIN Madonna (Sire).......... 1

19 Oct 85 HOUNDS OF LOVE Kate Bush (EMI).. 1

26 Oct 85 THE LOVE SONGS George Benson (K-Tel)..................... 1

2 Nov 85 ONCE UPON A TIME Simple Minds (Virgin) 1

9 Nov 85 THE LOVE SONGS George Benson (K-Tel)..................... 1

16 Nov 85 PROMISE Sade (Epic)..................... 2

30 Nov 85 THE GREATEST HITS OF 1985 Various Artists (Telstar) 1

7 Dec 85 NOW THAT'S WHAT I CALL MUSIC 6 Various Artists (EMI/Virgin) 2

21 Dec 85 NOW – THE CHRISTMAS ALBUM Various Artists (EMI/Virgin) ....2+

There have been 309 chart-topping albums since November 1958, each album staying at the summit for an average stay of 4.6 weeks. In exactly the same period, there have been 487 chart-topping singles, with an average length of stay at number one of only 2.9 weeks each.

Of the 309 number one albums, 42 have been Greatest Hits albums, and 31 have been compilation albums. The first Greatest Hits collection to hit the top was 'The Four Tops Greatest Hits' on 10 Feb 1968, and since then Greatest Hits albums have spent 191 weeks at the head of the lists, about one week in five. Abba have had three Greatest Hits LPs at the top of the chart, while the Beach Boys,

Diana Ross and the Supremes and the Stylistics have each had two number one 'Best Of . . .' albums.

The first compilation album to top the charts was 'Motown Chartbusters Vol. 3' on 14 Feb 1970, giving Tamla Motown the credit for pioneering both Greatest Hits packages and compilation albums in Britain. Since then, a further 30 compilation albums have totalled 121 weeks at the very top. The most successful compilation album in chart terms has been '20 All Time Hits Of The Fifties' which stayed at number one for a total of 11 weeks at the end of 1972.

In twenty years of releases, every studio album made the top three. This early photo of the Rolling Stones shows (left to right) Charlie Watts, Keith Richard, Mick Jagger, Brian Jones and Bill Wyman (LFI)

MOST NUMBER ONE HIT ALBUMS

12	Beatles
9	Rolling Stones
8	Abba
8	Led Zeppelin
7	Rod Stewart
6	David Bowie
6	Bob Dylan
6	Elvis Presley
6	Paul McCartney/Wings
5	Cliff Richard
4	Elton John
4	Police
4	Queen
4	Shadows
4	Status Quo
3	Boney M
3	Deep Purple
3	Genesis
3	John Lennon
3	George Mitchell Minstrels
3	Moody Blues
3	Gary Numan/Tubeway Army
3	Pink Floyd
3	Roxy Music
3	Slade
3	Barbra Streisand
3	T. Rex
3	Andy Williams

Simon and Garfunkel have scored two number one hit albums, and Paul Simon one more solo. Diana Ross and the Supremes have two number ones, and one more with the Temptations. Phil Collins has hit the top twice, as well as the three times with Genesis listed above. Bryan Ferry has one solo number one album to go with the three as lead singer of Roxy Music.

MOST WEEKS AT NUMBER ONE

163	Beatles
115	Cast of 'South Pacific' (Film Soundtrack)
70	Cast of 'The Sound of Music' (Film Soundtrack)
49	Abba
49	Elvis Presley
48	Simon and Garfunkel
43	Rolling Stones
27	Cliff Richard
27	Rod Stewart
22	Carpenters
22	Bob Dylan
21	Elton John
21	Shadows
20	David Bowie
19	George Mitchell Minstrels
18	Cast of 'Saturday Night Fever' (Film Soundtrack)
16	Paul McCartney/Wings

15	Barbra Streisand
14	Led Zeppelin
13	Beach Boys
13	Police
13	Cast of 'Grease' (Film Soundtrack)
13	Cast of 'West Side Story' (Film Soundtrack)
12	Adam and the Ants
12	Kids From Fame
12	Bob Marley and the Wailers
12	T. Rex
11	Queen
10	John Lennon
10	Diana Ross and the Supremes
10	Stylistics
10	Slim Whitman

This list excludes appearances on compilation albums.

MOST CONSECUTIVE WEEKS AT NUMBER ONE BY ONE ALBUM

70	SOUTH PACIFIC Film Soundtrack .... from 8 Nov 58
30	PLEASE PLEASE ME Beatles....from 11 May 63
23	SERGEANT PEPPER'S LONELY HEARTS CLUB BAND Beatles .... from 10 Jun 67
21	WITH THE BEATLES Beatles .... from 7 Dec 63
21	A HARD DAY'S NIGHT Beatles . from 25 Jul 64
19	SOUTH PACIFIC Film Soundtrack .... from 19 Mar 60
18	THE SOUND OF MUSIC Film Soundtrack .... from 1 Oct 66
18	SATURDAY NIGHT FEVER Film Soundtrack .... from 6 May 78
17	BLUE HAWAII Elvis Presley ..... from 24 Feb 62
14	SUMMER HOLIDAY Cliff Richard and the Shadows.............................. from 2 Feb 63
13	SOUTH PACIFIC Film Soundtrack ....from 15 Oct 60
13	BRIDGE OVER TROUBLED WATER Simon and Garfunkel................ from 21 Feb 70
13	GREASE Film Soundtrack.......... from 7 Oct 78
12	GI BLUES Elvis Presley............. from 8 Apr 61
12	ROLLING STONES Rolling Stones......................... from 2 May 64
12	LEGEND Bob Marley and the Wailers......................from 19 May 84
11	ABBEY ROAD Beatles............ from 4 Oct 69
11	BRIDGE OVER TROUBLED WATER Simon and Garfunkel................ from 16 Jan 71★
11	THE SINGLES 1969–73 Carpenters ....from 9 Mar 74
11	ELTON JOHN'S GREATEST HITS Elton John.......................from 23 Nov 74
10	THE SOUND OF MUSIC Film Soundtrack ....from 5 Jun 65
10	THE SOUND OF MUSIC Film Soundtrack ....from 16 Oct 65
10	THE SOUND OF MUSIC Film Soundtrack .... from 19 Feb 66
10	JOHN WESLEY HARDING Bob Dylan ....from 9 Mar 68
10	20 GOLDEN GREATS Beach Boys .... from 24 Jul 76
10	KINGS OF THE WILD FRONTIER Adam and the Ants .... from 14 Mar 81

★Includes 8 weeks at no. 1 when charts were not published because of a postal strike.

Total Weeks at Number One by One Album

115	SOUTH PACIFIC	Film Soundtrack
70	THE SOUND OF MUSIC	Film Soundtrack
41	BRIDGE OVER TROUBLED WATER	Simon and Garfunkel
30	PLEASE PLEASE ME	Beatles
27	SERGEANT PEPPER'S LONELY HEARTS CLUB BAND	Beatles
22	GI BLUES	Elvis Presley (Film Soundtrack)
21	WITH THE BEATLES	Beatles
21	A HARD DAY'S NIGHT	Beatles (Film Soundtrack)
18	BLUE HAWAII	Elvis Presley (Film Soundtrack)
18	SATURDAY NIGHT FEVER	Film Soundtrack
17	ABBEY ROAD	Beatles
17	THE SINGLES 1969–73	Carpenters
14	SUMMER HOLIDAY	Cliff Richard and the Shadows (Film Soundtrack)
13	WEST SIDE STORY	Film Soundtrack
13	JOHN WESLEY HARDING	Bob Dylan
13	GREASE	Film Soundtrack
12	THE ROLLING STONES	Rolling Stones
12	KINGS OF THE WILD FRONTIER	Adam and the Ants
12	THE KIDS FROM FAME	The Kids From Fame
12	LEGEND	Bob Marley and the Wailers
11	BEATLES FOR SALE	Beatles
11	20 ALL TIME HITS OF THE FIFTIES	Various Artists
11	ELTON JOHN'S GREATEST HITS	Elton John
11	GREATEST HITS	Abba
10	ROLLING STONES No. 2	Rolling Stones
10	20 GOLDEN GREATS	Beach Boys
10	ARRIVAL	Abba

Longest Climb to Number One

3 years 298 days *My People Were Fair And Had Sky In Their Hair, But Now They're Content To Wear Stars On Their Brows*
Tyrannosaurus Rex: from 13 Jul 68 to 6 May 72

2 years 67 days *40 Greatest Hits*
Elvis Presley: from 5 Jul 75 to 10 Sep 77

1 year 321 days *Fame*
Original Soundtrack: from 6 Sep 80 to 24 Jul 82

1 year 83 days *Tubular Bells*
Mike Oldfield: from 14 Jul 73 to 5 Oct 74

Eight other albums have taken 30 weeks or more to reach the top spot, as follows:
Rumours by Fleetwood Mac **49 weeks**
The Freewheelin' Bob Dylan **48 weeks**
Like A Virgin by Madonna **44 weeks**
Black and White Minstrel Show by the George Mitchell Minstrels **36 weeks**
Born In The U.S.A. by Bruce Springsteen **36 weeks**
Andy Williams' Greatest Hits **35 weeks**
Band On The Run by Wings **33 weeks**
And I Love You So by Perry Como **30 weeks**

Tyrannosaurus Rex hit number one with the longest titled album ever to hit the top only after it was re-released in 1972 as a double album with 'Prophets, Seers, Sages and the Angels Of The Ages'. Presley's album hit the top in the period immediately following his death. 'Tubular Bells' spent 11 weeks at number two before climbing to the very top, and 'Rumours' had spent 32 weeks in the Top Ten before hitting the number one slot. 'The Freewheelin' Bob Dylan' climbed to the top in its seventh chart run.

TYRANNOSAURUS REX

Most Hits Without a Number One Hit

51	JAMES LAST (who has had one number 2 hit)
28	SHIRLEY BASSEY (who has had one number 2 hit)
25	DIANA ROSS (who has had two number 2 hits)
22	NEIL DIAMOND (who has had one number 2 hit)
18	HAWKWIND (whose only Top Ten album reached number 9)
17	JIMI HENDRIX (who has had two number 2 hits)
16	JOHNNY CASH (who has had one number 2 hit)
15	SANTANA (who have had two number 6 hits)

Year by Year Review
1958 — 1985

1958 The American inventor Peter Goldmark was inspired to devise the long playing record while listening to classical music at a party. He realised he was always annoyed having to get up and change several 78s just to hear a complete piece. He thought there had to be a market for a single disc that could contain an entire symphony or sonata.

The eighteen albums that hit the chart in the last 8 weeks of 1958, the first weeks of *Melody Maker*'s Top Ten chart, demonstrated that Goldmarks's invention had other applications. None of the eighteen best-sellers was a classical orchestral performance! Thirteen were by adult male performers with wide audience appeal and five were of show business origin – that is, stage, screen or television.

The soundtrack to *South Pacific* was number one for each of the 8 weeks, a prelude to its equally total domination of the 1959 lists. The man with the most LPs to chart was Frank Sinatra, who touched the Top Ten four times. Elvis Presley had the most total weeks on chart, that is to say a sum of the runs of each of his hit LPs. Both 'Elvis Golden Records' and 'King Creole' were on every one of the eight charts.

The other artists who contributed to the all-male domain were Perry Como, Russ Conway, Mario Lanza, the American satirist Tom Lehrer, and Johnny Mathis. Perhaps Lanza was the closest to what Peter Goldmark had in mind: one side of his disc was the soundtrack to the film about the classical tenor Enrico Caruso, *The Great Caruso*.

1959 It can be whispered in reverent awe or shouted from the rooftops, but the achievement is so great it can not be conveyed in casual conversation: the original soundtrack to the film *South Pacific* was at number one for the entire year 1959. It led the list for every one of the 52 weeks, a feat which has never been matched. 'Here In My Heart' by Al Martino was on top of the singles scene for every chart in 1952, but the important qualification here is that there were no tables until 14 November.

'South Pacific' truly stands alone as the statistical star of the LP charts, though later discs would surpass it in sales. This family favourite boasted a wide range of memorable music, from the love ballad 'Some Enchanted Evening' (an American number one for Perry Como) to the novelty tune 'Happy Talk' (eventually a UK number one for Captain Sensible).

Film soundtracks were still the leading money-spinners in the LP market of 1959. The form was only a decade old, and soundtracks, Broadway cast performances and classical works were the most logical initial uses of Peter Goldmark's invention, requiring the additional space a long player could provide. The movie versions of *Gigi* and *The King and I* were notable winners in 1959, as was the New York stage production of *West Side Story*.

Rock-and-roll vocalists, previously content with singles, made further inroads into the album field, but Frank Sinatra still scored the most weeks on chart for a solo singer. Elvis Presley was a close second, registering an impressive success with 'Elvis' Golden Records'. The chart appearance of two LPs by Cliff Richard was the best 1959 showing by a young Briton.

'Curtain Up!', a compilation of stars from the London Palladium hosted by Bruce Forsyth, enjoyed a 13-week run, but the most impressive performance by a show business star was that of Peter Sellers, who spent 32 weeks in the Top Ten with two solo LPs and a further 5 with his colleagues the Goons.

1960 'South Pacific' dominated the album charts one more time in 1960, though not to the extent it had in 1959. It was in the best-sellers for every one of the 53 charts of the year, the only title to achieve that run, but it did occasionally let other discs take the top spot. Number one on the very first *Record Retailer* album chart, that of 10 March, was 'The Explosive Freddy Cannon', which fell in fragments the following week after giving Cannon the distinction of being the first rock-and-roll singer to have a number one LP. The second, Elvis Presley, may be a more predictable choice, but even he only managed 1 week at the summit, scoring with 'Elvis Is Back'. The other disc to interrupt South Pacific's streak was 'Down Drury Lane To Memory Lane', a nostalgic effort by the studio group 101 Strings.

Rock-and-roll made great progress in the long playing market in 1960. The previous year only four rockers had charted in the entire 12 months. This time five of the top six acts were rock stars, though the majority of chart artists were still not of this nature. Presley pipped Peter Sellers as the individual with most weeks on the chart, though Sellers would have ranked above Presley if the computation included his additional appearances with the Goons and Sophia Loren, not, one must add, on the same disc.

American guitarist Duane Eddy's surprisingly strong showing in fourth place should not be overlooked. The Shadows would be the only other rock instrumentalists to do well in a year-end tally.

1961 Commercial success does not guarantee artistic immortality, as the George Mitchell Minstrels have proved. Their *Black and White Minstrel Show* was an enormous success on television, record and stage, but an entire generation has grown up in, shall we say, the dark, about their achievements.

'The Black and White Minstrel Show' was the only album to stay in the chart for the whole of 1961. It accumulated 7 weeks at number one in four separate visits, while 'Another Black and White Minstrel Show' had a single mighty 8-week run at the top. Mass audiences loved the old-time performances of The Minstrels, many of whom blacked up to sing vintage popular songs. It was the dated nature of their material, as well as increased sophistication concerning racial matters, which spelled an end to large scale interest in the group in the late sixties.

Elvis Presley was the outstanding album artist for the second consecutive year, enjoying 22 weeks at number one with the soundtrack to 'GI Blues'. The granddaddy of film favourites, 'South Pacific', put in a final 9 weeks at the peak before retiring. It was a bumper year for original cast recordings of stage musicals, with a strong emphasis on the London stage.

'Oliver', 'Sound of Music' and 'Stop the World I Want to Get Off' all had lengthy runs with British rosters. 1961 saw hit honours for the well-remembered 'Beyond the Fringe' and the completely forgotten 'King Kong'. Even the London cast of 'Bye Bye Birdie' flew out of the wings and into the charts.

Frank Sinatra continued his series of fine years, entering the Top Twenty with seven titles on four different labels. Cliff Richard had three new top two successes and one happy hangover from 1960, 'Me and My Shadows'. '21 Today' was his first number one, though his mates beat him to the top by 6 weeks with their debut disc 'The Shadows'.

1962

Elvis Presley and the George Mitchell Minstrels overachieved again in 1962. The King of rock-and-roll notched up 18 weeks at number one with his 'Blue Hawaii' soundtrack, more time at the top than any other long player that year, and he ruled the roost for 6 more weeks with 'Pot Luck'. The Minstrels led the list with their new release, 'On Stage With the George Mitchell Minstrels', and then encored with their 1960 issue, the original 'Black and White Minstrel Show'. Their three albums tallied a total of 109 weeks in the chart, the first time any act had hit the century.

Compared to these two artists the rest of the field failed to flame, though 'South Pacific' again managed to appear in every one of the fifty-two charts. The new film sensation was 'West Side Story', surpassing its significant stage sales to pace the pack for 12 weeks. Four unusual multi-media successes were the soundtrack to 'It's Trad Dad', the original cast albums of the London production *Blitz*, and two Dorothy Provine sets inspired by her television series *The Roaring 20s*. Further evidence of the taste for trad was the appearance of a budget album at number one for 2 weeks, 'The Best of Kenny Ball, Chris Barber and Acker Bilk'. Barber and Bilk had appeared together on two fast-selling packages in 1961.

The Shadows achieved the fabulous feat of nabbing their second number one with their second effort, 'Out of the Shadows'. They shared credit on Cliff Richard's table-topping 'The Young Ones'. Cliff managed to top the Shads in weeks on chart thanks to his subsequent release, the literally timed and titled '32 Minutes and 17 Seconds'.

1963

Beatlemania spread like a flash fire in 1963, and the album chart showed its effects. The Fab Four's 'Please Please Me' seized the top spot on 11 May and held it for 30 consecutive weeks, to be replaced only by 'With the Beatles', which kept clear for a further 21. The Liverpudlians had come from nowhere to hold the premier position for 1 week shy of a full year. It was nothing short of a musical revolution: from their arrival until 1968, only one non-rock album would have a look at number one. A field that had been the domain of the soundtrack and cast album overnight became ruled by rock. It was hard to believe that 1963 had begun with 'The Black and White Minstrel Show' still in the lead.

With a couple of notable exceptions, the film and stage market dried up overnight. It is not surprising that they died in tandem, since the movie tracks were invariably Broadway shows adapted to the cinema. When the Great White Way stopped producing many memorable musicals, album sales dwindled

accordingly. 'West Side Story' was a survivor in 1963, charting through the entire year.

Cliff Richard was the weeks on chart champ this time, his total fed by three new successes. No one could have predicted that the second highest figures would be achieved equally by Elvis Presley and Buddy Holly. The Pelvis began twitching in anxiety as the soundtracks to three bad films did progressively worse. Holly, dead for four years, had always been a strong album seller, but really surged in 1963 when the poignantly-titled collection 'Reminiscing' joined the list of his other posthumous best-sellers.

Frank Ifield proved a one-year though not a one-hit wonder, reaching number three with two releases. He never came close again. Frank Sinatra rebounded with three top tenners, including a team-up with Count Basie that went to number two.

1964

The Beatles and Rolling Stones monopolized the number one position during 1964, making it the purest year for rock music in terms of holding the star spot. The only 12 weeks John, Paul, George and Ringo were not ahead with either 'With the Beatles', 'A Hard Day's Night' or 'Beatles For Sale', their chief competition was in front with the debut disc 'The Rolling Stones'. The fresh triumphs of 'A Hard Day's Night' and 'Beatles For Sale' gave the Beatles four number ones in four releases, a 100 per cent success ratio they maintained through all of their eleven official outings, though two other issues, a compilation and the 'Yellow Submarine' soundtrack on which they played only a part, fell short of the top. No other act has hit number one every time with as many records.

The Fab Four's quartet of hit LPs gave them 104 weeks on chart, the second time a century had been achieved. But even they were outdistanced in this regard by Jim Reeves. The American country singer had enjoyed two big albums to accompany his two strong singles in the first half of the year. After he died in a plane crash in July, nine further packages made the chart, six in a 4-week period. Gentleman Jim accumulated 115 weeks on chart in all, a record that would stand until 1968.

Third in the weeks on chart category was Roy Orbison, who enjoyed the distinction of seeing his 'In Dreams' set on every chart of the year, a feat attained for the second consecutive year by 'West Side Story'. Cliff Richard had only one new album, below average for his early years, and Elvis Presley definitely slipped as none of his three long players reached the top three.

1965

For the three middle years of the sixties only the Beatles, Rolling Stones, Bob Dylan and 'The Sound of Music' reached number one, trading off in a seemingly endless sequence. The first three were the rock artists who came to represent the spirit of the decade, while the last was a show business phenomenon that came, saw, conquered, and wouldn't go away.

The Beatles began the year on top with 'Beatles For Sale' and ended it there with 'Rubber Soul', having spent much of the summer there as well with 'Help'. Bob Dylan had the second highest total of chart-toppers, two, succeeding 'The Freewheelin' Bob Dylan' with his own 'Bringing It All Back Home', but his most impressive statistic was his 112 weeks on chart. Much of his back catalogue charted in late 1964 and 1965. Though primarily considered an album artist, he also logged five top thirty singles in 1965, his peak year.

Dylan's dear friend Joan Baez shared his success, with three charters to follow her 1964 debut. Infuriatingly for chartists, her winners confusingly included not just 'Joan Baez' but 'Joan Baez No. 5' and 'Farewell Angelina'. She taught Chicago all they knew about titles.

Though Miss Baez was the front-running credited female vocalist, Julie Andrews accounted for the greatest grosses with her soundtracks. 'Mary Poppins' spent the most weeks on chart of any 1965 title, 50, and 'The Sound of Music' began a run to rival that of 'South Pacific', accumulating its first 20 weeks at number one.

Sir Winston Churchill had a posthumous Top Ten LP, 'The Voice of Sir Winston Churchill'.

1966 Cash register tills came alive to 'The Sound of Music' in 1966. If the Beatles or Rolling Stones didn't have a new album, the star soundtrack of the sixties kept the number one position warm. It followed 'Rubber Soul' and preceded 'Aftermath'; it moved back in the aftermath of 'Aftermath' and before 'Revolver'. When the latter Beatles album had shot its shot, Julie Andrews and company skipped back to the top for the last 3 months of the year.

'The Sound of Music' was the only album to spend all of 1966 in the best sellers. It was as big an international phenomenon as a UK success. *Time* reported that it had sold seven million copies by Christmas, outmoving all other stage or screen sets, even the legendary 'South Pacific'.

The musical version of the Von Trapp family story was a timely purchase in any season, not linked to fad or fashion. The Beatles' unprecedented popularity, on the other hand, had made every one of their new discs an immediate must purchase. A short period of colossal concentrated sale would now be followed by a chart decline. Hence 'Revolver', a summer number one, was almost gone by Christmas. Parlophone, wanting a Beatles product for the major marketing month of the year, issued 'A Collection of Beatles Oldies' in December. However the fans weren't fooled. It peaked at seven, a commercial miscalculation.

The Beach Boys spent more weeks on the chart than anyone in 1966, with five long players accumulating 95 weeks between them. This success reflected their four consecutive top three singles. One album, the classic 'Pet Sounds', did better in Britain than America, reaching number two.

The other album artist of note was Herb Alpert, who garnered 89 weeks, but while his Tijuana Brass LPs loitered on the list they did not reach the highest chart positions.

1967 History remembers 1967 as the year of flower power and psychedelia. The only real evidence of this in the upper echelons of the LP charts was the tremendous success of the Beatles' landmark 'Sergeant Pepper's Lonely Hearts Club Band' and the considerable achievement of 'Are You Experienced?' by the Jimi Hendrix Experience.

'Sergeant Pepper', chosen the best rock album of all-time in two international critics' polls, spent exactly half the year at number one. The other 26 weeks were divided between the recurrent 'The Sound of Music' and the first time sets by the distinctly unpsychedelic Monkees. In a year when they had six hit singles and a cult television show, the 'fabricated four' reached the top with both 'The Monkees' and 'More of the Monkees'.

With only those four albums going all the way in 1967, it was a major achievement to get to number two. Hendrix and band did. Cream did respectably but not quite as well, earning Top Ten placings with their first two cartons of 'Fresh Cream' and 'Disraeli Gears'. The Rolling Stones surprisingly peaked at three with 'Between The Buttons'.

It was a fine year for easy listening and soul. In addition to 'Best Of The Beach Boys', records that rode the roster for all 52 weeks included the soundtracks of *The Sound of Music* and *Dr Zhivago* and 'Going Places' by Herb Alpert and the Tijuana Brass. Alpert paced the pack with 101 weeks on chart, though the Beach Boys were a close second with 97. Tom Jones had three Top Ten issues and the Dubliners, Irish singers enjoying a year of British popularity, had two.

1967 was the best year on record for Geno Washington, an outstanding live soul attraction. Otis Redding and the Four Tops also had strong chart performances, but they would do even better in 1968.

1968 The album chart lost its sense of discipline in 1968. In previous years the number of different artists who had reached number one, not counting performers on film soundtracks, could be counted on the fingers of one hand. This time no fewer than a dozen different acts went all the way, with occasional further appearances by 'The Sound of Music'.

The nature of the chart-toppers changed, too. Recently the number one spot had been the property of the world's outstanding rock talents. In 1968 Val Doonican, Tom Jones and Andy Williams managed to head the hordes. The Small Faces and Scott Walker enjoyed their only number one LPs, and Simon and Garfunkel tallied their first. The Four Tops, Otis Redding, and Diana Ross and the Supremes broke the all-white stranglehold on the top spot. The only black faces to have been there before were the made up ones of the George Mitchell Minstrels. Sadly, Redding's number one was achieved posthumously. Four albums charted after his death, two studio sets, a compilation, and a live LP.

For the fifth time in six seasons, the Fab Four had the Christmas number one, this year with the double disc 'The Beatles', often referred to as 'The White Album'. The Rolling Stones could reach no higher than three for the second straight year. Bob Dylan, on the other had, had a marvellous comeback from his motorcycle mishap, spending 13 weeks at number one with 'John Wesley Harding'.

Tom Jones had 135 weeks on the chart, the highest total yet achieved in any calendar year. Otis Redding also broke the previous high, set by another aeroplane casualty, Jim Reeves, by tallying 121 weeks. In the How Great Thou Were department, Elvis Presley only had 1 week on the chart in 1968, as did the George Mitchell Minstrels. The Mothers of Invention did better than both of them put together.

1969 For the third time the Beatles began and ended a year with different albums at number one. Their double LP 'The Beatles' ushered 1969 in and 'Abbey Road' showed it out. The 11 straight weeks the latter disc spent on top just before Christmas was the longest consecutive stint by any record since 'Sergeant Pepper'. 'Abbey Road's return to the summit the last week of the year marked the fifth occasion in 1969 when a former number one encored at that position. This statistic demonstrates the instability of the chart during these 12 months.

Familiar faces pacing the pack including Bob Dylan, who successfully flirted with country music in 'Nashville Skyline', the Rolling Stones, who managed a week out front with 'Let It Bleed', and Elvis Presley, who scored a glorious comeback with 'From Elvis In Memphis'. Other rock luminaries who led the list included Cream, whose farewell set 'Goodbye' had three separate appearances at number one, the Moody Blues, who scored the first of their three toppers, and Jethro Tull, making their only standout stint with 'Stand Up'.

But one cannot overlook the achievement of the easy listening mogul Ray Conniff, who spent 3 weeks ahead of the herd without the benefit of a hit single. Jim Reeves astonished all by registering the only number one of his career 5 years after his death. It should be noted, however, that his 'According to My Heart' was a budget album.

'Best of the Seekers' bested all competition on five separate occasions. The Australians had the most weeks on chart with a fairly feeble total of 66, three ahead of Simon and Garfunkel, who tallied their total without the benefit of a new release.

One LP most chartologists might not have thought of as a number one which did get there was 'Diana Ross and the Supremes Join the Temptations'. One LP most chartologists might have thought of as a number one which did not get there was the Who's rock opera 'Tommy', which had to settle for the second spot.

1970 Simon and Garfunkel were the mighty men of the new decade's first year. Britain's best-selling album of the seventies, 'Bridge Over Troubled Water', dominated the chart, spending 23 weeks at number one. The closest competitors, 'Abbey Road' and 'Led Zeppelin III', managed 5 weeks each. The S&G catalogue also sold handsomely in the wake of 'Water', giving the duo an astonishing 167 weeks on the chart in a single year, easily smashing Tom Jones' record of 135.

With the exception of the compilations 'Motown Chartbusters Vol 3 & 4' and the Christmas number one, 'Andy Williams Greatest Hits', every chart-topper was by a rock artist. The Beatles began their break-up year with 'Abbey Road' and parted with their spring smash 'Let It Be'. Fab Four fans obviously didn't want to say goodbye, buying enough various Beatle albums to give the group 122 weeks in the chart, the highest total of any year in their career. In parallel fashion, the greatest American star of the sixties, Bob Dylan, also had his last two number one LPs in 1970, those being 'Self Portrait' and 'New Morning'.

It was a banner year for what was then called progressive music. The Moody Blues had a number one and an admirable 115 weeks on the chart. Led Zeppelin flew over all followers with both 'II' and 'III'. Pink Floyd exploded with a real mother, 'Atom Heart Mother', and Black Sabbath won hosannas for heavy metal with their powerful 'Paranoid'.

The outstanding performance by an artist in a supporting role was by Johnny Cash. Though he did not get to number one the former Sun star did notch up 125 weeks on the chart as four albums entered on the heels of his phenomenally successful 'Johnny Cash at San Quentin'.

1971 'Bridge Over Troubled Water' was the outstanding album of yet another year, accumulating 17 weeks at number one, more than any other title. It was the only LP to appear on every one of the year's weekly tabulations.

Simon and Garfunkel works spent a total of 102 weeks on the chart during 1971, a sum exceeded only by the product of the prolific Andy Williams. The long-time hitmaker was at the peak of his career courtesy of his popular television series, and two different titles, 'Greatest Hits' and 'Home Loving Man', reached number one for him during the 12-month period. No other artist had more than one chart-topper this year, although three lots of uncredited session singers and instrumentalists did go all the way with budget compilations of cover versions. If anyone was involved with more than one of these productions, they have wisely remained silent.

Two ex-Beatles led the list with solo albums, Paul McCartney with 'Ram' and John Lennon with 'Imagine', though additional credits were given to Linda McCartney and the Plastic Ono Band, respectively. The Rolling Stones' first effort on their eponymous label, 'Sticky Fingers', gave them a one-for-one record. They continued their 100 per cent performance until their 1974 issue, 'It's Only Rock and Roll', only hit number two. The Stones' competitors for the title of the World's Greatest Live Rock and Roll Band, the Who, scored their only chart topper ever, 'Who's Next', while after a year of dominating the singles scene T. Rex managed an album number one in 'Electric Warrior'. Other acts enjoying outstanding years included Led Zeppelin, Rod Stewart, James Taylor, and the veteran Frank Sinatra. Only the 'My Way' man and Elvis Presley were still going strong from the original crew of 1958.

1972 Marc Bolan and a load of other people dominated the album charts in 1972. The T. Rex phenomenon was merely one aspect of genuine fan fervour. The appearance of five Various Artist LPs at number one was a triumph of marketing.

The year began with 'Electric Warrior' retaining the top spot. In May a double re-issue, 'My People Were Fair'/'Prophets Seers and Sages', grabbed the glory for a week, bearing the original label credit of Tyrannosaurus Rex. That an artist's old material released under an obsolete name could get to number one indicated the frenzied following T. Rex had at the time. The following set, 'Bolan Boogie', also went all the way. T. Rex were the first act to have three number one albums in 1 year.

Bolan's boys were one of four attractions to spend between 80 and 90 weeks on the chart in 1972. Cat Stevens did best with 89 in a year when no one hit the century.

Rod Stewart had his second good year as 'Never a Dull Moment' went to number one and 'Every Picture Tells a Story' continued a long run. These were the first two of six consecutive toppers by the leader of the Faces. That group's 'A Nod's as Good as a Wink' reached the second slot in 1972, narrowly missing an unusual double for Stewart. No artist had ever scored number ones as a soloist and a group member in the same year, though Cliff Richard had made it on his own and with the Shadows backing him. Paul Simon came close, touching the top with his eponymous solo debut in 1972, but 'Bridge Over Troubled Water' had just stopped making occasional appearances at number one.

Outside of the 'Concert for Bangladesh' triple album, the Various Artists compilations that led the list for 27 weeks, over half the year, were assembled by marketing firms for television advertising. This innovation in merchandising started a packaging trend that lasted for over a decade. Sales of this type of disc generally offered no indication of how popular taste in music was changing, as success was attributable to the impact of the commercial rather than the music itself.

 1973 David Bowie and Max Bygraves have never shared the concert stage, but they certainly were together in the 1973 album charts. The innovatory space rocker had six hit LPs that year, the singalong star five. Two of Bowie's efforts, 'Aladdin Sane' and 'Pin Ups', were number ones, while the resuscitated 'Hunky Dory' soared to three. Bygraves scored three Top Ten entries with his everybody-join-in approach to medleys of old favourites. One of his charters boasted perhaps the most ludicrous title of all-time, '100 Golden Greats'.

'The Rise and Fall of Ziggy Stardust and the Spiders From Mars' had broken Bowie big in '72. Now he ruled the album chart, accumulating an unprecedented 182 weeks on the list during '73 with the six different titles. This sum shattered the mark of 167 weeks set by Simon and Garfunkel in 1970. Ironically, the defunct duo still managed to total 104 weeks in 1973, three years after their break-up, with the potent pairing of 'Greatest Hits' and 'Bridge Over Troubled Water'.

The siblings from the States, the Carpenters, managed 88 weeks in the list to tie Max Bygraves for third, though the positions reached were less impressive. Elton John and Slade both achieved two number ones, Gilbert O'Sullivan his only one and Roxy Music their first. Rod Stewart nabbed one as a soloist and another as a member of the Faces, completing the odd double that had eluded him in 1972.

Perhaps the most telling statistic of the year is that twenty different albums reached number one. This new high suggested that even the outstanding artists were not dominating the charts as firmly as in the sixties, and that marketing departments had learned how to achieve great sales in a limited time period.

1974 Two artists who were already strong in 1973, the Carpenters and Elton John, surged in 1974. Richard and Karen accumulated 17 weeks at number one in four summit visits with 'The Singles 1969–73', the highest total since 'Bridge Over Troubled Water'. The bespectacled pianist, who had scored two number ones the previous 12 months, bagged another brace this time, reigning with 'Caribou' and the Christmas number one 'Elton John's Greatest Hits'.

Another keyboard wizard did a double. For the second successive year the previously unknown feat of hitting the heights both as a soloist and a group member was achieved. Rick Wakeman's last album with Yes, 'Tales From Topographic Ocean', was the year's first number one. That spring the synthesiser star topped the table again with his own 'Journey to Centre of the Earth'.

Dramatic evidence that the album and singles charts had grown far apart was offered in September. Mike Oldfield held the first two long player places with his new release, 'Hergest Ridge', and his 1973 classic, 'Tubular Bells'. The Osmonds were at one and two in the seven-inch stakes with their own 'Love Me For a Reason' and Donny and Marie's 'I'm Leaving It (All) Up to You'. Oldfield and Osmonds – two more different artists could hardly be imagined.

David Bowie narrowly nudged the Carpenters in the weeks on chart table in 1974, 107 to 106. In the process he picked up his third career number one, 'Diamond Dogs'.

The Beatles were close behind with 104, thanks to the year-long persistence of their 1973 compilations '1962–66' and '1967–70'. Paul McCartney was doubtlessly more pleased by the 7-week tenure at the top of Wings' 'Band on the Run'.

1975 The album and singles charts showed greater similarities in 1975 than in the immediate past. The three best-selling singles of the year were by the Bay City Rollers, Rod Stewart and the Stylistics, and all three artists also achieved number one LPs. 'Best of the Stylistics' spent more weeks in the Top Ten than any other disc, a statistic that startles until one recalls it benefited from a mighty marketing campaign that included considerable television advertising.

Other greatest hits albums that went to the summit courtesy of blurbs on the box included anthologies by Perry Como, Engelbert Humperdinck, Tom Jones and Jim Reeves; mass appeal singers logically benefited most from mass advertising. The one collection that went to number one naturally as a result of the artist's current popularity rather than artificial stimulus was 'Elton John's Greatest Hits'. By leading the list for the last 5 weeks of 1974 and the first 5 of 1975, the Pinner prodigy matched the Stylistics' 10 weeks over 2 calendar years. Elton was out front on his own with his total of 105 weeks on the chart, approached only by the slow-to-fade Simon and Garfunkel, whose back catalogue stayed around for one hundred more 7-day spells.

The year ended with Queen's 'Night at the Opera' pacing the pack. It included the Christmas number one single, 'Bohemian Rhapsody'. Status Quo, Led Zeppelin and Pink Floyd all lent the number one spot a heavier touch during the course of '75. Max Boyce translated his Welsh superstardom into disc sales with the first comedy number one ever.

1976 Beware of Greeks bearing gift tokens. There must have been a lot of them about in 1976, because Demis Roussos came from out of the Aegean blue to spend more weeks in the album chart than any other artist. The man-mountain scaled the survey with two top five entries, 'Happy to Be' and 'Forever and Ever', in reaching his total of 84 weeks, 1 more than Queen, 2 more than John Denver, and 3 more than Pink Floyd. Roussos also topped the singles chart with his 'Roussos Phenomenon' EP, the first time an Extended Play disc triumphed in that table.

The low magnitude of the leading weeks on chart total suggests that no artist dominated the field as David Bowie had only recently. This was indeed the case, as only Led Zeppelin zapped two number ones in 1976, both of which stayed on top for only 1 week. Were there a trend it would appear to have been in greatest hits compilations, with number one packages coming from Perry Como, Roy Orbison, Slim Whitman, Abba, the Beach Boys, and Glen Campbell. The legendary guitar star Bert Weedon actually made it all the way with a set of other people's hits. This information should not suggest that Weedon, Whitman, Como, Campbell or even the Beach Boys were enjoying a renaissance in singles sales, merely that television marketing of the greatest hits LP had reached the peak of its success. Only the 11 weeks spent at the summit by 'Abba's Greatest Hits', the highest sum of list leading weeks in 1976, reflected fame on forty-five. Indeed, the SuperSwedes were enjoying their best year on the singles chart.

'Rock Follies' and 'Stupidity' (by Dr. Feelgood) both reached the top without benefit of a hit single. For 'Rock Follies' the feat was doubly distinctive: the Andy Mackay — Howard Schuman score was the first television soundtrack to ever top the album chart.

1977

Marketing was the main matter when it came to getting to number one in 1977. Clever campaigns, with a heavy emphasis on television advertising, succeeded in helping several artists who had gone cold back to glory.

Slim Whitman, who had registered one hit single in 20 years, was once again brilliantly promoted to the premier long player position by United Artists promotion. The Beatles had their first summit scaler since 'Let It Be' with an extremely after-the-fact live album. Connie Francis and Bread, both of whom had fallen flat lately, had number one compilations. The role call of artists who vaulted to Valhalla with TV anthologies reads like a Hall of Fame: Johnny Mathis, Elvis Presley, Cliff Richard, Diana Ross and the Supremes, the Shadows, and Frank Sinatra. By its very nature this plethora of platters could only be issued once, so 1977 was the peak of this kind of catalogue culling.

The only number one greatest hits album that was part of the natural flow of an artist's output was Abba's. The SuperSwedes were on top for a total of 10 weeks, more than any other act or compilation. The Sex Pistols made history with their debut disc, 'Never Mind the Bollocks Here's the Sex Pistols', number one for 2 weeks in November despite some retail reluctance to display the provocative title. It was the first New Wave number one.

Pink Floyd bested Abba for most weeks on chart, 108 to 106, on the basis of their new number two, 'Animals', and their still-selling back list. In the year of his death Elvis Presley accumulated 95 weeks with an unprecedented eighteen titles, almost all re-entries.

1978

Two film soundtracks proved it was still possible for albums to achieve lengthy runs at number one, television advertising campaigns and a diverging market notwithstanding. 'Saturday Night Fever' stayed on top for 18 weeks, the longest uninterrupted reign since that of 'Sergeant Pepper's Lonely Hearts Club Band', and indeed there were fewer number one LPs in 1978, eight, than in any year since 1967, the time of the classic Beatles release.

'Grease' was the other movie megahit, spending 13 weeks at the head of the hits. Since John Travolta starred in both films, one might assume he was on the number one for 31 weeks of the year, the most by any artist since the cast of 'The Sound of Music' achieved the same figure in 1966. But though Travolta was shown on the cover of 'Fever', earning a royalty, he did not figure in the music. The Bee Gees, whose tunes dominated the motion picture, did not appear on the screen.

The real winner was the Robert Stigwood Organisation, which issued both films and both discs. The phenomenal sales these RSO albums and the singles from them enjoyed, encouraged the music business to expand, an inflation of overheads that proved financially ill-advised when no similar sellers followed in the next few years.

Boney M, who shocked the system by scoring a pair of chart topping singles in the same year, also enjoyed their most successful LP, 'Nightflight to Venus'. Abba earned 7 more number one weeks with 'The Album' and managed 112 weeks on chart during the year, clearly outdistancing all competition. Fleetwood Mac's 'Rumours', America's top record of 1977, finally managed 7 days at the summit in Britain.

1979

Nineteen different albums played musical chairs with the number one position in 1979, more than twice the total of toppers the previous year. No piece of product could compete with RSO's 1978 soundtracks in terms of length of stay at the summit. 'The Best Disco Album in the World', a Warner Brothers compilation released at the height of the disco craze and supported by television advertising, managed the longest stint, 6 weeks. Indeed, Warners as a company may have been the sales star of the year, managing to place three consecutive number ones at the top in their first week of release. Certainly the artists involved – Led Zeppelin, Gary Numan and Boney M – could not have been appealing to the same buyers.

The real star performers of 1979 were Abba, Blondie and the Electric Light Orchestra. The first two named each achieved two number ones, spending totals of 7 and 5 weeks ahead respectively. Gary Numan did nab one winner under his own name and another in his group Tubeway Army, but each of those only stayed in the lead for 1 week.

ELO's mark of merit was the 112 weeks spent on the chart by their various albums, including the number one 'Discovery'. The Jeff Lynne-led ensemble had their finest 12 months, enjoying four Top Ten singles as well. The only act to approach ELO in weeks on chart was Blondie with an exact century; Earth Wind and Fire trailed in third with 68.

'Bat Out of Hell' by Meat Loaf and Jeff Wayne's 'War of the Worlds' each spent the entire year on the chart as they headed for two of the longest runs in recent times. Neither album ever reached number one, but both ultimately outsold almost every disc that did in 1979.

 Twenty-three different albums led the list at some point during 1980, the most in any single year to date. The number one position was like New England's fabled weather: if you didn't like it, you could stick around for an hour and it might change. Johnny Mathis, Genesis and Rose Royce appeared in quick succession, and if the rapid variation from easy listening to rock to soul wasn't enough for the catholic consumer Sky followed with a kind of classical and pop hybrid that was impossible to categorise.

With more number one albums in a year than David Bowie has had images in a career, staying in front for even a month was an achievement. The Pretenders made it with their eponymous debut disc, and Roxy Music found 4 weeks in two stints with 'Flesh and Blood'. The star performers of the year were Police and Abba. The Bleach Boys had their second number one LP, 'Zenyatta Mondatta', and scored 116 on chart in total, far in front of the 70-week sum of runner-up AC/DC. The Super-Swedes once again had chart-toppers early and late in a year, registering in January with 'Greatest Hits Volume 2' and beginning a 9-week rule in November with 'Super Trouper'.

An extremely odd circumstance characterised the spring. For the entire season, albums had 2-week runs at number one and were then replaced. Seven LPs were in the spring string. The previous record for consecutive 2-week reigns had been a mere two, so this development was certainly curious if ultimately unimportant.

 To find the top album artists of 1981 one didn't have to look far beyond the letter 'A' in alphabetical browser bins. Abba began and ended the year at number one with 'Super Trouper' and 'The Visitors', extending their string of chart-topping LPs to 7. Adam and the Ants were the breakout act of the year, accumulating 12 weeks at the summit with 'Kings of the Wild Frontier', the longest leading stint. 'Kings' was also one of five long players to stay the course for the entire year. It was joined by previous Adam material and the end-of-year release 'Prince Charming' to give the Ants 87 weeks on the chart, a total topped only by Barry Manilow. The American balladeer bettered the Ant total by 5 weeks. Personal appearances and heavy promotion gave him a career peak in Britain several years after he had done his best at home.

One had to look hard to find evidence of the growth of techno-pop, the synthesised sound making great inroads in the singles market. 'Dare' by the Human League was the nation's best-seller for 1 week, but this was before the fourth single from the set, 'Don't You Want Me', became the year's Christmas number one and propelled its parent back up the chart in 1982. Ultravox, important pioneers of technopop, re-entered for another 48 weeks with 'Vienna' on the strength of the single of the same name.

There were oddities, as always. 'The Royal Wedding' of Prince Charles to Lady Diana Spencer was number one for a fortnight, twice as long as Motorhead managed with their equally live 'No Sleep Till Hammersmith', but the Royals never challenged the heavy metal merchants to a battle of the bands.

'Remember my name', Irene Cara advised in the title tune of the film *Fame*, 'I'm gonna live forever'. Well, almost. *Fame* itself proved to be more enduring than any of the young people in it.

When the BBC began broadcasting the American television series 'Fame', a spin-off from the Alan Parker movie, Cara's original version of the theme song zoomed to the top of the singles chart. The US label for her solo efforts, Network, did not have a UK distribution deal at the time, so the RSO soundtrack was the only LP available containing the hit. 'Fame' went to number one, and it seemed as if a quaint resuscitation of a former American hit had peaked quickly. It was actually only the beginning of a phenomenon.

BBC Records' 'The Kids From Fame' television cast collection, number two while the movie melodies were ahead, proceeded to lead the list itself. Fuelled by two Top Ten singles, this album sold over 850,000 copies by December, surpassing even the previous year's 'Royal Wedding' to become the BBC's best-selling long player.

RCA had leased the album because BBC1 could only plug vinyl with the BBC label, and they needed to establish the singing actors as a recording act. Mission accomplished, they issued a second TV platter, 'The Kids From Fame Again', and this also made the top three.

The sales success of the 'Kids From Fame' was peculiar to Britain. In contrast, the only LP that outsold theirs in the UK in 1982 was by a worldwide star. 'Love Songs' by Barbra Streisand was the year's best seller. That it did so well was mildly surprising, since it was a make-do collection with only two new songs assembled in lieu of new product.

ABC distinguished themselves by spending their first-ever week on the chart at number one with 'The Lexicon of Love'. The debut marked another first, the initial joint number one on the album chart. 'The Lexicon of Love' shared the spotlight with – yes – 'Fame'.

 Two of the greatest stars of the early seventies outpaced the pack this year, but whereas one, David Bowie, had already set album chart standards, Michael Jackson had previously been best known as a singles artist. Despite his string of Motown smashes the boy star had never enjoyed a Top Ten long player, either as a soloist or with the Jackson Five. He managed to reach number five in 1979 with 'Off the Wall', his solo start on Epic, but nothing prepared the world for what happened in 1983.

'Thriller' first entered the sweepstakes in December 1982, but by the end of its first month of release had only climbed to fifteen. It was only with the release of the second single from the set, 'Billie Jean', that the platter peaked. It scaled the summit three times for a total of 7 weeks and was the year's best-seller. Michael enjoyed 3 further weeks at number one when Motown's repackaged '18 Greatest Hits' proved popular during the summer. This compilation was credited to Michael Jackson Plus the Jackson Five, a brand-new billing, and gave Motown the LP sales this material had been denied earlier. This set was also one of the year's Ten Top sellers.

The fan fever which accompanied 'Thriller' pulled 'Off the

Wall' back for a long stint, gave 'E. T. The Extra Terrestrial' soundtrack, on which the artist appeared, a brief run, and lifted 'Michael Jackson 9 Single Pack' into the charmed circle, the first time exclusively seven-inch material had been listed as an album. The llama lover totalled 123 weeks on chart, a figure that would have beat all competitors in all but four previous years.

This year, however, David Bowie achieved a total eclipse of the chart, setting a new mark with 198. This staggering sum beat his old record of 182, established a full decade earlier in 1973. Although the chart had expanded to a top 100 during the interim, giving an artist a greater chance of re-entering the list at lower levels with a dated product, Bowie must be credited with having the only real golden oldie in the year-end 100, 'The Rise and Fall of Ziggy Stardust and the Spiders From Mars'. Nearly all his success this year came in the wake of 'Let's Dance', which entered at number one. Thirteen Bowie titles in all appeared in the fifty-three charts of 1983. Ten Bowie albums were in the week of 16 July, the year's greatest monopoly.

Phil Collins racked up 78 weeks on chart on his own and also did very well with Genesis, whose eponymous album went to number one. Meat Loaf followed closely with 76. His long-running 'Bat Out of Hell' was listed for yet another full year, moving up to fourth place on the all-time longevity list. Mighty sales figures were accumulated by Paul Young, whose 'No Parlez' went to the head of the class on three occasions, and Lionel Richie, whose 'Can't Slow Down' came out late in the autumn but was still one of 1983's Top Twenty.

Richard Clayderman, the French pianist cleverly marketed in both print and television, enjoyed two of the year's Top 100 and amassed 66 weeks on chart. He was far and away 1983's most successful instrumentalist.

The commanding position of the leading male soloists should not obscure the fact that thirteen of the year's twenty top albums were by groups. Culture Club were number one for 5 weeks with 'Colour By Numbers' and Men at Work toiled the same time at the top with 'Business As Usual'. Duran Duran only managed 1 week far of the field with 'Seven and the Ragged Tiger' but did stockpile 105 weeks on chart, more than any group save Dire Straits, who garnered 107 without issuing any new material.

Twenty-three different titles reached number one during 1983, more than in any previous calendar year. This was a clear indication that no single act dominated the twelve months. Even Michael Jackson's superlative showing in Britain was modest compared to what he achieved in the United States.

1983 was another year in which female artists did not come close to the levels of their male counterparts. Bonnie Tyler was the only female artist to spend even a single week ahead of the field, though Alison 'Alf' Moyet was the featured vocalist with two-week champs Yazoo. Barbra Streisand was the woman winner in weeks on chart with 57, but most of these were the final flings of 1982's list leader, 'Love Songs'. Dionne Warwick totalled 44 weeks as her comeback continued.

The most noteworthy variety of female achievement from a chart-watcher's point of view was the faddish popularity of a new form – the workout album. Two of the year's Top 100 were of this sort, 'Jane Fonda's Workout Record' and Felicity Kendal's 'Shape Up and Dance (Volume 1)'. Jackie Genova also charted with an exercise exemplar.

Another ingenius use of the LP form to make money came at Christmas when EMI and Virgin became the first two major companies to team up for a television-marketed compilation. 'Now That's What I Call Music' closed the year at number one and seemed certain to invite imitation in 1984.

1984

The face that dominated music advertising on television in George Orwell's dreaded year turned out not to be Big Brother but a pig. The porker was the meaty mascot of the EMI/Virgin anthologies 'Now That's What I Call Music'. These sets of recent hits were given heavy television exposure to generate short periods of intense sales activity.

The strategy worked. The first 'Now' ended 1983 and began 1984 at number one. The second moved into the penthouse in April and the third checked in during August. The three double albums spent a total of 15 of the year's 52 weeks on top, more than any individual act managed to achieve. 'Now 4' did well enough in its mere month of release to be one of 1984's Top Ten but was kept out of number one by CBS/WEA's even more lucrative imitative compilation 'The Hits Album/ The Hits Tape'.

No labels had ever placed three packages of recent hits at number one in the same year. Tamla Motown had reached the top with two 'Motown Chartbusters' volumes in 1970 and two of the 'Top of the Pops' collections of cover versions led the list a year later. K-Tel managed three chart toppers with programs of oldies in the marketing company's most visible year, 1972.

The success of the 'Now' formula was of a different nature than these previous collections. Tamla Motown was primarily a singles label and had only managed three number one LPs when it began its 'Chartbuster' series. The K-Tel campaigns recycled dated merchandise. 'Now' and 'Hits' promoted packages of fresh material, some still in the charts, by artists who nearly all had current albums of their own that might be hurt by the outside availability of their choicest cuts. In this auto-cannibalistic fashion leading British labels redirected the profits to be made from compilation albums back from independent marketers to their own coffers.

Television advertising also played a prominent part in the success of the longest-running number one of the year, Bob Marley and the Wailers' 'Legend'. Despite the Rastaman's legendary status the group had only achieved three Top Ten albums in his lifetime, leaving a large potential audience for a quality collection. 'Legend' proved to be that collection, spending 12 consecutive weeks at number one, the longest leading run the film soundtrack 'Grease' tallied 13 straight in 1978.

The top-selling album of 1984 was 'Can't Slow Down' by Lionel Richie. Though it was only number one for a fortnight it was near the top most of the year, fuelled by a succession of hit singles. The Motown marvel was one of an astonishing seven albums to stay on the chart for the entire year. These 52 week winners were 'Can't Slow Down', Michael Jackson's 'Thriller', Paul Young's 'No Parlez', Meat Loaf's 'Bat Out of Hell', Queen's 'Greatest Hits' and U2's 'Under a Blood Red Sky'. 'Thriller' and 'No Parlez' both returned to number one during 1984 for a total of four visits each. No long-player since 'The Carpenters 1969–1973' had gone to the head of the class on so many occasions. The eight-month gap between 'Thriller's' third and fourth stint at the summit was the longest interval since ten months separated turns by *The Sound of Music* soundtrack in 1968.

Though Lionel Richie had the year's best seller, other male artists also achieved outstanding feats. Billy Joel had the most albums on chart in a single week, six. They surged in sales during June to coincide with a visit to Britain and a televised Wembley Arena concert. Nik Kershaw managed two of the year's Top Fifty, Elton John two of the Top 100. Michael Jackson also had a brace of best-sellers, 'Off the Wall' continuing its revival. Combining the runs of his solo albums and the weeks in residence of Michael Jackson plus the Jackson Five's '18 Greatest Hits' gave a total of 136. Even crediting Michael with only half a share of the compilation's 29 weeks would put him ahead of the second most ubiquitous act, Dire Straits, who accumulated 116 weeks, still enough to place them in the all-time Top Ten for most in a single year.

Other groups with noteworthy performances included U2, who totalled an even 100 weeks on chart; Queen, who had two of the year's Top Fifty; and Wham! whose 'Make It Big' was one of the year's Top Five. The Smiths scored two Top Tens on the independent Rough Trade label and 'Welcome to the Pleasuredome' gave ZTT its first week at number one. Unlike Frankie Goes to Hollywood, ZZ Top had to work long and hard for a smash, and 'Eliminator' only reached the Top Ten in its 72nd week on chart.

It was not a great year for female soloists. None reached number one, though women did make the top spot as members of Eurythmics and the Thompson Twins. Sade had the biggest seller by a woman, 'Diamond Life', while Elaine Paige had two of the year's Top 100. Barbra Streisand accumulated 67 weeks on chart to lead the ladies.

Instrumentalists fared poorly. Richard Clayderman was the only non-vocalist in the year's Top 100. The French pianist had most weeks on chart, 30 in all.

A noteworthy development in lower regions of the chart was that the independent compilation company Street Sounds attained fifteen charters during the year. The devotional artist Bryn Ycmm had three new albums in, more than any other British act. 1984 was itself a star. It was the first year to have three hit LPs named after it.

1985

The long distance runner wasn't lonely in 1985. Nine albums remained on the chart for the entire fifty-two weeks, and four acts accumulated totals in excess of one hundred weeks on chart. The reason most marathon men and women stayed in stride was that their albums were mined for hit singles. With continued radio exposure, the LPs just kept selling.

Astonishing records were set. After a series of UK stadium dates Bruce Springsteen placed his entire catalogue of seven albums in the Top Fifty. Never before had an artist with that large a body of work got the lot that high. Springsteen finished the year with a total of 177 weeks on chart, the third best figure ever. 'Born in the U.S.A.' was one of the nine discs that saw the year through. It wound up the number four seller of 1985. Competing with The Boss for the title of Male Artist of the Year, Phil Collins finished with fewer weeks on chart, a still spectacular 131, but managed to nab the number two spot of the year-end tabulation with 'No Jacket Required'.

Bruce Springsteen reacting to the news that 'Born in the USA' had finally given him a UK number one. (Retna Pictures Ltd)

The top female artist of 1985. (Duncan Raban)

album both entered the Top Fifty. As noteworthy as her own success was the extremely strong showing by female artists in general. Seven of the year's top twenty were either by female soloists or outfits with female vocalists. Sade's two albums both finished in the Top Twenty. They were in the company of efforts by Alison Moyet, Kate Bush, Eurythmics and Tina Turner. Barbara Dickson also had a good year, with two of 1985's Top 100.

Dire Straits and U2 vied for Group of Year honours. Mark Knopfler's lot put in a special claim with the year's number one, 'Brothers In Arms'. 1985 was the third successive year in which Dire Straits exceeded 100 weeks on chart, a feat previously performed only by Simon and Garfunkel. During the three-year period 1983–85, Mark's men leapt from 33rd to 8th on the all-time list. Despite their achievements they were slightly pipped in weeks on chart by U2, 168 to 158. Both were among the half-dozen best figures ever achieved. The Irish band were also on a prolonged hot streak, having vaulted from 20 to 375 weeks on chart during the last three years.

Richard Clayderman retained his laurels as leading solo instrumentalist, but James Last bounced back as the top orchestra. It was also a good year for what might be called up-market material, with Andrew Lloyd Webber's 'Requiem', Leonard Bernstein's operatic version of 'West Side Story', and the Anderson/Rice/Ulvaeus 'Chess' all in 1985's Top 100.

The most successful broadcasting and charity event of all-time, Live Aid, achieved another distinction as the single happening that has most influenced the album chart. The deaths of Elvis Presley and Jim Reeves had previously brought many of their LPs back to the lists, but the sales effects of Live Aid were unprecedented. In the 27 July chart nine albums by acts in the concert re-entered the Top 100, four after a long absence, and twenty-one previously peaked packages suddenly surged. The act judged the finest by BBC audience research did best in sales, too. Queen's 'The Works' re-entered at thirty, 'Greatest Hits' bounced back fifty-five places, and lead singer Freddy Mercury's 'Mr Bad Guy' regained forty lost positions. U2 did even better than was theoretically possible, not only coming back with their first two albums to place all five of their LPs in the list, but entering with a US import, 'Wide Awake in America'. They now had more chart positions than official releases.

The impact of Live Aid was reflected in the chart through the summer. The craze of 1984, the TV compilations of recent and current hits, abated only slightly, with three EMI/Virgin 'Now' packages in the year-end Top Ten and two CBS/WEA Hits collections in the Top Twenty.

The whole country was talking about the Jones boys. The Welsh chorister with the unbroken voice, Aled, had three of the year's leading hundred hits. Howard, no relation, had one of the most unusual, the first smash LP comprised entirely of 12-inch mixes. Other outstanding male artists included Paul Young, whose two long players both finished in the year-end table. Both his 'No Parlez' and Lionel Richie's 'Can't Slow Down' continued lengthy runs. Meat Loaf's 'Bat Out Of Hell' finally fell from favour when 'Hits Out Of Hell' did well, but still managed to add 31 weeks to equal 'The Sound of Music' as the all-time high.

Madonna was clearly the female artist of 1985, her 'Like a Virgin' – the third best-selling set of the year – and her retitled first

THE PRINCE'S TRUST The best of Britain's album artists join forces to raise money for charity. (Brian Cook/Telstar Records)